PERFORMING THE BODY/ PERFORMING THE TEXT

Since the 1960s, visual art practices – from body art to Minimalism – have taken contemporary art outside the museum and gallery by embracing theatricality and performance and exploding the boundaries set by traditional art criticism. Such practices prompt us to reassess our ways of constructing meaning from art, making us receptive to the element of performance both in the processes of art production and in the act of interpretation itself. *Performing the Body/Performing the Text* explores the new performativity in art theory and practice, examining ways of rethinking interpretive processes in visual culture.

This collection undertakes two parallel projects: exploring art practices which *perform* the subject, and examining ways in which modes of performativity in contemporary art offer new models for interpreting artworks. Demonstrating how modernist art criticism attempts to fix the work with more stable aesthetic meanings, the contributors argue that interpretation needs to be recognized as much more dynamic and contingent. It does not come 'naturally' at the moment of contact with the artwork, but is worked out as an ongoing, open *performance* between artist and spectators, with meaning circulating fluidly in the complex web of connections among artists, patrons, collectors, and between both specialized and non-specialized viewers within the arena of encounter.

Offering its own performance script, and embracing both canonical 'fine' artists such as Manet, de Kooning and Jasper Johns, and performance artists such as Vito Acconci, Gunter Brus and the Sacred Naked Nature Girls, *Performing the Body/Performing the Text* offers radical re-readings of art works and points confidently towards new models for understanding art.

Amelia Jones is Associate Professor of Contemporary Art and Theory and the History of Photography at the University of California, Riverside. **Andrew Stephenson** is Course Leader and Senior Lecturer in the History of Art and Visual Theories at the University of East London.

Contributors: Fionna Barber, Lisa Bloom, Nao Bustamante, Gavin Butt, Jennifer DeVere Brody, Meiling Cheng, Coco Fusco, Michael Hatt, Amelia Jones, Jonathan Katz, Karen Lang, Reina Lewis, Joanna Lowry, Peggy Phelan, Christine Poggi, Donald Preziosi, Barbara U. Schmidt, Andrew Stephenson, Philip Ursprung, B. J. Wray.

PERFORMING THE BODY/ PERFORMING THE TEXT

Edited by

Amelia Jones and Andrew Stephenson

London and New York

First published 1999
by Routledge
11 New Fetter Lane, London EC4P 4EE

Simultaneously published in the USA and Canada
by Routledge
29 West 35th Street, New York, NY 10001

© 1999 Amelia Jones and Andrew Stephenson for selection and
editorial content; individual chapters to their authors

Typeset in Galliard by Solidus (Bristol) Ltd
Printed and bound in Great Britain by
Redwood Books, Trowbridge, Wiltshire

British Library Cataloguing in Publication Data
A catalogue record for this book is available from the British Library

Library of Congress Cataloging in Publication Data
has been applied for

ISBN 0-415-19059-2 (hbk)
ISBN 0-415-19060-6 (pbk)

CONTENTS

CONTENTS

PLATES

NOTES ON CONTRIBUTORS

Fionna Barber is Senior Lecturer in Art History at Manchester Metropolitan University. She has a long-standing interest in feminism and spectatorship and her forthcoming publications include an essay on Caillebotte, masculinity, and the bourgeois gaze for the Open University course, 'Art and Its Histories' (1999).

Lisa Bloom teaches at Josai International University in the Chiba Prefecture of Japan. She is the author of *Gender on Ice: American Ideologies of Polar Expeditions* (1993), editor of the anthology *Gender and Race Politics in Visual Culture* (forthcoming, 1999), and is currently working on a book about ethnicity and US feminist art.

Jennifer DeVere Brody teaches in the English Department at the George Washington University and is an associate editor of *Callaloo*. Her work has appeared in anthologies and journals and her book *Impossible Purities: Blackness, Femininity, and Victorian Culture* is forthcoming.

Nao Bustamante is a performance artist based in San Francisco. She has presented her work throughout the United States, Europe, Mexico, and Australia. Bustamante is also the curator of performance for New Langton Art Gallery in San Francisco.

Gavin Butt teaches modern and contemporary art and theory at Goldsmiths' College, University of London. He is currently completing his doctoral dissertation on the mutability of homo/hetero definition in American art and culture in the 1950s and 1960s.

Meiling Cheng teaches in the Theatre Department at the University of Southern California. She writes and publishes poems, short stories, and art criticism in both English and Chinese. She is currently working on a book entitled *Body Acts: Writing Extreme Performances*.

Coco Fusco is an interdisciplinary artist and writer based in New York. She has performed, lectured, curated, and published throughout North and South America, Europe, Australia, and South Africa and is the author of *English Is Broken Here: Notes on Cultural Fusion in the Americas (1995)*.

Michael Hatt teaches history of art at the University of Warwick. He has published on aspects of nineteenth–century American art and is completing a book on the male nude (forthcoming).

Amelia Jones teaches twentieth-century art and theory at the University of California, Riverside and is the author of *Postmodernism and the En-Gendering of Marcel Duchamp*

(1994) and *Body Art/Performing the Subject* (1998). She organized the exhibition and catalogue entitled *Sexual Politics: Judy Chicago's* Dinner Party *in Feminist Art History* (1996).

Jonathan Katz is chair of Lesbian, Gay and Bisexual Studies at the City College of San Francisco. He has written widely on queer art and theory in the postwar period. A political activist, Katz founded the Queer Caucus of the College Art Association and the Harvey Milk Institute and co-founded Queer Nation, San Francisco.

Karen Lang teaches at California Institute of Technology. She is the recipient of fellowships from the National Endowment for the Humanities and the Getty Grant Program, and has published essays on aesthetics and the history of the German monument.

Reina Lewis is Senior Lecturer in the Department of Cultural Studies at the University of East London. She is the author of *Gendering Orientalism: Race, Femininity and Representation* (1996) and co-editor with Peter Horne of *Outlooks: Lesbian and Gay Sexualities and Visual Cultures* (1996). Her current research is on 'Oriental' women writers in English and the limits of Orientalism.

Joanna Lowry teaches at the Kent Institute of Art and Design. She has published on contemporary art and photographic practice. Her current research concerns the relationship between photography and time.

Peggy Phelan is the author of *Unmarked: The Politics of Performance* (1993) and *Mourning Sex: Performing Public Memories* (1997). She co-edited *Acting Out: Feminist Performances* (with Lynda Hart, 1993) and *The Ends of Performance* (with Jill Lange, 1998). She teaches performance studies at the Tisch School of the Arts, New York University.

Christine Poggi teaches art history at the University of Pennsylvania. She is the author of *In Defiance of Painting: Cubism, Futurism, and the Invention of Collage* (1992) and many articles on modern and contemporary art. Her current research addresses Italian Futurism and contemporary performance art.

Donald Preziosi teaches courses on contemporary critical theory, modern visual culture, and museum studies in the Department of Art History at UCLA. His recent books include *Rethinking Art History: Meditations on a Coy Science* (1989) and *The Art of Art History* (1998).

Barbara U. Schmidt studied art history and literary criticism, completing her studies in 1994 with a doctoral thesis about the work of Miriam Cahn. She works as an independent scholar and curator in Munich, where she is presently teaching at the Academy of Fine Arts.

Andrew Stephenson is Senior Lecturer in Art History and Visual Theory in the Art, Design and Film History department at the University of East London. He has published on late nineteenth- and early twentieth-century English modernism, notably in *Impressionism for England: Samuel Courtauld as Patron and Collector* (1994) and *Fashioning the Ideal Body: Frederic Leighton and High Culture in Victorian England* (1998). He also co-curated the exhibition *Visualising Masculinities* at the Tate Gallery, London. His current research studies constructions of masculinity within English modernism, *c.* 1860–1960.

Philip Ursprung teaches art history at the Institute for the History and Theory of Architecture at the Swiss Federal Institute of Technology in Zurich. He studied in Geneva, Vienna and Berlin and his dissertation on German art criticism was published as *Kritik und Secession. 'Das Atelier', Kunstkritik in Berlin zwischen 1890 und 1897* (Basle, Schwabe 1996). He has also curated exhibitions of contemporary art. His current research is on the history of happenings and earthworks in the United States in the 1960s and 1970s.

B. J. Wray is a doctoral candidate at the University of Calgary, Canada. She is writing her dissertation on nationalism and sexuality in Canadian lesbian texts. She has edited a queer theory journal and has articles forthcoming in the second volume of *Unnatural Acts* (Indiana University Press) and *Camera Obscura*.

ACKNOWLEDGEMENTS

First and foremost the editors would like to acknowledge all of the contributors to this volume. Their unflagging responsiveness to our editorial interference, and willingness to engage performatively with our interpretive suggestions, made the process of organizing this volume pleasurable.

We give extra thanks, too, to the scholars who participated in the two panels that inspired the formation of this collection: the session 'Body Politics: Performativity and Postmodernism,' organized by Amelia Jones for the annual College Art Association conference in New York, February 1997; and the session 'Performance and the Performative,' chaired by Andrew Stephenson at the Association of Art Historians annual conference in London, April 1997. The CAA panel included earlier versions of the essays by Lisa Bloom, Jonathan Katz, Christine Poggi, and Barbara U. Schmidt in this volume, as well as a compelling response by Peggy Phelan. The AAH session was comprised of earlier versions of the texts included here by Fionna Barber, Gavin Butt, Karen Lang, Joanna Lowry, and Philip Ursprung, as well as papers by Amelia Jones and Reina Lewis addressing topics related to those essays they have written for this book. We give thanks not only to the speakers, but to the organizations – including our home institutions, the University of East London and the University of California, Riverside – which made the rich intellectual discussions prompted by these two panels possible.

Finally, we thank Rebecca Barden, editor, and her assistant, Alistair Daniel, at Routledge for their support, and the readers of the book manuscript, including Rebecca Schneider, for their excellent insights and suggestions.

Amelia Jones
Andrew Stephenson

ILLUSTRATIONS

INTRODUCTION

Amelia Jones and Andrew Stephenson

Performing the Body/Performing the Text is, in its broadest implications, a book of essays about how meaning *takes place* in the practices of visual culture – one that interrogates how art critical and art historical interpreters operate to legitimate their judgments as convincing or correct and attempts to offer different, more self-reflexive, models of reading. Since the 1960s, visual art practices, from body art to Minimalism, have opened themselves to the dimension of theatricality in such a way as to suggest that art critics and art historians might reassess our own practices of making meaning through an engagement with the processes of art production and reception as *performative*. In this way, artistic meaning can be understood as enacted through interpretive engagements that are themselves performative in their intersubjectivity. Thus, the artwork is no longer viewed as a static object with a single, prescribed signification that is communicated unproblematically and without default from the maker to an alert, knowledgeable, universalized viewer.

Instead, as much recent visual art and theory has underlined, the artist (as the first 'viewer' of the work) and subsequent viewers/interpreters are caught up within the complex and fraught operations of representation – entangled in intersubjective spaces of desire, projection, and identification. As classed, raced, sexed, and gendered (fully socialized and embodied) subjects, both artist and interpreter are imbricated within any potential determinations of meaning. The notion of the performative highlights the open-endedness of interpretation, which must thus be understood as a *process* rather than an act with a final goal, and acknowledges the ways in which circuits of desire and pleasure are at play in the complex web of relations among artists, patrons, collectors, and both specialized and non-specialized viewers.

As a consequence, this collection announces through its very title a commitment to the dual project of exploring practices that enact the body or subject in a *performative* fashion (*Performing the Body*) in order to point to the act of interpretation itself as a kind of performance (*Performing the Text*). The book, as noted, thus takes its initial inspiration from performative art practices. Performing the body in (or as) the work of art, as so many artists have done over the last three-and-a-half decades, exposes the fact that interpretation does not come 'naturally' at the moment of making contact with the artwork (any more than the artist 'naturally' injects her intentions or emotional affect into the forms of the work in a finalized or determinable way at the moment of creation). At the same time, such a performance of the body of the artist also points to the fact that the interaction among subjects, as mediated through the artwork (which in this case 'is' the artist), is hardly unaffected by the work's institutional and discursive stagings and more broadly construed social and political situations.

The secondary impetus for the bringing together of essays on the visual arts – essays that acknowledge rather than suppress the performative dimensions of meaning-making – is to build on the proliferation of studies addressing performance and performativity in other disciplines. *Performing the Body/Performing the Text* thus offers a way to revise art critical and historical studies via the insights of philosophy, theater and literary studies, cultural studies, and feminism as well as queer theory. Many scholars have made use of the linguistic notion of performativity, first developed by J. L. Austin and revised by theorists from Jacques Derrida to Judith Butler, to open up the process of meaning production with respect to narrative/temporal arts such as theater and film, or in relation to the experience of subjectivity and identity in the postmodern world.[1] Peggy Phelan, Lynda Hart, Rebecca Schneider, Sue-Ellen Case, and Jill Dolan (among others) have situated their intellectual inquiries in the domain of the performative gendered and sexed body, a body that is the 'center of semiotic crossings, which allows one to perceive, interpret and document the performative event.'[2] Within this matrix, critical writing itself is proposed and enacted as 'reimagining . . . the social bond' through its very performativity.[3]

While the issue of the performative has thus generated great interest across the humanities, it has not generally been addressed in art critical or historical writing (even though, as we have already argued, *practices* in the visual arts have consistently opened out the performative dimension of meaning production). Taking its cue from art practice, then, this project also borrows from interdisciplinary insights to intervene in the domains of art history and criticism. This anthology thus proposes that the viewing or embodied reception of visual artworks is a *process* that can be engaged as performative.

Adopting the notion of performativity as a critical strategy within the study of visual culture thus enables a recognition of interpretation as a fragile, partial, and precarious affair and, ultimately, affords a critique of art criticism and art history as they have been traditionally practiced. Since meaning is negotiated between and across subjects and through language, it can never be fully secured: meaning comes to be understood as a negotiated domain, in flux and contingent on social and personal investments and contexts. By emphasizing this lack of fixity and the shifting, invested nature of any interpretive engagement, we wish to assert that interpretation itself is worked out as a performance between artists (as creators, performers, and spectators of their work) and spectators (whether 'professional' or non-specialist). Borrowing again from theater studies, we are interested in focusing in on the 'complicity of the audience' – what Schneider has termed the 'subject/writer's complicity with her object; an engagement with her own embodied specificity, her habits of seeing and desiring' – in determining the meaning and social value of any cultural product.[4]

As 'professional spectators,' art critics and art historians have conventionally claimed to have decoded the artwork's 'true meaning' either at the first moment of contact or at the moment of some later, auspicious encounter. A historical or intellectual distance, it is sometimes argued, provides for a clearer sense of artistic imperatives. What needs to be realized is that such assertions of authenticity ultimately provide an interpretation that constitutes just one reading among many other (and competing) claims on the visual artwork. And, on the contrary, we would argue that, even when isolated in the trained hands (or, rather, before the 'professional' eyes) of the art critic or art historian as a 'privileged' expert witness, the object/image can hardly be convincingly argued to be static in its effects. Access to the position of making meaning is a crucial issue: one must locate the 'professional spectator' (the art critic and art historian) within the operative discursive conventions and a distinctive Western taxonomy (with all of the normative assumptions of race, class, gender, sexual orientation, and otherwise, that this entails) which serves to authorize and naturalize his readings as 'truthful.'

Through an emphasis on interpretation as a definitively *invested* kind of performance, we want both to emphasize the fetishistic, obsessive allure that the art object asserts upon such viewers (and open out the particular desires informing such structures of fascination) and to call for a cautious and critical self-reflexivity to be registered as part of the cultural identities being assumed as well as projected in the process of interpretation.[5] By focusing on interpretation as an exchange or negotiation, we hope to illuminate the undeclared assumptions of the usually heterosexual, white, Euro-American male art professional who, as a matter of course in pleading his case, overlooks the 'unnaturalness' and the incongruities of his position as a subject (and one who desires to identify particular meanings for particular, highly invested, reasons).

Such assumptions have come to be largely identified with the term 'modernism' and disseminated through the writings of formalist critics such as Roger Fry and Clement Greenberg;[6] after 1945, modernism in the visual arts came increasingly to be reduced in Euro-American discourse to a formalist, loosely Kantian model positing meaning as internal to (inherent in) the forms of the work of art as discerned by a trained yet objective interpretive eye. Such meanings were, in addition, claimed to be transcendent and abstract – definitively separate from the social and political realms. It is our contention that these strategies of naturalizing the interpreter's particular readings as inevitably correct or universally valid, and the concomitant veiling of the interpreter's stake in producing such readings under an armature of disinterest, continue to be structurally embedded in the practice of art criticism and art history, often even of the most seemingly enlightened and radical varieties.[7]

The critical authority of formalist modernism, which was structured through a loosely conceived extension of the Kantian premise that the interpreter must be neutral ('disinterested') in his relationship to the object to be judged, required the veiling of the body of the artist and, by extension, that of the interpreter: this dissembling functioned to ensure the occlusion of the viewer's interpretive desires to facilitate the claim of disinterestedness. Within this framework, meaning could be proposed as inherent to the forms of the object it supposedly inhabited; meaning was, then, simply waiting to be deciphered by the trained interpreter (who would in so doing authenticate the authority of his formalist model and so, by extension, himself as its practitioner). What this system ultimately demanded was the discrete suppression of the vicissitudes of interpretive desire – social investments, particular identifications, and personal biases – under the imperatives of critical rigor.

Of course, it has become somewhat of a truism in recent years that 'modernist formalism' is problematic in both philosophical and political terms. These previously dominant models of artistic value and meaning have been repeatedly and insistently questioned in art discourse and practices over the last decades;[8] however, as suggested above, we believe that these critiques have been incomplete to the extent that they have generally failed to acknowledge the continuation of a modernist desire to fix value in relation to the work of art. Even as Euro-American art history and art criticism have by and large shifted away from a value system based on abstract aesthetic ideals to one based on political efficacy (in terms of Marxian, structuralist, feminist, and other radical agendas), the majority of supposedly 'anti-' or 'post-' modernist analyses continue to veil the investments at work in posing particular values and meanings for works of art. What we hope to offer here is a more rigorous, more self-reflexive way to interrogate the undeclared assumptions built into modernist formalism, and, to a certain extent, often extended into even the most well-meaning (ostensibly politically radical) 'postmodern' analyses of visual practice.

Since the 1960s, the more explicit surfacing of the interpretive relationship via performative, embodied practices such as body or performance artworks, with their exaggerated eroticism and/or violence, has opened out this state of affairs. In a general sense, artistic practices have exploded beyond the boundaries staged by the disciplines of art history and art citicism in their attempt to codify a 'proper' type of art according to its supposed aesthetic and/or political value, addressing these limiting conditions through strategies such as the siting of the artwork in remote or temporary locations outside of the conventional art gallery and museum spaces; the expansion into temporality; the focus on concept over form; and the aggressive resurfacing of the artist's persona through the enactment of her or his body in or as the work of art. It is our contention that such work, by raising fundamental doubts about previous, prescriptive notions of the artwork as reducible to an essential and pure interrelationship of form and medium, openly implicates the art critic or historian in these regimes, thus undermining any claims for universality or the fixed truth value of particular interpretations. The interpreter is engaged and exposed in relation to her individual investments, institutional affiliations, and position in the art market in general. Further, we insist that the insights provided by artworks that encourage a recognition of the performative dimension of meaning production enable a radical rereading of potentially any artistic practice (including much earlier work) and the development of new models of interpretation that are sensitively open to this dimension.

As suggested, all of the essays in this book call for and attempt to enact a more nuanced and performative conception of artistic meaning as they address particular moments in the production and reception of visual artworks. In addition to undermining the authorizing principle of most art critical and art historical interpretation – that aesthetic, or for that matter political, value is determinable in a finalized way – this collection offers a range of possibilities for addressing bodies and subjects across the visual arts and their textual and institutional contexts.

We wish at the same time to avoid simply replacing the old model of art critical and historical analysis, which we have identified as authoritative and exclusionary, with a new orthodoxy. To this end, the actual modes of interpretation vary widely across the essays in this collection; they are joined together not by a unified or singular method, per se, but by a commitment to heterogeneity and to opening visual arts discourse to the expansive possibility of admitting ambivalence, confusion, and subversive diversities back into the structures of cultural arbitration and understanding. As Lisa Bloom writes in the introduction to her anthology *Gender and Race Politics in Visual Culture*, we are concerned to view visual culture as 'vital and living,' as something that is 'constantly being negotiated in everyday life' and which shapes our complex and charged relationship with the world.[9] In short, we propose a new way of *thinking* visual culture which would open it to desire and a productive lack of certitude that would encourage new critical perspectives to emerge.

Placed at the beginning of this collection, the essays by Karen Lang, Donald Preziosi, and Amelia Jones specifically address the ways in which art historical discourses and institutions have functioned as modernist machines for ensuring the smooth operation of this complex system by which the disciplines of art history and art criticism maintain their cultural authority at the expense of all subjects whose products fall outside of the domain of valued artistic practice. While Lang's 'Reason and remainders: Kantian performativity in the history of art' explores the veiled performativity of the philosophical foundations of art history and the 'idealized subject' produced by the aesthetic discourses that inform the discipline, Preziosi's 'Performing modernity: the art of art history' examines the ideological underpinnings of the modern museum. 'Performing modernity' points to the way in which this seemingly stable institution in fact performs a very particular – racist, sexist, and heterosexist – regime of intelligibility for its 'objects' of culture as well as for the subjects who appear to control it. Jones's essay 'Art history/Art criticism: performing meaning' focuses on the rise of Minimalism in the 1960s to highlight the moment at which modernist formalism came to its most powerful grip on art discourse – even as it began to be overtly challenged by these practices of engaging the body in relation to the work of art.

Essays by Reina Lewis, Michael Hatt, and Jennifer DeVere Brody focus on the ways in which race and ethnicity, completely repressed in modernist art historical and critical discourses (with their insistence on 'objective' interpretation and absolute systems of aesthetic and political value), can be critically resurfaced in order to interrogate disciplinary racism and ethnocentrism within histories of visual culture.[10] Reina Lewis's essay, 'Cross-cultural reiterations: Demetra Vaka Brown and the performance of racialized female beauty,' explores the performativity of racialized and ethnic identities in literary and visual art contexts, focusing on the written accounts of 'Oriental' female life produced in English by the Greek Ottoman woman Demetra Vaka Brown. Michael Hatt and Jennifer Brody contribute incisive analyses of the performativity of race in relation to US cultural history. Hatt's essay, 'Race, ritual, and responsibility: performativity and the southern lynching,' interrogates the significance of poststructuralist theories of performativity in relation to the specific – racially charged – historical example of the lynching of black men in the American south, ultimately calling for a re-evaluation of performativity in relation to historical culpability.

Brody's contribution, 'Shading meaning,' draws out our conception of the performativity of meaning production to theorize the intertwining of categories of race and gender – categories that, while central to the ways in which Euro-American subjects are portrayed in nineteenth-century art, popular culture, and literature, are most often masked in discussions of the same. Focusing on two major nineteenth-century art historical monuments – Edouard Manet's *Olympia* and Hiram Powers's *The Greek Slave* – and on blackface British minstrelsy, Brody resurfaces these categories to identify the ways in which white Euro-American masculinities have been constructed in relation to images of black female servitude. Normative subjectivity, then, becomes a question of continually reiterated *performances* of privilege via written texts and visual imagery.[11]

Essays by Gavin Butt and Fionna Barber expand the conception of performativity beyond performance or body art proper. Focusing on works produced within the 1950s New York art world, Butt and Barber explore the ways in which particular practices engage with performance to pleasurable ends such that the solicitation of pleasurable identifications can in itself (within the context of a rigidified, repressed modernist critical framework) lead to potentially radical effects. Gavin Butt's 'The greatest homosexual? Camp pleasure and the performative body of Larry Rivers' explores Rivers's self-performance as a self-identified heterosexual who adopted appropriated 'camp' signifiers as an act of pleasure and cultural empowerment in the context of developing 'hip' circles in 1950s New York. Fionna Barber's 'The politics of feminist spectatorship and the disruptive body: de Kooning's *Woman I* reconsidered' opens out the act of interpretation by interrogating how Barber herself, as a feminist, can take pleasure in viewing Willem de Kooning's savage depictions of seemingly mutilated women's bodies.

As noted above, in the 1960s and 1970s artists in Europe and the United States explosively and explicitly enacted their bodies in their works, surfacing the performative dimension of meaning production, including the highly invested circulation of racialized, gendered, sexed, and nationalized identities that accompanies any interpretive engagement. Focusing on this period, Philip Ursprung, in his '"Catholic tastes": hurting and healing the body in Viennese Actionism in the 1960s,' studies the important early performances of the Viennese Actionists, placing these within their complex historical and ideological contexts to argue that they both radicalized and reinforced a conservative postwar Austrian, Catholic, male subject. Lisa Bloom's 'Contests for meaning in body politics and feminist conceptual art: revisioning the 1970s through the work of Eleanor Antin' examines Antin's own performance of herself as racialized, a highly significant act for a white but also Jewish woman artist in the 1970s. Bloom uses Antin's work to explore how white ethnicity is interdependent on other social identities and mediated through institutional discourses of art history.

Peggy Phelan has asked in her book *Unmarked: The Politics of Performance* whether performing oneself necessarily entails cultural visibility and whether visibility is necessarily a desirable goal for subjects seeking to reject or transform their position of marginality, leading to the correlative question of whether a radicalization of culture might occur through the exploitation of a performative *in*visibility.[12] Several of the essays in this book intervene in the problematics of visibility/invisibility to explore the ways in which artists have enacted their bodies in/as the work of art to insist, whether consciously or not, upon the specific identifications of the subjects who participate in and give shape to culture. By performing particularized bodies (often highly marked in terms of race, gender, sexuality, nation, and/or class), artists may dramatically unveil the processes by which non-normative subjects are conventionally excluded from the canonical narratives of art history.

In 'Dismembership: Jasper Johns and the body politic,' Jonathan Katz focuses on Jasper Johns's 'performance' of body parts in his 1950s target pieces, engaging them interpretively as signs of a culture of repressed homosexuality. Johns's veiled, fragmented body parts thus signal the veiling of homosexual male subjects (such as Johns himself) in 1950s US art discourse. B. J. Wray's essay 'Performing clits and other lesbian tricks: speculations on an aesthetics of lack' studies a recent performance project – Holly Hughes's 'Clit Notes' – to explore the political issues at stake in making female genitalia visible through performance. Ultimately, Wray addresses the politics of a performative representation: do such enactments essentialize or suggest a lack of fixity in anatomically linked signifiers of female subjectivity?

In 'Renaming *Untitled Flesh*: marking the politics of marginality,' Meiling Cheng grapples directly with Phelan's argument regarding visibility, examining the problematic of identity politics in relation to how various identities are seen to register corporeally (visibly) in the performance practice of the 'Sacred Naked Nature Girls.' Cheng argues that this group explicitly intersects ethnicity, class, gender, and sexuality in their work and thus unhinges the assumed correspondence between 'appearance' and social or individual 'self.' Phelan, whose contribution here is the essay 'Andy Warhol: performances of *Death in*

America,' expands on the ideas she introduced in *Unmarked* and her more recent *Mourning Sex* to explore the representability of death itself and the capacity of Warhol's *Death in America* project to 'issue ... an invitation to the spectator to imagine her/himself as simultaneously dead and alive' through its performative engagement of spectatorial desires and fears.

The inclusion of a performance script – that of Coco Fusco and Nao Bustamante's 'Stuff' – is intended to provide a model of how subjects can be engaged and re-articulated through a performance art project that both draws the audience in through a seductive dynamic of identification but also provokes spectators by exposing the particularities of their racial, sexual, and gender affinities. This scripted scenario documents the performance itself, where, employing multiple media (theater, tourist narratives, slide projections, music), Fusco and Bustamante enacted themselves across multiple registers of inter-sectional identities to solicit spectatorial identifications and empathy as well as laughter. 'Stuff,' a parodic integration of discourses of tourism with exploded stereotypes of Latinas, exaggerates identities, making them overly 'visible,' but also points to their inevitably fraught, 'invisible' effects. 'Stuff' epitomizes the kind of performative practice that riotously overturns modernist formalism through its exuberant embrace of the corporeal, the kitsch, the feminine, the Latin, and the narrative as well as opening itself enthusiastic-ally to interpretive engagement and re-articulation.

The essays at the end of this collection address the ways in which advanced technologies of communication have been mobilized to 'perform' particular subjects in new ways in visual practice. Christine Poggi's 'Following Acconci/Targeting Vision' focuses on Vito Acconci's body artworks around 1970, highlighting his fascination with vision as a pheno-menological function of intersubjectivity. Acconci's manipulations of his body through photography, video, and performance art projects specifically investigate the intersubjective structures of vision – as these have been reformatted through technologies of representa-tion in the modern and postmodern eras. Joanna Lowry's 'Performing vision in the theatre of the gaze: the work of Douglas Gordon' and Barbara U. Schmidt's 'What sense do the senses make? Aspects of corporeality in the works of Miriam Cahn and Maureen Connor' focus on particular practices that surface the technological as a mediating factor in our experience of embodied subjectivities (including our own). While Lowry makes use of the Lacanian model of the gaze dominant in 1980s feminist theories of visual culture, Schmidt counters the better-known Lacanian model with a reciprocal, phenomenologically engaged notion of feminist practice developed via the work of Maurice Merleau-Ponty and film theorist Vivian Sobchack.

As suggested above, the very deployment of the term *performative* as understood in this collection proposes a dual critical project. First, it is one that opens out onto and questions the continuing assumptions of a reified conception of the artwork as a static object whose meanings are inherent in its form or structure and easily disclosed to the knowing interpreter. And second (and related to the first point), it scrutinizes the correlative assumption that the art critic or art historian has but to stage himself and his privileged 'eye' in a proper relationship to the work in order to decipher its semiotic codes (whether artistic or political and social) and elicit the work's 'true meaning' and cultural value, cloaking his findings in the legitimizing aesthetic rhetoric of an earlier interpretive regime, thereby securing his status as one of the professionalized select.

What the essays in this book collectively demonstrate is a skepticism towards such a stance. Together, they display an acute awareness of the thorny problematics of interpretation itself. The diversity of methods, materials, and objects of inquiry evident in these essays points to the impossibility of applying prescriptive notions of meaning and value to contemporary performance-oriented practices as well as to work from earlier periods. This diversity also undermines any desire to apply a methodological orthodoxy. Rather, these essays offer directions as to how the general issue of performativity has begun to transform the way we look at, engage with, and comprehend artistic practices of all kinds. Interpretation *is*, we would argue, a kind of performance of the object, while the performance of the body as an artistic practice *is* a mode of textual inscription. The body (as the corporeal enactment of the subject) is known and experienced only through its representational performances – whether presented 'live,' in photographs, videos, films, on the computer screen, or through the interpretive text itself. Interpretation, like the production of works of art, is a mode of communication. Meaning is a process of engagement and never dwells in any one place.

NOTES

1 See especially the collection of J. L. Austin's lecture notes, *How to Do Things with Words*, ed. J. O. Urmson and Marina Sbisa, Cambridge, Mass., Harvard University Press, 1975; Jacques Derrida, 'Signature Event Context,' in Derrida's *Margins of Philosophy*, tr. Alan Bass, Chicago, University of Chicago Press, 1982, pp. 307–330; Judith Butler, *Gender Trouble: Feminism and the Subversion of Identity*, London and New York, Routledge, 1990 and *Bodies that Matter: On the Discursive Limits of 'Sex'*, London and New York, Routledge, 1993. In performance studies, see Philip Auslander, *Presence and Resistance: Postmodernism and Cultural Politics in Contemporary America*, Ann Arbor, University of Michigan Press, 1992; Herbert Blau, *To All Appearances: Ideology and Performance*, London and New York, Routledge, 1992; Sue-Ellen Case, *The Domain-Matrix: Performing Lesbian at the End of Print Culture*, Bloomington and Indianapolis, Indiana University Press, 1996; Sue-Ellen Case, Philip Brett, and Susan Leigh Foster (eds), *Cruising the Performative: Interventions into the Representation of Ethnicity, Nationality, and Sexuality*, Bloomington and Indianapolis, Indiana University Press, 1995; Elin Diamond (ed.), *Performance and Cultural Politics*, London and New York, Routledge, 1996; Jill Dolan, *Presence and Desire: Essays on Gender, Sexuality, Performance*, Ann Arbor, University of Michigan Press, 1993; Peggy Phelan, *Unmarked: The Politics of Performance*, London and New York, Routledge, 1993, and *Mourning Sex: Performing Public Memories*, London and New York, Routledge, 1997; Lynda Hart and Peggy Phelan (eds), *Acting Out: Feminist Performances*, Ann Arbor, University of Michigan Press, 1993; and Rebecca Schneider, *The Explicit Body in Performance*, London and New York, Routledge, 1997. For a more extended theorization of performativity in the visual arts, see Amelia Jones, *Body Art/Performing the Subject*, Minneapolis, University of Minnesota Press, 1998.

2 Peggy Phelan, 'Introduction,' in *Acting Out*, p. 15. It is notable that, until recently, anti-racist and postcolonial theory has not tended to explore performativity as a critical mode of thinking about culture. The recent exceptions include Coco Fusco's *English Is Broken Here: Notes on Cultural Fusion in the Americas*, New York, New Press, 1995, which extends her performance work into cultural analysis, and Catherine Ugwu (ed.), *Let's Get It On: The Politics of Black Performance*, London, Institute of Contemporary Arts and Seattle, Bay Press, 1995, an exhibition catalogue with extended essays by Fusco, Ugwu, and others. Another major exception to this lacuna is the work of Trinh T. Minh-ha, which has been crucial to the opening up of the notion of race as intersectionally and performatively determined in relation to gender, sexuality, and class; see especially her book *Woman, Native, Other: Writing Postcoloniality and Feminism*, Bloomington and Indianapolis, Indiana University Press, 1989. White theorists of the performative have occasionally discussed racial difference as performative (see, for example, Peggy Phelan's chapter on Anita Hill and Clarence Thomas in *Mourning Sex*, pp. 95–118), but,

typically, issues of gender and sexuality tend to be the main focuses of white-dominated performance studies.

3   Phelan, 'Introduction', pp. 21–2; here, Phelan claims such 'reimagining' in particular for 'the performativity of feminist critical writing.' Schneider's *The Explicit Body in Performance* also explicitly stages its own arguments as performative; see her 'Introduction', pp. 1–10. In addition, Schneider's comments regarding an earlier draft of our introduction were invaluable.

4   'Complicity of the audience' is Herbert Blau's phrase in his eloquent Marxian analysis of theatrical performance and its historicization, *To All Appearances*, p. 3; the Schneider quotation is from the Introduction to Elin Diamond (ed.), *Performance and Cultural Politics*, p. 8.

5   Part of this self-reflexivity would involve acknowledging the long history in Enlightenment and post-Enlightenment thought of producing interpretations of the visual arts that reaffirm the supposed superiority of Western culture through, precisely, a complex dynamic of sexual and racial fetishism. As William Pietz has argued, '[t]he Enlightenment concept of fetishism [was a] fixated chiasmus that projected the spontaneous intentionality of subjective desire into inanimate material things'; the Enlightenment, Pietz argues, invented fetishism in order to denigrate the cultural products of, for example, African cultures as *other* to the aesthetic transcendence of European art. 'The unenlightened fetishist, apprehending the material world directly from the perspective of his or her material desires, lacking the capacity for disinterested judgment,' Pietz notes, was thus devalued for his 'lack of aesthetic discrimination' and easily subordinated, in both material and ideological terms, to the European – Kantian – subject. Pietz concludes that Kant's *Critique of Judgment* (1790) – the primary text informing the system of judgment in modernist art historical and critical analysis – can thus be viewed as a 'solution to the problem of fetishism,' in that it provides a model for the interpreter's claiming a disinterested authority over the visual object (rather than the 'primitive' subject's too-grossly embodied relationship with the 'fetish'). William Pietz, 'Fetish,' *Critical Terms for Art History*, Robert Nelson and Richard Shiff (eds), Chicago, University of Chciago Press, 1996, p. 199.

6   See, for example, Roger Fry, *Vision and Design*, London, Chetto and Windus, 1920, reprinted Oxford, Oxford University Press, 1981; and Clement Greenberg, *Art and Culture: Critical Essays*, Boston, Beacon Press, 1961.

7   This argument is fleshed out, and specific examples are given of the continuation of modernist assumptions in discourses of postmodernism, in Amelia Jones, *Postmodernism and the En-Gendering of Marcel Duchamp*, New York and Cambridge, Cambridge University Press, 1994, see especially chapter 2, 'Duchamp as "generative patriarch" of American postmodernists: the antimasculinist, antimodernist lineage,' pp. 29–62.

8   High points in this critique include the following: essays from the late 1970s and 1980s in the journals *Block* and *Screen* (including Mary Kelly, 'Re-viewing modernist criticism,' *Screen*, Autumn 1981, 22, 3: pp. 41–62); Francis Frascina (ed.), *Pollock and After: The Critical Debate*, New York: Harper & Row, 1985; Charles Harrison and Fred Orton (eds), *Modernism, Criticism, Realism: Alternative Contexts for Art*, London and New York, Harper & Row, 1984; Victor Burgin, *The End of Art Theory: Criticism and Postmodernity*, Atlantic Highlands, N.J., Humanities Press International and London, Macmillan, 1986; and Paul Wood, Francis Frascina, Jonathan Harris, and Charles Harrison (eds), *Modernism in Dispute: Art Since the Forties*, New Haven and London, Yale University Press and Milton Keynes, Open University, 1993. Notably, these are all publications in British venues and/or edited by British art historians some of whom are Marxian (sometimes feminist) in their impulse.

9   Lisa Bloom, 'Introduction,' *Gender and Race Politics in Visual Culture*, Minneapolis, University of Minnesota Press, forthcoming, manuscript p. 8. We are indebted to Lisa Bloom for sharing this text with us before its publication.

10   The notion of race as a complex system of identities negotiated through visual images is explored at length in the essays collected in Lisa Bloom's anthology *Gender and Race Politics in Visual Culture*; see especially essays by Inderpal Grewal, Shawn Smith, Irit Rogoff, and Jennifer González. In addition to the scholars in Bloom's anthology, those mentioned in note 2 above, and the myriad scholars working on race and nation in cultural studies, the essays in the London-based journal *Third-Text* and the work of Homi Bhabha, Lola Young, Judith Wilson, and Jennifer Brody have also been crucial in expanding the analysis of racial identities in this direction.

11 On subjectivity as an ongoing process of continually reiterated codes of sexual identity, see Butler's *Bodies that Matter*.

12 Phelan, *Unmarked*; see especially chapter 1, 'Broken symmetries: memory, sight, love,' pp. 1–33.

1

REASON AND REMAINDERS

Kantian performativity in the history of art

Karen Lang

TO M.L.R.H., *IN MEMORIAM*

> Just as the capacity of representation is the measure of domination, and
> domination is the most powerful thing that can be represented in most
> performances, so the capacity of representation is the vehicle of progress and
> regression at one and the same time.
>
> (Horkheimer and Adorno, *Dialectic of Enlightenment*, 1947[1])

In a well-known passage Kant equates the moral law within the subject to the starry
heavens above him. Arguably the philosopher's most famous utterance aside from the
categorical imperative, 'the starry heavens above me and the moral law within me'
concludes the second volume of his critical philosophy, the *Critique of Practical Reason*, of
1788. It is useful to follow Kant at length on this point, for in this conclusion he offers us
the essential contours of an idealized Kantian subject:

> Two things fill the mind with ever new and increasing admiration and awe, the
> oftener and more steadily we reflect upon them: the starry heavens above me and
> the moral law within me. I do not merely conjecture them and seek them as
> though obscured in darkness or in the transcendent region beyond my horizon: I
> see them before me, and I associate them directly with the consciousness of my
> own existence. The former begins at the place I occupy in the external world of
> sense, and it broadens the connection in which I stand into an unbounded
> magnitude of worlds beyond worlds and systems of systems and into the limitless
> times of their periodic motion, their beginning and their continuance. The latter
> begins at my invisible self, my personality, and exhibits me in a world which has
> true infinity but which is comprehensible only to the understanding – a world with
> which I recognize myself as existing in a universal and necessary (and not only, as
> in the first case, contingent) connection, and thereby also in connection with all
> those visible worlds. The former view of a countless multitude of worlds
> annihilates, as it were, my importance as an animal creature, which must give back
> to the planet (a mere speck in the universe) the matter from which it came, the
> matter which is for a little time provided with vital force, we know not how. The

11

latter, on the contrary, infinitely raises my worth as that of an intelligence by my personality, in which the moral law reveals a life independent of all animality and even of the whole world of sense – at least so far as it may be inferred from the purposive destination assigned to my existence by this law, a destination which is not restricted to the conditions and limits of this life but reaches into the infinite.[2]

Whereas the experience of the starry heavens 'annihilates' the 'importance' of the subject by reminding him of his inevitable mortality, or to use the words of Kant, the fact that he 'must give back to the planet . . . the matter from which it came,' the moral law elevates the subject out of his station as 'a mere speck in the universe' and into the possibility of infinity.[3] The subject in his infinity is thereby rendered akin to the cosmos in its vastness, while he is also endowed with the capacity to grasp a seemingly infinite totality. It is this idealized subject, and not the subject constituted by a duality of reason and nature, that is championed by Kant.[4] Guided by the moral law as a regulative principle, the idealized Kantian subject discovers his superiority and his 'universal and necessary connection' to the universe in the contemplation of the starry skies.

Kant will follow a similar paradigm in his analytic of the sublime. In the third volume of his critical philosophy, the *Critique of Judgment*, of 1790, the starry heavens will be replaced by an object whose vastness or might will initially overwhelm the subject; the 'moral law within' will be translated into the idea of 'a higher purposiveness,' occasioned by the experience of the sublime. Just as 'the moral law within' lifts the subject out of his own animal nature, so in the experience of the sublime the subject discovers his superiority over and above nature. In Kant's second and third *Critiques*, mortality gives way to morality as nature is traded for reason.

According to Kant, the subject desires to live in accord with reason's demands, and it is reason's 'peculiar fate' to press itself toward questions and ends it often cannot answer or attain.[5] What Kant calls this 'peculiar fate' is, however, anything but a failing. As Susan Neiman remarks, the 'autonomy of the principles of reason permits them to function as a standard by which experience can be judged: by providing a vision of intelligibility that the given world does not meet, they urge us to continue our labors until this idea is attained.'[6] In his three *Critiques* Kant demonstrates how reason operates as a regulative principle, guiding understanding, moral action, and judgment. Operating on the world rather than constituted through it, reason provides the possibility of organization and so shapes the world according to its own moral image.[7]

Unlike the faculty of the understanding, which enables the subject to feel at home in the world, reason is not of the natural world, nor is it at home in it. The faculty of understanding is directed toward knowledge of the world as it is, whereas the efforts of reason are exerted in the name of the future – toward the world as it should be, or will one day become. Reason and nature are therefore constituted as separate spheres in the Kantian system. For Neiman, this 'duality of reason and the world' makes Kant's philosophy 'profoundly modern.'[8] While a duality of reason and nature is certainly constitutive of the Kantian subject, 'the unity of reason' is his ascendant principle. As a result, the Kantian subject is not so much implicated in nature as transcendental to it.

Whereas for Rousseau and others of Kant's contemporaries, freedom is located in nature and in a 'natural' state of unalienated wholeness, for Kant freedom lies in the reverse direction – in a prospective moral end which the subject only begins to move toward once reason has released him from the 'womb of nature.'[9] In the concluding passage of the

Critique of Practical Reason, Kantian freedom is located at a telling point along this trajectory. Progressing from the 'starry heavens above me' to 'the moral law within me,' Kant charts a path from nature to reason that opens onto vistas of infinite possibility once the 'animality' of the subject is left behind. The autonomy of the Kantian subject is predicated on this break from nature, and the illusion of the autonomy of the subject is maintained only in so far as the subject's relation to nature has been minimized, or covered over. Not permitted to linger in the realm of nature, the Kantian subject stands to reason, in both senses of the phrase.[10]

While the idealized Kantian subject transcends nature within, and dominates nature without, nature nevertheless remains. In *Bodies that Matter,* Judith Butler describes the mechanisms whereby '[w]hat is refused or repudiated in the formation of the subject continues to determine that subject. What remains outside the subject, set outside by the act of foreclosure which founds the subject, persists as a kind of defining negativity.'[11] As the 'defining negativity' of the Kantian subject, nature forms the underside of the idealized subject as well as an unimagined detour from the creation of a fully rational and moral world. Consequently, nature must be warded off. The idealized Kantian subject, or the movement from nature to reason, must be continually performed.

For Kant, the performance of the subject is one of discovery rather than of struggle. What the subject discovers is his moral worth in the shape of his own reason. Highlighting reason over nature, and the domination of nature through reason, Kant describes the movement from nature to reason as one forever in the service of the idealized subject. In this sense, the discovery of the moral law, or of 'a life independent of all animality,' might be termed a Kantian historical sign: a sign of progress, indicating that humankind is improving.[12] Yet the idealized Kantian subject actually represents himself to himself in the form of his own domination. Considering the domination of nature by the subject in a favorable light, Kant views the movement from nature to reason as a story of progress. Following Horkheimer and Adorno, on the other hand, one can see in Kantian performativity the traces of regression.

In *Dialectic of Enlightenment,* published in 1947, Horkheimer and Adorno describe the mythic origins and contemporary effects of Enlightenment progress. The book begins with 'Odysseus or Myth and Enlightenment,' an excursus by Adorno on Homer's epic wanderer.[13] Odysseus, whose sense of self is fragile and who struggles to preserve the newly constructed self against the overpowering forces of nature, served well as an illustration of Adorno's account of the mythic origins of enlightenment. For Horkheimer and Adorno, the turning points of Western civilization are marked by the emergence of new peoples or classes who have succeeded in ever more strenuously repressing their fear of 'uncomprehended, threatening nature,' a fear which is itself the creature of attempts to objectify and materialize nature. Myth is reduced to 'superstition,' and the domination of nature is made into the absolute purpose of life. Yet as Adorno demonstrates in his excursus, the domination of nature entails a certain sacrifice on the part of the subject himself: the nature Odysseus slays in the external world – most memorably captured in his episode with the Sirens – is, at the same time, the nature he sacrifices within himself.[14]

For Odysseus as well as for the Kantian subject, the journey into rational subjectivity entails an overcoming of internal and external nature. While Odysseus slays nature through the cunning of reason, the Kantian subject confronts nature in the aesthetic experience, only to find himself superior to it. This is most powerfully demonstrated in Kant's analytic of the sublime. Unlike their philosophical forebear however, Horkheimer and Adorno do not view the overcoming of nature as an unequivocal sign of progress. Instead, they consider the movement from nature to reason dialectically.

As *Dialectic of Enlightenment* indicates, the production of a self occurs only once instinct – or nature – has been overcome by reason, and this is registered through the exercise of self-consciousness. For the 'proto-bourgeois' Odysseus, and so Horkheimer and Adorno argue for all subsequent bourgeois subjects, self-consciousness thus occurs at the expense of the subject's own nature.[15] Odysseus signals the achievement of self-consciousness by the beating of his breast, thereby making clear that his victory is one over his own nature. Rather than submit to the rule of the instincts and desires, the newly self-conscious Odysseus is able to exercise more thoroughly his faculty of reason and so to win his battle with the forces and manifestations of nature he encounters. Yet as Horkheimer and Adorno make clear in their nightmare vision of an instrumental reason run amok, in time this reason comes to dominate the subject himself. Considered in this way, 'representation is the vehicle of progress and regression at one and the same time.'[16] As progress, representation indicates the slaying of an internal and external nature that had formerly dominated the subject; in its denial of nature and of the space between things, however, representation is regressive.[17]

Homer's *Odyssey* and the Kantian philosophical enterprise indicate how the subject of reason is perforce male.[18] Nature, on the other hand, is customarily gendered female.[19] The realm left behind in the triumphant march toward rational subjectivity and Enlightenment progress, nature makes her appearance in the history of art in the guise of personification. Kantian performativity in art history will therefore be a drama played out between male and female, wherein the female will be equated with nature, while the male will serve as artist, philosopher, or ideal spectator. To be sure, the conflation of woman and nature, indeed the personification of nature, is not a natural fact. Rather these constructions, and the artistic conventions to which they have given rise, dramatize the need to secure the idealized Kantian subject from the internal and external nature that continually threatens his undoing. It is to this act of securing that I would now like to turn.

In the history of art we encounter reverberations of the philosophical journey of the Kantian subject, or so it appears when we consider three graphic works by German artists of the late nineteenth and early twentieth centuries. In Max Beckmann's pen and pencil drawing of February, 1946, *Walk (The Dream)* (Plate 1.1), the artist depicts himself taking a nocturnal stroll along a high bridge.[20] Beckmann vividly described a long walk in his diary during the month this drawing was made, noting how 'the sea was once again the sea and said good day Mr. Beckmann.'[21] In the chasm separating the darkness on the left-hand side of the drawing from the light on the right, a colossal, supine female form lies across an expanse of water. The night walker, who steps off the end of the bridge, is poised to fall into the lap of a recumbent nature. Like the song of the sirens, the personification of the sea beckons to this latter-day Odysseus, who appears to have no option but to fall, as his journey into the light has been pre-empted by the very disjuncture of the bridge itself.

In Max Klinger's 1900 etching and aquatint, *The Philosopher* (Plate 1.2), we find a similar *mise en scène*.[22] The third in a suite of prints entitled 'On Death, part II,' the Philosopher is conceived along with the ruler and the genius (artist) as an exemplary individual.[23] Klinger depicts the philosopher, perhaps a self-portrait, standing naked and upright beside an image of a colossal, supine woman. As in the drawing by Beckmann, the image of female nature in Klinger's print is suspended between solid ground on one side

Plate 1.1 Max Beckmann, *Walk (The Dream)*, 1946. Collection Sophie Franke, Munich

and water on the other, just as her form marks a divide between regions of darkness and light. Shifts in scale, such as those of the woman and the philosopher who stands upright beside her, and combinations of vertical hatching and ink washes, produce a richly textured, fantasy world. As in so many of Klinger's prints, the focus in *The Philosopher* is on a decisive moment, one that suggests a narrative not directly revealed.[24]

Concentrating the action in the print on a moment of beholding, Klinger presents the philosopher reaching beyond the personification of nature to the lighted realm, and to his own mirror image, on the other side of her body. As if to underscore the separation of woman and man, of nature and reason, Klinger's image of a slumbering nature does not

Plate 1.2 Max Klinger, *The Philosopher*, 1885/1900. Museum der bildenden Künste, Leipzig

find her reflection in the mirror, a visual fact made all the more poignant by her monumentality relative to the questing male figure. Taking his inspiration from the writings of the German philosopher Arthur Schopenhauer, particularly his *Parerga and Paralipomena*, Klinger here depicts the limits of self-recognition.[25] According to Schopenhauer, the only true path for philosophy is through the interiority of the subject. The subject can, however, never know the knowing subject, since one can never be both knower and known subject simultaneously.[26] Separated from himself as an onlooker, the philosopher enacts the disjuncture between the perceiving subject and the object of his knowledge. It is nature, personified through the body of a woman, and her realm, namely the murky waters of imagination and the indeterminate, which shape the space between darkness and light, between the merely perceiving subject and the truth that is the object of his pursuit. As nature, the slumbering woman is likewise an emblem of mortality, and, according to Schopenhauer, it is death that offers the only release from the separation of subject and object.

In the manner of an idealized Kantian subject the philosopher in Klinger's print accommodates the limits of self-recognition by standing to reason over and above internal and external nature. It is reason that drives the philosopher to know the truth, yet what he discovers is merely his own reflection.[27] Nature, slayed and slumbering, does not figure in this reflection – she is, after all, not reflected in the mirror. What is depicted in Klinger's print is an act of representation and of domination: of the representation of knowledge, of the domination of nature in pursuit of that knowledge. It is the configuration of knowledge we find in Descartes, the *cogito ergo sum*, wherein thinking defines subjectivity, and nature is at best an absent presence. Performing as an idealized subject, Klinger's *Philosopher*

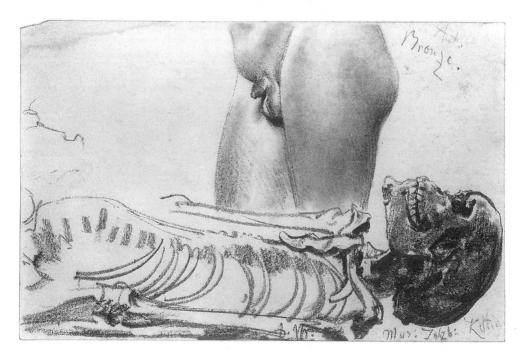

Plate 1.3 Adolph Menzel, *Skeleton of a Celtic Woman and Detail of a Statue in Salzburg Museum, c.* 1887. Kupferstichkabinett, Berlin

17

reflects himself as himself, and not as nature, or what he is not. (A = A, and not B.)

If Klinger's philosopher remains suspended between the moment of beholding and recognition, then Adolph Menzel's drawing of 1887, *Skeleton of a Celtic Woman and Detail of a Statue in Salzburg Museum* (Plate 1.3), provides us with the point of view of the artist-recorder and the art historian.[28] In this suggestive drawing of objects in storage in Salzburg Museum, Menzel brings together two objects which would surely never be placed in such close proximity in any 'rational' museum display.[29] Menzel had a habit of incessantly recording the world around him, and was especially interested in the sidelines of life – in the objects, details, and fragments that comprise the diurnal and the incidental. Whether Menzel simply recorded the position of the skeleton and the antique bronze as he found them in the storage bin of the museum is not known. What is certain, however, is that he found the juxtaposition of these objects intriguing, perhaps precisely because of the ironic commentary they seem to make on the supposedly rational nature of museum display.

Given the customary conflation of woman and nature, it should come as no surprise that Menzel depicts a female skeleton. In this instance, nature has been more than tamed: Menzel's drawing presents not a Celtic woman so much as sheer, inanimate matter. Placed beside the very upright bronze, whose biological sex leaves no room for debate, the artist provides us with a provocative configuration. Menzel does not enact the drama of his own subjectivity (although we could well argue that we see its traces here). Instead, and akin to the art historian, the artist has found a suggestive juxtaposition and has delineated his chosen figures with a fine objectivity. Menzel, the artist-recorder, is not implicated in nature. In keeping with his Kantian counterpart, his viewpoint on his subject is transcendent, thus affording him a certain measure of objectivity.

Herein lies the performance of the subject in Kantian philosophy and in art history. If the drawing by Beckmann demonstrates how nature beckons, then the philosopher of Klinger's eponymous print has warded off the lure of nature through transcendence. In bridging the divide through his own reason – and not troubling over the fact that what he discovers is merely his own reflection – Klinger's philosopher performs as an idealized subject. The works on paper by Beckmann, Klinger, and Menzel not only echo the trajectory of the idealized Kantian subject, they also tell us about the history of art as a disciplinary practice. Like Klinger's philosopher, or *a fortiori* Menzel the artist-recorder, the art historian stands over and above the work of art. Avoiding the lure of the image, he employs his own brand of Odyssean cunning. Renouncing the fusion of subject and object that troubles the experience of fetishism, in the discipline of art history the rational subject of aesthetic judgment confronts the art object with a certain detachment. In this way, the elevated status of the art object – what might be termed the idol in the history of art – is met by the cool gaze of the humanist, while the distance necessary for a truly aesthetic experience is structurally maintained.[30]

The idealized Kantian subject, the philosopher of Klinger's print, the 'objective' art historian, these are all constructions through which the subject is at once established and vacated. Drained of its own nature – of its own corporeality – the subject is accorded through reason a transcendent position on both 'the starry heavens above me' and the artistic object. This has not always been the case, however. As Hans-Georg Gadamer reminds us in *The Relevance of the Beautiful*: 'our recourse to ancient thought helps us to see that in art and the beautiful we encounter a significance that transcends all conceptual thought.'[31] It was Kant who reversed the terms of this equation. His 'Copernican revolution' in philosophy laid out the conditions of the possibility of knowledge, moral action, and judgment for a subject conceived as transcendental to a world of objects.

The Kantian turn toward the (rational) subject did not merely establish and impoverish an idealized subject. In this process the art object was stripped of its magical qualities – it was overcome by reason – thus safely removing it from the realm of fetishism. Because of the interrelation between the work of art and the beholder, reinvesting the work of art with its magical qualities, or what George Steiner has termed its 'real presence,' would be akin to investing the art historian with a body.[32] This embodiment would include a more richly varied 'topography of the self,' one offering more than mere reason.[33] Since how we perform the body greatly determines how we perform the text, refashioning the subject, the art historian, would likewise enable us to re-envision objectivity.

After all, to borrow Lewis Hyde's evocation, 'we are only alive to the degree that we can let ourselves be moved.'[34] If the art object, which has the essential capacity to move us, is denied this capacity in 'scientific' modes of analysis and description in the history of art, then we have robbed the art object – and ourselves – of its primary mode of address. In this sense, the polarity of objectivity and subjectivity presents a circuit of false alternatives in the history of art. Seeking the stamp of a scientific rigor, the discipline of art history has historically sought methodologies that turn on objectivity. Art criticism, on the other hand, has traditionally been the realm where subjectivity has been allowed to reside. At our historical moment, I propose that we attempt to bring these two strands of our practice together. To this end, we might consider what the historian of science Evelyn Fox Keller has described as 'a pursuit of knowledge that makes use of subjective experience ... in the interests of a more effective objectivity.'[35]

In this essay I have tried to show how the performance of the Kantian subject, or the move from nature to reason, involves a certain overcoming of the subject himself, as well as a domination of internal and external nature. Reason may incessantly push the subject beyond his current limits, and toward the moral law, but the idealized Kantian subject cannot help but succeed in his self-projection. For, in the philosopher's systematics, thought is self-contained: understanding and reason reside within the Kantian subject as a self-enclosed system set over and against a world of objects. In the performance of the idealized Kantian subject, nature is therefore assimilated into a subjectivity that literally creates its own world.[36] But what if nature were not so much a phenomenon assimilated into an idealized subjectivity, or dominated in mental or physical representations, as an unassimilable remainder? Though Kant denies nature a foothold in the constitution of an idealized subjectivity, he nevertheless indicates how nature and reason lie at the foundations of the subject. Keeping within the frame of German idealism, Kant – to be sure – views reason rather than nature as the foundation for critical knowledge.

Yet just as assuredly as Kant secures the ascendant position of reason, and so the architectonic of his systematics, he sets up a paradox: Kant denies the body in the formation of subjectivity but clings to the body of the subject as the site of reason, and so of freedom.[37] Recall the conclusion to the *Critique of Practical Reason*, where we find the philosopher's subject contemplating an overwhelming vastness, leaving his own nature behind, and in so dividing himself from himself, finding self-preservation through discovery of the moral law. This divided subject – the subject of reason – is nevertheless tied to the body it has renounced, for it is out of the body that subjectivity arises. Leaving the body behind, the idealized Kantian subject trades mortality for morality. Whereas the embodied being signals the inevitability of death, disembodiment allows for the transcendent vistas of reason. Dominating nature, the subject thus conquers his own fear of death, but he does so at the expense of a separation from himself that is never final, but only spectral. In this sense, too, Klinger's *Philosopher* might be considered an emblem of the performative moment of an idealized subjectivity.

The Philosopher demonstrates that the purely transparent structure of self-consciousness, of recognizing oneself as oneself, actually involves a misrecognition: the lighted realm of freedom and the darker realm of necessity are, in fact, not congruent; they may be considered so only at the expense of nature. It is nature, then, that lies at the limits of self-recognition. As the limit that cannot be grasped in reflection, nature figures as part of the pre-reflective subject, or the subject before subjectivity. For the pre-reflective subject, nature constitutes the ground that unites and separates.

We can follow this thread by returning to *The Philosopher*, focusing this time on the viewpoint of the figure in the lighted realm at the left-hand edge of the image. Like his counterpart, the luminous philosopher on the left stares into the dim space in front of him. Yet whereas the lighted realm reflects only the searching male figure, the darkened, right-hand side of the print contains both the philosopher and the personification of nature. Surrendering to the illusion of Klinger's image, we could say that the philosopher in the lighted realm perceives more than his own reflection: he perceives the pre-reflective subject as his own identity, an identity he has shed in the movement from nature to reason. From the viewpoint of the figure on the left, *The Philosopher* might therefore be seen as not so much reflecting himself as himself (A = A, and not B), but as identifying himself in that which he both is and is not (A = A and B). In this model of identity rather than subjectivity, mind (A) resides along with nature (B) in a configuration of identity wherein – as the copula suggests – the subject is conceived as on the one hand, mind, and on the other hand, nature. By recognizing the nature effaced in an idealized model of subjectivity, the subject discovers the aspect that connects him to the cycle of nature and the fact of mortality. Nature thus becomes the determining ground, binding the philosopher to himself and to the external world in a relation of identity and difference that does not position the subject over and against a world of objects so much as indicate their interrelation.[38]

While it can be argued that Klinger provides a model of identity in the viewpoint of the philosopher at the left-hand side of the print, he nevertheless accentuates the shedding of nature as a constituent element of subjectivity.[39] Displaying an erect male figure beside a recumbent female form, Klinger sets up a gendered relation that clearly indicates the ascendancy of the male and the role of reason for self-consciousness. Identity is consequently undercut as it is indicated, and, as in the other depictions of genius in Klinger's print cycle, an idealized subjectivity is favored. Indeed, Klinger's *Philosopher* does not unravel when read from left to right, as subjectivity does not for Schopenhauer. Like Klinger's scene of representation, Schopenhauer's own philosophy is caught between two ways of conceiving the subject.

According to Schopenhauer, aesthetic experience offers a transition from the painful reign of the subject's own will to the Will of the world, a fundamental reality that exists beneath the veil of phenomenal appearance.[40] In order to apprehend the Will in aesthetic contemplation, the subject must actively 'tear itself free from the service of the will,' and so from 'the principle of sufficient reason,' to 'lose [itself] entirely in [the] object.' When subject and object are merged, '[t]hus at the same time, the person who is involved in this perception is no longer an individual, for in such a perception the individual has lost himself; he is the *pure*, will-less, painless, timeless subject of knowledge.'[41] For Schopenhauer, aesthetic experience thus proceeds from active to passive modes, finally resting with the 'pure subject [of a will-less knowing].' If art is understood as a representation of the Will, then the underlying Will never changes, but is conceived as the ground of truth the subject apprehends through aesthetic contemplation. As Cheryl Foster rightly remarks: 'The respect for an *aesthetic* way of knowing, as an alternative to the more familiar scientific way of knowing, is one of the most potent but neglected lessons to be drawn from Schopenhauer's work.'[42] Whereas 'an aesthetic way of knowing' underlines the attraction of subject and object, a 'scientific way of knowing' focuses on the differentiation between elements, thus setting the subject off from the world.

In Schopenhauer's philosophy aesthetic contemplation clearly offers a means of identity with the underlying world of ideas, and so a glimpse of a greater unity of which the subject is also a part. Still, Nietzsche complained of Schopenhauer's 'residually humanistic refusal totally to immerse himself in the flux,'[43] with the result that his philosophy remains caught between the worlds it seeks so assiduously to bridge. Like the Kantian subject confronted by the 'starry skies above,' Schopenhauer offers the 'vastness of the world' only to accentuate the subject's 'triumph over its world': 'The vastness of the world, which previously disturbed our peace of mind, now rests with us; our dependence on it is now annulled by its dependence on us.'[44] As in Klinger's print, the subject of Schopenhauer's philosophy may release himself to the Will of the world, yet, in self-consciousness, he reflects his domination of the external world. Once again, subjectivity ultimately rests with a transcendental rather than with a corporeal subject, that is to say, with a subject who knows the world rather than with a subject in the world.

The philosophies of Kant and Schopenhauer are intriguing for the ways in which they signal and deny embodiment. Schopenhauer's subject of aesthetic contemplation, the pure subject of a will-less knowing, is defined through a bodily will that becomes suspended in the space of the aesthetic experience, only to rise up again, for the world 'is dependent on us' – the subject. While Schopenhauer goes further than Kant in conceptualizing nature as the determining ground of truth, he nevertheless allows the subject to dominate the nature it seeks to feel and apprehend. In this way nature, which may initially overwhelm the subject, may never be the cause of his undoing.

Another view of of the subject and nature is found in the work of the contemporary video artist Bill Viola. In a manner akin to Schopenhauer's description of the aesthetic object as representation, Viola's video projects present different views of the same underlying substance.[45] But whereas Schopenhauer conceives of aesthetic representation and natural appearance as so many variations of the world of the Will, or of the Platonic Ideas, Viola finds the ground of truth in nature itself, a nature at once internal and external. Inspired by the writings of Christian mystics, Zen Buddhists, and other philosophers, Viola presents the subject as at once embodied and in flux, prey to interior and exterior forces that are beautiful, haunting, uncanny. It is these forces, and so nature itself, to which the subject surrenders in his work. In Viola's video art we view the subject in nature and subject as nature.

Conceiving the subject and nature together, Viola views art as 'a whole-body, physical experience' in time.[46] Temporality plays a leading role in his work, for it allows him to follow the development or unraveling of subjects across visual fields that correspond to both human time and timelessness. Vision is thus not solely equated with our point of view. Instead, vision leads to realms of 'unseen images' that emanate from temporal and supra-temporal registers of existence, from the conscious and the unconscious memory.[47]

21

Indeed, as Ursula Frohne suggests, Bill Viola 'is concerned . . . with an aesthetic encounter with the world in its most comprehensive, and also metaphysical sense. . . . The pictorial patterns of memory that Viola understands as equivalent to a super-temporal, or de-temporalized, level of existence that is, as it were, assumed into a sort of cosmic infinity, can hardly be understood without taking into account the perpetual resonance of metaphysical longing.'[48]

The modern subject, cleaved from internal and external nature, responds with 'metaphysical longing' for a perceived unity of existence now lost, for an imaginary unity with nature. Yet the subject is cleaved, and so it is constitutively unable to join permanently with nature, but only to long for this re-union. If, as the German romantic poet Novalis claimed, 'all philosophy is homesickness,'[49] then Viola's art is a gift from a homeland lost in modern society, a homeland conceived not as a golden age, but as the phenomenon of nature itself. In this way, Viola's creations offer the possibility of a transitory reconciliation with internal and external nature. What we are offered is therefore not redemption, but a medium through which to recognize what we have forgotten, and consequently yearn for through 'metaphysical longing.'

Stations of 1994 (Plate 1.4) is an evocative case in point. In this large-scale installation the viewer is plunged into a darkened space and surrounded by five channels of video projected onto five translucent screens. On each screen a figure is shown suspended upside down in water, picked out from the surrounding darkness by a strong cross light. We hear the interior of this aquatic world through sound projection, as we watch the figures emerge, float adrift, and disappear from the screens with varying frequency, only to then

Plate 1.4 Bill Viola, *Stations*, 1994. Zentrum für Kunst und Medientechnologie, Karlsruhe

plunge back into the water to repeat the approximately thirty-minute cycle of the installation. The projected figures – a boy, a young woman, a young man, a pregnant woman, and an old man – represent the stations of earthly life. Whereas the figures on the screens are shown upside down, they are reflected upright on granite slabs positioned on the floor in front of each screen.

In contrast to Klinger's *Philosopher*, Viola's *Stations* does not offer a single viewpoint, or, as in Klinger's print, one that can be relayed back and forth along the axis of a single line. In place of a stationary viewpoint, we are offered a visual environment that invites the engagement of the eye and the body, and of our movement in space. *Stations* confounds a transparent notion of reflection: while the bodies on the screens correspond – in reverse – to those fixed on the surfaces of the granite, on the polished stone surfaces we see ourselves and the reflection of a body that is not our own.[50] Reflection, seeing oneself as oneself, is here also seeing oneself as another. Like the philosopher on the left-hand side of Klinger's print, in *Stations* one perceives identity in that which one is and is not.

Rather than an overcoming of nature by the subject, *Stations* presents subjects suspended in nature and invites us to contemplate the implications of their immersion. Although chronological age and gender are indicated, the subjects on the screens are equally unmoored from temporality. Viola asks us to suspend our knowledge of the technological origins of *Stations* and instead to contemplate this liminal space as simply posited rather than fabricated. When experienced as merely posited, *Stations* becomes a theater of technological illusion and metaphysics, an environment wherein the human subject's relation to temporality and mortality are the primary subjects of artistic legerdemain. To quote Viola, in *Stations* an 'initial surface appearance of eerie, serene beauty resides over a deeper disturbing aspect of muted violence and disorder, with the unrooted, isolated, free-floating bodies evoking an eternal state between dream and death.'[51] *Stations* speaks of a nature that exists not as a world of objects tamed for a transcendental viewer, but as a realm that includes and exceeds a subject who is asked to ponder identity and difference, temporality and the supra-temporal, and life and death as part of his or her own existence.

In *Stations* the subject is not established and vacated, but reminded of its corporeality. In a similar vein, Viola's art does not invite a transcendent point of view or an 'objective' analysis so much as beckons for bodily participation on the part of the beholder. Earlier models of historical meaning sought the royal road to objectivity – and so of truth – in the transcendence of the interpreter's historical position and, with it, the temporal distance separating historian and object of investigation.[52] In Viola's art the viewer is likewise invited to bridge the separation of subject and object, but only as a means to interpret the works according to her or his own point of view. Because Viola's work turns on a reflexive model of meaning, it suggests that understanding itself 'is not to be thought of so much as an action of subjectivity, but as the entering into an event of transmission in which past and present are constantly mediated.'[53] In this way – and importantly – neither subjectivity nor meaning are denied, nor are they conceived as transcendental or unitary. Instead, subjectivity and meaning are conceived through their interrelation, and specifically through a non-idealized, historically bounded, corporeal subject.

Using the latest video and sound technology, Viola trains his sights, and ours, on a modern condition of metaphysical longing: the artist both acknowledges the separation of subject and object and indicates the connection of the subject to the life cycle of nature. Nature, coursing through Viola's video art as an unassimilable remainder, is thus a fundamental and unfathomable phenomenon offered up for understanding, not an object or concept to be dominated. Gadamer's perspective, which he termed philosophical hermeneutics, strikes a resonant chord with Viola's own work and writings. In an essay published in 1966, Gadamer makes clear that 'our task is to reconnect the objective world of technology, which the sciences place at our disposal and discretion, with those fundamental orders of our being that are neither arbitrary nor manipulable by us, but rather simply demand our respect.'[54] Whereas the duty of the idealized Kantian subject is to transcend internal and external nature, Gadamer and Viola advocate the re-emergence of the subject in nature. The task of this subject, which, as Gadamer indicates, is also our own charge, might therefore be as follows: to cultivate rather than to dominate, and in so doing, to reunite reason and its remainders.[55]

NOTES

I should like to thank Amelia Jones and Andrew Stephenson for their sustained engagement with this project, and Amelia Jones for her helpful editorial comments. I would also like to extend my gratitude to my family for their support. Unless otherwise indicated, all translations are mine.

1   M. Horkheimer and T. Adorno, *Dialectic of Enlightenment*, 1947, tr. John Cumming, New York, Continuum, 1987, pp. 34–5.
2   I. Kant, *Critique of Practical Reason*, tr. Lewis White Beck, New York, Liberal Arts Press, 1956, pp. 161–2. On this passage, see also H. Blumenberg, *The Genesis of the Copernican World*, tr. Robert M. Wallace, Cambridge, Mass., and London: MIT Press, 1987, pp. 52–64; and Rudolf Unger, '"Der bestirnte Himmel über mir ...." Zur geistesgeschichtlichen Deutung eines Kant-Wortes,' in Albertus University, Königsberg in Prussia (ed.), *Immanuel Kant: Festschrift zur zweiten Jahrhundertfeier seines Geburtstages*, Leipzig, Dieterich'sche Verlagsbuchhandlung, 1924, pp. 340–70.
3   While I find it highly unsatisfactory to refer to an exclusively male Kantian subject, this is how Kant characterizes the subject. For historical consistency, I will follow Kant's designation. On the problem and implications of sexual difference for the idealized Kantian subject, see U. P. Jauch, 'Schopenhauer oder Kant. Geschlechterdifferenz zwischen Zeitkritik und Zeitgeist,' in W. Schirmacher (ed.), *Schopenhauer in der Postmoderne*, Vienna, Passagen Verlag, 1989, pp. 49–58.
4   For an extended critique of the foundational premises and idealized construction of the Kantian subject, see my article, 'The Dialectics of Decay: Rereading the Kantian Subject,' *Art Bulletin*, September 1997, lxxix, no. 3, pp. 413–39.
5   Kant begins the first edition of the *Critique of Pure Reason*, (A viii): 'Human reason has the peculiar fate [das besondere Schicksal] in a species of its knowledge [in einer Gattung ihrer Erkenntnisse]; it is burdened with questions that it cannot dismiss – for they are assigned to it by the nature of reason itself – but which it also cannot answer, for they exceed [übersteigen] the power of human reason altogether.' Cited in P. D. Fenves, *A Peculiar Fate: Metaphysics and World-History in Kant*, Ithaca and London, Cornell University Press, 1991. (I have followed Fenves's improved translation of this passage, though I have substituted 'exceed' for 'overstep' in translating *übersteigen*.)
6   S. Neiman, *The Unity of Reason: Rereading Kant*, New York and London, Oxford University Press, 1994, p. 92.
7   Kant's idea of a 'moral image of the world' was shaped to a large extent by his reading of Jean-Jacques Rousseau. Rousseau believed that without a moral image of the world to guide the thoughts and actions of humanity, human beings would fall prey to skepticism, or waver in despair. Kant translates Rousseau's theory into a regulative idea of reason. On the Kantian moral image of the world, see D. Heinrich, *Aesthetic Judgment and the Moral Image of the World: Studies in Kant*, Stanford, Stanford University Press, 1992, especially pp. 3–28; and S. M. Shell, *The Rights of Reason: A Study of Kant's Philosophy and Politics*, Toronto and Buffalo, University of Toronto Press, 1980, pp. 20–32.

8   Neiman, *The Unity of Reason*, p. 203.

9   I. Kant, 'Conjectural Beginning of Human History,' in Lewis White Beck (ed.), *Kant on History*, New York, Macmillan, 1985, p. 59.

10 What has been described as Kant's 'humanist turn,' or his turn away from nature and toward the subject, has profound implications for the constitution of the subject and for the separation of the subject from the natural world. To use the words of Richard Kearney, *Poetics of Modernity. Toward a Hermeneutic Imagination* (New Jersey, Humanities Press, 1995): 'Henceforth, fundamental questions of value gravitate less around external reality than around inward conditions of human consciousness. This anthropocentric reduction is epitomized in a semantic shift in two operative terms of modern thought – "transcendental" and "subjectivity." After the humanist turn, "transcendental" sheds its traditional reference to a real order of value "out there" and refers instead to an inner order of human experience, understanding, or imagination. Likewise, "subjectivity" undergoes a reversal of meaning from its old metaphysical connotation, as that which underlies the solidity of things (*hypokeimenon/subjectum*), to its modern connotation of immanent human activity' (p. 2).

11 J. Butler, *Bodies that Matter: On the Discursive Limits of 'Sex,'* London and New York, Routledge, 1993, p. 190.

12 On the Kantian historical sign see, for instance, I. Kant, 'The Contest of the Faculties,' in H. Reiss (ed.), *Kant: Political Writings*, tr. H. B. Nisbet, Cambridge, Cambridge University Press, 1991, pp. 176–90ff.

13 See note 1. A nuanced translation of Adorno's excursus by Robert Hullot-Kentor appears in *New German Critique*, Spring/Summer 1992, no. 56, pp. 109–35. Hullot-Kentor is in the process of translating Adorno's writings into English. See the new translation of *The Odyssey* by Robert Fagles, New York, Viking, 1996.

14 In addition to Adorno's excursus, see also M. Horkheimer, *Eclipse of Reason*, New York, Continuum, 1947, especially chapter 3, 'The Revolt of Nature.'

15 Horkheimer and Adorno, *Dialectic of Enlightenment*, p. 48. Compare Odysseus's beating of his breast to Georges Bataille's conception of the erotic, which he declares can only be suppressed through rational work. G. Bataille, *Erotism: Death and Sensuality* (1957), tr. M. Dalwood, San Francisco, City Lights Books, 1986.

16 Horkheimer and Adorno, *Dialectic of Enlightenment*, pp. 34–5. See also Horkheimer, *Eclipse of Reason*, where he observes that it is with Socrates that the 'subject begins to think of himself – as opposed to outward reality – as the highest of all ideas' (pp. 134–5).

17 In *Dialectic of Enlightenment*, Adorno also describes the regression of the subject *vis-à-vis* society. As Robert Hullot-Kentor remarks in 'Notes on *Dialectic of Enlightenment*: Translating the Odysseus Essay,' *New German Critique*, Spring/Summer 1992, no. 56, 'Adorno formulates the dialectic of enlightenment as the process by which the domination of nature results in the regression to nature in the form of a society that is second nature; history as domination is a natural history that recreates barbarism' (p. 105).

18 In this sense, *The Odyssey* and the idealized Kantian subject might be considered as part of the development of modern individualism. On the mythic nature of analogous male heroes, see I. Watt, *Myths of Modern Individualism: Faust, Don Quixote, Don Juan, Robinson Crusoe*, Cambridge and New York, Cambridge University Press, 1996.

19 The gendering of nature, of course, has its own history, one that goes back to Aristotelian definitions of feminine matter and masculine mind. On the gendering of nature and its implications, see E. Bronfen, *Over Her Dead Body: Death, Femininity and the Aesthetic*, London and New York, Routledge, 1992; C. Merchant, *The Death of Nature: Women, Ecology, and the Scientific Revolution* (1980), San Franscisco, Harper & Row, 1990; S. B. Ortner, 'Is Female to Male as Nature is to Culture?' in M. Zimbalist Rosaldo and L. Lamphere (eds), *Woman, Culture, and Society*, Stanford, Stanford University Press, 1974, pp. 67–87; and D. Summers, 'Form and Gender,' in N. Bryson, M. A. Holly, and K. Moxey (eds), *Visual Culture: Images and Interpretations*, Hanover and London, University Press of New England, 1994, pp. 384–411.

20 Beckmann signed his drawing 'Beckmann/A46,' indicating his exile in Amsterdam, and on the verso he wrote, 'Spaziergang 7. Februar 46.' Beckmann drew a similar configuration of a monumental nude stretched across a ground in his lithograph 'The Fall of Man' ('Südenfall'), plate 14 of his 1946 series, 'Day and Dream.' For an illustration of this lithograph, see J. Hofmaier, *Max*

Beckmann: Catalogue raisonné of his Prints, Bern, Gallery Kornfeld, 1990, pp. 862–3.

21 In Amsterdam on February 6, 1946, Beckmann wrote in his diary: 'War in Zandvoort und zu Fuss nach Overveen, ziemlich anstrengend, aber das Meer war wieder Meer und sagte guten Tag Herr Beckmann. Auf Schienen und Brücken Schwindel, ziemlich wenig weh.' Cited in F. Erpel, *Max Beckmann: Leben im Werk. Die Selbstbildnisse*, Munich, C. H. Beck, 1985, unpaged.

22 Between 1885 and 1909 Klinger created the twelve etchings that comprise 'On Death, part II,' though certain ideas date back to 1879. A first edition of the print cycle, published in 1898, included six prints. Three more prints were published in 1904, and the rest, including *The Philosopher*, followed in 1910. A study for *The Philosopher*, in black ink and dated 1885, contains the inscription 'SAPIENTER/IGNORABERIS.' See M. Klinger, *Bestandkatalog der Bildwerke, Gemälde und Zeichnungen im Museum der bildenden Künste Leipzig*, Leipzig, E. A. Seemann Verlag, 1995, p. 207. 'On Death, part II' is a continuation of the theme of the print cycle, 'On Death, part I,' first published in 1889. In the first part of the cycle Klinger focuses on images of death conceived as an unexpected stroke of fate. In 'On Death, part II,' Klinger moves from an exterior consideration of death – as a force that strikes coincidentally – 'to a more encompassing view, one in which the incidents of the first series are given over to the depiction of larger principles, such that exterior horror is now opposed to inner resolution, thus making possible a harmonious conclusion' (Max Klinger in H. W. Singer, *Zeichnungen der Max Klinger, Meister der Zeichnung*, vol. 1, Leipzig, 1912, p. 89). On the artist's preoccupation with, and renderings of, death, see T. Matuszak, 'Todesdarstellungen im graphischen Werk Max Klingers,' in *Max Klinger*, loose-leaf exhibition catalogue, Kunsthalle Bielefeld, Universitätskunstsammlung Göttingen, Kunsthalle Tübingen, and Museum Wiesbaden, 1976–7, pp. 289–96. On the theme of death in German art of the nineteenth century, see H. Beenken, *Das Neunzehnte Jahrhundert in der deutschen Kunst*, Munich, Verlag F. Bruckmann, 1944, pp. 234–46.

23 The ruler, the genius (artist), and the philosopher are conceived in 'On Death, part II' along with images of plague, war, and misery, for, according to the artist, 'with the summa of recognition of respect grows the capacity for suffering.' On this point, and on the positioning of the plates in the cycle as a whole, see D. Finselberger, 'Untersuchungen zu Opus XIII, "Vom Tode II,"' in *Max Klinger*, pp. 297–303.

24 This point is lyrically described by Giorgio de Chirico, 'Max Klinger,' in M. Carrà, *Metaphysical Art*, tr. C. Tisdall (New York and Washington, Praeger, 1971), as he writes in 1921 on another of Klinger's prints: 'As I have already said, it possesses the dramatic sense of certain moments in the cinema in which people inhabiting tragedy and modern life appear frozen in the spectrality of a moment, scenes that are terrible and real' (p. 133).

25 '... so ziemlich der ganze Zweite Teil *Von Tode* is das Resultat der langgepflegten Lektüre der *Parerga und Paralipomena*. Die gehörten lange Zeit zu meinem täglichen literarischen Futter ....' Letter from the artist, cited in *Max Klinger. Wege zum Gesamtkunstwerke*, Mainz, Verlag Philipp von Zabern, 1984, p. 286; original citation from H. W. Singer (ed.), *Briefe von Max Klinger*, Leipzig, 1924, p. 205. On Schopenhauer's influence on the artist, see A. Dückers, *Max Klinger*, Berlin, Rembrandt Verlag, 1976, pp. 67–8; A. Hübscher, 'Betrachtungen zu den beiden zentralen Problemkomplexen Tod und Liebe in der Graphik Max Klingers – in Verbindung mit seinen Theorie über Grafik,' Ph.D. dissertation, University of Halle, 1970, pp. 100–10; and M. Michalski, *Max Klinger. Künstlerische Entwicklung und Wandel weltanschaulicher Gehalte in den Jahren 1878–1910*, Augsburg, AV-Verlag, 1986, pp. 7–14.

26 A. Schopenhauer, *Parerga und Paralipomena*, Gesamtausgabe, vol. v, pp. 24 and 54. Cited in Dückers, *Max Klinger*, 67.

27 As Klinger puts it in S. Wega Mathieu (ed.), *Max Klinger. Leben und Werk in Daten und Bildern* (Frankfurt am Main, Insel Verlag, 1976), 'the searching man reaches over the earth (female nature) for the universe and finds only his own reflection.' ('Der forschende Mensch greift über die Erde (weibliches Wesen) hinweg nach dem Weltall und findet nur sein eigenes Spiegelbild'), p. 154. Consider, as well, the words of G. W. F. Hegel from *Aesthetics: Lectures on Fine Art*, tr. T. M. Knox, Oxford, Oxford University Press, 1975, 'man draws out of himself and puts before himself what he is ... in order ... to enjoy in the shape of things ... an external realization of himself' (p. 31). For an interesting comparison to Klinger's *Philosopher* that brings into question the model of subjectivity contained in his image, see Cindy Sherman's *Untitled Film Still #56* of 1980, and Amelia Jones's analysis of it in her essay, 'Tracing the Subject with Cindy Sherman,'

in A. Cruz and E. A. T. Smith (eds), *Cindy Sherman Retrospective*, Los Angeles, Museum of Contemporary Art, 1997, pp. 37–8.

28 Menzel's drawing is signed at the center-bottom, A. M., and annotated in the upper right, 'Ant: Bronze,' and in the lower right, 'Mus: Salzb: Keltin.'

29 F. Forster-Hahn, 'Public Concerns, Private Longings: Adolph Menzel's *Iron Rolling Mill* and *Studio Wall*,' unpublished essay, p. 9. See also her essay 'Adolph Menzel: Readings between Nationalism and Modernity,' in C. Keisch and U. Riemann-Reyer (eds), *Adolph Menzel, 1815–1905: Between Romanticism and Impressionism*, New Haven and London, Yale University Press, 1996, pp. 103–12; and W. Hofmann (ed.), *Menzel – der Beobachter*, Munich, Prestel Verlag, 1982.

30 These and other aspects of aesthetic experience are explored in a book project I am preparing, provisionally titled, *Cool Idols: Aesthetics, Subjectivity, and the Making of Art History*.

31 H.-G. Gadamer, *The Relevance of the Beautiful and Other Essays*, tr. N. Walker, R. Bernasconi (ed.), Cambridge, Cambridge University Press, 1986, p. 16.

32 G. Steiner, *Real Presences*, Chicago, University of Chicago Press, 1991.

33 Charles Taylor, 'The Moral Topography of the Self,' in S. Messer, L. Sass, and R. Woolfolk (eds), *Hermeneutics and Psychological Theory*, New Brunswick, Rutgers University Press, 1988, pp. 298–320. In her recent writings, Susan Buck-Morss also argues for an inclusion of somatic or bodily knowledge in aesthetic experience. See her essays, 'Aesthetics and Anaesthetics: Walter Benjamin's Artwork Essay Reconsidered,' *October*, Fall, 1992, vol. 62, pp. 3–41; and 'The City as Dreamworld and Catastrophe,' *October*, Summer, 1995, vol. 73, pp. 3–26.

34 L. Hyde, *The Gift: Imagination and the Erotic Life of Property*, New York, Vintage Books, 1983, p. 20.

35 Cited in S. Bordo, *The Flight to Objectivity: Essays on Cartesianism and Culture*, Albany, State University of New York Press, 1987, p. 103.

36 On the one hand, Kant's claims demonstrate the epistemological and scientific hubris of the late eighteenth century, a time when it was felt that nature could be entirely known and classified. On the other hand, by designating something that cannot be known, Kant's *Ding an sich*, or thing-in-itself, the noumenon in an otherwise phenomenal world, diverges from such claims for complete knowledge. Yet I contend that the *Ding an sich* actually functions in the Kantian system in the same way as the a priori: the thing-in-itself allows the subject to understand the world even though the subject can never know it. We might say, then, that although the *Ding an sich* points to an inaccessible knowledge, as a structural element in Kantian systematics, it nevertheless facilitates intellectual mastery.

37 In Hegel's slave and the development of his 'unhappy consciousness,' we encounter a similar paradox. Judith Butler's 'Stubborn Attachment, Bodily Subjection: Hegel on the Unhappy Consciousness' (in T. Rajan and D. L. Clark (eds), *Intersections: Nineteenth-century Philosophy and Contemporary Theory*, Albany, State University of New York Press, 1995) describes how in 'the passage from bondage to unhappy consciousness,' the body of the slave is '[n]o longer subjected as an external instrument of labor, [yet] the body is nevertheless still split off from consciousness. Reconstituted as an interior alien, the body is sustained through its disavowal and as that which for consciousness must remain disavowed' (p. 181). Butler's essay has informed my own thinking on Kantian subjectivity.

38 I have adapted this model of identity from Schelling's philosophy. See F. W. J. Schelling, *Ausgewählte Schriften*, M. Frank (ed.), Frankfurt, Suhrkamp, 1985, 6 vols; and the 'Stuttgart Seminars,' tr. and ed. T. Pfau, in *Idealism and the Endgame of Theory: Three Essays by F. W. J. Schelling*, Albany, State University of New York Press, 1994, pp. 195–243ff. A lucid introduction in English to Schelling's philosophy is Andrew Bowie's *Schelling and Modern European Philosophy: An Introduction*, London and New York, Routledge, 1993.

39 To this end it is interesting to consider the final print of Klinger's cycle 'On Death, part II,' *On Beauty (An die Schönheit)*, which illustrates a naked man kneeling on grass before a wide expanse of ocean. Here Klinger indicates how man finds deliverance from life, and fulfillment of his longing, by entering into the universe ('im Eingehen in das All'). As opposed to *The Philosopher*, then, who, according to Klinger, 'reaches over the earth (female nature) for the universe [das Weltall] and finds only his own reflection,' in the final print of the cycle fulfillment is indicated for a subject who enters into the universe [das All]. For an illustration of this print, see Dückers, *Max Klinger*, p. 73.

40 Schopenhauer's distinction between the will of the subject and the Will of the world repeats Kant's separation of phenomenal and noumenal worlds. Yet whereas Kant believed that the subject could never know the noumenal world of the *Ding an sich*, or the thing-in-itself, Schopenhauer contends that one can know the Will of the world through an inner will within one's own body.

41 A. Schopenhauer, *World as Will and Representation*, vol. 1, sec. 34, tr. E. F. J. Payne, New York, Dover Publications, 1966, pp. 178–9. Friedrich Nietzsche in the *Genealogy of Morals*, tr. W. Kaufmann and R. J. Hollingdale (New York, Vintage Books, 1969) undoubtedly had this very passage in mind when, in 1887, he wrote the following admonition: 'Henceforth, my dear philosophers, let us be on guard against the dangerous old conceptual fiction that posited a "pure, will-less, painless, timeless knowing subject"', p. 119.

42 C. Foster, 'Schopenhauer and Aesthetic Recognition,' in D. Jacquette (ed.), *Schopenhauer, Philosophy, and the Arts*, Cambridge and New York, Cambridge University Press, 1996, p. 142. Not surprisingly, Schopenhauer accords the genius a special role in aesthetic perception. On the genius, see Foster, 'Schopenhauer and Aesthetic Recognition,' pp. 141–3.

43 Rajan and Clark (ed.), *Intersections*, p 32.

44 Schopenhauer, *World as Will and Representation*, vol. 1, sec. 39, p. 205.

45 Alexander Pühringer in A. Pühringer (ed.), *Bill Viola* (Stuttgart, Ritter Klagenhurt Verlag, 1994) amplifies this point: 'Viola's work *appears* in singular "works", but it *is* one *whole*, a work in progress.... [The] conceptual or spiritual *ground* that appears in the works may be identical but it is not shown in identical ways; the works exhibit, rather, different *aspects* of it, that is, of the *human condition*', p. 78.

46 'Art has always been a whole-body, physical experience. This sensuality is the basis of its true conceptual and intellectual nature, and is inseparable from it.' Bill Viola in conversation with Otto Neumaier and Alexander Pühringer, 'Putting the Whole Back Together,' in Robert Violette in collaboration with the author (ed.), *Bill Viola: Reasons for Knocking at an Empty House. Writings 1973–1994*, Cambridge, Mass., MIT Press, 1995, p. 265.

47 'Unseen images' is Bill Viola's descriptive phrase for his art, and the title of an exhibition of his work. See M. L. Syring (ed.), *Bill Viola: Unseen Images/Nie gesehene Bilder/Images jamais vues*, Düsseldorf, Kunsthalle Düsseldorf, 1992.

48 U. Frohne, 'Motifs of Time: An Anthology of the Time Phenomenon in Contemporary Art,' in H. Klotz (ed.), *Contemporary Art. The Collection of the ZKM: Center for Art and Media Karlsruhe*, Munich and New York, Prestel, 1997, p. 45. I would like to thank Ursula Frohne, as ever, for her stimulating intellectual exchange, and for her help in securing materials.

49 'Philosophy is essentially homesickness – the universal impulse to be home.' *Pollen and Fragments: Selected Poetry and Prose of Novalis*, tr. A. Verslius, Grand Rapids, Phanes Press, 1989, p. 56.

50 This experience would be especially striking for a non-white viewer, since Viola represents the stations of earthly life with an all-white cast. In this sense, the artist remains within a 'humanist' frame of reference that imputes universality for a Caucasian subject, and in so doing, effaces isses of race and ethnicity along with non-white subjects.

51 Bill Viola, in *Bill Viola*, curated by D. R. Ross and P. Sellars, New York, Whitney Museum of American Art in association with Flammarion, 1998, p. 112.

52 Here I refer to models of historical interpretation developed by the German historians Leopold von Ranke and Wilhelm Dilthey.

53 H.-G. Gadamer, *Philosophical Hermeneutics*, tr. and ed. D. E. Linge, Berkeley and Los Angeles, University of California Press, 1977, p. xvi.

54 H.-G. Gadamer, 'The Universality of the Hermeneutical Problem,' in Gadamer, *Philosophical Hermeneutics*, p. 3.

55 To this end, I affirm an original sense of 'culture,' as articulated by Hannah Arendt in her essay, 'The Crisis in Culture: Its Social and Political Significance,' in *Between Past and Future: Eight Exercises in Political Thought* (1954; London, Penguin, 1985), where she writes the following: 'Culture, word and concept, is Roman in origin. The word "culture" derives from *colere* – to cultivate, to dwell, to take care of, to tend and preserve – and it relates primarily to the intercourse of man with nature in the sense of cultivating and tending nature until it becomes fit for human habitation. As such, it indicates an attitude of loving care and stands in sharp contrast to all efforts to subject nature to the domination of man', pp. 211–12.

2

PERFORMING MODERNITY
The art of art history

Donald Preziosi

As we have come to appreciate, modernity cannot be understood apart from its continuing juxtapositions and superimpositions with many different anti-, pre-, and post-modernisms. We are still only beginning to learn to speak cogently, critically, and usefully of the complexities of modernity, since, in the deepest sense, the performance of the contradictions making up our modernity constitutes who and what we are and what we imagine ourselves and our lives and our dreams to be. Among the more indispensible of these practices have been those extraordinary inventions of the European Enlightenment: art, art history, and museums.[1]

I want to outline here a number of propositions regarding just how essential the phenomena we conventionally label 'art,' 'art history,' and 'museums' have been to the fabrication and maintenance – the *performance*, in fact – of the modern world in all of its facets. At the same time, it may become clear that the very possibilities of modernity's alternatives are equally entailed in the labor of art and art history-making, and of collecting and exhibiting.

What has it meant to live in a world in which virtually anything could be plausibly 'exhibited' in a museum, and in which virtually anything could be designated and serve *as* a museum? Just exactly what kind of world is that? What kind of places, and what kind of roles were we, as subjects, as bodies, exhorted to fill and play in such a world? It still remains barely imaginable, despite so many claims or desires to the contrary, as to what kinds of alternative realities there might be: modernity, after all, always will be the present, and presence itself, in one form or another.

From a Eurocentric perspective, art history came to be constructed and construed as a universal empirical science, systematically discovering, classifying, analyzing, and interpreting specimens of what came thereby to be naturalized as a 'universal' human phenomenon. It was devoted to investigating the 'natural' artisanry or 'art' of all peoples, or rather all those peoples and cultures invented by art historians, samples of which came to be arranged relative to each other both in museum space and more generally in the more extensive, encyclopedic, and totalizing space-time of what I will call here *museography*.

I am going to use this term as an umbrella to refer to a very broad, interrelated set of modern(ist) practices, professions, and institutions, from academic art history, aesthetic philosophy, art criticism, museology, exhibition and exposition, tourism, and the heritage, fashion, and infotainment industries (I will stop short momentarily of including history-writing, novels, sexualities, religions, and ethics, but would like you to remember these seemingly detached objects as we go along). What I want to call attention to by speaking in this manner is the comonplace understanding that all specimens of 'art' in this

29

vast and unsurpassable archive sit as if they were delegates or 'representatives' – that is, as *representations* – in a congress of imaginary equals, as the myriad of manifestations making up a 'Universal World History of Art.' To each came to be alloted a plot and display space, a platform or a vitrine, a web site or home page – in short, a place and address in an aestheticized ethical historical evolution of human civilization.

Of course it was always apparent that this vast, virtual museum had a narrative structure, direction, and point: all its imaginary spaces lead to the modernity of a European nationalist present, which constitutes the apex or observation-point; the *vitrine* within which all else is visible. Europe, in short, constructed itself *as* the museum space within which non-European objects become specimens, where their (reformatted) visibility was rendered legible. Europe, that is, as the *brain of the earth's body*.

European aesthetic principles – in the guise of a reinvented generic neo-classicism (or what in art schools in the nineteenth century came to be promoted as 'universal principles of good design') – constituted the self-designated unmarked center or Cartesian zero-point around which the entire virtual museographic edifice of modernity circulates, on the wings of which all things may be plotted, ranked, and organized in their differential particularities.

There was no 'outside' to this: all alien objects were ranked as primitive, exotic, charming, or fascinating distortions of a central classical (European) canon or standard – the *un*marked (and seemingly un-classed, seemingly un-gendered, etc.) point or site toward which all others may be imagined as aspiring. It may also be imagined as a kind of Möbius strip which at first glance appears to have two surfaces – the normal and the exotic, the familiar and the other – but which in reality has but one continuous side. Art history and museums are epistemological technologies; instruments for the production of cogent and convincing knowledge; optical devices of the most brilliant design and conception.

What was pragmatically afforded by this universal museographic archive was the systematic assembly or re-collection of artifacts destined to be constru(ct)ed as material *evidence* for the elaboration of a universalist language of description and classification: the vocabulary, grammar, and syntax, in fact, of what we know today as the discipline of art history. Even the most radically disjunctive differences among things could be reduced to differential and time-factored qualitative manifestations of some pan-human capacity; some collective human essence or soul. Differences could be reduced to the single dimension of different (but ultimately commensurate) '*approaches* to art or artistic form' (the Inuit, the French, the Mexican, the gay, the German, the Greek, the Chinese, etc.). Each work pedestalized as approximating an ideal, canon, or standard (the theoretical and ideological justification for the modernist social practice that came to be called 'art criticism' was thus born, occluding while still instantiating the magic realisms of exchange value).

In short, the hypothesis of art as a 'universal' human phenomenon was clearly essential to this entire enterprise of commensurability, intertranslatability, and (Eurocentrist) hegemony. Artisanry in the broadest and fullest sense of 'design' was positioned – and here of course archaeology and palaeontology had their say – as one of the defining characteristics of humanness. The most skilled works of art, therefore, must be seen as the widest windows onto the human soul, affording the deepest insights into the mentality of the maker, the most lucid delineations of the maker's ethical identity, and thus the clearest refracted insights into humanness as such. This assumption of universality was complementary to the proposition that there must exist essential linkages between objects and subjects, so that to speak of an art was to speak of a people, class, race, or gender.

The art of art history was thus *simultaneously* the instrument of an Enlightenment universalist vision of humanity, *and* a means for fabricating qualitative distinctions between individuals and societies. Understanding just how all this worked (and still works) may be the most pressing problem facing the profession of art history today, for what constitutes the most minute and commonplace things we do and imagine as art historians (what we in fact *perform* daily) are refractions of this breathtakingly massive and powerful dream. A dream founded, like modernity itself and as such, as the repression of the impossibility of representation.

Essential to the articulation and justification of art history as a systematic and universal human science in the nineteenth century was the construction of an indefinitely extendable *archive*, potentially coterminous (as it has since in practice become) with the material or so-called 'visual culture' of all human groups everywhere and at all times. Within this vast imaginary museographical artifact or edifice (of which all museums are fragments or part-objects) every possible object of attention might then find its fixed and proper place and address relative to all the rest. Every item might thereby be sited (so as to be susceptible to citation) as referencing or indexing another or others on multiple horizons (metonymic, metaphoric, or anaphoric) of useful association. The set of objects displayed in any exhibition (as with the system of classification of slide or photo collections) is sustained by the willed fiction that they somehow constitute a coherent 'representational' universe, as signs, substitutes, or surrogates of their (individual, national, racial, gendered, etc.) authors.

The pragmatic and immediately beneficial use or function of art history in its nineteenth-century origins was the production of pre-modernity; *the construction of a past that could be effectively placed under systematic observation for use in staging and politically transforming – that is, performing – the present*. A past that could be imagined as bearing a causative relation to the present, yet at the same time a pre-modernity that could be imagined to be a detached object, 'independent' of the analytic gaze of the present. Common to the practices of museography and its component art histories and museologies was a concern with spectacle, stagecraft, and dramaturgy; with the locating of what could be framed as distinctive and exemplary objects, so that their relations among themselves and to their original circumstances of production and reception could be vividly imagined and materially envisioned in a cogent and useful manner – useful above all to the production of certain modes of civic subjectivity and responsibility. (The problematics of historical causality, evidence, demonstration, and proof constituted the rhetorical scaffolding, the 'labanotation' as it were, of this nexus of social and epistemological technologies.)

Needless to say, much of this was made feasible by the invention of photography – indeed, art history, not to speak of museums (and, indeed, 'art' itself as we know it today) are in a very real sense the children of photography. Photography has been equally enabling of the discipline's fraternal nineteenth-century siblings, archaeology, anthropology, and ethnography. It was photography which made it possible not only for art historians but for whole populations rapidly and efficiently to *think (art) historically* in a sustained and systematic fashion, thereby setting in motion the stage machinery of an orderly and systematic university discipline: that psycho-mechanical disciplining of seeing and vision that we know by the name of art history.

Photography most especially made it possible to usefully envision 'objects of art' as *signs*. The impact of photography on determining the future course of art historical theory and practice was as fundamental as Marconi's invention of the wireless radio sixty years later

31

in envisioning the basic concept of arbitrariness in language: linguists of the 1890s very rapidly saw that Marconi's radio paved the way for a fundamental rethinking of the key concepts of modern linguistics.

A clear and primary motivation for the massive archival labor of what I am calling here museography was the assembly of material 'evidence' justifying the construction of narratives or historical novels of social, cultural, national, racial, or ethnic origins, identity, and development. The membrane separating the novelist, the actor, and the art historian – those siblings separated at their Enlightenment birth – is in fact exceedingly thin and porous. The professional art historian was a key instrument for scripting and giving voice to that archive, providing its potential users, both lay and professional, with maps, charts, itineraries, and safe and well-illuminated access routes into and through it. Museums became a key art of this museography, and this House of Historicist Memory has evolved as a paradigmatic instrument for making the visible (socially) legible: for 'reading' what you are seeing in a properly disciplined manner.

Museums and art history work in this way. Their objects – these framed and storied artifacts or monuments – were invested with a(n ethnically specific) decorum, wherein they would be legible and would 'speak' to (and through) us in a disciplined manner. These objects would be legible as *object-lessons*, as 'illustrating' (or 're-presenting') desirable and undesirable social relations in the (perpetually) modernizing nation (whose faults, it may be added, would rarely seem to lie in its nature, but rather mainly in the relative abilities of its citizens to 'realize' the national ideal or potential: ask not what your country can do for you; ask what you can do for your country).

Artworks, monuments, archives, and histories became the *sites* where the hidden truth of the citizen, the modern individual subject, could seem to be (re)discovered and read. In this regard it would be fair to say that the art historical object is the *elsewhere of the subject*, the place where it came to be imagined that unsaid or unsayable truths about their makers (and about ourselves as their 'viewers' or users) are already written down. Why else would the labor of reading a novel, watching a play or film, or walking (performing) a museum be seen as socially useful unless it were framed as resulting in the (proper) discovery of the 'truth' of individuals (nations, ethnicities, races, genders): truths revealed to be somehow magically inhering 'in' objects and products, available for discovery and decipherment by the astute.

Such a 'science' (to give this mode of magic realism its nostalgic nineteenth-century designation) did not however exist as a *single* professional field. Rather, it emerged as a facet of the generic protocols for the performance of modernity as such; appearing to neutrally and naturally exemplify 'method' itself. It – and I refer here again to what I am designating collectively as museography – existed at such a scale as to be invisible in the ordinary light spectrum of individual perceptions. The overall museographical project could be known and recoverable today through an archaeological examination of traces and effects dimly legible in its later twin professional and institutional progeny (separated, so to speak, at their disciplinary birth), namely, history and psychoanalysis.

But it may also be rendered legible through the construction of a truly effective critical history of that key discursive practice – art history – that was always in a very powerful manner a unison of the two before their more recent schism, and that in its oscillatory and paradoxical *modus operandi* even today, continues to bridge, albeit at times in the dark, what has since become their difference. The oscillations between what became history and psychoanalysis – *are* that bridge; the name of the bridge is art history.

Traces of this superimposition are palpable most especially in that ambivalent and paradoxical *object* that has constituted the *art* of art history since the Enlightenment, with its perpetual oscillation between the ineffable and the documentary, the eucharistic and the semiotic.

Modernity is thus the the performance of the ethics and politics of identity, at every scale from the person to the race. It exists as a virtual site constituting the *edge* between the material residues, relics, and dreams of the past and the adjacent dream space of the future. It is what is perpetually in-between two fictions: origins in an immemorial past and the destiny of its to-be-fulfilled future. The fundamental labor of the nation and its parts (that cyborg entity conjoining the organic with the artifactual) was to use the image of its (future) fulfillment as a rear-view mirror oriented backwards, so as to reconstitute its origins, identity, and history as the reflected source and truth of that projective fulfilled destiny – a room all of whose walls, and whose floor and ceiling, are mirrored.

What is thus realized in the history of the nation-state and of the nation's citizens and material objects is not the past definite of what it was, since it is no more, or even the present perfect of what it has been in what it currently is; rather it is the future anterior of what the nation-state and its subjects and objects shall have been for what they are in the process of becoming. The modern performative technologies of knowledge-production known as art, art history, and museums were founded upon a very particular ideology of representational adequacy, wherein objects and their exhibitionary formatting in museological or discursive space were presumed to more or less faithfully 'embody' or 'reflect' some set of external affairs; some 'real' history, spirit, or mentality which, it was imagined, pre-existed its portrayal or *re*-presentation.

However fragmentary, temporary, or terse the collection or exhibition, it exists today within parameters of expectation established by over two centuries of museums, galleries, salons, fairs, expositions, displays, and visual and optical demonstrations and experiments of many familiar kinds. Every exhibition, every museum, is commonly imagined today to be a fragment, or a 'selection' out of, some absent and fuller whole – commonly, the life-work of an artist or producer or of an entire civilization, nation, culture, or race. Every item in this space is a *specimen* – a member of a class of like objects which are imagined to bear traces of some family resemblance.

Each mode of modern exposition is in its own way the successor to, or a modern version of, one or more older 'arts of memory,' some of which are of very great antiquity in the West (for example the use of lanternslides, which predates art history as a profession). All such modes of exposition and display are facets of an interrelated, co-constructed, and mutually defining network of social and political practices and epistemological technologies that together make up the vast enterprise of modernity. Just as the set of practices which came to be orchestrated together as the modern museum may have had separate and distinct antecedents, so too may it be useful to understand the museum, art, and art history as components of a system of social and epistemological technologies whose coordination and interrelation came about in connection with – in fact as essential to – the fabrication and maintenance of a very specific kind of sociopolitical entity – the modern nation-state. To practice art history is to perform modernity.

Like politics, art, museums and art history make promises they cannot keep, while weaving and fascinating us into the fictions that constitute the realities of modern social life. All forms of museography are predicated upon the repression of the impossibility of representation. It is within the convoluted space of that paradox that making, exhibiting, and interpreting must be attended to if we are ever to see, let alone create distance from, our modernity [(assuming that might be desirable): the modernity of the bourgeois nation-state whose only exits found so far have all been part of the exhibition itself, painted on the walls].

What I am suggesting is that we attend to 'art' and its 'histories' as fundamental mechanisms for the legitimizing of existing social orders through the articulation and presentation of those orders (national, ethnic, racial, individual) as the *realization of a dream* – not our dream as such, but in fact the dream of our Other(s): *the dream of our dead ancestors*, which is imagined to be fulfilled and realized (or thwarted and postponed) by our own modernity, which, however, is by nature and design uncompletable.

Comprehending the past of the profession of art history – seeing through art history, in both senses of the term – is essential to productively imagining its future, should it have any. So much would seem obvious. But to do so effectively would mean at the very least abandoning certain easy academic habits of imagining art history as some kind of straightforward 'historical' or 'scientific' practice – as simply a history of ideas about art, or as genealogies of individuals who had ideas about art and its 'life' and its 'history,' or as an episode in the evolutionary adventure of the history of ideas – as increasingly refined protocols of interpreting objects and their histories and their makers: all those 'theories and methods' from Marxism to feminism, or from formalism and historicism to semiology and deconstruction; and all those disciplinary object-domains from fine art to world art to visual culture, which with hindsight all seem so very much cut from the same loose and leaky cloth. In the final analysis, all these distinctions amongst disciplinary perspectives are much less significant than their underlying similarities and structural and functional complementarities.

Art history was a complex and internally unstable enterprise throughout its two-century-long history. Since its beginnings, it has been deeply invested in the fabrication and maintenance of a modernity that linked Europe to an ethically superior aesthetics grounded in eroticized object-relations. It *was* a crucial instrument in allaying European anxieties about cultural relativism, wherein Europe (and Christendom), in their expanding and bewildering encounter with alien cultures, might have been reduced to being but one reality among many. The museographic invention of modernity – a process that is still ongoing – was a means of repressing relativity and of articulating a messianic millennialism in which Europe and its extensions would constitute the apotheosis and fulfillment of all histories: of everybody's history – 'modernization' as everybody's fate.

Generally speaking, museology and art history are instrumental ways of distributing the space of memory. Both operate together on the relationships between the past and present, subjects and objects, and collective history and individual memory. These operations are in aid of transforming traces of the past superimposed upon the present into a storied space wherein the past and present are imaginatively juxtaposed, where their hypothetical relationships cannot *not* be construed as succession and progression; cause and effect. Where, in other words, the illusion that the past exists in and of itself, somehow immune from the projections and desires of the present, might be sustained as the most powerful and seductive of modernist fantasies.

Such a project has obvious and direct psychoanalytic resonances, which I'll allude to briefly by noting that this pre-modern object of our desire, this authentic (and authoritative) 'past,' recognized as an Other in our present, and as the cause of our desires as citizen-subjects, is re-articulated and displaced as being outside of ourselves, as a separate (and hence commodifiable, and (art) historicizable) object. At the same time, that object (what Lacan termed *object [petit] a*, and which he also very remarkably and, fittingly for our purposes, here, termed *agalma* (which means 'statue' in Greek), is a paradoxical, *virtual* object – a veritable eucharistic object. That object is what has come to be articulated in modernity as *art;* or in art as modernity.

The art of art history and museology became an instrument for thinking representationally and historically; for making history capturable and collectible; for imagining a certain kind of historicity commensurate with the (now universally exported) nationalist teleologies of European modernity. To appreciate the extraordinary power and massive success of this ideological enterprise, this astonishing sleight-of-hand, we would need to articulate in fine detail what precisely was most deeply at stake two centuries ago in the invention of the modern nation-state. What came to be the canonical art of art history was indeed a magical and paradoxical object, perfectly suited to being an 'explanatory' documentary or historical instrument in the enterprise of fabricating and sustaining the modern nation and its (similarly 'statuesque') epitome, the citizen-subject.

(What is entailed here is what might also be described as the aestheticization of social and political life, and the embodiment of social desires; although to put it in these terms still implies that the latter somehow pre-exists the former, which is contrary to what I am suggesting here, namely that 'aestheticization' and modern social life, identity, and nationality are co-constructions.)

It is crucial to appreciate that this 'art' cannot be seriously understood in isolation from the field of relationships within which it originally came to have meaning. Art was the complementary (civilized) foil to its implicit and imaginary obverse, that enigma of the Enlightenment, the (uncivilized) fetish. It was a powerful instrument for legitimizing the belief that what you see in what you make is what in some deep, essential way you truly 'are,' the *form* of your work being the *physiognomy* of your truth. At the same time, it provided a powerful instrument for making plausible the proposition that Europe was the brain of the earth's body, and that all outside the edifice of Europe constituted its prologue. Of course that external anterior, that Other, was the necessary support and defining instance of what constituted its presence, its 'modernity.'

The term fetish ultimately derives from the Latin adjective *factitius* (used by Pliny to refer to that which is the result of art or artifice), through the Portuguese (*feiticaria*, a term applied to West African 'witchcraft' and idol-worship), the word *fetisso* referring to small objects or charms used in trade between West Africans and Europeans. Its early modern meaning may have more to do with a late Latin sense of the term as something imitative of natural properties (like sound, as in onomatopoeia). At any rate, it came to be constituted as the uncivilized (read 'black') anterior to the imaginary (read 'white') 'disinterestedness' of European aesthetics. They imply one another and cannot be understood in isolation from each other. Their dyadic *complementarity* has served as the skeletal support of all that art history and its art have been for the past two centuries.[2]

There are some structural and systemic parallels, for example 'sex.' If sexuality came, during the nineteenth century, to be privileged in European medical discourse as of the essence of the self – the innermost truth of one's personality – fine art came to be its civilized and complementary obverse: the very mark of civilized interaction between subjects and objects. In modernity, moreover, art and sex are *commensurate*. Like sex, art became a secret truth to be uncovered about all peoples everywhere, an omnipresent, universal mark of humanness linking the caves of Lascaux with the imagineering studios of

Los Angeles – a fictitious unity, surely, yet an immensely powerful and durable one: one of the weight-bearing walls of our modernity. You are not only 'what you eat' or what you make, consume, or collect, but you are also, and especially, what you desire. As with sexuality, with art you desire what you imagine the 'desire' of the object itself to be – 'what it wants to be.' Consumption as the quintessential modernist performance.

Historically, artwork and fetish came to occupy opposite poles in what was nonetheless a spectrum of continuities from disinterestedness to idolatry, from the civilized to the primitive. Neither one, in short, can be understood in isolation from the other. What I am suggesting is this: art did not exactly precede art history like some phenomenon of nature 'discovered' and then 'explained' by an empiricist science. Art history, aesthetic philosophy, museology, and art-making itself were historically co-constructed social practices whose fundamental, conjoint mission was the production of subjects and objects commensurate with each other, and possessive of a decorum suitable for the orderly and predictable functioning of the emergent (bourgeois) nation-states of Europe.

At the same time, this extraordinary enterprise afforded the naturalization of an entire domain of rhetorical devices (from 'style' to 'genre' to 'period' to 'genius' to 'intentionality') which could be employed as instruments or servo-mechanisms for manufacturing and scripting the histories of all peoples through the systematic and disciplined investigation of their cultural productions. Museography was grounded upon the associations of similarity and contiguity that might be mapped amongst archived specimens. They demonstrated, in effect, that all things could be understood as specimens, and that *specimization* – as a species of 'representation' – could be an effective prerequisite to the production of useful knowledge about any thing. That which was not representable was not human: the in-human, sub-human, super-human, or extra-human.

The museological and art historical archive, in other words, was no passive storehouse or data bank; it was rather a critical instrument in its own right – a dynamic device for calibrating, grading, and accounting for variations in continuity and continuities in variation and difference. The epistemological technology of this museographical archive was and remains indispensible to the social and political formation and maintenance of the nation and to its various legitimizing paradigms of ethnic autochthony, cultural uniqueness, and social, technological, or ethical progress (or decline) relative to real or imagined Others.

It works, in part, this way. The enterprises of mythic nationalism required a belief that the products of an individual, studio, nation, ethnic group, class, race, or gender should share demonstrably common, consistent, and unique properties of form, decorum, or spirit. Correlative to this was a paradigm of temporal homogeneity: the thesis that an art historical period or epoch would be marked by comparable similarities of style, thematic preoccupation or focus, or techniques of manufacture.

All of this would only make sense if time itself were framed not simply as linear but rather as progressively unfolding, as framing some epic or novel-like adventure of an individual, people, nation, or race. Only then would the notion of the 'period' be pertinent, as standing for a plateau or stage in the graded development of some story. The period would mark gradual changes in things – as the gradual change or episodic transformation of that thing or that 'spirit' underlying things.

Museology and museography fabricated object-histories as surrogates for or simulacra of the developmental histories (the pre-modernity) of persons, mentalities, and peoples. The period was an episodic part of an historical novel or novella that served to demonstrate and delineate significant aspects of the character, level of civilization or of skill, or the degree of social, cognitive, or ethical advancement or decline of an individual, race, or nation.

Art historical objects have thus always been *object-lessons* of documentary import insofar as they might be deployed or staged as cogent 'evidence' of the past's causal relationship to the present, enabling us thereby to articulate certain kinds of desirable (and undesirable) relations between ourselves and others. No longer overtly discussed in art historical discourse in this regard is the (silent) contrast between European 'progress' in the arts in contradistinction to the coincident 'decline' of Europe's principal Other in early modern times, the (comparably multinational and multiethnic) world of Islam.

It is in this connection that we may understand the enterprises of museography - and in particular of its componential facets known as art, museums, and art history, as having served as a very powerful and effective modern(ist) *concordance* of politics, religion, ethics, and aesthetics. It still remains virtually impossible, at the end of the twentieth century, *not* to see direct, causal, and essential connections between an artifact and the (co implicative) moral character and cognitive capacity of its producer(s). Such idealist, sexist, essentialist, racist, and historicist assumptions, which were so explicitly articulated in museology and art history in their historical origins, still comprise the covert subtext of contemporary art historical and critical practices, underlying many otherwise distinct or opposed theoretical and methodological perspectives. And despite the best intentions.

The modernist nation was crafted as the ark of a people: a finite and bounded artifact with a trajectory in time, a storied space; museums and art history as its cybernetic or navigational instruments, as optical devices allowing each citizen-passenger (who is also always permitted to perform the role of captain of his or her own fate) both to see behind the ship, the direction whence it came (its unique and singular past; its 'heritage'), and to imagine steering and guiding it forward along the route seemingly projected and implied by its prior history, the reflection back from a vanishing point (origins) on to the point of fulfillment in an ideal future. Never mind that such a horizon point is always equally far away however close we seem to come: the visual mirage in the noonday blankness of the present.

Art, then, came to be the common frame, the parergonal product, within which all human manufacture could be classified, fixed in its proper places, and set into evolutionary motion in the historical novel of the nation. In one sense, the art of art history is the Latin of modernity: a universal medium of (formerly religious, latterly scientific) truth; at the same time a gold(en) standard, mean, or ideal canon, relative to which all forms of (manu)facture are anticipatory, relative to whose ideal realities each utterance is an approximation, as each plant is a realization of certain ideal botanical internal relationships, written down in precise vocabulary and syntax in some big book, in Latin.

Historically, this was nothing less than a brilliant gesture and a massively devastating hegemonic act: *this transformation of the world into not simply a 'picture' but into an image of what would be visible from the very specific central-point perspective of Europe masquerading as the present of the world's past, as the (naturally) evolved order of things.* A making of Europe into the brain of the earth's body and a site for the collection, containment, and taxidermy of all the things and peoples of the world: the most thoroughgoing and effective imperialist gesture imaginable; the co-option of all possible ethnocentrisms.

To see through art history, to see through museology, would be to come to a position of necessarily forgetting and dis-membering art history, so that the accomplishments, affordances, and effects to which art, art history and museums contributed so centrally in fabricating and maintaining our world can be more truly and clearly re-membered. At the same time we may be capable of more fully appreciating art history for what it has been – one facet of a dramaturgical practice (which I have called here museography) central to the performance of our modernity.

NOTES

1   Issues raised in this essay are discussed at greater length in D. Preziosi, 'The Art of Art History,' in D. Preziosi (ed.), *The Art of Art History*, Oxford, Oxford University Press, 1998, pp. 507–527.
2   See W. Pietz, 'Fetish,' in R. S. Nelson and R. Shiff (eds), *Critical Terms for Art History*, Chicago and London, University of Chicago Press, 1996, pp. 197–207.

3

ART HISTORY/ART CRITICISM
Performing meaning

Amelia Jones

I am interested in this essay in excavating the deep structures of art critical judgment, structures that inform and motivate the mutually intertwined discourses of art history and art criticism. Historically, institutionally, and ideologically linked through the Enlightenment-based logic of viewing, classifying, and hierarchizing (visual) objects according to a schema of relative values, art history and art criticism ultimately rely on a powerful apparatus of repression. As Jane Gallop has argued,

> The problem with . . . criticism is not [the critic's] . . . rebellion, not the violence or the desire to possess, but that all too often we see only the aftermath of the rebellion, when the critic is instated in his superiority over the needy work of art. . . . [T]hat moment [can be called] 'interpretation'. . . . But what has been forgotten, what has been covered over, is that the interpretive gesture with its assumption of superiority over a mute object is always based upon a prior rebellion against the object's power. It is the aggression and the desire in that rebellion which constitute the most authentic encounter with the object's power, where we experience not only the object's force but equally our own powerful drive to understand, to possess, that which moves us so intensely.[1]

Gallop's insights are applicable to art history as well since, as it is conventionally practiced, art history by and large relies on art critical modes of determining value – modes derived loosely from Kant's *Critique of Judgment*, and its subsequent refinements in German, French, English, and US aesthetic theory (from Hegel to Fry, Greenberg, and beyond).[2] While most art historians would prefer not to admit it, the practice of art historical analysis most often assumes certain values determined via an art critical model of a 'disinterested' judgment practiced by a learned interpreter who veils his investments in the service of objectivity.[3] This mode of judgment continues to be structural to evaluations of contemporary art, which – even as they claim 'post-' modernity – tend to reiterate these Enlightenment-based assumptions of modernist criticism, even as they replace notions of 'aesthetic' value with an avant-gardist conception of 'political' value or efficacy; political like aesthetic judgments aim to secure meaning and value and are thus threatened by the anxious uncertainty put into play by the performative, theatrical dimension of meaning production.[4] This essay explores what happens to the prevailing mode of judgment when it is posed in relation to works of art that exaggerate this dimension.

Art history and art criticism thus work to frame a set of practices via interpretive acts that are legitimated through the suppression of the investments – the desires – of the interpreter. As Gallop's quote suggests, this suppression marks what, on a psychic level, is a *repression* of inconvenient ('forbidden, powerful, . . . embarrassing'[5]) desires; or, perhaps more accurately, it marks a projection of these desires onto art objects and their making subjects – an imputing of these desires to the artist her/himself. When the 'objects' of art are theatrical or flamboyantly open in their feverish solicitation of spectatorial desire (especially when the objects of art are also its subjects, in the case of body art[6]), this repression is made difficult and judgments crack open, showing the gaps in logic still informing our ways of making meaning for works of art.

The Kantian notion of disinterested judgment requires a pose of neutrality (a repression and veiling of desire) on the part of the interpreter. For Kant, aesthetic judgment must, by definition, be 'devoid of all interest,' since desire marks a judgment as mere liking: '[e]veryone has to admit that if a judgment about beauty is mingled with the least interest then it is very partial and not a pure judgment of taste.'[7] Kant's model instantiates the Cartesian opposition between mind and body, clearly distinguishing between contemplative, disinterested aesthetic judgment and embodied, sensate, interested, contingent, and therefore individualized and non-universal judgments.[8] Pure aesthetic judgment ('pure judgments of taste') must not be sparked by interested desires.[9] At the same time, Kant recognizes that judgments of taste are necessarily subjective (in the sense of being 'of the subject'), a recognition that conflicts with our notion of disinterestedness as 'objectivity.' For Kant, it is the aesthetic that must bridge the chasm of contradictions opened between the 'subjective' and the 'universal': 'a judgment of taste must involve a claim to subjective universality . . . if [he who judges] proclaims something to be beautiful, then he requires the same liking from others; he then judges not just for himself but for everyone.'[10]

Aesthetic judgment is precisely the mode of logic through which European 'man' takes account of the uncodifiable; it relies on the containment of the objects of art analysis: the regulation, in Terry Eagleton's words, of the 'dense, swarming territory' beyond the sway of human reason, the 'whole of our sensate life together, . . . how the world strikes the body on its sensory surfaces.'[11] This sensual 'territory,' if left unbounded, would destabilize the Enlightenment subject by eliciting potentially uncontrollable spectatorial desires that would expose his contingency on the world and indebtedness to his own desires (the interestedness of his interpretation). Thus, even though aesthetics was born 'as a discourse of the body,' it becomes primarily a mode of eliminating corporeality and its uncertainties from our relationship to the world of sensual objects: whether scarily primitive fetishes, feminine, low-class 'kitsch,' beautiful 'high art' works – or, in postmodern parlance, radical, politically efficacious *texts*.[12]

As Kant and his followers recognize, the removal of the desiring, sensate body (of both artist and interpreter) from the project of aesthetic judgment or interpretation is crucial to this absence of interest and to the requirement of universality implicit in aesthetic judgments of taste: if the individual, desiring body were implicated in these judgments, they would clearly be interested and particular rather than universal. In the twentieth century, the attempted repression or re-assignment of desire has operated to confirm the authority of the art historian/art critic, who labors to maintain the illusion of disinterestedness such that her judgments seem inevitable and 'correct' and the qualities she assigns to practices as 'inherent' to them rather than interpretively negotiated or corporeally invested. While the art historian/art critic will surely always fail in this project, her role as cultural arbiter (as privileged Western subject), authorized to construct a frame that defines quality at the cost of excluding that which ostensibly has lesser or no value, rests on this illusion of control.[13]

In his monumental study, *Distinction: A Social Critique of the Judgement of Taste* (1979), the French sociologist Pierre Bourdieu makes a crucial contribution to an understanding of what is at stake in the claims of disinterestedness authorizing art historical and art critical analysis – precisely through interrogating modes of spectatorial engagement. Bourdieu points out the threat of popular culture to class hierarchies: 'the object which "insists on being enjoyed". . . neutralizes both ethical resistance and aesthetic neutralization; it annihilates the distanciating power of representation, the essentially human power of suspending immediate, animal attachment to the sensible and refusing submission to the pure affect. . . .'[14] Bourdieu's study emphasizes the class implications of such structures of distancing (which are also, as I have suggested above, structures of containment). It is the maintenance of distance (boundaries of containment) that enables the upper classes to differentiate themselves from the masses' supposed lust for the crudely sexual and the immediately enjoyable rather than the aestheticized.

Clement Greenberg's now infamous attempt in 'Avant-Garde and Kitsch' (1939) to legitimate his own 'taste' (and thus, by implication, his social position) through his opposition of 'ersatz' culture, or kitsch, and 'true' culture epitomizes the dynamic Bourdieu identifies.[15] Furthermore, inasmuch as 'kitsch' is widely associated with women's crafts and the debased, 'primitive' cultural preferences of 'lower class,' often non-Euro-American ethnic groups, it points to the way in which gender and ethnicity are always already implicated in distinctions of class associated with 'taste.'[16] The psychic dimension of aesthetic judgment as a strategic mode of *othering* (of producing boundaries to define white, upper-middle class, masculine culture as superior in relation to a debased – non-white or 'primitive,' lower class, feminine – alternative) is relatively clear. Bourdieu stresses the psychic stakes within Anglo-patriarchy of maintaining the myth of disinterestedness: 'pure pleasure – ascetic, empty pleasure which implies the renunciation of pleasure' is proper to the aesthetic experience, as opposed to the disgust linked with the enjoyable, kitsch object, which removes 'the distance . . . between the representation and the thing represented [and threatens] . . . the loss of the subject in the object.'[17] It is crucial, then, for the art critic/art historian to claim 'pure pleasure,' to avoid acknowledging his investments in the determination of meaning: 'the loss of the subject in the object' threatens not only the interpreter's claim to authority, but his very coherence as a subject (who is implicitly masculine, white, heterosexual, upper middle class, etc.).[18]

What happens, then, when works of art solicit *im*pure bodily pleasures? overtly stage their relationship to the viewer as corporeal, invested, mutual, intersubjective? What happens when these works pose themselves in a threatrical mode: one that, by definition, acknowledges their contingency on an 'audience,' an 'other willing to be cast in the role of auditor [or spectator],' who sees, hears, and takes as well as makes meaning from them? What happens when works of art mark themselves, in their theatricality, as only ever 'rehearsals,' never final or fixed but always open to the muddying whirlpools of spectatorial desire?[19] Predictably, one of the first things to occur in such cases is the development of a renewed mode of judgment (aesthetic, political, or otherwise) to *close down* the threat of this 'feminine' openness of the theatrical (in its calling on an overt spectatorial relation of 'waiting, . . . rehearsal and masquerade') for, '[l]ike other feminine forms in patriarchal cultures,' works that open up the performative dimension of meaning production are 'seen as something that needs control, even policing.'[20] In the following section, I explore one of these modes of policing theatricality and attempt to interrupt its effects by offering my own, highly invested and overtly contingent readings of particular works of art–readings that, while unseemly in their lack of professional decorum, I hope will be convincing at least in their openness and self-reflexivity if not in the meanings they offer.

THE BODY RE-EMERGES: THE CASE OF MICHAEL FRIED

At the risk of being perceived as beating a dead horse (dead in the letter, but one still unfortunately all too 'present' in the underlying assumptions of contemporary art discourse), I would like to turn at this point to a particular, well-rehearsed example of the tautological reasoning that subtends modernist formalist art historical and art critical analysis. Michael Fried's well-known 'Art and Objecthood' (1967), a veritable manifesto of Greenbergian modernism (uttered just at the moment in which artistic practices such as Minimalism and body art were rendering Greenberg obsolete), is an important object of analysis precisely because it stages so obviously and with such rhetorical flair the oppositional logic and lack of self-reflexivity that continues to characterize the practices of art history and art criticism.[21] Ironically, Fried's essay – which excoriates the 'theatricality' of Minimalist art – is itself highly theatrical and thus exposes while it attempts to veil Fried's investment in closing down the engagements that these works so aggressively solicit.

The spare, minimal objects of Fried's denunciation – including Robert Morris's *Untitled (Ring with Light)* (1965-6), a huge (97-inch diameter) circular form in gray fiberglass, with fluorescent light gleaming from two vertically cut slices in the substance of the circle, and Tony Smith's *Die* (1962), a six-foot cube in steel – hardly appear outlandish enough to have inspired his almost hysterical attack.[22] They are certainly not apparently 'feminine,' 'kitsch,' 'primitive,' or otherwise (in Bourdieu's terms) apparently insistent of being enjoyed. However, Fried interprets such works as paradigmatic of a debasement of the pure aesthetics of modernism, a debasement that, not incidentally, takes place precisely through the objects' supposed evacuation (again, Bourdieu's terms) of 'both ethical resistance and aesthetic neutralization,. . . . [of] the essentially human power of suspending immediate, animal attachment to the sensible . . ."

It is these objects and their kind, then, that Fried, with a startling lack of self-awareness, differentiates from modernism, which he positions as both 'good art' and 'art' *tout court*. Minimalist works (which he labels 'literalist') are 'ideological' (as opposed to the 'wholly manifest' objects of modernism); 'anthropomorphic' (versus the putative self-sufficiency of 'good,' that is, modernist, art); 'corrupted and perverted by theatre,' and, ultimately, 'antithetical to art.'[23] Rather than rehearsing these epithets here, I want to focus on a few key moments of Fried's virtuosic if hyperbolic critique in order to expose the assumptions he cleverly covers over with the veil of authority provided by a loosely Kantian structure of aesthetic judgment.

In order to stage this oppositional hierarchy of good and bad, art and non-art, and to naturalize it as compelling and truthful, Fried explicitly conflates ontological questions with aesthetic ones: 'I would argue that what modernism has meant is that the two questions – What constitutes the art of painting? And what constitutes *good* painting – are no longer separable.'[24] With this gesture, Fried strategically veils his own assumptions by eliding the *ontology* of the objects, their properties as objects that are to be considered as

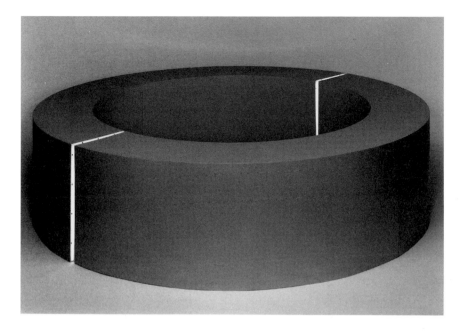

Plate 3.1 Robert Morris, *Untitled* (Ring with Light), 1965–6. Fiberglass and fluorescent light; 24 in × 14 in × 97 in. Dallas Museum of Art, General Acquisitions Fund and matching grant from National Endowment for the Arts

Plate 3.2 Tony Smith, *Die*, 1962. Steel painted black; 6 ft × 6 ft × 6 ft. Private collection. Photograph by Geoffrey Clements, courtesy of Paula Cooper Gallery, New York. © Tony Smith Estate

art, their self-evident 'art-ness' and 'thing-ness,' with their value, thus implying that the value (which is determined through a set of highly motivated assumptions on Fried's part) is somehow *inherent in the ontological structure of the works themselves.*[25]

This aesthetic 'value' (which, again, Fried conflates with the very art-status of the work) is assigned to works of art on an extremely tenuous ground. Peeling away the layers of inflated rhetoric and authoritative posing, the reader gleans that the sole criterion of a work's value is whether or not it is 'capable of compelling conviction.'[26] Needless to say, in Fried's tendentious view, 'literalist' works fail to compel conviction: while 'the literalists have largely avoided the issue of value or quality. . . . , within the modernist arts nothing short of *conviction* – specifically, the conviction that a particular painting or sculpture or poem or piece of music can or cannot support comparison with past work within that art whose quality is not in doubt – matters at all.'[27] Failing to comprehend how or why artists could seek to 'avoid the issue of value or quality' (and it is key that Fried defines this as an avoidance rather than taking it up as a potential challenge and questioning these terms altogether) and might be willing to expose their 'uncertainty' as to what 'art' might be or mean, Fried can only view Minimalist objects as *failing* the goal that he has predetermined for any work that situates itself in relation to discourses of art. The authoritative description of art *whose quality is not in doubt* exposes to view the a priori assumption of 'quality' (one that Fried has told us is contingent on his particular notion of 'conviction') that tautologically subtends his subsequent attributions of aesthetic value. The work is good, the work is art, only if it attains the conviction – the quality that 'is not in doubt' – which is apparently obvious, natural, transcendent, and yet which apparently only Fried can adequately define.

It is no accident that Fried, who is brilliant in some of his observations if, in my view, completely wrong-headed in his conclusions, introduces 'Art and Objecthood' with a long quotation from a book about Jonathan Edwards, a clergyman and theologian practicing in early eighteenth-century North America.[28] On first glance, this explicitly religious reference seems bizarrely out of place. Returning to it after reading the article, however, the reference seems curiously apt; though it is difficult to imagine that Fried could have been deliberately ironicizing his own maintenance of essentially theocratic assumptions in his critical practice, as he seems to take himself extraordinarily seriously throughout the essay, the religious overtones read at this point as an explicit reminder of these assumptions. One can return to the epigraph after perusing the last few sentences of the article as a whole, which read as follows:

> This essay will be read as an attack on certain artists (and critics) and as a defense of others. And of course it is true that the desire to distinguish between what is to me the authentic art of our time and other work ... has largely motivated what I have written. In these last sentences, however, I want to call attention to the utter pervasiveness – the virtual universality – of the sensibility or mode of being that I have characterized as corrupted or perverted by theatre. We are all literalists most or all of our lives. Presentness is grace.[29]

In relation to this hyperbolically metaphysical claim for the authority of 'presentness' as 'grace,' the citation of Jonathan Edwards's theological wisdom ('it is certain with me that the world exists anew every moment' and the assurance of this is that 'we every moment see the same proof of a God as we should have seen if we had seen him create the world at first') takes on new significance. Whether consciously or not, Fried has signaled to us that his critical authority in debasing Minimalism as 'non-art' is shored up by a tenuous logic whose truth claims rely ultimately on a blind belief in the speaker's singular access to transcendent meaning: I see the world as new; I believe God creates the world as new; therefore, God exists. For Fried, this would translate as: [I say] Minimalism is theatrical; [I say] theatricality is bad or non-art because it engages the spectator rather than being wholly manifest; [I say] therefore, Minimalism is non-art. Fried's logic, which is predicated on the veiling of the 'I' of his assertions so as to naturalize them as transcendentally, universally true, is based entirely on his own responses – highly invested and specific in relation to New York art world politics in the 1960s.[30]

Modernist art history and art criticism, as Fried so incisively, if seemingly inadvertently, illustrates, are ultimately theocratic regimes, in which the artistic interpreter stages himself in the position of the one true reader who may discern the meaning or value of a work of art according to seemingly unassailable – 'neutral' and 'disinterested' – criteria (the degree to which a work 'compels conviction' in Fried's case). As Bourdieu's model suggests, this particular technology of meaning production is intimately linked to the development of bourgeois culture. Fried's ultimate recourse to religious metaphors exposes his participation in a system that is ultimately a highly specific extension of capitalism – a system that sells aesthetic value as a fixed commodity and, correlatively, increases his own cultural capital as arbiter of taste.[31]

Finally, the particularity of Fried's metaphysics is established in relation to his notion of 'presentness.' It is 'presentness' that Fried aligns with (good) modernist practices, in that they give themselves to the viewer instantaneously, 'wholly manifest' at every moment.[32] Presentness, however, is not by any means opposed to absence but to the 'presence' invoked by 'literalist' works, a presence Fried excoriates not for its plenitude (that would be 'presentness') but, paradoxically, for its *lack*. The 'literalist' object lacks, precisely, in its theatricality: in its acknowledgment that it does not contain its own inherent significance and value, in its overt dependence on, even embrace of, spectatorial desire as a condition of its meaning and value, and, in Peggy Phelan's terms, in its 'feminine' openness and solicitation of a spectatorial relation of 'waiting, . . . rehearsal and masquerade.' While Fried excoriates the 'corruption' and 'perversion' he identifies with the theatricality of Minimalism, these are precisely the qualities I argue here (out of an almost diametrically opposed set of values) to be its greatest offering.

Notably, Fried further anticipates my formulation of the value of work that is theatrical (or, we might say, 'performative') by noting that theatricality links 'figures as disparate as Kaprow, Cornell, Rauschenberg, Oldenburg, Flavin, Smithson, Kienholz, Segal, Samaras, Christo, Kusama.'[33] It is no accident that almost every one of these 'theatrical' artists participated in bodily performances that, like 'literalist' art, opened the work of art, in this case as the body of the artist itself, to spectatorial desire. Once again I find myself agreeing with his categorization (which, from the point of view of one interested in postmodern visual culture *as performative*, has a convincing explanatory force), but feeling repelled by his implicit and naturalized conclusion that these artists are therefore inevitably trivial and of no interest.[34]

Fried, insistently refusing to acknowledge his own participation in the views and interpretations that he propounds, has made clear that he sees the embrace or acknowledgment of spectatorial relations as a nefarious influence (writing more recently, '[i]n the years since "Art and Objecthood" was written, the theatrical has assumed a host of new guises and has acquired a new name: post-modernism,' and 'boy was I right about art moving towards theater!'[35]). In contrast, I want here – reading through Minimalism – to produce a tentative model for an alternative, self-reflexive critical and historical practice: to argue for a particular kind of value that Fried strategically neglected (a kind of value I openly acknowledge to be *contingent* on my particular investments). That is, while Fried, given his starting premise, could only vehemently reject Minimalism for its theatrical embrace of spectatorial relations, I want to reverse Fried's value system to argue that this highlighting of the spectatorial relation that Fried so rightly perceived to be the downfall of his particular kind of modernism can only be viewed in a positive light from a feminist, post-colonial/anti-racist, queer, and class-conscious point of view.

My basic assumptions in making this argument are as follows: that any work that is contextualized and experienced in such a way that it breaks down the capacity of art historians and art critics to claim authority for themselves, by naturalizing and univer-salizing their interpretations as 'true,' can be engaged as a radical and positive contribution to global culture. I want to suggest that we can learn from the frightening openness and theatricality of particular works, producing a new kind of art writing (of art historical or critical interpretation) that is itself theatrical or performative, destructuring the very premises of the modern subject by activating rather than suppressing the multifarious differences that give shape to contemporary life.[36] Interpretation is a mode of translation – incommensurable with but also inextricably bound up in the life-world of the objects it addresses.[37] It is a transubstantiation of verbal and visual signs which chiasmically intertwines subjects, not the final word. I am convinced that, if we acknowledge the performativity of meaning production – opening ourselves to visual art works as fully embodied sensuous experiences rather than closing them down through reified models of aesthetic or political judgment, fixing them in a matrix of predetermined values, we will find ourselves in a different and more productive relationship with visual culture. We will find ourselves in a relationship that *moves us* (in both senses of the word) rather than securing us in one rather well-worn place.

REREADING MINIMALISM

As Fried's rhetoric suggests, the Minimalists themselves were deeply informed by phenom-enology and proposed Minimalism as a radical rethinking of subject/object relationships. What Fried does not explore is the fact that the Minimalist object was staged in the mid- to late 1960s within a discursive context invested in opening out the formerly veiled structures of viewing and interpretation. As Robert Morris writes in his important 'Notes on Sculpture, Part 2' (1966), '[t]he awareness of scale is a function of . . . comparison. . . . Space between the subject and the object is implied in such a comparison . . . it is just this distance between object and subject that creates a more extended situation, for *physical participation becomes necessary. . . .*' Morris continues, arguing for the large scale of Minimalist works as a strategic method of spectatorial engagement: 'Things on the monumental scale [place] . . . kinesthetic demands . . . upon the body.'[38]

Expanding upon Morris's phenomenological ideas, I would like to engage with several Minimalist pieces through a specifically feminist, phenomenological model of reading. This is a model that fundamentally asserts an *intersubjective* engagement among and between objects and subjects and a coextensiveness of body and mind. It is a model that, in the words of Judith Butler, proposes the body as an 'essentially dramatic structure which can be "read" in terms of the more general life that it embodies ... the "place" in which possibilities are realized and dramatized, the individualized appropriation of a more general historical experience ... a modality of reflexivity....'[39] Minimalism and its corollaries (among which I would include body art) draw on this phenomenological notion of the body (which, in phenomenological terms, is also understood as the self) as a 'modality of reflexivity' to propose the interpretive relation as a reflexive exchange. In the terms of Maurice Merleau-Ponty, 'my body ... is what opens me out upon the world and places me in a situation there.... [it] opens itself to others ... to co-existence...';[40] the Minimalist object provides a 'situation' of intensive engagement that encourages the acknowledgment of the *contingency* of the body/self on its environment (Merleau-Ponty's 'situation,' which he calls elsewhere 'the flesh of the world'[41]) and thus, correlatively, of the environment as it comes to mean through the experience of the body/self. It is precisely this contingency that Fried anxiously attempted to ward off with his proclamations of Minimalism as non-art.

Returning to two of the monuments cited in Fried's critique, Morris's *Untitled (Ring with Light)* and Tony Smith's *Die*, I would like to perform an entirely different set of meanings around them, looking through the felicitously distorting prism of feminism and phenomenology. It is surely no accident that I have never (or don't remember ever having) seen either of these works in the 'flesh.'[42] My phantasmatic projections, otherwise known as interpretations, can thus be viewed as pure fantasy; or, they can be engaged as votive offerings nurtured from my own capacity to imagine and throw myself corporeally (via cognitive processes) into the arms of works I may or may not have 'really' seen. Either way, they are offered as overt, even aggressive, translations – as metaphorical rather than 'definitive.'

Fried points to Morris's work as an example of the 'blatantly anthropomorphic' quality of Minimalist works, their 'apparent hollowness' and implication of 'an inner, even secret life.'[43] For Fried this secretiveness is to be disparaged in that it is disempowering, exposing his own contingency on the situation of interpretation. He cannot *master Untitled (Ring with Light)* but can only hope to engage it experientially (an experience he attempts to close down through definitive proclamations that substitute for it the label of non-art). But what if we were to walk metaphorically around the piece and allow our sense of intimidation and, perhaps, confusion come to play overtly in our interpretation of the work?[44] What if we were to explore our feelings of dis-ease in relation to the object – at once disconcertingly large and blank – before us? It neither tells a story nor memorializes a famous figure; it appears (Fried's anxieties aside) to be the opposite of coyly seductive, refusing to allow itself to be interpretively possessed.

It is arguable whether there is a verbally identifiable 'meaning' lodged in this experience at all, but, as a trained art historian, I will inevitably try to recreate in some fashion what I encounter there. I might personally interpret my uneasiness in the presence of the Minimalist object in the first instance as a reflection of the aggression apparently built into monumental sculpture, and, in the second, of the uncomfortableness, indeed, of the suggestion of meaning as a hidden, unattainable proposition. However, I read both of these as metacritical: the Minimalist object makes me aware of my bodily/cognitive response to monumentality in general; further, I read the 'hiddenness' of this particular piece to be an ironic reference to the modernist formalist idea of meaning as embedded in the 'interior' of the work's set of forms, to be discerned by the trained and privileged interpreter. I have to respect this piece, then, which seems so cleverly to stage its relation to me before the fact (and yet this 'a priori' is only defined by me a posteriori, in the [metaphorical] experience and in the text).

Viewed from the point of view of the late 1990s, this piece comes to have another set of references. It resonates for me as a kind of mocking reference to the commodification of Minimalist forms by multinational capitalist culture in the 1980s. At 24 inches high, *Untitled (Ring with Light)* begins to feel like a bench in a corporate lobby, encouraging my passivity and soliciting my semi-supine form to ensconce itself on the mute, vacuous surface of the curve. Yet, the fluorescent light is a bit too bright, even jarring, and thus ruptures the sensation of vapid seduction (but in a manner consistent with the excesses of corporate culture: it reminds me of the just-too-much sensorial input of the shopping mall, with its complex and often disorienting arrangement of slick metal or plastic surfaces and shrieking explosions of light and reflections; I've never liked shopping malls).

In painted plywood and fiberglass, after all, this piece boasts some pretty low-tech elements in its fabrication and materials; unlike Fried, who is so certain about what he sees, I can't quite situate myself relative to its ambivalent objecthood. The donut can become a black hole, its empty center mocking the lack of centeredness it inspires in my now anxious body/self. Once traversed, it urges me to move on. The slits both beckon and repel. Other than sitting on its broad rim, or attempting to step across its fat lip (it is 14 inches deep) and probably injuring myself in the process, I cannot penetrate its mysteries nor get a good clean view of this hole, with its dry and humorless edges. There isn't 'lack' there, nor is there 'presence,' but, rather, a kind of potential non-space that incorporates time and the flux of my experience.

Tony Smith's 1962 *Die* is an enormous steel cube the height (six feet) of a relatively tall man or a very tall woman. Fried's essay cites Smith's comments in response to questions about *Die*:

Q: Why didn't you make it larger so that it would loom over the observer?
A: I was not making a monument.
Q: Then why didn't you make it smaller so that the observer could see over the top?
A: I was not making an object.[45]

This idea of 'not monument'/'not object,' Fried argues, exposes the 'latent or hidden naturalism, indeed anthropomorphism' that 'lies at the core of literalist theory and practice.'[46] So, paradoxically, this huge cube becomes a 'surrogate person – that is, a kind of *statue*,'[47] and, for Fried, this can only be a bad thing, since a statue solicits the viewer, opening the interpretive relation to all sorts of infelicitous (potentially even homoerotic – think Rodin's *Balzac*) desires. But what if we look at the cube as simply *acknowledging* the fact that the human observer will always engage with objects (with what Merleau-Ponty calls, again, the *flesh of the world*) as in some way extensions of herself. Why would it be a bad (indeed, Fried suggests, execrable) thing to admit that we engage actively with the flesh of the world through our own embodied perceptual apparatus? Why try to deny this? What is at stake in such a denial?

What if I looked at *Die* as a kind of *flesh*: a kind of *industrial* flesh, marking my own experience in a world largely made up of human-oriented machine-made things? – a world the rest of which can only appear through the lens of such industrialized subject-object-ification?[48] What if I experience this cube as a weighty solid, dwarfing my particular human form (which is only 5 feet 6 inches)? After all, can we assume that *every subject*

48

would experience this cube as 'not looming' and 'not visible'? It is looming to me but would be rather manageable to basketball star Michael Jordan, who could not only easily see across its top but could probably climb on top of it with relative ease (thus, in turn, monumentalizing himself further by using *it* as a pedestal to his massive, statuesque athlete's body/self). Something tells me that Jordan would experience *Die* as architectural, environmental, as a potential extension of his already commanding body/self, rather than as 'theatrical' and 'anthropomorphic' (my guess is that Fried is not much over six feet). In the same way, I would bet (based on my past attempts to teach such works, via slides, in class lectures at the University of California) that the vast majority of urban youth in US cities today would interpret *Die* as a small-scale metaphor of the intimidating hideousness of the blank, distantly International Style projects they are often forced to inhabit.

Maybe there are other kinds of looking, other ways to *make meaning* of such an object. After all, as Merleau-Ponty observed, my body is neither a thing nor an idea but 'the measurement of the things. . . . [M]y body sees only because it is a part of the visible in which it opens forth. . . .'[49] *Die* exposes me to the fact of my own contingency: I am *seen by it* (as 'part of the visible) even as I see and experience its mass – and it sees me differently than it sees other subjects. It *makes me small*, even as it marks Jordan's superiority-of-flesh (one needn't wonder how it made Fried feel). I want to take *Die* away from Fried, to transform it into an object that points to my body – our bodies – in their vast geographical/spatial/experiential differences; that points to the ways in which corporate (as well as corporeal?) repression can turn into a socially embedded kind of engagement; that points to the shift of meaning from the mute sign (of 'presence,' in Fried's terms) into the activating embrace of absence.

I translate *Die* for a politics of cultural engagement. I stage *Die* as instantiating the capacity of any artwork to open out the intersubjectivity of interpretation as an exchange, the contingency of our interpreting bodies/selves on the particularities of the environments in which we experience works of art as well as on the specificities of these works in their relation to our bodies (that is, specificities that are not inherent, in that they have no meaning until engaged). A throw of the dice (plural: die) opens meaning to chance.[50]

Die has been refigured (translated) before, but by artists whose works are, naturally, not of interest to theorists of the aesthetic such as Fried: artists who are women. These artists have placed themselves at *Die*'s feet, not in prostration but in order to surface the Minimalist object/monument as *flesh*. From Eva Hesse's *Accession II* (1967), a more intimate (30 $3/4$ inch-high) open cube of galvanized steel and internally protruding fingers of rubber tubing, to Rachel Lachowicz's *Lipstick Cube* (1990), a diminutive 8-inch cube in red lipstick, women artists have opened out the effects of Smith's huge cube (there's something about it that seduces us women, not into compliance, but into a mode of defiant appreciation). Hesse draws us in via the sense of touch, pretty thoroughly thwarted in *Die* by its scale and rudely ungiving, brushed metal surfaces; we are now lured *inside* this cube (which is open, its antennae-like, grasping rubber tubing viewable from the top).[51] Lachowicz draws us in by the lips, urging us to bend down, all the way down, to this crushable mass of red. Far from the industrialized intimidation of *Die*, here (and I speak with authority, having vivid memories of encountering this piece myself[52]) we come to fear our own bodies as potentially deadly masses. Lowering ourselves (but holding ourselves just a breath away) we want to moisten our lips with its dense, luscious color; as with *Die*, the surface is mass. Surely a man would relate quite differently than a woman to the seductions of *Lipstick Cube*: would he want to kiss it, eat it, wear it?

Plate 3.3 Rachel Lachowicz, *Lipstick Cube*, 1990. Cast lipstick; 8 in × 8 in × 8 in. Photograph courtesy of Shoshana Wayne Gallery, Santa Monica, California

I experience *Die* as marking out what Merleau-Ponty calls the *chiasmus*: the 'reversibility of the seeing and the visible.' The chiasmus is 'that point where the two metamorphoses cross what we call perception is born, so there is a reversibility of the speech and what it signifies.' Within this reversibility, 'the signification is what comes to seal, to close, to gather up the multiplicity of the physical, physiological, linguistic means of elocution, to contract them into one sole act,' which we call interpretation.[53] This interpretive intertwining, this chiasmus, 'manifests itself by an almost carnal existence of the idea, as well as by a sublimation of the flesh.'[54] The carnal instantiation of ideas and simultaneous sublimation of the flesh that come together in what I am calling interpretation precisely unhinge Fried's readings, which rely on 'disinterestedness' rather than acknowledgment. It is precisely this coextensiveness of the carnal and the cognitive, the embodiment of the interpretive act, that I am performing – against the grain of Fried's repressive act – via Minimalism itself. We are embodied, particular in our identifications; we are flesh and part of the flesh of the world. As such, we *change* the things we encounter: I hope I have changed *Die* for you, my reader (no mean feat to transubstantiate a block of steel the size and weight of an elephant).

PERFORMING AN ENDING

This essay has concerned itself with artistic interpretation. I have focused on a particular, highly charged, case of aesthetic judgment, interrogating Michael Fried's 'Art and Objecthood' – which now has a kind of epochal presence in discussions of 1960s and 1970s art – in order to expose its assumptions and argue for an alternative way to engage with visual art works. As will be evident from my rereadings of Minimalist objects, my proposed alternative, a feminist phenomenological approach, is deeply invested in *performing meaning* so as to acknowledge and surface, rather than suppress and veil, meaning as a process, an ongoing exchange.[55] In turn I hope my interpretations invitingly open themselves to further engagement; my experiences of Morris's and Smith's works are certainly open to debate. I adopt here the words of Julia Kristeva, who has noted, 'Meaning

50

is made infinite by desire. I am not therefore a dead subject, a wise interpreter, happy and self-annihilated in a uniform totality. I am subject to Meaning, a non-Total Meaning, which escapes me.'[56] I too have offered myself up for translation.

Within the alternative mode of interpretation I have argued for here, the escape of 'Meaning' from our grasp – its excess and heterogeneity – would be understood as part of the limiting structure of our analysis, with its inevitable attempt to convince *our* interpreters that we have something to say that is valuable (or, as Fried would say, 'compelling') at this moment in time. Finally, rather than resting on its own veiled assumption of normativity, this project would, by its very nature, enact a deep engagement with – and thus evince a deep respect for – the psychic/corporeal specificities that, on the one hand, position each of us differently in the matrices of culture and, on the other hand, are themselves continually open to reinterpretation. Works of art, in this sense, would be viewed as extensions of bodily/verbal communication in the broadest sense and the question of what is allowed to be called art and what not would be obviated. Rather than being labeled 'right' or 'wrong,' interpretations themselves would be held responsible for their participation in a circuit of desires and meanings that might or might not change how subsequent readers understand the objects at hand as well as the processes that shape their significance.

NOTES

1. Jane Gallop, 'Psychoanalytic Criticism: Some Intimate Questions,' *Art in America*, November 1984, vol. 72, no. 10, p. 11.

2. My interpretation of this trajectory of aesthetic theory is indebted to the work of Karen Lang and Donald Preziosi, including their essays in this volume. Lang's examination of the philosophical underpinnings of art history has also been worked through in her essay, 'The Dialectics of Decay: Re-reading the Kantian Subject,' *Art Bulletin*, September 1997, vol. 79, no. 3, pp. 413–439, and in her Ph.D. dissertation, 'The German Monument, 1790–1914: Subjectivity, Memory, and National Identity,' for UCLA, 1996. Donald Preziosi's ideas on this subject can also be found in his book *Rethinking Art History: Meditations on a Coy Science*, New Haven, Yale University Press, 1989, and his essay 'The Art of Art History,' in *The Art of Art History*, ed. Donald Preziosi, Oxford, Oxford University Press, 1998.

3. While I adopt the common understanding of twentieth-century art criticism as having Kantian bases, it is crucial to note how the productive complexities and ambivalences that comprise Kant's aesthetic have been suppressed in modernist formalist – as well as postmodernist – models of judgment, which tend to take the notion of disinterestedness simplistically as meaning simply 'objectivity.' Kant's model builds on, even as it attempts to subdue, the impossibility of 'objectivity' while it insists on sensorial 'disinterest.'

4. I discuss the continuation of modernist assumptions in so-called postmodern judgments at length in my book *Postmodernism and the En-Gendering of Marcel Duchamp*, New York and Cambridge, Cambridge University Press, 1994; see especially chapter 2.

5. J. Gallop, 'Psychoanalytic Criticism,' p. 10. Gallop uses these words to characterize the desires engendered by the sexual charge of subject matter, but they are clearly relevant to the broader effects of visual objects/images in general.

6. I explore this particular case at length in *Body Art/Performing the Subject*, Minneapolis, University of Minnesota Press, 1998. My discussion of Kant here is revised from this book.

7. Immanuel Kant, *Critique of Judgment* (1790), tr. Werner S. Pluhar, Indianapolis, Hackett Publishing Company, 1986, pp. 45, 46.

8. René Descartes' Enlightenment dictum 'I think therefore I am' poses the mind, in its pure, disinterested judgments, as transcending the loathsome, uncontrollable desires of the body. In his 'Meditations' (1641), Descartes leads the viewer through his supposedly disinterested

contemplation of his own cognitive processes and objectifies himself as a thinking being. While he acknowledges that he cannot successfully 'efface from . . . thought all images of corporeal things,' he nonetheless makes claim to 'consider them as being vain and false; and thus communing only with myself, and examining my inner self, I shall try to make myself, little by little, better known and more familiar to myself. *I am a thing which thinks.* René Descartes, *Discourse on Method and The Meditations*, tr. F. E. Sutcliffe, London and New York, Penguin Books, 1968, p. 113.

9. 'Both the agreeable and the good refer to our power of desire and hence carry a liking with them, the agreeable a liking that is conditioned pathologically by stimuli [i.e. is sensate in nature] ... A judgment of taste, on the other hand, is merely *contemplative*' (Kant, *Critique of Judgment*, p. 51). Paradoxically, given the role of vision in such judgments, it is, Kant stresses, the *sensate body* that must be suppressed or eradicated from the picture in order for the claim of purely disinterested, 'universal' aesthetic judgment to function. In his excellent and provocative book *Downcast Eyes: The Denigration of Vision in Twentieth-century French Thought*, Martin Jay describes poststructuralist philosophy precisely in terms of the resistance to this Enlightenment focus on disembodied vision (Berkeley and Los Angeles, University of California Press, 1993).

10. Kant, *Critique of Judgment*, pp. 54, 55. As I understand it, Kant's argument is tautological: a judgment that isn't universal would imply particular investments, therefore it can't be a judgment of aesthetic taste; a judgment that involves sensate experience or involves particular investments (needs, desires), by its very nature can't be aesthetic since the aesthetic judgment must be universal.

11. Terry Eagleton, *The Ideology of the Aesthetic*, Oxford and Cambridge, Basil Blackwell, 1990, p. 13.

12. Ibid., p. 13. As Eagleton eloquently argues, aesthetic judgment (and perhaps especially Kantian theory) developed as an attempt to 'rescue the life-world from its troubling opacity to reason' (p. 17), linking the newly articulated modern subject to the world of things through a new kind of reason that inevitably contradicts itself, being both free of corporeal desires ('disinterested') and fundamentally sensual, attached to the world of things through sensual perceptions. It is relevant to my argument in this essay, that in the twentieth century it is *phenomenology* that most usefully extends the work done by Enlightenment philosophy in trying to theorize the link between human subjects and the world; Eagleton discusses the importance of Husserl in this regard (see pp. 17–19).

13. I discuss feminist body art's potential to break out of this frame in 'Interpreting Feminist Bodies: The Unframeability of Desire,' *in The Rhetoric of the Frame: Essays Towards a Critical Theory of the Frame in Art*, ed. Paul Duro, Cambridge and New York, Cambridge University Press, 1996, pp. 223–241. See also Lynda Nead's powerful extension of this notion *vis-à-vis* the female nude in *The Female Nude: Art, Obscenity and Sexuality*, London and New York: Routledge, 1992.

14. Pierre Bourdieu, *Distinction: A Social Critique of the Judgement of Taste* (1979), tr. Richard Nice, Cambridge, Harvard University Press, 1984, p. 489.

15. Clement Greenberg, 'Avant-Garde and Kitsch' (1939), *in Art and Culture: Critical Essays*, Boston: Beacon Press, 1961, pp. 3–21.

16. Thus, extending Bourdieu, it is equally clear that aesthetic 'disinterestedness' can function to eradicate racial and sexual difference from the realm of 'human' experience. As William Pietz has argued, Kant's *Critique of Judgment* (1790) might be viewed as a means of coping with the colonial era's incursion of non-European (especially African) cultural values into the fabric of European life – as a 'solution to the problem of fetishism,' a means of *disavowal* aiming to devalue and so ameliorate the increasingly obvious effects of class, cultural (and, I am arguing, sexual) difference. Just as the masses yearned indiscriminately for 'capitalized economic objects as the magical source for wealth and value,' so the 'primitive' fetishist lacked the capacity for 'aesthetic discrimination' and thus for the 'moral autonomy and true freedom' which characterized the enlightened European subject – defined as such through the model of aesthetic judgment. William Pietz, 'Fetish,' *in Critical Terms for Art History*, ed. R. S. Nelson and R. Shiff, Chicago, University of Chicago Press, 1996, pp. 199, 201.

17. Bourdieu, *Distinction*, pp. 491, 488. Strategies of distancing or containment paradoxically link up both to the radical cultural theories of avant-garde artists and writers such as Bertholt Brecht

and to the dangerous othering that takes place in and through nationalist ideologies perpetrated by regimes such as Hitler's National Socialist party; for a brilliant analysis of the consequences of the strategy of distancing otherness in proto-Fascist 1920s Germany, see Klaus Theweleit, *Male Fantasies*, vols. 1 and 2, tr. Erica Carter, Chris Turner, and Stephen Conway, Minneapolis, University of Minnesota Press, 1987 and 1989.

18. Given this litany of characteristics aligned with normative subjectivity, my alternation of gender pronouns throughout this essay may seem confusing. This strategy is meant to stress these characteristics as socially experienced identifications, not essential identities (to suggest, that is, that women art historians can be just as authoritarian as men). At the same time, it is important not to elide the issues of privilege, marginality, and oppression – to recognize the cultural and social benefits that do tend to accrue to subjects who adopt or exploit these normative identifications.

19. This passage and these terms are drawn from Peggy Phelan's eloquent *Mourning Sex: Performing Public Memories*, London and New York, Routledge, 1997, p. 31.

20. Ibid.

21. Michael Fried, 'Art and Objecthood' (1967), reprinted in *Minimal Art: A Critical Anthology*, ed. Gregory Battcock, New York, E. P. Dutton, 1968, pp. 116–47. Notably, Peggy Phelan addressed Fried's theory of theatricality in her eloquent response to the panel 'Body Politics: Performativity and Postmodernism,' which I organized for the College Art Association meetings in New York City in 1997; Christine Poggi's paper published in this volume, also originally given on my panel, specifically addresses Fried's essay as well. Finally, Henry Sayre cites Fried's article in the introduction to his book *The Object of Performance: The American Avant-Garde Since 1970*, Chicago, University of Chicago Press, 1989, pp. 6–7. The critique of Fried in relation to performative works of art is thus hardly new, but I hope to frame it differently, looking again specifically at his response to Minimalist objects in the context of the historical development of modes of judgment outlined above.

22. In fact, Fried hardly discusses actual Minimalist works; his entire critique seems to be based on the Minimalists' writings (mainly those of Morris and Donald Judd) more than on their objects, and he more or less reads these texts through the philosophical context provided by the Minimalists themselves, with an authoritarian Greenbergian gloss. Furthermore, in an egregious show of contempt for Morris and Judd, he conflates their writings, stating in an early footnote that to differentiate these two very different thinkers would have been to 'litter the text with footnotes'; (Fried, 'Art and Objecthood,' p. 117).

23. Ibid., pp. 145, 128, 136, 125. It is in teaching this material that one is reminded how counterintuitive Fried's logic is (a counterintuitivity that I suggest exposes the deep ideological investments motivating Fried's analyses). The idea that these enormous metal hulks would be dismissed as theatrical and thus, in conventional terms, feminized, is most often baffling to those uninitiated into the particular language and gender-loaded assumptions of modernist formalism. On Nietzsche's excoriation of theater as feminine and lower-class, see my discussion in *Postmodernism and the En-Gendering of Marcel Duchamp*, p. 19.

24. Fried, 'Art and Objecthood,' p. 124.

25. It is on this level that Marcel Duchamp's ready-made gesture becomes relevant: the ready-made teaches us (in a lesson we are apparently still not ready to hear) that value is never inherent in the structures of the work but, rather, is interpretively negotiated according to highly invested, commercially and ideologically motivated structures of value.

26. Fried, 'Art and Objecthood,' p. 124. Elsewhere, he makes recourse to the even more dubious criterion of 'sheer rightness'; see his response to T. J. Clark, 'How Modernism Works,' in 'Critical Exchange I: The Politics of Modernism,' *The Politics of Interpretation*, ed. W. J. T. Mitchell, Chicago, University of Chicago Press, 1983, p. 238.

27. Fried, 'Art and Objecthood,' p. 142.

28. He credits the quote only as coming from Perry Miller's *Jonathan Edwards*; ibid., p. 116.

29. Ibid., p. 147.

30. As T. J. Clark has pointed out, Fried's readings rely on metaphysical 'appeals to "intuition",' where 'the intuition *is* the religion' that one must simply take on faith as true. See T. J. Clark's convincing Marxian critique of Fried's essay, and their rather heated exchange as a whole, in 'Critical Exchange I: The Politics of Modernism,' this passage on p. 248. See also Annette

Michelson's savage critique of Fried, whom she accuses of idealism, prescriptiveness, a preoccupation with the canon, and 'identification of aesthetic decisions with moral choices,' in 'Robert Morris: An Aesthetics of Transgression,' *Robert Morris*, Washington, D.C., Corcoran Gallery of Art, 1969, pp. 19, 23; and Hal Foster's critique via avant-gardism in 'The Crux of Minimalism' (1986), revised and republished in *The Return of the Real: The Avant-Garde at the End of the Century*, Cambridge, Mass. and London, MIT Press, 1996, pp. 50–56.

31. Raymond Williams offers another convincing interrogation of aesthetics as an apparatus of bourgeois capitalism in his book *Marxism and Literature*, Oxford, Oxford University Press, 1977. Clark's convincing critique of Fried's authoritarianism links it to a particular set of class assumptions, in 'Critical Exchange I: The Politics of Modernism,' pp. 239–48.

32. Fried, 'Art and Objecthood,' pp. 146, 147.

33. Ibid., p. 130.

34. It is perhaps unfortunate for Fried that he makes this judgment while lauding the work of Anthony Caro as the epitome of high modernism. Fried's apparent gaffe in assigning Caro the premier position in Western contemporary art (gaffe, if one assumes importance is linked to the extent to which an artist is relevant to subsequent artistic developments) bears an obvious parallel to Baudelaire's infelicitous choice of Constantine Guys, who has otherwise completely faded from view, as the exemplar of advanced modernism in artistic production in his epochal essay 'The Painter of Modern Life' (1863), in Charles Baudelaire, *The Painter of Modern Life and Other Essays*, tr. and ed. Jonathan Mayne, New York, De Capo, 1964, pp. 1-40.

35. The first part of this quotation is Fried in 'Critical Exchange I: The Politics of Modernism,' pp. 233–4; the second part ('boy . . . !'), Fried in *Discussions in Contemporary Culture*, no. 1, ed. Hal Foster, Seattle, Bay Press, 1987, p. 84.

36. Here, I am again indebted to the terms set forth by Peggy Phelan in her book *Mourning Sex*; see especially her comments on 'mimicry' as 'the fundamental performance of this cultural moment,' an idea I am in turn 'mimicking' in my call for a new way of writing about art that itself mimics the performative effects of Minimalism, body art, etc. (p. 12).

37. Jacques Derrida has written extensively on the problematic of translation; in *Dissemination* (tr. Barbara Johnson, Chicago, University of Chicago Press, 1981), he argues that '[a]ll translations into languages that are the heirs and depositories of Western metaphysics' – such as aesthetics! – thus produce on the object of interpretation (in the case of *Dissemination*, Plato's *pharmakon*) 'an *effect of analysis* that violently destroys it, reduces it to one of its simple elements by interpreting it ... in the light of the ulterior developments it itself has made possible' (p. 99). This insight perfectly describes the tautological aspect of Fried's interpretation – translation – of Minimalism into 'theatrical' or 'literalist' art.

38. Robert Morris, 'Notes on Sculpture, Part 2' (1966), reprinted in Morris, *Continuous Project Altered Daily: The Writings of Robert Morris*, London and Cambridge, Mass., MIT Press, 1993, pp. 13–14; my emphasis. It is no accident that Morris was active in experimental dance and performance in the 1960s, literally proposing his body as a site of spectatorial engagement. For an excellent overview of this trajectory in Morris's career, see Maurice Berger, *Labyrinths: Robert Morris, Minimalism, and the 1960s*, New York, Harper & Row, 1989.

39. Judith Butler, 'Sexual Ideology and Phenomenological Description: A Feminist Critique of Merleau-Ponty's *Phenomenology of Perception*,' in *The Thinking Muse: Feminism and Modern French Philosophy*, ed. Jeffner Allen and Iris Marion Young, Bloomington: Indiana University Press, 1989, pp. 86, 89.

40. Maurice Merleau-Ponty, *Phenomenology of Perception* (1945), tr. Colin Smith, New York and London, Routledge, 1962/1995, p. 165.

41. Maurice Merleau-Ponty, 'The Intertwining – The Chiasm,' *in Visible and the Invisible* (*c.* 1959–60), tr. Alphonso Lingis, ed. Claude Lefort, Evanston, Northwestern University Press, 1968, especially p. 144.

42. I am embarrassed to say I cannot remember seeing Morris's *Untitled (Ring with Light)*, although I am sure I must have, as I viewed the entirety of the Morris retrospective held at the Solomon R. Guggenheim Museum in New York in 1994. Apparently, a sense of bodily fatigue at encountering a lifetime's worth of complex, phenomenologically engaging works prevented me from actually 'seeing' some of them.

43. Fried, 'Art and Objecthood,' p. 129.

44. In its attempt to incorporate, rather than suppress or regulate, the anxieties opened up by the experience of Minimalist objects, my reading here clearly differs not only from Fried's but also from the rather narrowly determined feminist analysis of Minimalism as necessarily masculinist by Anna Chave in her 'Minimalism and the Rhetoric of Power,' *Arts Magazine*, January 1990, vol. 64, no. 5, pp. 44–63. I am, obviously, sympathetic to Chave's feminist impulse but reject her interpretive model, which proposes that a masculinist authority is 'implicit in the identity of the materials and shapes the artists used, as well as in the scale and often the weight of their objects' (p. 44). On the one hand, I argue that, by posing meaning as inherent, Chave performs the same kind of *interpretive authoritarianism* as Fried; on the other hand, Chave's polemic clearly has a certain force in terms of its in-depth interrogation of the national and art-world politics motivating the rhetoric of Minimalism during the 1960s.

45. Fried cites this ('Art and Objecthood,' p. 128) from Morris's citation of it in 'Notes on Sculpture, Part 2,' p. 11.

46. Fried, 'Art and Objecthood,' p. 129.

47. Ibid., p. 128.

48. Actually, one could argue that even this notion of industrialized bodies/selves is now outmoded and that a kind of cybernetic body/self has replaced it. Minimalism – unlike its high-tech Los Angeles corollary, the 'Light and Space' work of the 1960s – thus dates itself as a comment on industrial capitalism even as it was being replaced by a more slippery mode of subjectification. The Los Angeles work, by artists such as Judy Chicago, Larry Bell, and Robert Irwin, is equally phenomenologically engaging but is produced with 'postindustrial' materials developed by the aerospace industry, largely located in southern California. This work has yet to be integrated into the histories of 1960s art, Minimalism, and body art.

49. Merleau-Ponty, 'The Intertwining,' pp. 152, 153–4.

50. This locution is obviously a reference to Stéphane Mallarmé's poem, 'Un coup de dés jamais n'abolira le hasard' (1897), a favorite among the Surrealists for its self-reflexive metacommentary on poetry itself; the poem offers an approach to meaning I am linking to Minimalism. On this poem and its relationship to Surrealism, see Neil Baldwin, *Man Ray: American Artist*, New York, Clarkson Potter, 1988, p. 151.

51. Anne Wagner discusses the *Accession* series precisely in terms of their tactile and physical beckoning, noting that the first version of this piece was destroyed by the visitors who felt compelled to climb into it. There is also a picture of Hesse, illustrated in Wagner's chapter, bending over the edge of the cube. See Wagner, 'Another Hesse,' in *Three Artists (Three Women): Modernism and the Art of Hesse, Krasner, and O'Keeffe*, Berkeley and Los Angeles, University of California Press, 1996, pp. 258, 260.

52. On display at Shoshana Wayne Gallery in Santa Monica in the early 1990s.

53. Merleau-Ponty, 'The Intertwining,' p. 154.

54. Ibid., p. 155.

55. As the work of phenomenological philosopher Martin Heidegger reminds us, 'all interpretations are in time, and the temporal situation governs and is part of the interpretation itself . . . interpretation is not a subjective domination of the text. It is a striving to let the text be, or to listen.' This is a paraphrasing of Heidegger's general theory of hermeneutics in Hazard Adams and Leroy Searle, *Critical Theory Since 1965*, Tallahassee, Florida State University Press, 1986, p. 757.

56. Julia Kristeva, 'Psychoanalysis and the Polis,' *in The Politics of Interpretation*, p. 92.

4

CROSS-CULTURAL REITERATIONS

Demetra Vaka Brown and the performance of racialized female beauty.[1]

Reina Lewis

ORIENTALISM AND ORIENTALIZATION

Much of the interest generated by theories of performativity has centred on questions of gender identity and of theatrical spectacle, whether it be formal or informal drag performances, theatre, film, or performance art. In this piece, I want to use the emphasis on the instability of identity foregrounded by theories of performativity to think about the construction of racialized and ethnic identities in literary texts. My study here relates to writings in English by 'Oriental' women in the early twentieth century who wrote about segregated Muslim life for a (by definition, non-Muslim) Occidental audience. I am particularly interested in how writers use descriptions of female appearance and beauty to present a series of racial and ethnic Oriental identities that they clearly think will be only partially comprehensible to their Occidental readership. Their efforts to explain localized Oriental differentiations of race and ethnicity – that are unremittingly gendered and classed – to a readership of presumed outsiders may be suggestive for an analysis of how the reiterative qualities that Judith Butler sees as essential to performative gender identities can be applied to race and ethnicity.[2]

So, what I want to do in this still somewhat exploratory piece is to think about how female beauty is racialized in relation to who is looking at the point of both production and of reception. What gender, racial, and ethnic identificatory codes are being activated and how does the text position the reader in relation to them? When the main claim to fame of these books is that they can sell themselves as the 'accurate' revelation of a still largely hidden world authenticated by the 'real' Oriental status of their female authors, I want to ask how much manoeuvrability their authors have in relation to the types of identification with which they align themselves. When they explicitly and implicitly invoke European visual art in the depiction of Oriental women, is it useful to consider the emerging regime of representation in relation to discussions of the embodiment of performative spectacle? Do the authors' fluctuating processes of identification with and separation from the variously racialized female subjects of their books tell us something new about the functioning of those contradictory and shifting processes of identification that have emerged as central to discussions about performativity?[3] As this essay proceeds, I hope to analyse the identificatory positions for authors and readers that are produced in and by these sources and to think about how we might reconceptualize the Orientalist gaze as plural rather than singular, and as polysemic in its potential to produce diverse positions of spectator pleasure and identification.

My source material consists of written accounts of segregated life penned in English by Oriental women and published in North America and Europe for an Occidental audience. Although there are also accounts from the nineteenth century,[4] this essay is concerned with two early twentieth-century sources, both of whom were Ottoman subjects and wrote between 1900 and 1940. Halide Edib Adivar was Turkish and involved in the formation of the republic with Kemal Mustapha Atatürk. She wrote two volumes of autobiography, published initially in London in 1926 and 1928, several novels and much journalism. Demetra Vaka Brown was a Greek Ottoman raised in Istanbul, who emigrated to the United States at the age of seventeen in 1894 and wrote three memoirs/travel books and several novels. Her two volumes about Turkish women, *Some Pages from the Life of Turkish Women* and *The Unveiled Ladies of Stamboul*, published in 1909 and 1923, were both written on the occasion of protracted visits back to Turkey.

Many of the books that form part of my larger project are illustrated, largely with location shots and sometimes with pictures of the authors, but they are all characterized by a highly visual style of literary description through which different types of Oriental women are displayed for the reader. It is my contention that these descriptions institute a regime of representation – the presentation of Oriental women by Oriental women – that we can analyse in relation to the dominant modes of Orientalist spectacle with which we are more familiar. Moreover these images also set up a series of racialized ethnic and national differences that splinter the dominant version of a generic Orient or Oriental. With this in mind, I shall be exploring how these localized differences, which the texts often assume will be invisible to Occidental readers, function in the construction of an alternative Oriental femininity, and assessing the implications of this construction for the textual self-inscription of their authors. I am thinking about beauty in relation to a series of looks that, in a number of different ways, gender and racialize both the objects of the gaze and the owners of the look.

First, I want briefly to lay out the Orientalist discursive conditions in which these texts emerged. Although the sexualized display of the Oriental female body was a central strand of Western Orientalism, fully developed and well-known by the second half of the nineteenth century, I would not want to characterize this as a display whose only audience was male. I agree with many other scholars in the field who argue that the dominant codes of Orientalist art prioritize a male visual pleasure and that this is bound up in the construction of imperial identities and the subjective investment in imperial power relations.[5] None of that is contested: pictures by male artists such as Jean-Léon Gérôme, Eugène Delacroix, John Frederick Lewis, Ludwig Deutsch (see for example Gérôme's *Slave Market*, c. 1867, Plate 4.1) were prevalent in the salons and academies of Europe.[6] But I want to think about women consumers too, since exhibitions were also attended by women of the middle and upper classes and by some from the working class – and the work of key Orientalists would have had an even wider circulation via print and periodical reproduction.[7] So it is clear that we are talking about an audience in which women as well as men looked at Orientalized female bodies and were well schooled in the logic of the Orientalist fantasy harem.

Plate 4.1 Jean-Léon Gérôme, *Slave Market*, c. 1867, oil on canvas, 84.3 × 63cm. Stirling and Francine Clarke Art Institute, Williamstown, Massachusetts

It is evident that Western women produced Orientalist imagery too. In previous work I have studied representations of the Orient by European women artists in order to resituate what is still often seen as a masculinist Orientalist gaze in relation to differences of gender.[8] I want briefly to invoke those paintings now in order to signal that there was a painterly female Orientalist gaze in operation in the nineteenth century, the products of which circulated in the same venues as paintings by Delacroix, Ingres or Gérôme. These female-originated works would have been seen by women and men viewers. What is important about the reception of these works for my argument is that, whether they liked them or not, critics nearly always read their female point of origin as essential to their meaning. The logic of the Orientalist obsession with the harem – a sexualized space forbidden to Western men – meant that women were assumed to have a privileged access because of their gender. Thus, works understood to be based on a woman artist's visit to a harem were universally understood to bear traces of her privileged access to the forbidden site.

Of course, this rationale was applied with some discretion. Harem scenes by artists like Elisabeth Jerichau-Baumann or Henriette Browne (see Plate 4.2) who were known to have travelled to the Orient were treated differently from odalisques by Sophie Anderson or other women artists not known to have travelled East. Although gender was seen as a determining element of the paintings, not every critic accepted women artists' versions of the harem. Even those writers who deplored Browne's harem scenes found that to challenge the veracity of her accounts they inevitably had to marshal conflicting 'evidence'

Plate 4.2 Henriette Browne, *Une visite (intérieur de harem, Constantinople, 1860). A visit (Harem Interior, Constantinople, 1860)*, 1861. Oil on canvas, 86 × 114cm. Photograph courtesy of Sotheby's, London

provided by another woman artist or writer. It is this almost ethnographic authority that accrues to the female Orientalist gaze that I shall come back to in the case of Oriental women writers, not least because their access to any claim of pseudo-scientific authority was at best partial.[9]

Clearly, there was a market for women's Orientalist art – even though this supplementary Orientalism challenged as many cherished male fantasies as it upheld. So, dominant Orientalist discourse can be reconfigured as heterogeneous and contested rather than homogeneous and monolithic. It is also apparent that from the 1860s there was a market for written accounts by Oriental women. I want to think about this body of material not so much as a straightforward alternative to dominant Orientalism, but as a reverse or counter discourse, in which the terms of the dominant discourse are challenged by cultural agents who have experienced their effects from the other side. All these women were highly educated and literate in at least one European language and they were clearly familiar with Western stereotypes about the East. When they engage with the West they do so as subjects whose sense of self as Eastern or Oriental is formed by the Orientalist lens through which they know their Western interlocutors view them. So when they decide to write in English for a target Occidental audience (as well as their Oriental readers), they are clearly and self-consciously engaging with an Orientalist discourse whose positioning of them as inferior and exotic they set out to challenge. As such, they are operating within the orbit of Orientalist discourse while at the same time trying to refashion its terms to their own purpose without being entirely contained within it.[10] But as we shall see, this is a dangerous game.

On the plus side, if the logic of Orientalism accords Western women observers an enhanced veracity, then Oriental women who can also report first hand must have an even higher 'truth' status – a fact reflected in the way their accounts are marketed in terms of their ethnic credentials with titles that identify them as the memoirs of 'a Turkish woman' or 'an Arabian Princess'. Like the artistic convention of referencing locations in the titles of paintings to signal a precise and ostensibly authentic geography, these book titles aim for a similar, but literary, appeal to ethnographic authority. But on the negative side, women of any sort had trouble establishing themselves as objective observers as Billie Melman has demonstrated.[11] The mode of scientific neutrality cultivated by the new social sciences such as ethnography and anthropology was generally coded as masculine and therefore inaccessible to women, whose knowledge was typified as emotional and subjective. Women were caught up in a double bind whereby the gendered privilege that gave them access to knowledges/experiences denied to men in the field compromised their chances of identifying with a detached scientific objectivity on which the new disciplines rested their claim to authority. Not only were women's knowledges diminished as 'empathetic' and 'intuitive' rather than 'observational' and 'scientific', but they also risked being contaminated by a too great proximity to the object of study. It was difficult to inscribe objective distance at the same time as one's claim to partial authority was based on an experiential coda that was relentlessly gendered.

For all that the European woman was at one remove from the nascent superiority of the ethnographer's gaze, the woman coded as Oriental was situated even further from any space of cultural authority. This begs the question: how did 'Oriental' women insert themselves into a Western representation system and does this have anything to do with the representation of female beauty?

Before I pursue that discussion, I have to ask who is the Oriental woman?[12] I am using the term 'Oriental' with inverted commas to signify that it is to be understood as a constructed, relative term, not simply as one of neutral, geographic description. Of course, one could also put inverted commas around 'woman', but I am taking it as read that we understand gender and femininity to be constructed terms of identification, rather than biological essentials. 'European' is, of course, a similarly non-natural category. The easiest way to think about this is as a classification for one who has been Orientalized; that is a subject racialized in the specific terms of an Orientalist discourse, which is, of course, gendered. The non-fixity of the designation 'Oriental woman' is also important, as we shall see in relation to the internal, local differentiations between Oriental women. So, for example, Halide Edib Adivar, who identifies herself as Oriental, is a Turkish Muslim who starts off her life as an Ottoman subject and later, with the establishment of the Republic in 1923, becomes a Turkish citizen. Demetra Vaka Brown also calls herself Oriental and Ottoman yet, though born and raised in Turkey, is of Greek Christian descent. And although Vaka Brown professes a great affinity with segregated life, it is vital to acknowledge that she is not Muslim and knows segregated society only as a visitor to Muslim houses. Eschewing narrow stereotypes in both their work we see deployed a broad range of other Oriental and Occidental gendered ethnicities (such as Armenian, Albanian, Perote – the 'non-ethnic' Turks and foreigners living in the Pera region of Constantinople, Syrian, negro, and Circassian) all of which are portrayed as having different meanings for Oriental or Occidental readers.

Obviously, this shifting set of identifications is important for an Orientalist discourse that sets such store by an authenticity whose guarantee rests on ethnic, Orientalist, and gender allegiances. How can the concept of performativity help us to think through these varieties of racial and ethnic identities? In unpicking some of these complex positionings Vaka Brown, who was writing from the United States, emphasizes that she is Oriental by creating an affinity between herself and all that is best about Turkish Muslim female life. Thus, to her Occidental readership she may appear to be a reliable observer-participant (American enough to give judgments, Oriental enough to gain privileged access). But to Oriental Muslim readers she is more partisan. This is evident in Halide Adivar's objection to Vaka Brown's version of harem life and to her romanticization of polygamy. Writing bitterly of the misery that polygamy brought to her childhood when her father took a second wife, Halide says:

> Although this dramatic introduction of polygamy may seem to promise the sugared life of harems pictured in the 'Haremlik' [American title of *Pages*] of Mrs Kenneth [Vaka] Brown, it was not so in the least. . . . On my own childhood, polygamy and its results produced a very ugly and distressing impression.[13]

Included in the first volume of Halide Adivar's memoirs, written while in exile in Britain and after she had fallen out of favour with the Atatürk regime, this passage is obviously intended for the benefit of a European and American audience since it was not translated into Turkish until the 1950s.[14] Claims to authority rest on Halide Adivar's firsthand experience of segregated life and her direct involvement in revolutionary politics. The old customs of elite gracious and segregated living that Vaka Brown glorifies are not for her. Instead her journey towards emancipation and her public contribution to changing sexual politics – which she, like Vaka Brown, stresses must be developed in specifically Turkish terms – chronicle her changing consciousness.[15]

It seems to me that of all the writers I have read, Halide Adivar has the least trouble establishing an ethnographic authority. As one whose identity meshes with all the variable terms that constitute the sign Oriental woman – Ottoman, Turkish, Muslim, female – her claim to authenticity is a powerful one. She uses her firsthand experience to dispute the 'sugared' vision of harem life for which Demetra Vaka Brown is nostalgic, and yet at the same time she stresses the relative autonomy of even segregated women. One consequence is that the question of contamination by the object of study is not as acute for Halide Adivar as it is for Vaka Brown. However, what is difficult to work out is how far this authenticity is undercut by the very Orientalness that guarantees it, since Halide Adivar is neither a native informant nor an ostensibly objective Western observer. While, in the concluding section of this essay, I shall be discussing how using theories of performativity may help us to understand these competing claims to authenticity, for now, let me just signal how Halide Adivar's status as a modern, educated, and in some ways 'Westernized' subject might also mitigate against her 'Orientalness'.

Against Halide Adivar, Vaka Brown's status as Oriental is quite differently inflected. As a self-designated Oriental woman, she presents herself as an explorer in a bewildering display of association with and disassociation from other Oriental women. Returning to Turkey after six years in the United States, she writes:

> I had returned to my native land with new ideas and a mind full of Occidental questioning, and I meant to find things out. Many of my childhood friends had been Turkish girls: them I now looked upon with new interest. Before, I had taken them and their way of living as a matter of course. . . . I had lived among them, looking upon their customs and habits as quite as natural as my own. But during my stay in America I heard Turks spoken of with hatred and scorn, the Turks reviled as despicable, their women as miserable creatures, living in practical slavery for the base desires of men. I had stood bewildered at this talk. Could it possibly be as the Americans said, and I never have known it?[16]

Immediately we are told that she is like and not like the Oriental object of inquiry. What troubles her in this passage is that the Turks are reviled by her new neighbours, the Americans. As we shall see, this resituating of her previously unproblematic partial identification with Turkish women continues to destabilize her narratorial position.

REGIMES OF REPRESENTATION: IMAGING THE ORIENTAL WOMAN

All the Oriental women writers assume that ethnic difference exists and can be read from the body and behaviour. Sometimes they observe national characteristics in men (Halide Adivar contrasts the brave endurance of Turkish soldiers to the 'childishness' of their Arab counterparts) or in children (Halide detects obvious differences between Turkish, Kurdish, and Armenian children). Vaka Brown, notably in her fiction, paints a world that is split by ethnic and national divides as much as it is by religion. (Her novel *In the Shadow of Islam* is peopled by irritating Armenians, heroic but pleasure-loving Greeks, duplicitous Turks, betrayed Albanians.[17]) But most often these differences are registered through the representation of women, and there are many references to a hierarchy of beauty in which

Circassians and Abyssinians are the most beautiful and 'Negroes' the least. This occurs in other nineteenth-century sources, such as that of Emily Said-Ruete, herself the daughter of a Circassian slave mother and Arab royal father, and in twentieth-century accounts, particularly Vaka Brown's. Noticeably, Halide Adivar is the most restrained in this regard – her main representation of racialized difference is in the depiction of 'Negroes' in the Ottoman empire and of Hindu women in India.[18]

The most conspicuous exponent of the construction of different female beauties is Demetra Vaka Brown, who institutes a gallery of female portraits that, even when they represent Turkish women as superior to American women, emphasize their difference. On her first visit to the polygamous harem of some old friends she enthuses:

> [they were both] sweet, commonplace women – not very different by nature from many commonplace American friends I have, whose lives are spent with dressmakers, manicures, masseuses, and in various frivolous pursuits. . . . Except for the absence of men, I might almost have been visiting an American household. What difference existed was to the advantage of the Turkish girls. They were quite natural and spontaneous. . . . They read a lot of French novels, without pretending that they did it for the sake of 'culture'. They took everything naturally and enjoyed it naturally. There was no unwholesome introspection – that horrible attribute of the average half-educated European and American woman. They never dreamed of setting the world aright.[19]

References to the superior 'naturalness' of Turkish women occur in the work of a number of Oriental writers. Occidental writers also compare the ease of manners in Turkish women favourably to the affectation of over- or mis-educated Western women. Given that by the 1910s and 1920s, many of these accounts are evaluating Western feminism and its potential applicability to the East, I am interested to trace how this implicit critique of the modern 'new woman' is received by Occidental readers.

One significant feature perhaps allied to this subject is that Vaka Brown's descriptions become more and more Orientalized and eroticized. In the following scene, Vaka is trying to insist to her childhood friend Djimlah that women do have a soul:[20]

> She [Djimlah] laughed scornfully. 'You little petal of a flower, woman has no soul . . . she is all emotions and senses."

> If an ugly girl had spoken as Djimlah spoke, it would have been very repulsive; but the radiant loveliness of the girl could not fail to modify the impression made by her words. While speaking, she would clasp her hands above her head, the sleeves falling away from her white arms; she would half close her eyes, in a way that made the light shining through them softer; and her lips forming her words were fresh and crimson, like a rose with the dew on it. The Greek in me, looking at her, forgave her words – one of the judges who liberated Phryne, because she was so beautiful, may have been an ancestor of mine.[21]

Vaka Brown offers a sexualized description of the Oriental woman posing as an odalisque and aligns herself with a male sexualized gaze by adopting the position of Phryne's judges who forgave her her crimes when her naked beauty was revealed to them (a motif also popular with Orientalist artists such as Gérôme). The fancy flourishes of 'little petal' etc., which already by page 60 pepper the text to underwrite the reality of Vaka Brown's Oriental experiences, are simultaneously invoked as one of the pleasures of the Oriental *mise en scène* (honeyed language, excessive and exotic complement being expected tropes along with lovely ladies) and criticized in an invocation of stereotypical Oriental wiliness and duplicity. The reference to Phryne ends with the words:

> And she [Djilmah] prefaced all her blighting remarks with such endearments as 'little crest of the wave,' 'little mountain brook,' or 'flower of the almond tree'. It was as if I were being taken to a slaughter-house through a rose-conservatory.[22]

It is as if Vaka Brown, who five lines earlier aligned herself with Phyrne's judges, is now herself the prisoner. But she does not just switch from judge to prisoner; later she becomes the agent who will enact the judgment or punishment, when she is irritated by another Turkish woman, Aishe. Aishe's refusal to take seriously Vaka Brown's suggestion that she pursue her painting studies in Paris, and her response to every suggestion or explanation with an idiotic 'What for?', anger Vaka Brown. And even the author's intrinsic Greek appreciation of female beauty cannot save the Turkish woman from her punitive fantasy:

> She was very beautiful; not of the Turkish type, but of the pure Circassian, with exquisite lines and a very lovely, musical voice, and of things on this earth I am most susceptible to physical beauty. At that particular moment, however, I should have derived great pleasure if I could have smacked her pretty mouth. [23]

In these passages, Vaka Brown is positioned first as magnanimous judge/connoisseur of female beauty, second as sacrificial lamb, and third as both judge and executioner. But we, dear readers, are not the only ones who find this confusing. After she leaves Aishe, Vaka Brown goes to her room feeling

> rather bewildered. Orientalism was like a labyrinth: the more I advanced in it, the more entangled I became. One woman after another was confronting me with a new problem, a new phase of life; and I felt stupid and incapable of understanding them. It hurt my vanity, too, to find how small I was in comparison with them. I should have liked really to sell myself to them for a year, merely to be able to live with them continuously, to try to understand a little more of their lives. They interested and charmed me: there was so much worth understanding. There was so much of the sublime in them, which is lacking in our European civilization. I felt petty and trivial every time I found myself facing one of those conditions which they understood so well.[24]

Vaka Brown's oscillating and clearly fantastical relationship to the Oriental women she describes reveals the tensions of her position. Like any Westerner she can be 'bewildered' by the illogical maze to which the Orient was often likened, yet she is also drawn to Oriental women and wants to identify with them. This potential loss of (Westernized) self is not simply the projective fantasy common to Western Orientalism, since for Vaka Brown the Orient is already experienced as part of self. In representing herself as enslaved by Turkish women's sublime beauty Vaka Brown attests to the hold that the Orient has over her but, despite her alleged preference for the luxurious calm of Occidental life, she is not in Turkey to stay, 'for he who tastes of American bustle can never again live for long without it.'[25] The passage's high-blown language and emotive imagery of total surrender suggests an investment that is strongly libidinal, an element which comes through even more strongly later in the book.

As the book progresses the generic painterly allusions used for the odalisque-like Djimlah are replaced with more overt references. A quite specific visual reference is introduced as Vaka Brown describes her first encounter with she whom she calls the 'Rossetti woman', at a bath-house party thrown in Vaka Brown's honour.

> I was especially attracted by a certain woman, whose type I had never met in flesh and blood before. To say that she looked like a Rossetti painting would be doing her scant justice, yet it was of the Blessed Damosel [sic] I thought when I saw her.[26]

The woman begs Vaka Brown to visit her and of their next meeting Vaka Brown writes:

> There was a pathos in her voice that I had not detected at our previous interview. Rossetti's poem came back to me, and I said aloud, gazing at her beauty:
>
> 'Her body bore her neck as the tree's stem
> Bears the top branches; and as the branch sustains
> The flower of the year's pride, her high neck bore
> That face made wonderful with night and day.'
>
> 'Why do you say those lines?' my hostess asked.
> 'Because you make me think of them.'
> 'Do you mean that I look like Rossetti's paintings?'
> 'I rather think you look like his poems: you are the embodiment of them.'
> 'And am I this to you?'
> 'Yes, you are this to me. Ever since I first saw you I have been drawn to you. By rights I ought to be somewhere else tonight [Vaka Brown is meant to be travelling to Russia], but I am with you. It was of you I was thinking when you came into my room. Do you know, I do not even know your name. That does not matter, though, for to me you are my Rossetti lady.'
> The Turkish woman sat on a divan, near me, her fingers playing with my loose hair.
> 'You are a sweet-scented little bride,' she said irrelevantly. 'Where is the bride-groom, little one?'
> 'Your slave just gave me a heliotrope bath,' I explained: 'and as for the bride-groom, I am afraid his grandsire died heirless.'
> '*Yavroum*, you are a very dear person, and I hope some day you will know the joy of being a wife.' She was silent for a long time, and then asked, suddenly: 'Shall I tell you why I insisted so strongly at the bath-party that you should come to see me?'
> 'Then it wasn't because you liked me?'
> 'Yes, indeed, little flower of the pomegranate tree. The minute my eyes met yours

I knew that I liked you, and I knew that you belonged to us Oriental women. That is why I asked you to come. I wanted to ask you to do something for me, something which I can only trust to you.[27]

What type of position is Vaka Brown taking up in relation to this 'Rossetti' woman? What other regime of representation does the reference introduce? The tragic vision of female beauty by which Vaka Brown is spellbound reconfigures the Orientalist trope of the unhappy odalisque. Here the odalisque is pictured within an Occidental Pre-Raphaelite mode of imagery noted for its exotic/Italianate vision of mysterious, if not doomed, passionate female beauty. What is intriguing here, is that the stanza Vaka Brown quotes comes not from 'The Blessed Damozel' but from another long poem by Dante Gabriel Rossetti, 'The Last Confession' (originally written 1849, later revised and published 1870). Although Rossetti painted two versions of 'The Blessed Damozel' (Plate 4.3), there is no painting to accompany 'The Last Confession', so the confusion between visual and literary analogies applies to more than Vaka Brown's reported conversation. That Vaka Brown is able to characterize the woman as 'like a Rossetti painting' is not surprising: the Pre-Raphaelites were known for a particular vision of a full-lipped, enigmatic but fleshly female type, whose monumental forms stared out from numerous paintings. As critics have pointed out, the Pre-Raphaelite investment in the figure of the woman as muse and in a vision of femininity that was mysterious and unavailable said more about their own preoccupations than the actual women they so mythologized.[28] Notably, this was not a vision of a normative and reproductive femininity. So what we have here is the self-conscious invocation of what was by the early twentieth century a highly recognizable nineteenth-century image of femininity; one that was redolent of grandeur, transgressive passion, undying love and, often, tragedy.

The stanza from which Vaka Brown quotes comes from the most intensely and overtly eroticized section of 'The Last Confession'. The poem tells the story of an Italian freedom-fighter who makes his final confession to a priest. He had, eleven years earlier, adopted an abandoned girl child, whom he raised and loved. The quoted stanza comes just at the point in his narrative when the speaker tells of the moment when he realized that the girl he had rescued and raised had turned into a desirable woman. His paternal love – 'the father's, brother's love' – turns into a man's love, as he notices for the first time that her body had matured and her beauty no longer reminds him of child angels but of lovely women. The stanza before Vaka Brown's quotation concludes with a revelation of her developing breasts:

> And drew her long hand through her hair, and asked me
> If she was not a woman; and then laughed:
> And as she stooped in laughing, I could see
> Beneath the growing throat the breasts half-globed
> Like folded lilies deepset in the stream.

The next stanza continues

> Yes, let me think of her as then; for so
> Her image, Father, is not like the sights
> Which come when you are gone. She had a mouth

Plate 4.3 Dante Gabriel Rossetti, *The Blessed Damozel*, 1875–8, oil on canvas, 174 × 94cm, with predella. Fogg Art Museum, Harvard University, Cambridge, Massachusetts. Photograph courtesy of the Bridgeman Art Library, London

Made to bring death to life, – the underlip
Sucked in, as if it strove to kiss itself.
Her face was pearly pale, as when one stoops
Over wan water; and the dark crisped hair
And the hair's shadow make it paler still:–
Where the moon's gaze is set in eddying gloom.
Her body bore her neck as the tree's stem
Bears the top branches; and as the branch sustains
The flower of the year's pride, her high neck bore
That face made wonderful with night and day.
Her voice was swift, yet ever the last words
Fell lingeringly; and rounded finger-tips
She had, that clung a little where they touched
And then were gone o' the instant....[29]

I put Vaka Brown's quoted passage in context because the erotic charge of the material she has selected cannot be ignored – even if it is taken out of its context in one poem and attributed to another. It is after this section that the narrator murders his beloved, having subsequently heard her give a coarse and womanly laugh from which he 'deduces' that she is no longer an innocent.[30] Why does Vaka Brown, I wonder, choose to invoke two poems which both deal with the (doomed) beauty of a dead woman? To what extent was the Pre-Raphaelite obsession with doomed, or even dead female beauties available to women?[31] Although the Pre-Raphaelites rarely ventured into overtly Orientalist subjects, the trope of the enigmatic and fated woman could be combined with the morbidity stereotypically attributed to Oriental woman, as could the idea of a death-inducing passion. But to what is Vaka Brown alluding by the introduction of Rossetti into her Oriental scene?

I think it is very significant that at the culmination of this highly charged exchange, the 'Rossetti woman' identifies and claims Demetra Vaka Brown as 'belong[ing] to us Oriental women'. The problem that plagues Vaka Brown throughout her book is whether her ethnic and racialized identity is stable and is recognizable – to herself, to the characters in the book, and to the book's readers. While it is precisely her ability to perform both Occidental and Oriental identifications that makes her book a marketable product, it is also quite obviously troubling to the narrator to be so insecure and unstable. The authorial identity constructed within the text requires both a closeness to and a distance from the Orient and Oriental femininity: the proximity is simultaneously one which the narrator desires, not least on behalf of her readers, and something to be avoided, or else she will be one of *them* and will risk being denigrated along with the Turks.

One further feature which demands to be discussed at this point is, How do we as late-twentieth-century readers deal with the queerness evident in this passage and yet hold on to a sense of what it might have meant to its original audience? Vaka Brown frequently depicts herself being touched and fondled by the Turkish women she spends time with (they hold her hand, sit close to her on divans, play with her hair) which, while it clearly activates the lesbian subtexts that were a common feature of Western harem narratives (though less so in women's accounts), also disassociates the narrator and hence by implication Vaka Brown from any actual queerness. This is possible, I think, because in the terms of this text the homoerotic elements serve to emphasize the being-there-ness of Vaka Brown as narrator without tainting her as too sapphically Oriental. While the text's performance of the familiar lesbian codings associated with the Oriental woman is perhaps part of Vaka Brown's presentation of herself as Oriental within the classificatory system recognizable to the West, she works to desexualize these most overtly masculinist stereotypes and to turn them to her own advantage. In her fiction and travel accounts, physical closeness is presented as typical of Oriental female manners – on a similar register of local authenticating detail as frankness in discussion and charming hospitality. Her ability to recognize all of these features as typical is one of the things that establishes the accuracy of her accounts. But, in seeking to authenticate herself as someone familiar enough with Oriental living and trusted enough by Oriental women to have valuable insider knowledge in the context of a physical intimacy redolent of such titillating images as J. A. D. Ingres's the *Turkish Bath*, Vaka Brown risks becoming part of the Oriental spectacle. And if she does become part of the spectacle, what happens to the distance necessary for the establishment of the ethnographic authority which, at other moments in the book, she clearly desires?

It is for this reason that Vaka Brown tries repeatedly both to invoke the stereotypes that make the Oriental woman recognizable and to challenge and invalidate their negative aspects. Her distressed bewilderment in the passage I quoted earlier – could it have been like this all along 'and I never have known it' – is reminiscent of the impact of shame discussed by Eve Kosofsky Sedgwick in her article 'Queer Performativity: Henry James's *The Art of the Novel*'.[32] In this she draws on Silvan Tomkins to argue that shame is an affect central to the formation of identities. Although what is considered shaming will vary across cultures, the result, she suggests, is the same: if shame 'is a bad feeling attached to what one is: one therefore *is something* in experiencing shame'.[33] Most importantly for my analysis, the affect of shame is not only prompted by shame at one's own behaviour but may also be activated by witnessing the shaming of another. In this light, the shame Vaka Brown feels at the belittlement of the Turks sets up the problematic of her book. Is she an Oriental woman or not? Can she risk this identification, when the shaming instance of having Turks re-presented to her through American eyes (as well as her own ambivalence about identifying with the Orient) has actually tarnished a previously acceptable identification? Her ambivalence about being identified with the Turkish women is not just another example of the problems of contamination faced by Occidental women travel-writers as they attempted to claim the objectivity of an ethnographic authority. Rather, it signals the distress of a subject in the making that is under threat of being forced to give up an already only partial identification with a desired (and, in the context of her teenage emigration to the United States, nostalgic) Orientalized self. The customs of the Turks were only looked upon as 'quite as natural as my own', they never actually *were* her own.

But this partial ownership was a source of pleasure and pride: evidenced by the fact that Vaka Brown was not only active on behalf of Greek-American philanthropic causes, but also toured the country speaking about her Oriental experiences. Nevertheless, her decision to write this and other books suggests a strong desire to retain the Oriental self that has been partially diluted by her emigration to the United States; yet Vaka Brown must also perform as an American and enact her new, dare I say diasporic, identifications in terms that her host country could tolerate. The threat of contamination by the East, which I referenced earlier in relation to Occidental artists and writers, is indeed present in Vaka Brown's account, as I have shown. But here contamination works two ways: she also risks having her Orientalness contaminated by too much American-ness. It is in this light that the eroticized conquest of her by the Rossetti woman needs to be seen: it is not just that Vaka Brown wants her to *like* her, but that she wants her to *claim* her, and, to claim her in such a way that her Oriental and Occidental qualities are recognized. It is important to note that the Rossetti woman has sought her out to help in a custody case over her daughter[34] – something that she feels only a liberated part-Occidental woman could manage. Thus, for the twice displaced Vaka Brown, already somewhat 'other' as a Greek in Turkey, and then again as Oriental in America, comes proof that her performance of a complex racialized identification has been properly recognized. I think that the display of Oriental femininities offered in the book serves to mark out for an audience assumed to be less than expert the reiterative elements essential to the racialized and ethnic performative identifications in relation to which Vaka Brown wants to be situated.

The ambivalence of her identification as Greek and Christian, which was tolerable in Turkey because there was a context for the comprehension of those identifications (although there were tensions felt by many Greek Ottoman subjects), is rendered trouble-some once she is relocated to America, where she is interpellated as Oriental within an Orientalist discourse that cannot recognize her differentiated Oriental subjectivity.[35] Shamed by the prejudice against Turks, which also threatens to envelop her if Americans persist in failing to recognize her performance of a nuanced Greek-Ottoman identification, Vaka Brown proffers a defence of Turkish women that is successful enough partially to redeem her Oriental roots, without capitulating entirely to the lure of the harem and too much contamination. In this context we can see why writing about subsequent visits caused her more problems in terms of her multiple identifications. When she returns to report again in 1921, Vaka Brown is strongly disapproving of the emancipated women she sees this time. This makes sense not only in terms of the conservative politics she demonstrated in other arenas, but also psychically, since it is through an alignment with the old life-style of the elite harems that she can best demonstrate the particular Orientalized identification that she craves.[36] Her displeasure with the unveiled Istanbul shop-girls of 1921 takes a tone of such personal affront that I cannot avoid speculating about the psychic loss she feels at the demise of a system of segregated life that was never hers in the first place, but in which she clearly had an over-determined investment and personal allegiance. But that's another story.

CONCLUSION: PERFORMATIVITY AND TRANSCULTURATION

In 'Critically Queer', Judith Butler argues that performative actions only stand any chance of success if they have accumulated '*the force of authority through the repetition or citation of a prior, authoritative set of practices*'.[37] Following Derrida, she insists that the performative statement relies for its success on conformity to an 'iterable model'; in other words, the norms through whose reiteratation performativity works must have a history and be recognizable. The sources I have been discussing raise the question of whether perform-ativity can work across cultures and languages and in terms of racial and ethnic identifications. This is not to say that a different culture will not have the regulatory and discursive modes of power that spur reiterative performative actions, but that, in trying to enact new identities, subjects risk remaining unrecognizable if their codings do not translate across cultures. The history of the identificatory terms reiterated by both Halide Adivar and Demetra Vaka Brown is largely unavailable to their Occidental audience. This renders it either meaningless (what is 'Perote', anyway?) or inaccurate (the struggle over the term 'harem', for example, illustrates how the word's associations in the Occident are quite different from its meaning in the Orient).[38] Demetra Vaka Brown is trying to give voice to a different form of Oriental femininity from that standardized by dominant Orientalist discourse. Yet the terms of intra-Oriental differentiation which are so important to her vision of her particular racialized space have no comparable iterative history and hence meaning in the Occident. While some designations, like Circassian, might be familiar in the West, their particular histories would have carried different resonances in the Orient. There, their power as a distinguishing term among Oriental identifications was not overlaid with the same force of Orientalism, which attaches to each and every Oriental identification a similarly charged racialization. In trying to use these terms Oriental writers find themselves stuck between explaining the nuances of the classifications as they see them and simultaneously challenging the blanket deformations of Orientalist structures of comprehension. In this light, Vaka Brown's oscillation between being of or separate from the Orient reveals both the lure of performative identificatory processes[39] and the limits of the performative once it attempts to transculturate.

This is where the problem of authenticity returns. If we think about authenticity performatively, we can see that the set of previously sanctioned codings whose reiteration signals authenticity will be differently constituted for different audiences. Halide Adivar's writing typifies this dilemma. She is simultaneously trying to present herself to an Occidental readership as an authentic Oriental woman (which requires that she reiterate and reconfirm signs of Orientalness that the West can recognize) and at the same time trying to discredit Vaka Brown's performance of Orientalness (by arguing that Vaka Brown's signs of belonging would not be recognized by an Oriental audience). But Halide Adivar is not only struggling because she is trying to codify herself within two overlapping but separate discourses – to be an authentic Oriental in both local/Oriental and Occidental terms – the problem is generic.[40] Like the deadening effect of repeating a stereotype (in which one can only ever approximate but never quite fit a previously set classificatory mould), the invocation of authenticity will each time slightly miss the mark. Since the iterative elements of a performative action have to be familiar to the viewer before they can make sense, the 'authentic' Oriental woman who wants her performance to be recognizable to the West must relate herself to a series of already available stereotypes operating within a previously existing Western classification system. Since every performative repetition is a dynamic intersubjective event, it will succeed or fail depending on who is involved and what histories and individual qualities they bring to their participation in the event. Furthermore, such stereotypes, as Emily Apter highlights in 'Acting Out Orientalism', are the 'Achilles heel' of performativity.[41] Using Homi Bhabha's emphasis on the stereotype's role in processes of subjectification, Apter argues that each new attempt to repeat the stereotype will *qua* Bhabha be a 'deadening' mismatch. The experience of not quite matching will alienate the subject from the image rather than tie them securely to it. If we think about authenticity as performative, we can see that it opens up the idea of the reiterative as not only referring back to but as also always misfitting, not quite matching, a prior or imagined 'original'. The difficulty of being authentic is that one can never actually make a match, one can only ever approximate. And it is this dilemma that is so clearly manifested in my sources. What both Vaka Brown and Halide Adivar underscore is the impossibility of totally reproducing a prior model – since when this is combined with a transcultural scenario the inbuilt problem becomes even more complex.

It is not just that cross-cultural iterations (like all iterative elements) need an interpretive community that can recognize and understand them. The gap between the Oriental performer and the Occidental viewer/reader emphasizes the always intersubjective quality of the processes by which a performative action is decoded. Where the different agents do not share a set of codings, the performance breaks down. The ways in which the stereotype misfits will not only be different each time, but the gaps and frayings from the original will themselves be differently recognizable to differently formed subjects. Hence, Halide Adivar's rejection of Demetra Vaka Brown's claim to fit the mould of the authentic harem respondent is couched both in terms of the mismatch of Vaka Brown's performance to Halide Adivar's own experience (coded as truly authentic and Oriental) and in relation to Halide's own attempt to remake the mould of the real Oriental woman to which she aspires. This quest to create alternative iterable qualities for a new type/image of Oriental women is also addressed to a 'home' audience of Oriental readers who will be able to read her self-representation within a different classification system. But, can the Western-educated and European-dressed Halide alter the terms of an Orientalist frame sufficiently for her primary Occidental audience to recognize the performative qualities she reiterates, without herself being deadened by the powerful stereotypes she must invoke in order to replace them?

It is in this light that the erotics of Vaka Brown's interaction with the Rossetti woman can be rethought. Like Halide Adivar, Vaka Brown has to operate within already existing codes and sometimes risks being overpowered by the stereotypes she invokes (as in her depiction of the homoerotic Rossetti scenario). This passage activates a lesbian theme that was clearly a well-established trope of Orientalist representation. By so doing this act may in part serve to mark her authenticity because she reiterates a code easily recognized in the West. In addition, because of the way that she does this she is aligned with a masculinist classificatory gaze that works through the aesthetic (and racializing) 'appreciation' of female beauty (one associating her with a higher order of knowledge than that usually attributed to women). But the Sapphic Orient is a dangerous trope to perform as it risks coding Vaka Brown as a sexualized object within the depicted scene. I do think that the text is partly successful in securing Vaka Brown as the observer and not the observed, which is one of its aims. But this separation from the Oriental object is put at risk once the Rossetti woman fulfils its other aim by identifying and claiming Vaka Brown as an Oriental woman. The dangers of being located as part of the (in this instance sapphic) Orient are clear. Although Vaka Brown wants her performance of Orientalness to be recognized, she wants it to be nuanced and remade in her own terms; not just to exist as an endlessly invalidating/alienating mismatch of existing stereotypes. The adoption of an objectifying gaze that classifies and evaluates the beauty of the Oriental women she surveys is one way that Vaka Brown can claim authenticity on both (feminine) experiential and (masculine) objective grounds. This lets her occupy a more validated knowledge position through which to authenticate herself, while at the same time she is recognized as the owner of a body of knowledge that is self-experience. The Rossetti woman fully understands the nature of Vaka Brown's Oriental identity and it is the intense desire of the text that this be recognized – at the very moment when Vaka Brown's appropriation of an eroticizing masculine-coded gaze is at its most pronounced and most interactive – that produces the libidinal charge of the narrative. The queerness so evident to our modern eyes is a result of her appropriating this masculine gaze in a book that is utterly bound by a gender-specific authenticating convention that can never overlook her femininity.

We cannot know, nor really need to know, whether Vaka Brown did herself engage in same-sex acts, or even whether she was conscious of the queer dynamics of her writing.[42] But we can productively explore how the difficult-to-translate iterative elements of Orientalist stereotypes were open to a series of interventions that reveal glimpses of the different status that these performative tropes might have had in different discursive situations. In this light, claims to authenticity destabilize not only the stereotypes of the West – even as writers who invoke them risk being incorporated into them – but also hint at the different histories and cultural meanings that could be attached to those performances. The possibilities offered by a homoerotic or homosocial engagement between Orientals in an Oriental setting can only be guessed at when represented in a source such as that published by Demetra Vaka Brown. Her mainly Occidental readership would have been ill-equipped to read her interaction with the Rossetti woman outside of the Western associations of the iterative terms she deploys. Whereas Halide Adivar's self-presentation as progressive and modernizing Oriental woman also introduces the internal debate about the Kemalist adoption of a Westernizing model of progress,[43] this resonance can be more easily held by the text, I think, than the rogue eroticization of Vaka Brown's harem interlude. Perhaps it is not just that the revolutionary Halide Adivar has a different political agenda from the nostalgic and conservative expatriate Demetra Vaka Brown (nor that one really is more authentically Oriental than the other and so more entitled to tell it like it is), but that Halide treads a more careful path between the volatile iterative elements whose transculturated performance is revealed to be so precarious.

NOTES

1. This paper has greatly benefited from my discussions about performativity and authenticity with Wendy Leeks and with the editors of this volume, all of whom I thank.
2. J. Butler, *Gender Trouble: Feminism and the Subversion of Identity*, London: Routledge, 1990.
3. See also A. Brah, *Cartographies of Diaspora: Contesting Identities*, London: Routledge, 1996.
4. Melek-Hanum *Thirty Years in the Harem: or the Autobiography of Melek-Hanum, Wife of H.H. Kibrizli-Mehemet-Pasha*, (1872), 2nd edn, Calcutta, Lewis and Co., 1888. Melek-Hanum, *Six years in Europe: Sequel to Thirty Years in the Harem*, London, Chapman & Hall, 1873. E. Said-Ruete, *Memoirs of an Arabian Princess: Princess Salme bint Said ibn Sultan al-Bu Saidi of Oman and Zanzibar* (1888) London, East-West Publications, 1981.
5. L. Nochlin, 'The Imaginary Orient', *Art In America*, May 1983. O. Richon, 'Representation, the Harem and the Despot', *Block*, no.10, 1985. Ç. Tawardos, , 'Foreign Bodies: Art History and the Discourse of Nineteenth-Century Orientalist Art', *Third Text*, nos. 3/4, Spring/ Summer 1988, pp. 34–44.
6. Though Orientalist visual culture had a market throughout Europe, one must not forget that there were internal divisions within European Orientalism. Apart from the historical differences that marked the development of Orientalist art in relation to different levels of state or private patronage in France and England, for example, one cannot ignore the tendency in the nineteenth century for critics to read nearly everything in relation to apparently detectable signs of national taste, morality, talent, and so on. See L. Thornton, *The Orientalists: Painter Travellers 1828–1908*, Paris: ACR Edition, 1983; P. Mainardi, *Art and Politics of the Second Empire: The Universal Expositions of 1855 and 1867*, New Haven: Yale University Press, 1987; L. Nead, *Myths of Sexuality: Representations of Women in Victorian Britain*, Oxford: Blackwell, 1988.
7. On forms of popular Orientalism see also J. M. Mackenzie *Orientalism: History, Theory and the Arts*, Manchester: Manchester University Press, 1995.
8. R. Lewis, *Gendering Orientalism: Race, Femininity and Representation*, London, Routledge, 1996.
9. One could also consider here the role of photography in the 'accurate' depiction of the harem.

See S. Graham-Brown *Images of Women: The Portrayal of Women in Photography of the Middle East 1860–1950*, London: Quartet, 1988; and M. Alloula, *The Colonial Harem*, Manchester: Manchester University Press, 1987.

10. I thank Lois McNay for helping to clarify this point.

11. B. Melman, *Women's Orients: English Women and the Middle East, 1718–1918. Sexuality, Religion and Work*, Basingstoke: Macmillan, 1992. See also S. Mills, *Discourse of Difference: An Analysis of Women's Travel Writing and Colonialism*, London, Routledge, 1991.

12. R. Lewis, 'Authorship, Authenticity and Transculturation: Reading Ottoman Women's Cross-Cultural Representations of Segregated Life', forthcoming 1999.

13. H. Adivar Edib , *Memoirs of Halide Edib*, London, John Murray, 1926, pp. 144–5.

14. It was available in English in Turkey after her rehabilitation upon Ataturk's death in 1939.

15. On Halide Adivar's differing representations of polygamy in her fiction see S. Paker, 'Unmuffled Voices in the Shade and Beyond: Women's Writing in Turkish', in H. Forsås-Scott (ed.), *Textual Liberation: European Feminist Writing in the Twentieth Century*, London: Routledge, 1991. For more on how Turkish women depict Western feminism see R. Lewis 'Writing the Racialised Self? Ottoman Women Writers and Western Feminism, 1872–1926' in P. Cohen (ed.) *New Ethnicities; Old Racisms*, London, Zed Books, 1999.

16. D. Vaka Brown, *Some Pages from the Life of Turkish Women*, London, Constable, 1909, pp. 12–13.

17. D. Vaka Brown, *In the Shadow of Islam*, London, Constable, 1911.

18. H. Adivar Edib, *Inside India*, London, George Allen & Unwin, 1937. Both Halide Adivar and Vaka Brown use the term negro. On some occasions this refers to what we would now call African-Americans, but on others it appears to refer generically to all Africans. This is particularly confusing since both authors also make distinctions between different African Continental nationalities and ethnicities, such as Nubian and Abyssinian.

19. Vaka Brown, *Some Pages from the Life of Turkish Women*, p. 28.

20. Vaka describes Djimlah as one to whose 'vigorous and original mind' she had been 'attracted' in her youth. The issue of whether Islam allows that women have a soul is a recurring pre-occupation of most Occidental women writers. Grace Ellison also covers it; see G. Ellison, *An Englishwoman in a Turkish Harem*, London: Methuen, 1915.

21. Vaka Brown *Some Pages from the Life of Turkish Women*, pp. 60–1.

22. Ibid., p. 61.

23. Ibid., p. 102.

24. Ibid., p. 127.

25. Ibid., p. 221.

26. Ibid., p. 234.

27. Ibid., pp. 251–3.

28. D. Cherry and G. Pollock, 'Woman as Sign in Pre-Raphaelite Literature: A Study of the Representation of Elizabeth Siddall', *Art History*, June, 1984, vol. 7, 2, pp. 206–27; D. G. Riede, *Dante Gabriel Rossetti Revisited*, New York, Twayne, 1992.

29. D. G. Rossetti, 'The Last Confession' (1842–70) in W. G. Rossetti, *The Works of Dante Gabriel Rossetti*, London: Ellis, 1911, p. 48.

30. Although I have previously characterized the typical Pre-Raphaelite heroine as unlike a normative regime of representation that ran between the angel in the house (the chaste and asexual bourgeois wife and mother) and the cautionary tale of her counterpart, the fallen woman, the 'Last Confession' is clearly a poem concerned with a woman assumed to have fallen. There is not space here for a more detailed discussion of either the Rossetti poems or the painting, so let me just signal the debate to be had about the erotic investment in the event of the fall and the potentially countercultural meanings of some of Rossetti's phallic sirens.

See also L. Pearce, *Woman/Image/Text: Readings in Pre-Raphaelite Art and Literature*, Hemel Hempstead: Harvester Wheatsheaf, 1991.

31. On the wider cultural context of the Pre-Raphaelite valorization of women's ill health as beautiful and on the cult of the dead woman as muse, see E. Bronfen, *Over Her Dead Body: Death, Femininity and the Aesthetic*, Manchester: Manchester University Press, 1992. See also Pearce, *Woman/Image/Text* on the potential pleasure available to twentieth-century women consumers of Rossetti's work.

32. E. Kosofsky Sedgwick, 'Queer Performativity: Henry James's *The Art of the Novel*, *GLQ*, vol. 1, 1993, pp. 1–16.

33. Ibid., p. 12, original emphasis.

34. The woman, who had been happily married, was wooed by an English nobleman while her husband was away, and ran away with him. They married and had a daughter, but after two years the woman repented and wrote to her Turkish husband begging forgiveness. He travelled to Scotland to reclaim her and her new daughter, at which point the Englishman committed suicide. The problem she now faces is that his mother, the Duchess, war s the daughter to return to England (or Scotland). The Rossetti woman wants Vaka Brown to write to the Duchess explaining that the girl will be raised in Turkey as an 'Osmanli noblewoman', and may return to England as an adult if she wishes. I note in passing that in this instance the dead lover is the husband, not the damozel, as in the poem referenced and that, unlike the woman in 'The Last Confession', this Rossetti woman is presented as having made a happy romantic alliance on her own terms – despite the potentially destructive implications of her illicit passion.

35. See Kalogeras on the different problems of being identified as Greek within the context of emergent anti-immigrant prejudice directed at the American Greek community. Y. D. Kalogeras, 'A Child of the Orient as American Storyteller: Demetra Vaka Brown', in R. Parkin-Gounelas (ed.), *Working Papers in Linguistics and Literature*, Thessaloniki: A   University Press, 1989.

36. D. Vaka Brown, *The Unveiled Ladies of Stamboul*, Boston: Houghton Mifflin, 1923.

37. J. Butler, 'Critically Queer', *GLQ*, vol. 1, 1993, pp. 17–32, p. 19, original emphasis.

38. Even as Oriental women challenged the institutions of segregation, they were hampered in their quest for international support by the impossibility of translating for the Occident the meanings that harem had for them aside from the power relations of Orientalist discourse.

39. Not that, as Butler emphasizes, performative processes of identification can be thought of as entirely voluntaristic. One must recognize the non-consensual elements of interpellation and the force of the unconscious, Butler 1993, 'Critically Queer'.

40. It should be clear here, I hope, that I am regarding all claims to authenticity as imagined and discursive rather than actual or achievable. For a summary of responses to what some see as the problem of the 'real' Orient in Said's *Orientalism*, see Lewis, *Gendering Orientalism*. E. W. Said, *Orientalism*, Harmondsworth: Penguin, 1978.

41. E. Apter, 'Acting Out Orientalism: Sapphic Theatricality in Turn-of-the-century Paris', in E. Diamond (ed.), *Performance and Cultural Politics*, London: Routledge 1996.

42. This is not, however, to evacuate the lesbian codings from the text. I do not have time here for the lengthier discussion of how sapphism works as a trope within Orientalist discourse and the different pleasures it makes available to its different audiences. At this point I would just like to signal that an awareness of the queer pleasures available to readers now needs to co-exist with a historicized reading concerned both with temporality (how those codes might have registered at the start of the century) and with space (how they were differently meaningful for Oriental and Occidental audiences). In the latter case, the example of Demetra Vaka Brown serves to remind us of the congruences between those two spatialized placements.

43. On the debates in Turkey about the move towards modernization on a Western model, presented by some as a return to a more truly Turkic pre-Islamic tradition, and its relationship to the development of female emancipation see: K. Jayawardena, *Feminism and Nationalism in the Third World*, London: Zed Books, 1986; D. Kandiyoti, (ed.), *Women, Islam and the State*, Basingstoke: Macmillan, 1991; J. S. Shaw and E. K. Shaw, *History of the Ottoman Empire and Modern Turkey*, vol 2, *Reform, Revolution and Republic*, Cambridge: Cambridge University Press (2nd edn) 1994.

5

RACE, RITUAL, AND RESPONSIBILITY
Performativity and the Southern lynching[1]

Michael Hatt

There will be no speech from
the scaffold, the scene must
be its own commentary.[2]

The power (of performance) is not the function of an originating
will but is always derivative.[3]

In a recent essay, the philosopher Judith Butler has posed an enormous challenge to scholars, thinkers, and lawyers concerned with the question of race hatred. In a brilliant, complex, and difficult argument, Butler explores deep contradictions in the liberal idea of free speech and analyses how the ideological basis of 'hate speech' is replicated in the judicial process that purports to oppose it. By offering an analysis grounded in a critique of the subject derived from Nietszche, Derrida, and J. L. Austin, she suggests that to presume a straightforward culpability for racism by a given person necessitates an adherence to an Enlightenment model of the subject that is unsustainable. In other words, the apparent ease with which blame can be apportioned in one instance may be at the cost of being able to mount a philosophical critique of the subject and, therefore, of the question of speech itself.

In this essay, I want to challenge Butler and attempt to refute her argument by looking at its implications for the late-nineteenth-century lynching. My position is clearly very different from hers, and in a sense is underpinned by a defence of liberal humanism; hence, I suppose, by a pragmatism that is prepared to pay a philosophical price. Nonetheless, it should also be clear that the very fact I am engaging with Butler's argument is proof of the seriousness with which I think her intervention in the debate must be taken. I shall first offer an account of lynching as a performative ritual, using Austin's theory of performative speech – essentially, that certain types of utterance enact rather than describe or name – and I shall then go on to give my reasons for thinking Butler's argument misguided. Between these two tasks, the notion of performativity will function as a hinge, acting both as a topos of my essay and as an analytical tool.

Lynching has a long history, but it reached its peak in the American South in the 1890s. This peak is represented both by the number of lynchings – at least 1,500 in that decade – and by the scale of the lynchings as public events. While earlier forms of lynching had involved small mobs or posses or bands of vigilantes, it was in the 1890s that the lynching became a mass spectacle with, sometimes, thousands of participants. Although not all victims were black, the majority were, and it was black victims who drew the biggest and most excited crowds. Moreover, the contemporary debate about the practice is almost exclusively concerned with a race-specific structure of white mob and black victim. The specific nature of this *fin de siècle* lynching points to the fact that although it was often dismissed as a relic of the Old South, a reminder of its backwardness and refusal to modernize, it was in fact a very modern ritual, albeit one that reasserted antebellum white supremacy in an age when African Americans were nominally free citizens, recognized constitutionally as human beings.

For most people, I suspect, the term lynching brings to mind some scene from a film, perhaps a western; an unceremonious affair involving a few men on horseback, a rope, and a tree. In fact, lynching was a long and complex ritual of torture and extreme violence. There would be a procession as the terrified victim was dragged from his place of capture to the site of execution; the body would then be mutilated, and stabbed with knives, corkscrews, forks, or other weapons; eyes would be gouged or burned out; parts of the body would be severed; and the victim could be burnt with hot irons all over the body and in the mouth and throat. After this appalling violation of the body, the victim would be burned alive, although hanging and shooting were also used as methods of execution. After death, the body might be mutilated further, or riddled with bullets, and pieces of the charred flesh would be kept as souvenirs. These were often given to children as mementoes, as were ears or fingers or toes, or pieces of charcoal from the pyre. Keepsakes were made photographically, as the examples here show (Plates 5.1 and 5.2). One is a drawing made from a photograph of a lynching in Kentucky in 1893; the other image is a souvenir postcard from a hanging in Alabama in 1891. These events, then, were public spectacles, often advertised in local papers. Railways would even lay on special services sometimes to ferry people there and back. Many lynchings had a carnival atmosphere; folks could dress up, take picnics, and bring along the kids since it was considered family entertainment. While these events are often assumed to be vernacular or popular justice, and were classed so at the time, lynchings nearly always involved authority, either by the presence of leading citizens such as doctors and judges, or by the very fact that the authorities turned a blind eye. Although Tennessee, for example, instituted anti-lynching legislation in 1897, by 1905 no charges had yet been brought under it.[4]

The most common justification for lynching was an allegation of rape, a crime which included any kind of sexual or even social dalliance. At times it only needed a white woman to declare that a black had been discourteous or looked at her insultingly for a mob to take action. So incensed were locals by these breaches of decorum and the defilement of pure white womanhood by the negro that only this kind of rough justice would suffice as retribution. This was not the only misdemeanour that was punished in this way – almost as many lynchings were for murder, and offences such as theft and disrespect to a man could cause similar responses – but it was rape that, in contemporary discussions, was most frequently alluded to as the inciting action. It hardly need be said, of course, that these were crimes that were almost never proven and one can only assume that most of the time they had no basis in fact.[5]

Lynching has been subject to various analyses, and the diverse interpretations of the ritual and its purpose appear to pose a problem for the historian of the South. In brief, so many contradictory motives seem to be at work in the lynching, it becomes difficult to

Plate 5.1 Lynching of C. J. Miller at Bardwell, Kentucky, July 7, 1893, from Ida Wells-Barnett, *A Red Record*, 1895

Plate 5.2 Scene of Lynching at Clanton, Alabama, August 1891, from *A Red Record*

present a definitive account of the form and its social and political use. For example, it has been described as a simple expression of racism in an unenlightened society; it has been discussed in terms of the specific racial tensions that arose in the wake of Reconstruction; it has been subject to psychological readings, such as John Dollard's famous 'frustration-aggression' thesis – that is, that blacks become a focus for irrational white aggression – or to psychoanalytically inclined accounts that emphasize sexuality and gender. It is also open to a number of social historical interpretations as symptomatic of shifting economic fault lines, related to patterns of employment and economic hardship. Poor whites, for instance, viewed free blacks as competitors for jobs, and thus had to recognize them as humans, rather than a subhuman species; the lynching not only reinstated a sense of white superiority, but also worked to mitigate the black threat to white labour. Richer whites, planters and landowners, may have found a reign of terror useful in ensuring a cowed, docile, terrified black labour force as ready to submit to white demands as they were under slavery. Moreover, white farmers could rely on racism as a means of distracting exploited whites from issues of class inequality. This multiplicity of possible readings has, perhaps, opened up the question of what the *real* motive is, what the fundamental purpose of the lynching is.[6] It seems to me that this very question is mistaken, and the idea of the lynching as a performance is exactly the theorization that can explain why.

The ritual nature of the lynching and the self-conscious sense of participating in a spectacle, either as actor or viewer – although, of course, this boundary is blurred – meant that debate, discussion, and argument were unnecessary. The process of naming the victim, parading him through the streets, forcing a confession, and then torturing and killing him, followed by the desecration of the body, took the place of any verbal procedure of establishing guilt and justifying punishment in moral terms. The substitution of ritualistic action for moral or juridical debate had two important functions. First, it meant that different motives and interests could be served. For poor whites who saw the black as an economic threat, for those who wanted to cast the black back into a subhuman position, for rich or for poor, every desire was satisfied by the ritual, and the very absence of debate ensured that no particular interest group was either omitted or given priority. By substituting the gestural for the verbal, by dealing with the body rather than the person, specific ideological differences could all be accommodated by the performative nature of the lynching. Each of these white positions could be satisfied, and this process, in turn, occluded tensions between whites. White unity could be endorsed, and economic and political differences could be glossed in the fantasmatic identification with an imaginary whiteness set in opposition to the blackness being destroyed. The performance becomes a concrete argument that cuts the Gordian knot of legal, moral, and political debate, and asserts a unified constituency of whiteness, providing no space for any objection or expression of disapproval or outrage. The ideological importance of this is clear: it posits a caste- or race-based social structure which displaces class issues, and subsumes different white points of view. Discontent, hatred and dissatisfaction could be projected onto the black body, which would then be dismembered, and the reification of the black endorsed a sense of self for the white crowd, as if whiteness and subjecthood were synonymous. Thus, the lynching was not simply a rebuttal of black citizenship, attempting to refute the constitutional redefinition of the black as a free American, but a refusal of black subjectivity. The two images are both suggestive of this. In each picture, it is whites who recognize each other as subjects across the picture plane. The spectator is positioned as white, as part of the mob around the body in the photograph, while the drawing mimics a particular art convention as one of the crowd stares out at the viewer and points to the body, drawing them into the image like a grotesque parody of Parmigianino's *Vision of St Jerome*, positioning them as participants. At the centre of these intersubjective exchanges are dead black bodies, endorsing the idea that the recognition of personhood entails whiteness. It is the literally objectified black that provides the basis of white intersubjectivity. It is also this that is at stake, I believe, in the hysterical desecration of the black body. The mob does not simply wish to see a dead black body, since this implies the absence of a living subject, but seeks to reduce the body to dead flesh, to a form that is unrecognizable as a person.

Second, the ritual functioned as its own legitimation. Whereas in a court of law the question of guilt would have to be debated and questioned, here the very fact of the lynching was tantamount to the proof of guilt. This has a strong connection with a certain southern tradition brilliantly discussed by Kenneth Greenberg in his book *Honor and Slavery*. Greenberg describes the Southern system of honourable behaviour as essentially superficial: the surface was seen as the truth of the matter. He tells an anecdote of a man who, on receiving an unwelcome visitor at his home, simply declared 'I am not at home.' For the visitor to question this would have been a slur to the man's honour and would have resulted in a duel and social disruption. Therefore, the honorable way of behaving was to leave, to show that the man's words – 'I am not at home' – were believed.[7] The lynching works according to the same logic; it takes the antebellum code and ritualizes it in a modern form. In effect, it makes a statement that is impervious to challenge. To question the charge of rape would be to dispute the purity and goodness of Southern womanhood; to question the behaviour of the crowd would be to threaten their honour; and to make a charge of injustice or barbarism would be unacceptable. Because Southern women *are* pure and true, because Southern men *are* honorable, because the South *is* just, no challenge can be made. The very act of saying something makes it fact, provided it is spoken from a position invested with the necessary social, political, or institutional power.

In these examples, action stands as an *ex post facto* justification of itself. There is no question of an underlying truth or falsity in the claim to be absent, the claim of rape, or the claim of the lynch victim's guilt. The very saying of the words 'I am not at home,' or 'I was raped,' or 'He is guilty' is sufficient, in the sense that the very articulation, according to Southern codes of honour, is proof of legitimacy. To question the statements, to ask whether there is an underlying truth status different from the verbal veneer is an unacceptable mode of inquiry. The lynching itself bears this structure in that its legitimacy is made plain in its very performance. The lynching itself stands as the reason for the lynching, and the transmutation of inquiry into hatred, into bodily violence, is a performed justification. In this way, opposition to the lynching, from writers and commentators whether white or black, is silenced.

Here, perhaps, is our first hint of why Austin's notion of the performative is helpful. The performative utterance is one where what is spoken performs an act.[8] For example, when a child is baptized and the priest says 'I baptize thee,' his words are not a description of what he is doing, but constitute the actual baptism itself. Now, in utterances describing actions, their validity may be assessed by matching the statement to a state of affairs in the world. If I say 'I am walking,' you assess the truth of my words according to whether I really am walking or whether I am sitting down or standing still. But the performative speech act is neither true nor false; the very issue of falsity is not a criterion by which the speech act can be assessed (and clearly this constitutes one of the most telling attacks on the logical positivist model of language which was, after all, Austin's principal target). To ask if the priest's declaration 'I baptize thee' is true or false is akin to asking whether the act of walking is true or false, and while statements *about* walking can have such status, it is nonsensical to say that walking itself is true. Of course, the performance of the lynching is not performative in a strictly Austinian sense, since Austin is concerned with language and his theory of the performative is about a particular category of utterance. Nevertheless, the lynching functions in an analogous manner for the participants. The lynch mob behaves as if their actions stand apart from any independent assessment of truth or falsity. Instead of verifying the cry of rape, the confession, and the guilt of the victim, the ritual seems to assert that verification has been replaced by performativity, a radically counter-rational or counter-Enlightenment strategy which sets different criteria of validation.

The congruence with antebellum codes of behaviour also underlines the use of the lynching in consolidating a sectional identity in the aftermath of defeat in the Civil War and the presence of the North as social and legislative overseers. In effect, many Southerners saw the North as a colonial power, and the North–South divide is made apparent in attitudes to these rituals. First, in the South this is seen as real justice as opposed to the Northern insistence on juridical process. The new freedoms that the North has insisted upon for blacks (which, by the 1890s of course, had been removed by Jim Crow legislation) are negated by Southern justice. This is the way things are done in the South, and reaffirms a racial, or perhaps more accurately a racist, tradition in a new guise. Interestingly, many commentators in the North, while appalled by lynching, never actually questioned the guilt of the victims. Instead they attacked the practice as juridically unacceptable. The barbarism of lynching was criticized – and again this was a way of locating the South as a rather backward region that required Northern intervention – but blackness was credited as a problem. James Cutler, for instance, whose 1905 book *Lynch Law* is a thorough historical and sociological account of lynching which condemns the practice, discusses the seasonal nature of lynching, that is, that it happened most frequently in the summer months. Cutler does not put this down to the fact that the weather is better for dragging off innocent men to the stake, but that the agricultural field work that blacks do at this time of year leads to disagreements, bad temper, and, consequently, crime. In other words, he accepts that the crimes are committed. The quesion for him is not 'Why are there more lynchings in the summer?' but 'Why is there more black crime in the summer?'.[9]

Here too we might begin to see potential comparisons with Austin in relation to the power invoked by the performative. Austin makes it quite clear that the performative only works – that is, something is only *done* with words – under conditions where the speaker has the authority to speak performatively. For instance, when a priest says to the bride and groom before him 'I now pronounce you man and wife' he is indeed marrying them; but if an actor were to stand before them, perform the part of priest and utter the same words, the statement would not be performative, but rather an unauthoratative performance of the performative. This is one of the conditions Austin refers to as 'felicity', which stands in place of truth or falsity as the index of validity in a performative utterance. In the ritual of the lynching, similarly, felicity rather than truth is invoked as the crucial criterion. When the victim confesses under extreme duress and in agony, the authority of the mob to force these words and their felicitous power to accept them become the key indices rather than the question of whether the confession is true or false. One might almost stretch the analogy and, just as Austin challenged the verification theory of logical positivism, so verification is not at issue in the confession; it is rather that the confession is used in the ritual as a part of the unfolding drama.

The photographic souvenir provides another concrete example of this division between verification and felicity. In Alabama, the photograph was produced not only as a memento of an act of justice, but a memory of having participated in that act, of having performed it. Even if the viewer was not literally there, such an image functioned as a means of inclusion. This is because the souvenir is not merely a separate citation of the act; instead, the making and taking of souvenir objects, whether it be a visual image or a piece of the body, was part of the ritual itself. One might say that the image itself aspires to a performative status. Like the confession, the souvenir photograph is sufficient proof of black criminality and white justice done. In the North, and in anti-lynching discourse in the South, the opposite pertains. Both the images reproduced here were included as illustrations in Ida Wells-Barnett's famous attack on the practice, her pamphlet *A Red Record* of 1895,[10] and in the context of a political tract produced and circulated in the North, performativity loses its power. Wells-Barnett's essay was an attempt to precipitate anti-lynching legislation and action, and so for her these pictures are not a concrete example of the lynchers' power to act and of their righteousness, but a document offering evidence of their injustice and brutality. It thus provides verification, furnishing proof of the truth of Wells-Barnett's argument.

Wells-Barnett edited a newspaper titled *The Free Speech* in Memphis, which campaigned vigorously against lynching. This campaign made her so unpopular that local white men destroyed the paper's presses and made it clear to her that if she remained in the city she would be a target for violence. Like so many other anti-lynch protestors, both black and white, Wells-Barnett was forced to move to the North.[11] Of course, this is not difficult to explain. The presence of anti-lynching agitators was clearly unacceptable to the white racist community, and anyone stirring up trouble – particularly a black – would inevitably face harrassment. But there is another aspect of the black intellectual which may have troubled white supremacists, an aspect which also points to a further ironic division between performative felicity and verification. As we have seen, Southern manners, the Southern code of honour and Southern justice all took the surface as equivalent to the truth. A person's behaviour or words were not to be tested against an external reference, such as a particular state of affairs in the world, for validation. It is this, I have claimed, that makes these protocols symptomatic of performativity. This is not the case, however, with the black. Indeed, the very opposite applies. Whatever his or her behaviour, the black was defined according to a set of fixed principles whereby the surface was seen to occlude the truth. For example, there was the retrogressionist paradigm, an argument that outside the institutions of slavery and white control, the black would revert to his true and authentic nature, namely that of the beast from the jungle. Other biological and pseudoscientific arguments similarly identified the essential and immutable nature of the black. Whites believed that the superficial appearance and actions of the black were a veneer covering the truth of the black's animal and degraded nature. In each case, these theories of the negro posit a fundamental truth for which any behaviour serves as verification. An act of violence, even in self-defence, is a sign of animality; a refusal of violence is essential unmanly and, therefore, subhuman cowardice; and even politeness is merely a sign of the black's ability to dissimulate and thus hide his true nature.

The black, then, is positioned outside the performative and given a fixed identity. He is also denied agency, and this, as we have seen, reaches its apogee in the reification of the body as it is dismembered and reduced to a set of souvenirs in the lynching. We have also seen how the lynching worked to construct an imaginary unified Southern whiteness, and here is the corollary of that: an imaginary singular blackness. Just as white difference was masked by the performance, the single black body stands for all blacks, similarly denying internal differences in the category of blackness. This is clearly a means of controlling, of consolidating, and maintaining a strict racial hierarchy, and of disabling challenges to white supremacy. The problem of the black intellectual, such as Wells-Barnett, is that her intelligence, her ability to argue and reason, and her active participation in political matters are not only a threat to a specific practice, but to the very conception of the black. It is almost impossible to decribe such a figure in terms of predominant black stereotypes. Hence, lynching, or exile effected by the threat of lynching, again deploys performativity in order to disallow any challenge to its legitimacy and to maintain a racial economy where white and black are defined as distinct undifferentiated groups.

Performativity in the lynching is thus an alternative to debate, reason, and argument. Its ritual violence is a means of accommodating class conflict and reasserting a nostalgia for a utopian antebellum South where the only difference that mattered was black versus white; class is occluded by caste, and a white Southern identity is acted out. However, this issue of the performing of *identity*, or, rather, the performative constitution of identity, is a notion that must not be taken at face value. Indeed, it is around this point I want to take issue with some recent theoretical accounts of the performative (and here I am discussing only those accounts that specifically take Austin's idea of performative speech as their starting-point). My argument will be that misapprehension of Austin's philosophy, and its misuse as an analogy for the performing of an identity, can lead to ethical tangles which are unacceptable.

There seems to be some confusion in recent work in cultural studies as to what a performative actually is. One could argue that this confusion is inherent in Austin's own work, as Austin himself discovered in trying to consolidate the boundary between the performative and the constative and his subsequent development of his philosophy into speech act theory.[12] However, even working within the terms laid down by Austin in *How to Do Things with Words*, many thinkers simply get it wrong. Even Judith Butler displays an apparent inability to wrench herself free of the notion of reference; she refers to the performative's ability to 'generate that which it names,'[13] but the point is it does not name, it performs. Although she says, quite rightly, that in the case of a performative 'one cannot reasonably ask for a "referent"', her argument insistently invokes sense and reference, and this is, of course, what Austin's notion of performativity precludes.[14] Indeed, Austin introduced the term exactly to overcome the limitations of a sense-reference model of language and to allow the recognition of speech as an act.

Beyond this kind of misconstrual, there is a more profound issue. Eve Sedgwick uses the idea of performativity as analogous to the constitution of identity.[15] Just as there is no distinction between speech and act in a performative statement – as in when the articulation of marrying a couple actually constitutes the act of marrying them – so, Sedgwick claims, in identity there is no distinction to be made between a behaviour (a performance or a citation) and a subject. But this analogy is false. The relationship between performance and subject is not analogous to that between speech and act in performativity. To take an example, a man who declares 'I am gay' does not at that moment become gay – the likelihood is he says 'I am gay' because he is or feels himself to be gay. In saying 'I am gay' he may change the social recognition of his sexual status, and he may feel differently about himself, but saying 'I am gay' is not being gay. We might say that the statement requires Austin's three criteria of authority, sincerity, and evidence of commitment in subsequent action. Sedgwick's position has much more in common with the ontological behaviourism of Gilbert Ryle; like him, her target actually seems to be Cartesianism, and, following his famous argument, like Ryle she seems to want to replace the 'ghost in the machine' with a subject that has no privileged access to its self and is constituted by an accumulation of behaviours.[16]

Judith Butler argues similarly, if more subtly, that the subject is produced by the performative; that a given act is not the function of an originating will, but 'a citation', an imitation of a prior act or behaviour. It is as if the act performs the subject rather than vice versa, with the subject 'temporarily produced as the belated and fictive origin of the performative'.[17] Thus, she argues in relation to race hatred, there is a difficulty in prosecuting certain actions, since the perpetrator is dispersed across different subjects and essentially finds its origin in a tradition rather than a single subject. The fact of citation means that no originary and singular point of responsibility can be found. However, the consequences of this argument for racial violence – such as a lynching – are disastrous and while Butler clearly has no truck with racist violence (and I must emphasise that this argument in no way attempts to implicate her in racism or to impugn her political credentials) I shall suggest that her philosophical position ironically echoes the position of the lynch mob.

First, as I have already discussed, the subject is not produced by the citation; that is, the subject does not suddenly come into being. Of course, social rituals position people and provide roles for them. But this is not to say that persons are empty vessels whose subjecthood is coterminous with such positioning. To use terminology more fashionable than Austin's, there is always already a subject there, shaped by innumerable social and physical forces, which exists in a dialectical relationship with the citation; and the citation, in turn, has to contend dialectically with other desires, beliefs, motives, and so on. The figure in the Kentucky lynching illustration attempts to interpellate the viewer as a subject of the lynching, but it would be naive to suggest that interpellation therefore simply happens. Indeed, one might claim that the acceptance of a role, that citation itself, is a *validation* of subjecthood rather than a production of it. Butler's account rather suggests that, as with an Austinian performative, the subject is only there because of what is said or done; that identity and act are one, just as utterance and act can be one. But, as we have seen with our example of the man who declares his gayness, what is said or done takes place because it is deemed appropriate to the subject. For this reason, an Austinian analysis implies rather the opposite to Sedgwick and Butler. While the idea of performativity does not necessarily entail a notion of an authentic and unchanging subject, the performative, as we have seen in Austin's terms, does require 'felicity', and the grounds for this would seem to lie in agency.

Second, to return to the arena of racist violence, the agent of such an outrage, as with the perpetrators of and accessories to the lynching, clearly has a responsibility in choosing to make that citation. While there may be no original act, there clearly is a willed act in the decision to cite, a decision on the part of the agent to position him- or herself in a given genealogy. In other words, it would be possible for them to act in other ways. Clearly, we are heading here into one of philosophy's thorniest and most impenetrable problems, and this is not the forum to address fully the questions of free will and its compatibility or incompatibility with determinism. I am not suggesting that we need to accept a model of action which relies on a simplified notion of the will as the basis of an authentic, uninflected agency; rather, I would claim that it is not a question of *either* willed intention *or* citation, but rather of the will-to-repeat. It is this that constitutes the moral choice racists make, and although that choice cannot be defined as a simple, single mental act, this is surely because, first, will and citation are not mutually exclusive, and, second, subjectivity and agency are not mutually reducible.

Crucially, this brings us to the question of responsibility. Just as Butler disperses the point of responsibility, so did the lynchers themselves. By acting as a group, by ritualizing racist action as a community event, no inciting moment of blame – no originating will, if you like – could be identified. Again, this is not to align Butler with the lynchers, which would be a disgraceful suggestion, but it is to point to an irony that arises when a certain liberal philosophy and post-humanism meet; an irony I am clearly attributing to Butler's deconstructive strategy (which is perhaps the reverse of the troubling irony to which Butler points so forcefully). Butler's position leads to a defining of responsibility as philosophically intractable, rather than as socially intractable. I would argue strongly that the absence of a centre of responsibility in the lynching is socially and ideologically created by the group themselves as a deliberate strategy, and that to assert a philosophical equivalence is to unwittingly endorse that strategy. This is not to say that we can simply ignore philosophical problems if they cause us difficulty, but rather that an analysis of lynching that followed Butler might fail to see the social bases of the philosophical issue; for instance, that the lynch mob relied on a dispersal of responsibility as a crowd and as part of a tradition both to refuse culpability and to ensure that it was the victim's body that became the physical object in which responsibility, guilt, and violence could be located.

The Austinian notion of performativity, then, could be a useful tool for a sustained analysis of the Southern lynching and its success as an ideological structure. Southern honour parodies the performative in its evasion of the issue of truth or falsity in favor of a 'felicitous' use of language, as do the invocation of authority and power, and the refusal of reason in favour of a festival of bodily degradation. While those in the North may try to rationalize and debate, even within a broadly racist paradigm such as James Cutler, in the South the act has sufficient authority to banish argument. This is nonetheless a problematic analogy, and, in the end, what I am really arguing for here is a questioning of how performativity is currently deployed, and the need, as I see it, for a recuperation of human-ism. The performative should not be used for a dispersal of the subject but as a means of apprehending the subject's dialectical relationship with ideology.[18] Indeed, the subject is a precondition for performativity not least in the creation of criteria for felicity and of the power structures that authorize it. To argue that the case of lynching could not, hypothetically, be prosecuted is, ultimately, to risk accepting the terms of the lynchers. To say that the truth or falsity of motive is mitigated by repetition or citation; to declare that such sadism is not willed; to deny agency as a fundamental problem in dealing with racist violence; all these risk mimicking the evasive manouevres of the Southern mob. To shift one's ground to a common-sense notion of responsibility may seem reactionary, and may be viewed as philosophically naive, but I hope my use of Austin has proved to be neither. In cases of racist violence, we cannot allow the critique of agency or subjectivity to dissolve the question of culpability. We cannot allow the scene of race hatred to be its own commentary.

NOTES

1. Some of the material here is taken from 'To a Man, a Race, and a Cause: St Gaudens's *Shaw Memorial*', the 1996 Tomas Harris Lectures, University College, London. My thanks to Professor David Bindman and the Department of History of Art at UCL for inviting me to speak.

2. Thom Gunn, 'No Speech from the Scaffold', in *Selected Poems 1950–1975*, London and New York, 1979, p. 76.

3. Judith Butler, 'Burning Acts – Injurious Speech', in Andrew Parker and Eve Kosofsky Sedgwick eds, *Performativity and Performance*, New York and London, 1995, p. 205.

4. For full accounts of lynching rituals see W. Fitzhugh Brundage, *Lynching in the New South: Georgia and Virginia, 1880–1930*, Urbana and Chicago, 1993; Herbert Shapiro, *White Violence and Black Response: From Reconstruction to Montgomery*, Amherst, 1988; George C. Wright, *Racial Violence in Kentucky, 1865–1940: Lynchings, Mob Rule and 'Legal Lynchings'*, Baton Rouge and London, 1990; Joel Williamson, *The Crucible of Race: Black–White Relations in the American South since Emancipation*, New York and Oxford, 1984; Neil R. McMullen, *Dark Journey: Black Mississippians in the Age of Jim Crow*, Urbana and Chicago, 1989. Details of Tennessee's anti-lynching legislation is from James Elbert Cutler, *Lynch-Law: An Investigation into the History of Lynching in the United States*, New York, 1905, p. 237.

5. Some recent accounts have concentrated upon the impugned sexual motive and, in conjunction with accounts of the castration of victims, have linked the lynching to the erotic economy of the South. While desire was surely at work, evident in the delight in the manipulation of the black body and the obvious sadism of the ritual, these psychoanalytical writings tend to confuse literary representations of the lynching, where castration is a common motif, with the historical ritual itself, where victims were more usually mutilated in other ways. For a rich and suggestive account along these lines see Trudier Harris, *Exorcising Blackness: Historical and Literary Lynching and Burning Rituals*, Bloomington, 1984. For a less successful and historically imprecise account, see Robyn Wiegman, *American Anatomies: Theorizing Race and Gender*, Durham and London, 1995, pp. 81–113.

6. For a fine account of these various positions, see Stewart E. Tolnay and E. M. Beck, *A Festival of Violence: An Analysis of Southern Lynchings, 1882–1930*, Urbana and Chicago, 1992. There is also a useful overview in Brundage, *Lynching in the New South*, pp. 9–48. John Dollard's 'frustration-aggression' thesis underpins his *Caste and Class in a Southern Town*, Garden City, NY, 1949.

7. Kenneth S. Greenberg, *Honor and Slavery*, Princeton, 1996, pp. 31–2.

8. Austin's theory is most fully set out in *How to Do Things with Words*, Oxford, 1962. See also, 'Performative Utterances', in J. L. Austin, *Philosophical Papers*, J. O. Urmson and G. J. Warnock (eds), Oxford, 1979, pp. 233–252. For a masterly discussion of the topic, see G. J. Warnock, 'Some Types of Performative Utterance', in Isaiah Berlin *et al.*, *Essays on J. L. Austin*, Oxford, 1973, pp. 69–89.

9. Cutler, *Lynch-Law*, p. 165.

10. Ida Wells-Barnett, *A Red Record: Lynchings in the United States, 1892–1893–1894*, Chicago, 1895.

11. For a full account, see Alfreda M. Duster (ed.), *Crusade for Justice: The Autobiography of Ida B. Wells*, Chicago and London, 1970.

12. See, for example, the paper 'Constative-Performative' in John Searle (ed.), *The Philosophy of Language*, Oxford, 1971, pp. 13–22. This essay marks a transition from the performative-constative model to Austin's later emphasis on the perlocutionary and the illocutionary. As Stanley Cavell points out, it is the primacy of the perlocutionary that provides another important focus in Butler's essay: Stanley Cavell, *A Pitch of Philosophy: Autobiographical Exercises*, Cambridge, Mass. and London, 1994, pp. 183–4.

13. Butler, 'Burning Acts', p. 204.

14. Ibid., p. 198; compare Timothy Gould's critique of J. Hillis Miller along similar lines in his excellent essay, 'The Unhappy Performative' in Parker and Sedgwick, (eds) *Performativity and Performance*, p. 25.

15. Eve Kosofsky Sedgwick, 'Queer Performativity: Henry James's *The Art of the Novel*', *GLQ*, no.

1, 1993, pp. 1–16, and Andrew Parker and Eve Kosofsky Sedgwick, 'Introduction: Performativity and Performance' in Parker and Sedgwick (eds), *Performativity and Performance*, pp. 1–18.

16. Gilbert Ryle, *The Concept of Mind*, London, 1949. Another comparison one might make, and a philosophically much tougher one, is with the Wittgenstein of the *Philosophical Investigations*.

17. Butler, 'Burning Acts', p. 203.

18. I take my lead here from Alexander Saxton's indispensible *The Rise and Fall of the White Republic: Class Politics and Mass Culture in Nineteenth-Century America*, London and New York, 1990, pp. 1–18.

6

SHADING MEANING

Jennifer DeVere Brody

It sometimes happens that one may learn something useful about works of art from translation into another medium, especially when these appear to be vulgarizations.

(Martin Meisel[1])

Categorizing is not the sin; the problem is the lack of desire to examine the categorizations that are made ... the problem is the failure to assume responsibility for examining how or where we set our boundaries.

(Patricia Williams[2])

The premise of this volume is that critical praxis is *performative* – that 'artistic meaning can be understood as enacted through interpretative engagements that are themselves performative in their intersubjectivity.' (Introduction, p. 1). Similarly, this essay translates a black vernacular understanding of 'reading' in which to read is to critique or 'throw shade.' Such an understanding allows us to see that every act of reading is a (re)reading or translation and therefore *all* texts are open to revision(s). As Gayatri Spivak explains, 'Under the figure of RAT (reader-as-translator), [one tries] to limn the politics of a certain kind of clandestine postcolonial reading, using the master marks to put together a history.'[3] This essay performs a similar reading of 'master marks' through its focus on reception and reading *as* acts of translation. Although this text appears to be relentlessly black and white, readings of it may clear its opacities and/or shade its meanings.

In her book, *Playing in the Dark: Whiteness and the Literary Imagination*, Toni Morrison explains that figures of blackness are bound inextricably to corresponding images of whiteness. She writes: 'Through significant underscored omissions, startling contradictions ... one can see that a real or fabricated Africanist presence was crucial to [Anglo-American and European constructions of whiteness].'[4] Like Morrison, I read through a black feminist lens that colors the conventional readings of classic works of art as pure, perfect abstractions and recodes them as 'mere' cultural artifacts which, along with other cultural detritus, may be seen as expressing popular anxieties about race, gender, sexuality, and nationalism. In my discussion of the impossible attempts to fix pure forms of whiteness and white forms of purity, I show how some differently positioned cultural readers have unmasked the presumed, assumed and prescriptive aspects of the following artistic texts: American sculptor Hiram Powers's the *Greek Slave* (1847), blackface British minstrelsy, and Édouard Manet's *Olympia* (1863). Moreover, my exploration of verbal and/or visual translations and changes to these 'original' works highlights the concept of 'impure' vulgarization. I want to mention my own desire to point out and play up the impossiblity of producing a fixed, pure, static and/or stable identity since all performances are tainted by history, reception, and differences.

PETRIFYING PURITY

There is overwhelming evidence to suggest that nineteenth-century Euro-American artists had an obsession with the Pygmalion story. The myth of the Greek sculptor Pygmalion and his statue (identified as Galatea in Jean-Jacques Rousseau's eighteenth-century version of the myth) was ubiquitous – many variations of this story (it was reworked most famously by George Bernard Shaw in his play of the same name) continue to circulate.[5] The story of the sculptor Pygmalion begins with the artist working on a beautiful statue that he wishes to 'bring to life' (perhaps literally, perhaps metaphorically). He prays for assistance and the female nude comes to life whereupon Pygmalion falls instantly in love with her. The narrative of Pygmalion underscores the idea that the artist is the 'first viewer' of the work. The Pygmalion myth binds together a father/creator with his femininized creation and is referenced in the racialized readings of several 'female' statues shown in London at the Great Exhibition of 1851.

Hiram Powers's sculpture the *Greek Slave* took center stage at the Exhibition and generated unequivocal praise. Powers intended his nude to represent a chaste Christian girl awaiting her fate with dignity. She was meant to represent the triumph of purity over adversity, as the narrative the artist wrote to accompany the statue stressed. Powers explained that the Greek slave depicted in a moment of contemplation as she is about to be sold to a Turkish harem, was 'a pure abstract human form tempered with chaste expression and attitude . . . calculated to awaken the highest emotions of the soul for the pure and beautiful.'[6] Powers's use of marble sculpture along with the cleansing trope of classicism kept some viewers from reading his slave in more crass, materialist terms. Although numerous critics testified to the success of Powers's intentions, the *Greek Slave* was not immune to such debasement. The following discussion reflects the impossibility of creating absolute purity.

For many viewers, the idealized figure of the female slave was hailed as the pinnacle of female purity (Plate 6.1). Displayed on a pedestal in the main court pavilion, the statue received as much adulation as it had previously when in the 1840s it had been exhibited in twelve cities throughout America.[7] Exhibited *un*painted, the sculpture was revered and described by Elizabeth Barrett Browning as 'passionless perfection . . . [that would strike the viewer with] thunders of white silence.'[8] The values attributed to sculpture and the way in which the debate about its inherent properties was cast, tell us much about 'pure' forms and their link to moral and ethical issues about purity. Suturing, reifying, setting in stone the analogies between whiteness and perfect hardness, critics in and of nineteenth-century Anglo-American culture commented on the connections among whiteness, beauty and purity.[9] For half a century, parlors from Boston to San Franscisco held miniature copies of the *Greek Slave* in Parian marble. Henry James recalled that the figure 'so undressed, yet so refined, even so pensive, in sugar-white alabaster, [was] exposed under little glass covers in such American homes as could bring themselves to think such things right.'[10] Reproductions (of reproductions it turns out) of Greek sculpture abounded also in museums, public parks, and even on stage.

The color white was related to the 'material' in an equation that reads as follows: White = pure = solid = cold = complete = perfect. These concept-metaphors were equated and understood as being not only analogous, but synonymous. Charles Dickens and George Eliot spoke about the beauty of sculpture – of its pure white forms, smooth unblemished surfaces, its unchanging solid structure; they spoke simultaneously of an idealized form of

Plate 6.1 Hiram Powers, *Greek Slave*, Düsseldorf Gallery, New York City, 1847. Engraving by R. Thew (detail). Courtesy of New York Public Library

white beauty that denoted not only specific artworks but also a nationalistic ethos, in which 'the whiteness of statuary [was used] as an emblem of purity.'[11]

An exception to the overwhelming reverence the statue evoked in both America and England was the cartoon by an anonymous illustrator in *Punch* magazine. A satirical engraving of Powers's marmoreal masterpiece appeared in the journal with the following title and caption: 'The Virginian Slave, intended as a companion to Powers's Greek Slave' (Plate 6.2). In contrast to the idealized classical perfection noted so often by viewers of Powers's marmoreal creation, the *Punch* cartoon reads/transforms and/or translates his pure Greek slave into a debased Virginia slave. This vulgar translation drew upon several

THE VIRGINIAN SLAVE.

INTENDED AS A COMPANION TO POWER'S "GREEK SLAVE."

Plate 6.2 The Virginian Slave, from *Punch*, 1851. Courtesy of the Huntington Library

different kinds of varying, unstable tensions inherent in the 'original' version (original appears in quotations because Powers sculpted six versions of the piece).

The sculpture depicts the slave with her eyes cast down demurely; in the engraving, her eyes confront the viewer; her wide-eyed almost caricatured gaze suggests the stereotyped image deployed in blackfaced minstrel shows. Indeed, the latter is a minstrelized version of the demure gaze. Moreover, the explicit references to an American state (the phrase 'e pluribus unum' and an American flag accompany the *Punch* version) debase and defile because these details make the image geographically specific, contemporary rather than 'universal' and 'transcendent.' The translation of the Greek (English) slave into the Virginian (American) slave exemplifies how some English viewers thought of themselves as English and white in contrast to the Americans, who were viewed as 'black.'

Whereas the Greek slave was intended to and indeed did appear as the essence of purity, the Virginia slave lampooned such high cultural sentiment by disrobing its allegory to reveal its mundane references. Where one is white the other is black; where one is three-dimensional, the other is two-dimensional; one exalted, the other debased; one emblematic of England (by virtue of being Greek), the other emblematic of a particular version of America (by being black); one redolent of the past, the other rooted in the present; one enduring – marmoreal, one ephemeral – sketched on paper; one nude, one naked; one Ideal, one real; one pure, one impure. These images demonstrate the difficulty of stabilizing what turn out to be unstable forms and readings. And yet, in the language used to describe this figure there is an almost blind praise for its pure, *white* presence. The pure and perfect whiteness of the Greek slave, to judge by some contemporary reviews, was viewed as one of the artwork's most salient features.

Despite Powers's efforts to transform the impure situation unequivocally into a pure one he was not successful, as the *Punch* cartoon illustrates. Many viewers were able to fill in the blank of the erased, salacious aspects of the slave's story. They may have been aware of the fact that the invocation of a slave could never distance itself from its illicit thematics or its black, sexually licentious trace. These viewers defiled Powers's pure figure with prurient gazes. Thus did they exchange with the slave image, transforming it and reading it in a performative manner so that how they read and the lenses through which they viewed the statue were inextricably related to 'what' they saw.

The visual interrelatedness between black and white is mirrored in the linguistic meanings of these terms. The complex relationship between blackness and whiteness is seen in the etymology of the word 'black,' which in English has been confused with the medieval term 'blac', meaning 'white' or 'pale.' The *Oxford English Dictionary* notes that 'black' is a word of difficult history. In old English, it was written with the long vowel blāc – 'which was easily confused with blăc which meant 'pale' or shining white . . . [in medieval manuscripts] the words were often distinguishable only by the context, and sometimes not by that.'[12] This archaic and confused etymology of the word 'black' is cited here in an effort to point out the ways in which meaning is never stable but, rather, is constructed and reconstructed through repeated references.

Thus, purity, like the terms black and white, is a chimerical concept. The *Oxford English Dictionary* defines purity as:

> I. a. not mixed with anything else; free from admixture or adulteration; unmixed, unalloyed, often qualifying names of colours; b. not mixed with or not having in or upon it anything that defiles, corrupts, or impairs; unsullied, untainted, clean;

c. visibly or optically clear, spotless, stainless, clear transparent, d. intact, un-broken, perfect, entire. [There is a wide range of sense here but *lines of division cannot well be drawn among quotations, many of which unite more than one shade of meaning*]

(italics added)

This definition underscores that purity as a concept-metaphor is not pure. It is defined always through negation. Moreover, the invocation of any of the terms, as seen above and in our earlier examples, denotes more than one register of meaning. The visibility of perfect whiteness (or blackness) may be merely the suppression and denial of blackness (or whiteness). Still, the impossible desire to see pure forms as such – to see the whiteness of white and the blackness of black – is expressed in a letter that playwright Henrik Ibsen wrote to British writer Edmund Gosse. Ibsen wrote:

> We are no longer living in the age of Shakespeare. Among sculptors there is already talk of painting statues in the natural colors. Much can be said both for and against this. I have no desire to see the Venus of Milo painted, but I would rather see the head of a Negro executed in black than in white marble. Speaking generally, the style must conform to the degree of ideality which pervades the representation.[13]

This statement concurs with my reading of the desire to see 'blacks' as black, and 'whites' as white. The belief that black and white are binary oppositions, or exact opposites, is a long-standing cultural fiction. In his eighteenth-century philosophical inquiry on the sublime and the beautiful, Edmund Burke asserts: 'Black and white may soften, may blend, but they are not therefore the same. Nor when they are so softened and blended with each other or with different colors, is the power of black as black or white as white so strong as when each stands uniform and distinguished.'[14] The desire for permanent perfect purity comes to be preferable to the permeable imperfect impurity – whether 'white' or 'black.'

The firm conviction that led many Victorian viewers to associate whiteness with purity is demonstrated in the reception of another sculpture, John Gibson's *Tinted Venus* (1850), which was also shown at the Great Exhibition. As actual Greek sculpture had been, Gibson's statue was painted and thus appeared as the color of (white) flesh. The painted surface of the sculpture was read by Victorians as vulgar and vile. Elizabeth Barrett Browning thought the *Tinted Venus* 'rather a grisette than a goddess.'[15] The sculpture invoked invective. Its (white) flesh tones intoned indecent sexuality. Its color conveyed concupiscence. This is ironic because, if purity and authenticity are related, the Victorians, in their reverence for Greece, selected to worship a 'false' representation of the antique. Like Englishness itself, which was an 'imagined community' (to use Benedict Anderson's term), the tradition of all-white (unpainted) Greek sculpture was an invention.[16]

The debate about originals and copies, rooted in Platonic dialogues, is related to this discussion. In an age already replete with reproductions of ruined pasts (epitomized by the eighteenth-century reconstructions of ancient ruins) and with advanced technologies capable of mass-producing copies of antique statuary, the Victorian conception of the classical past was thoroughly compromised. The concern generated by the difficulty of recovering a pure past is expressed in Walter Benjamin's essay 'The Work of Art in the Age of Mechanical Reproduction' (1936), where he notes that:

even the most perfect reproduction of a work of art is lacking in one element: its presence in time and space, its unique existence at the place where it happens to be. This unique existence of the work of art determined the history to which it was subject throughout the time of its existence. . . The presence of the original is the prerequisite to the concept of authenticity.[17]

Powers's use of marble sculpture is a way of effacing another version of his subject and reflects the impossibility of creating absolute purity. As Benjamin's essay makes clear, a pure recovery of the past is impossible. Even the so-called original Greek statues were often either copies of other Greek statues or Roman reproductions of Greek statues. As Richard Jenkyns notes,

> The experience of seeing the Elgin Marbles and other authentic Greek statuary – the Venus de Milo, the Winged Victory of Samothrace, the sculptures of the Delphi and Olympia were all 19th century discoveries – gradually taught the world that the antique statues which it had most revered were reproductions, and sometimes not very good reproductions. Moreover, most people's knowledge of art before the 19th century had been a knowledge not of originals but of casts, copies, and engravings.[18]

The ersatz is the only possible authentic form given that a petrified, pure past is impossible.

CASTING THE DYE

Just as the performance of pure perfect whiteness was read within and against discourses of pure but imperfect blackness, the practice of white blackface minstrelsy sought to maintain differences that were inherently unstable. Blackface minstrelsy may be read as a text that shows how

> the coloniser is no longer self-sufficient in the sign of 'whiteness'; in order to be projectively (politically) powerful, it has to enter into a discourse of whiter-than-whiteness: a form of excessive or overidentification that turns the imperial subject around upon itself to face the *impassability* of its own desire.[19]

For, in minstrel shows, white performers controlled blacks by playing them, miming difference in order to make it their own. As Roland Barthes theorizes,

> unable to imagine the Other . . . he comes face to face with him, he blinds himself, ignores or denies him, or else transforms him into himself . . . any otherness is reduced to sameness. The spectacle . . . where the other threatens to appear in full view, become[s] a mirror. This is because the Other is a scandal which threatens his essence. . . . Sometimes – rarely – the Other is revealed as irreducible: not because of a sudden scruple, but because *common sense* rebels: a man does not have a white skin, but a black one. . . How can one assimilate the Negro. . . ? There is here a figure for emergencies: exoticism. The Other becomes a pure object, a spectacle, a clown.[20]

Barthes's suggestive reading relates to minstrelsy. The first strategy he describes for diffusing the threat of difference requires the white man self-reflexively to 'blind himself' to blackness. The second strategy, perhaps the essence of minstrelsy, is to erase the distance by pretending to become the other. A third strategy, reserved for 'emergencies,' allows one to recognize forms of black power – 'a man has a black skin' – if only to make this difference into a 'pure object.' In this strategy, the Other is stereotyped safely as an exotic primitive whom the civilized man may take delight in denigrating.

In the relentlessly classed society of England, wealth could at times 'cancel' racial subjugation especially for the non-Irish. The depiction of elite black figures was put up in order to reaffirm the lower-class status of particular white figures; however, upper-class blacks turn out to be less valuable than those with white skin, even if lower-class. From Charles Dickens's biting critique of Mrs Jellyby, who cared more for the poor blacks in Africa than for her own family at home, to the lower-middle-class whites who resented upper-class English sympathy for and involvement in abolitionism – English men of means who spared charity for 'those dear bracks [sic]' were castigated by the lower-class English poor who resented having to compete with 'foreign' causes. In bids to help 'little England,' blackface minstrelsy was used to consolidate alliances that privileged white racial features over class differences (hence the ultimate privileging of even the Irish figures with 'white' faces over blacks). A similar strategy was used by middle-class white feminists in their bid for suffrage in the United States, which had granted the vote to black men first.

A cartoon from the British weekly journal *The Lantern* illustrates this idea (Plate 6.3). The cartoon shows a poor London family 'blacking up' in order to simulate the numerous roving 'negro' street minstrels, few of whom were actually black, but who begged with greater success than did those with white faces. The caption for the image has the 'head of the family' state: 'That's right, Polly! Give him a lick of paint – There ain't no color goes down now but Uncle Tom's. Niggers [sic] is up – Whites is down.' Beyond the convoluted inversions of Up and Down as signs of value, such tensions between class and race are apparent even in abolitionist discourse, which often analogized class and race, making the 'blacks' stand-ins for the more pressing, national concern of *white* slavery. Drawing on the tradition established in the slave narratives, the scene compares the status of working-class whites in England with black slaves in the Americas. White authors such as Thomas Carlyle, in his tract 'On the Nigger Question,' argued that the 'white slaves' of England lived in worse conditions than the 'Quashees gorged on melons, lounging in sunny climes.' By contrast black authors such as Mary Prince and Harriet Jacobs tended to note the freedoms accorded British workers in the same period. Comparing 'white' and 'black' slavery was common in British minstrel shows.

European audiences seemed to identify with the 'black' characters only by reading such figures as fundamentally 'white.' Although minstrel performers and abolitionists had different goals, at times, they shared the same discourse about blacks. Drawing on the idea that black skin was merely an external marker of difference, both groups were interested in articulating the buried whiteness of the enslaved black African's body. Indeed, Eric Lott has claimed that 'without minstrelsy, Harriet Beecher Stowe's *Uncle Tom's Cabin* could not have existed.'[21] This ability to erase and/or emphasize the black slave features is manifested in Stowe's narrative and is mentioned explicitly in an article written in 1853, just after Stowe's text became a bestseller in England. The essay discusses the effect of *Uncle Tom's Cabin* in Europe by stating:

Plate 6.3 *The Black Dodge*, from *The Lantern*, 1853. Courtesy of the Stowe-Day Library, Hartford, Connecticut

The color of the heroes of the tale was soon lost sight of by the European reader. His passions are stirred by the wrongs of injured individuals – men like himself. . . . All he notes is the oppression they are painted as suffering. Without any extraordinary effort of imagination he draws a plausible analogy between the conditions of his own fellow-countrymen and that of the Uncle Toms of romance.[22]

Here we see the strategy outlined by Frantz Fanon when he wrote, 'For the black man there is only one destiny. And it is white.'[23] In fact, this rereading erases the black man in order to read him as human, universal, 'white' – which ironically is an act of dehumanization.

Similarly, in 1852, the anonymous author of *Uncle Tom in England; Or, A Proof that Black's White*, a novel that 'may be looked upon as an Echo, or Sequel to "Uncle Tom",' elects to extend the abandoned or abbreviated story of Susan, Emmeline, and Cassy, each light-skinned mulattaroon characters from the original novel. This homage demonstrates that the greatest sympathy was reserved for the whitest characters in the book.[24] As the preface explains:

After Emmeline's escape with Cassy, Mrs Stowe dismisses her with a few words, in which she is stated to have become the wife of a mate of a vessel. The Author of 'Uncle Tom in England' could not help feeling that something more was needed, from the interest centered on her character, than that she should be *mated* off in this way. . .

(emphasis in original)

An abolitionist tract *par excellence*, this novel which, in true social protest form, concludes with 'actual' documents, speeches, and testaments to the horror of slavery, also suggests a rationale for the English entanglement with America. The special 'relationship' is articulated in racialist terms based on paternalism, Anglo-American racial nationalism, and the perceived moral superiority of the English. In one of the speeches printed at the end of the volume, the passionate abolitionist intones:

If the good works of Englishmen may excite emulation in the breasts of their brethren of France, Germany, and Spain, how much greater will be their influence upon a people speaking the same tongue, having the same common origin, and united to each other by the links of the most inseparable kind? . . . . England, perhaps, more than any other nation owes a duty to America and certainly no other people can perform such a duty so effectively as the English. We owe it, then, as a duty to God and to man, and to the Americans especially, to speak out against the dreadful oppression of which the black slave is a victim.[25]

The 'white man's burden' expressed so clearly in this quotation also signals the boundaries of whiteness that stretch across the Atlantic to form the roots of an international white brotherhood.

The practice of white men pretending to be black women on stage was common. How are the supposedly distant categories of the white man and the black woman related in such performances? Perhaps the close proximity creates the possibility of their approximating one another. The practice of white male impersonation of black women may be read as a form of miscegenation. Taking on the body of a black woman, the white man unites with or perhaps expresses his own repression of blackened femininity.[26] So too, like the Pygmalion story, such representations reveal the latent desires to create and control differences. Such impersonations are complex: they expose the multiple and contradictory readings of blackness and femininity that circulate in circum-Atlantic culture, to use Joe Roach's resonant phrase.[27]

Blackface cross-dressing brings into play a multiplicity of illicit crossings. The account of the black female slave Ellen Craft who actually escaped slavery dressed as a white master has been discussed in her own slave narrative, *Running a Thousand Miles for Freedom*, as well as in William Wells Brown's fictional *Clotel, or the President's Daughter*.[28] Craft literally gained her freedom through white male impersonation. White male minstrels gained a figurative freedom through their impersonations of black women. In an effort to control black women and the threat of both sameness and difference, the performances of some white men as black women distanced through proximity. So too, in a homoerotic context, such performances may have made another white male body 'safe' for sexual play. When representations of blackness, femininity, whiteness, and masculinity collide, the white man playing the part of the black woman comes face to face with the forbidden. This is so because the evocation of one category carries with it the other – because blackness, femininity, and illicit sexuality are related.

While there is certainly a pleasure in disguise and disidentification apparent in these cross-dressed, cross-racial performances, there may also be a more fundamental motive for this phenomenon. I shall argue that these performances served to define and produce white masculinity. Consider as an introduction to this argument, Paul de Man's discussion of Saussure's analysis of the hypogram, a Greek term meaning 'to underscore by means of makeup the features of the face.' De Man writes:

> This usage is not incompatible with his own adoption of the term which by analogy underscores a name, a word, by trying to repeat its syllables and thus giving it another artificial mode of being added . . . to the original mode of the word. Hypographein is close in this meaning to prosopon, mask or face. Hypogram is close to prosopopeia, the trope of apostrophe . . . provided one assumes . . . the stable existence of an original face that can be embellished or supplemented by the hypogram. But prosopon-poeine means to give a face and therefore implies that the original face can be missing or nonexistent. The trope which coins a name for a still unnamed entity which gives face to the faceless is . . . catachresis. That a catachresis can be a prosopopeia in the etymological sense of giving face.[29]

This idea is expressed in the black vernacular phrase 'giving face,' which means to cast one's face as a mask (this term was appropriated by Madonna for her Blonde Venus tour which featured the hit-track 'Vogue').

The disruptive relationship between blackness and whiteness enacted in minstrelsy 'subjects' the white and the black in different ways. The white man becomes a subject through the subjection (as in ridicule and objectification) of the black. By giving a face to what is an abstracted, objectified, and actually absent black female, the white male creates and expropriates the black other, thereby reproducing and supplementing white male identity; the white male thus 'subjects' the black female to his desires. Where neither existed previously, the performance creates both figures in an asymmetrical play of power. Whereas black women are absent presences (they are seen, but never present), white men are present absences (they are present but not seen as themselves). In the minstrel show white men 'make up' (invent) black women by putting them on and, simultaneously, white men make up the category white men by putting black women on. This performance works in two directions at once. Putting on and making up, creatively deforming differences between black and white so that the source of the categories of pure white and pure black is revealed to be the same – a projection of white desire. The process of differentiation is everywhere displayed in the performative practice of minstrelsy.

By imitating black people, pretending to copy black forms, white practitioners mixed up the difference between imitation and original. For their intents and purposes, the blacks they performed were the (un)real thing.[30] Indeed, the entire practice of blackface minstrelsy as it was performed in England had everything to do with the construction of Englishness. Taking on the guise of an-other was a sure way to discover oneself or at least to attempt to define through negation what one might be if not who one was.

As a means of distancing and controlling, 'white' men became 'black' women, white played black and white played white in a triple play whose sameness of 'before and after' in front of and behind the mask was in fact mediated by the show of blackness. The exaggerated difference of the temporary turn might have been part of the pleasures of blackfaced shows. In order to 'become white' one consciously became black in a gesture of becoming so that, retroactively, one would be what one 'is' or should have been. It is then the ritual of blackening up and whiting out that becomes the arbitrary arbiter of difference. The performance of black femininity fills in momentarily the nothing that was the before of white masculinity: 'Difference is not engendered in the space between identities; it is what makes all totalization of the identity of a self or the meaning of a text impossible.'[31] Pretending, putting on, producing/performing the play of differences acknowledges and recognizes the power of pretense (pre-tense). After the fun has been displayed, the natural returns with a greater force as *naturalized* in contrast to the unnatural performance of blackness – a process similar to that noted in the previous discussion about the *Greek Slave*.

The tradition of masking one's face was transformed when British performers actually began putting on 'white' face. Female performers went beyond the use of face make-up and began to dye their hair blonde. 'Ada with the Golden Hair' was a popular, exclusively English, minstrel song that recorded this practice:

> Oh! Ada, do you love me?
> Tell me if you love me.
> She said, I love you;
> Which made me feel so queer,
> As we walked in Brompton Square.
> Her eyes so blue, her feet so small,
> I thought I should die right there.
> She took my arm – oh, yes she did,
> Ada with the golden hair.
>
> One day I called on Ada,
> My sweet little Ada,

> Dear little Ada.
> Her Mamma told me she was dying;
> I thought I should drop right there.
> I rushed up-stairs – Ada screamed out,
> 'Just come in if you dare.'
> 'Are you dying, my dear?'
> 'Why you silly,' she said,
> 'I'm only *dye*-ing my hair!'
> (from 'Ada with the Golden Hair', 1868)[32]

This peculiarly British minstrel song furthers our discussion of the problematics of the appearance of purity. Beginning in the 1860s, several white men played black women as 'beautiful' blonde women in America. After the Civil War, the performer known as the 'Only Leon' was said to set the fashion for New York society matrons with his consummate style. Playing one of the increasingly popular 'yella gal' parts, Leon set a precedent for rarified forms of beauty. In the early part of the century, the ideal Victorian heroine had dark hair as did Jeanie Deans in Walter Scott's popular novel, *The Heart of Midlothian* (1819). Minstrelsy helped to usher in the cult of the blonde, which explains some of the significance of Ada dyeing her hair blonde.

Hair has long been considered a signifier of race, class, and gender as well as a marker of feminine sexuality. In European culture blonde hair, in particular, has been associated with forms of idealized femininity. The so-called 'style/politics' of hair makes it an important marker of cultural differences. Nineteenth-century commentary about 'the blonde,' the fair and golden-haired, tended to associate blondness with both purity and power: 'The Blonde Venus has ... usurped not merely black vigor, but male privilege. [Her] mythification elevates [her] over white men as well as black women, while borrowing crucial characteristics of each. Female blondness integrates categories of blackness and maleness.'[33] This statement by James Snead in reference to a provocative reading of Marlene Dietrich's famous performance in Von Sternberg's film *Blonde Venus* (1932) as the apotheosis of the blonde seems to have a precedent, if not a corollary, in the performances of the minstrel troupe known as the British Blondes.

The roots of the cliched concept of the blonde, an Anglo-American invention, reach back to the nineteenth century as well as to the circum-Atlantic vortex in which whiteness covers over blackness.[34] It is a truism that the best blondes were 'originally' brunettes.[35] Like the Victorian fashion of whitening one's skin – an effect achieved by the ingestion of arsenic and/or the application of powder – blonde beauty was made up, a fabrication of British culture. Snead observes that when Dietrich emerges from her gorilla suit in the infamous 'Hot Voodoo' number, she 'does not use her own hair, but instead wears a *blonde* Afro wig. The frizzy blonde hair, and her harmony with the "African" women in the chorus line indicate that, despite having entirely removed the gorilla suit, she has now assumed some of the attributes of her "black" get-up. Indeed, the subtle joke intended here is that, as a blonde *femme fatale* she is conceivably more threatening to the white male than a black gorilla would be.'[36] The use of the blonde wig is like the stategy of dying one's hair in an effort to emphasize difference – to make the whiteness of whiteness visible.

Lydia Thompson, the founder of the burlesque troupe known as the British Blondes, required each of the shapely performers in her company to peroxide her hair.[37] 'The old association of blondness with innocence now became both a way of legitimizing the new sensuality and of heightening it by combining both purity and voluptuousness . . . [when the British Blondes' hair was described as] golden clouds which envelop all imperfections.'[38] This reading resonated a comment made in 1899 by the German gynecologist Carl Heinrich Stratz, in which he elaborated the aesthetic appeal of light hair which complemented the soft contours of the woman's body.[39]

The erotic charge of the British Blondes derived from the traces of blackness in their hair, the vestiges of the minstrel show in their burlesque variety show, and their assumption of masculine power.[40] The British Blondes evoked comparison with grisettes, soubrettes, and courtesans – all figures of the demi-monde. William Dean Howells likened the Blondes to 'creatures of an alien sex.'[41] Other contemporary reviewers of the group commented that '[t]o justify wearing tights, the women all played male roles [often they were kings, vagabonds, soldiers, pirates and] they spoke with impeccable upper-class British accents.'[42] At once hyper-feminine and erotic in their attempts to play with modes of masculinity, the astounding success of the British Blondes suggests the effectiveness of the ironic purification and idealization of exaggerated whiteness. Their hyper-white femininity was, at its base, impure, because it was 'black.'

OUT OF THE SHADOWS: OLYMPIA IS MADE

Manet's *Olympia* (1865) (Plate 6.4) is a painting of a 'white' courtesan (known as Victorine Meurent) and her 'black' maid bringing a bouquet of flowers to her mistress.[43]

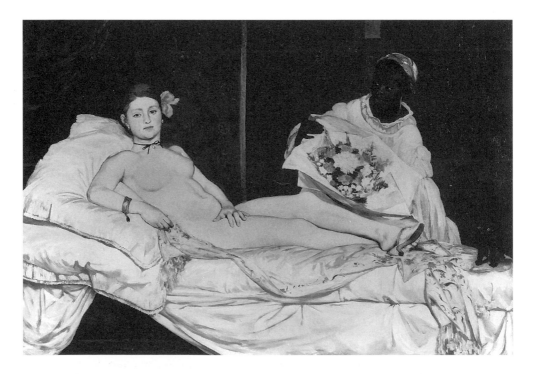

Plate 6.4 Édouard Manet, *Olympia*, 1863. Courtesy of the Musée d'Orsay, Paris

The body of the black servant grounds and informs the white woman; the two figures are projections of one another, perhaps depicting a white male fantasy that always reads these figures in relation to each other. Rather than seeing the black woman as the literal re-presentation of the white woman with a black heart (interior) – with a white veneer and dark interior – we might read these figures as inversions of each other. They share a similarly debased social status. They are understood as figures *in relation to* culturally volatile terms of black and white. Linda Nochlin describes Manet's odalisque:

> Thin, tense and chilly she embodies a timely idea of elegant artificiality and, with her mules, her velvet ribbon, her black cat and Negro servant carrying a token of admiration up to her boudoir, is very different . . . from . . . idealized nudes. . . .
>
> [Manet] transform[s] the orchid, flower of lasciviousness, and the black cat, promiscuous beast, from *hidden symbols* into *natural accessories* of the mid-nineteenth-century demi-mondaine, although the chilly aura of luxurious perversity may . . . take us back . . . to a work like Girodet's crystalline *Danae*, or forward to the *femmes fatales* of the *fin de siècle*.[44]
>
> (italics added)

Nochlin lists the black woman as a possession of the white woman; however, one could also argue that the black woman's assumed hypersexuality possesses the white woman, stains her black in nearly every reading. She is thus re-possessed, re-constituted as white (black) prostitute.

The dominant concern in critical analyses of the painting is not with the black background, but with the white forefigure. Presumably, audiences who have viewed Manet's *Olympia* do not desire the black woman in the background – they seem only to see the lasciviousness of the 'obvious' object – namely, Olympia herself. Lorraine O'Grady argues this point in her piece, 'Olympia's Maid', when she states that,

> [the non-white woman is] castrata and whore . . . [her] place is outside what can be conceived of as woman. She is the chaos that must be excised, and it is her excision that stabilizes the West's construct of the female body, for the 'femininity' of the white female body is insured by assigning the non-white to a chaos safely removed from sight. Thus, only the white body remains as the object of a voyeuristic, fetishizing male gaze. The non-white body has been made opaque by a blank stare.[45]

Oscillating between obliteration and obligation, Olympia's maid has been minstrelized, not only in nineteenth-century cartoons, but also in Picasso's 1901 (per)version of Manet's masterpiece in which Olympia is re-presented *as* black in an exaggeration of the elements more subtly suggested in the original.[46] Notably, Herb Hazelton's *Marilyn Monroe as Olympia* – a 1964 American translation of the painting – includes a pancake-bearing 'Aunt Jemima' Mammy figure and a white cat (Plate 6.5). In this version, Olympia's plain face and reddish-brown hair have been replaced by the bold face and bleached blonde hair of Marilyn Monroe, whose supine figure is identical to Manet's 'original.'[47] These translations, like the one read by O'Grady, assume that the black object is not sexualized, or rather is so sexualized that she must *only* represent the 'black' sexuality of the white woman with whom she appears. Readings of the black female body, therefore, can be seen as the vehicles needed for the (re)productive performance of 'white' sexuality. In short, black

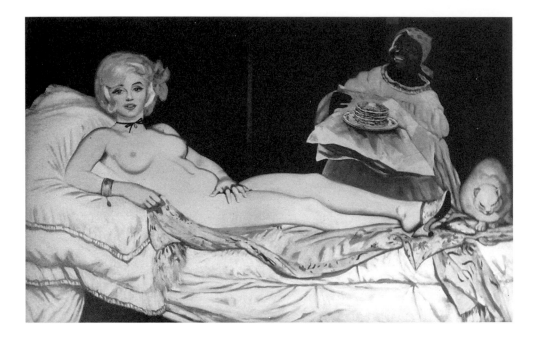

Plate 6.5 Herb Hazelton, *Marilyn Monroe as Olympia*, 1964. Provenance unknown

women become 'vestibular to culture . . . because the black female remains exotic, her history transformed into a pathology turned back on the subject in tenacious blindness.'[48]

These readings of Manet's *Olympia* bring together many of the concerns of this essay: reading as translation, interracial desire, and performances of racialized sexuality. The white male artist/creator's complicated conception of the powers of the 'white-black' *femme fatale* speaks directly to the related issues of blackness and femininity that are compounded (literally) in the signification of the 'black woman' understood as both a visually and morally compromised woman. In reading diverse instances in which the desire for purity is manifested through ultimately unstable, racially-coded representations of female bodies, or through complex intersubjective projections of desire, this essay reveals how certain differences are made absolute (and absolutely different) through the impossible, performative process of purification. More specifically, by looking at texts that constitute white sculptures, blackface minstrelsy, and the text of the 'blackened' femme Olympia, we can speculate about how forms and figures of 'black' femininity functioned to reproduce not only whiteness and masculinity, but also the performative boundaries of gender, race, and sexual propriety.

NOTES

1   Martin Meisel, 'The Material Sublime: Jon Martin, Byron, Turner, and the Theater,' in Karl Kroebler and William Walling (eds), *Images of Romanticism: Verbal and Visual Affinities*, New Haven, Conn., Yale University Press, 1978, p. 211.
2   Patricia Williams, *The Alchemy of Race and Rights*, Cambridge, Mass., Harvard University Press, 1991, p. 102.

3 Gayatri Chakravorty Spivak, 'The Politics of Translation,' in *Outside in the Teaching Machine*, London and New York, Routledge, 1993, p. 200.

4 Toni Morrison, *Playing in the Dark: Whiteness and the Literary Imagination*, Cambridge, Mass., Harvard University Press, 1992, p. 4.

5 Richard Jenkyns, *Dignity and Decadence: Victorian Art and the Classical Inheritance*, Cambridge, Mass., Harvard University Press, 1992, p. 107.

6 Joy Kasson, 'Narratives of the Female Body: The Greek Slave,' in Shirley Samuels (ed.), *The Culture of Sentiment: Race, Gender, and Sentimentality in Nineteenth-Century America*, New York, Oxford University Press, 1992, p. 178.

7 Kasson, 'Narratives of the Female Body: The Greek Slave,' p. 173.

8 Quoted in Richard Jenkyns, *Dignity and Decadence*, p. 106.

9 See, for example, Richard Dyer, *White*, London and New York, Routledge, 1997.

10 Henry James quoted in Oliver W. Larkin, *Art and Life in America*, New York, Holt, Rinehart & Winston, 1949, p. 181.

11 Jenkyns, *Dignity and Decadence*, p. 104.

12 According to medievalist Ralph Hanna the translation of these terms is 'a matter of interpretation.' He claims that he struggled for three years over whether a figure turns 'black' or 'pale' in his translation of *Julian of Norwich*. (Personal conversation, 22 January 1997.)

13 Henrik Ibsen quoted in Bernard F. Dukore (ed.), *Dramatic Theory and Criticism: Greeks to Grotowski*, New York, Holt, Rhinehart & Winston, 1974, p. 560.

14 Edmund Burke, *A Philosophical Enquiry in the Origin of Our Ideas of the Sublime and the Beautiful*, London, R. and J. Dodsley, 1764, p. 124.

15 Jenkyns, *Dignity and Decadence*, p. 107.

16 Benedict Anderson, *Imagined Communities: On the Origin and Spread of Nationalism*, London, Verso, 1983.

17 Walter Benjamin, 'The Work of Art in the Age of Mechanical Reproduction,' in *Illuminations: Essays and Reflections*, ed. Hannah Arendt, tr. Harry Zohn, New York, Schocken Books, 1968, p. 220.

18 Jenkyns, *Dignity and Decadence*, p. 106.

19 Homi Bhabha, 'Day by Day . . . with Frantz Fanon,' in *The Fact of Blackness: Frantz Fanon and Visual Representation*, ed. Alan Read, Seattle, Bay Press, 1996, p. 199.

20 Roland Barthes, *Mythologies*, tr. Annette Lavers, New York, Hill & Wang Publishers, 1987, p. 152. Other excellent readings of the attractive powers of mimesis include Michael Taussig's *Mimesis and Alterity: A Particular History of the Senses*, London and New York, Routledge, 1993, and Judith Butler, *Bodies That Matter: On the Discursive Limits of Sex*, London and New York, Routledge, 1993.

21 Eric Lott, *Love and Theft*, New York, Oxford University Press, 1995.

22 Anonymous news article from the Harry Birdoff collection, Stowe-Day Foundation Library, Hartford, Conn.

23 Frantz Fanon, *Black Skin, White Masks*, tr. Charles Lam Markmann, New York, Grove Press, 1967, p. 10.

24 Anonymous, *Uncle Tom in England; Or, A Proof That Black's White*, London, William Tyler, 1852.

25 Ibid., p. 210.

26 For superb readings of late twentieth-century performances of 'blackface crossdressing,' see Carole-Anne Tyler, 'Boys Will Be Girls: The Politics of Gay Drag,' in Diana Fuss (ed.), *Inside/out: Gay and Lesbian Studies*, New York, Routledge, 1994, and contemporary commentators of Jennie Livingston's film, *Paris is Burning* – especially Peggy Phelan, 'The Golden Apple,' in *Unmarked: The Politics of Performance*, London and New York, Routledge, 1994, and Philip Brian Harper, 'The Subversive Edge: Paris is Burning, Social Critique, and the Limits of Subjective Agency,' *Diacritics*, Summer–Fall 1994, vol. 24, no. 2–3, pp. 90–103.

27 See Joe Roach, *Cities of the Dead: Circum-Atlantic Performance*, New York, Oxford University Press, 1996.

28 William Craft and Ellen Craft, *Running a Thousand Miles for Freedom* in Arna Bontemps (ed.), *Great Slave Narratives*, Boston, Beacon Pres, 1969, pp. 271–331, and William Wells Brown, *Clotel*, New York, University Books, 1969.

29 Paul de Man, 'Hypogram and Inscription,' in *The Resistance to Theory*, Minneapolis, Minn., University of Minnesota Press, 1986, p. 44.

30 It was not until later in the century that 'real' negro performers, such as the Fisk Jubilee Singers, were valued for their authenticity. It is no accident that Ralph Ellison wrote of minstrelsy in his collection of essays 'Shadow and Act', given this particular relation established in such blackface performances, New York, Random House, 1993.

31 Barbara Johnson, *The Critical Difference: Essays in the Contemporary Rhetoric of Reading*, Baltimore, Johns Hopkins University Press, 1980, p. 5.

32 G. W. Moore, *The St. James's Hall Veritable and Legitimate Christy's Minstrels Christmas Annual*, London, 1868.

33 James Snead, Colin McCabe and Cornel West (eds), in *White Screens, Black Images: Hollywood from the Dark Side*, London and New York, Routledge, 1994, p. 71.

34 The metonymic use of the term 'blonde' epitomized in scenes from *Invisible Man* shows both how this term was femininized and juxtaposed with images of black masculinity. Also relevant to this discussion is Ellison's famous description of 'optic white' paint which cannot be made without the addition of a drop of black dope. See Ralph Ellison, *Invisible Man*, New York, Vintage International, 1990, Chapter 10, pp. 196–205.

35 See Dyer, *White*, p. 38.

36 James Snead, *White Screens, Black Images*, p. 72.

37 Lois Banner, *American Beauty*, Chicago, University of Chicago Press, 1983, p. 121.

38 Ibid., p. 124.

39 Wendy Cooper, *Hair: Sex, Society, Symbolism*, New York, Stein & Day Publishers, 1971, p. 75.

40 For a related discussion of the blonde wig as an erotic commodity, in this case in the performance of Marlene Dietrich in Von Sternberg's film, *Blonde Venus*, see Mary Ann Doane, *Femmes Fatales: Feminism and Psychoanalysis*, London and New York, Routledge, 1991, pp. 209–48.

41 William Dean Howells quoted in Lois Banner, *American Beauty*, p. 123.

42 See Lois Banner, *American Beauty*, p. 123.

43 For a fascinating discussion of the term courtesan in relation to Olympia see T. J. Clark, 'Olympia's Choice,' in his book *The Painting of Modern Life: Paris in the Art of Manet and his Followers*, Princeton, NJ, Princeton University Press, 1984, pp. 116–17.

44 Linda Nochlin, *Realism*, London: Penguin Books, 1971, p. 203.

45 Lorraine O'Grady, 'Olympia's Maid: Reclaiming Black Female Subjectivity,' in Joanna Frueh, Cassandra Langer, and Arlene Raven (eds), *New Feminist Criticism*, New York, Harper Collins, 1994, pp. 152–70.

46 Charles Bernheimer's reading of the painting in 'Manet's *Olympia*: The Figuration of Scandal' helps to explain the appeal of this portrait by providing numerous contemporary readings of the picture, see *Figures of Ill Repute*, Cambridge: Harvard University Press, 1989.

47 So too, Hazelton's translation recalls the novel and film 'Imitation of Life' that has been so important to unthinking the representations of racial authenticity in America. See Lauren Berlant, 'National Brands/National Bodies: Imitations of Life,' in Hortense Spillers (ed.), *Comparative American Identities*, London and New York, Routledge, 1991, pp. 110–40. Another translation, this time into a different medium (painted wood and cardboard), is Larry Rivers's *I Like Olympia in Black Face* (1970), which Richard Powell describes as a '*tableau vivant* burlesque of *Olympia*.' Rivers's doubled two-dimensional construction has one 'black' face Olympia and one 'white' face Olympia. See Powell, *Black Art and Culture in the Twentieth Century*, London, Thames & Hudson, 1997, p. 146. Given my discussion of the roots of blondeness in burlesque, Rivers' reading/translation of Olympia makes sense. For more on translation of *Olympia*, see Alan Krell, *Manet*, London, Thames & Hudson, 1996, pp. 50–62.

48 Hortense Spillers, 'Interstices: A Small Drama of Words,' in Carol Vance (ed.), *Pleasure and Danger: Exploring Female Sexuality* (New York, Pandora Books, 1989), p. 76.

7

THE GREATEST HOMOSEXUAL?

Camp pleasure and the performative body of Larry Rivers

Gavin Butt

In an article entitled 'Wonder Boy and his Many Sides' which appeared in *Life* magazine in October 1958, the artist Larry Rivers is photographed in a quadrupled image of himself as jazz saxophonist, painter, sculptor, and 'nightclub emcee' (Plate 7.1).[1] The performance of such diverse professional identities by a single individual provides the magazine with its novel and newsworthy angle on the popular image of the artist.[2] It is Rivers as an exceptional 'many-sided' individual – his many 'talents', his many 'lives' – which earn him

Plate 7.1 'Wonder Boy and His Many Sides,' in *Life* magazine, October 20, 1958, vol. 45, no. 16, pp. 100–1. Photograph by Peter Stackpole (courtesy of Katz Pictures)

the appellation of art world 'wonderboy'. That a single artist could be seen to have so many personae and, moreover, that he is able to 'juggle them with such dexterity', is what *Life* invites its readers to marvel at with 'awe'. The photographic spread gives representational form to this noteworthy multiplicity by cleverly incorporating four different exposures on a single sheet of film, with Rivers adopting a different pose for each one. Thus Rivers's many sides appear within the logic of photographic construction as the multiple exposures contained within a single, apparently seamless, image. Such professional 'many-sidedness' is seen by *Life* to have its aesthetic corollary in the 'countless fragmentary images of people and objects' in his paintings which, the magazine remarks, 'seem as many-sided as the painter himself'. As a backdrop to Rivers's performative photographic posing is his 1956 painting *The Athlete's Dream*, which the article refers to as a portrayal of 'two of his friends, glimpsed in elusive, shifting attitudes'. In this way both the photograph and the painting within the photograph, foreground the multiplicity of 'Rivers' in life and in art (or indeed as they co-mingle in *Life*).[3] But just as *Life* appears to surface the performative *dis*continuity of 'Rivers' – either through the different personae of artist, saxophonist, compere, etc., or through the shifting definition of the subjects in his painting – it simultaneously attempts to unify them under the auspices of familiar art historical constructions of artistic authority. Even as 'Rivers' appears performatively mobile across different (at least quadruple) personae, he is also construed by the article as the centred *author* of such performances. *Life* defers to Rivers's authorial voice in positioning them as exterior facets of an 'inner' essential self, as outer expressions of some 'deep' (and deeply familiar) construction of artistic subjectivity: 'I think . . . in my life and my art', Rivers is quoted as saying, 'there's a central Larry Rivers running through everything.'

But rather than following the suggested hermeneutic closure here, positioning Rivers's performances as the differential surfacing of some deep and continuous artistic subjectivity and subordinating the performative within metaphysical models of authorial identity, what I want to propose is that 'Rivers' emerges within *Life* and elsewhere (including, I hope, within my own interpretative discourse) as a 'campy' performance of subjectivity.[4] Indeed, the apparent privileging of Rivers's 'authentic' voice by *Life* can be seen to become unhinged as it too becomes infected with the logic of camp performance – thereby appearing as a linguistic 'pose' of one of Rivers's many personae.[5] In figuring the many within the one – in figuring the posing at the very heart of artistic being – *Life* is witness to the aporetic tensions between the way Rivers *is* and the way he *acts*.[6] The one who *is* Larry Rivers appears as coincident with the many roles which he *enacts*, just as the performance of shifting identity in Rivers's painting appears as commensurate in kind with the performative enactments which go to make up Rivers's life.[7] In highlighting the performative dimension of Rivers's 'self' and his 'work', and the complex ways in which these can be seen to fold back onto one another, *Life* foregrounds the tensions which have had serious consequences for Rivers's canonical position within art history.

Though assured a place in Irving Sandler's 1978 book on second-generation art, *The New York School*, Rivers's work occupies only a marginal position within the history of postwar American art.[8] Even one of Rivers's critical defenders, Sam Hunter, never seems quite sure if his art is fully redeemable to modernist canons of 'greatness', posing too many antinomies between a lofty grand manner and a 'more light-hearted' autobiographical tendency; between 'disciplined craft' and 'hedonism'; between sincerity and irony to sit easily within any canonical positioning.[9] Betty Kaufman, writing in *Commonweal* in 1960, echoes Hunter's remarks and is typical of the generally cautious appraisal of Rivers's work in the face of its apparently intractable contradictions.[10] Here, it is Rivers's 'intuition' which is seen to be at odds with his 'sense'; his undoubted facility as a painter and draughtsperson contrasted with his seeming lack of ability to harness it in any meaningful or focused manner. 'His footwork is dazzling', she writes, 'but he has no knockout punch.' This is not to say that his work is not ambitious but rather to say that its ambition seems almost inversely related to the level of its achievement: 'the more ambitious the enterprise, the more dispersed and insubstantial the result.' In this way, Kaufman takes his work to be 'haunted by the banal, the superficial and the show-off' even as his 'real quality as a painter and a draughtsman . . . place him beyond real ridicule.' Therefore, she concludes, she can't quite work out whether she is witnessing 'the making or undoing of a major talent'. This is typical of the way in which Rivers's work has been viewed as a problematic mixture of talent and pretension; as that which risks its significance and authenticity by appearing to slide into the affected and the histrionic. It is as if Rivers's work, like Gertrude, 'protests too much' to be taken seriously, but by the same token does not appear to be theatrical *enough* to be dismissed out of hand by its would-be modernist detractors.

Rivers's artistic 'personality' has played a key role in fuelling these troublesome uncertainties surrounding his work. His refusal to abide by the dominant image of the male artist in the 1950s – his appearance on a television quiz show; his involvement in jazz music; his drug-taking; his tendency for self-aggrandizing and self-mythologizing statements – made him a problematic candidate for the artist subject position as constituted within Abstract Expressionist circles.[11] For rather than appearing surly, anguished and inward-looking in the manner of Jackson Pollock, Rivers emerged as brash and audacious, and rather anticipated Warhol in the formulation of the artist as a kind of celebrity personality. Thus, as Hunter has written: 'The tendency under the circumstances is for commentators to emphasise the public entertainer, and to take the private artist and his work with something less than a full measure of seriousness.'[12] This 'something less' is what I want to ponder in relation to a certain embodiment of camp performance by Rivers; one peculiar to the social and cultural contexts of American bohemia in the 1950s.

'THE PERFECT CAMPER'

In 1965 *Newsweek* wrote that Larry Rivers was 'a stereotype of the modern bohemian whose life is an affectionate parody of yesteryear's sophisticated values. That's what is called 'camp' nowadays, and Larry Rivers seems the perfect camper.'[13] As 'the perfect camper', Rivers represented, at least to *Newsweek*, the very embodiment of a new bohemian type which began to take shape in American culture in the late 1940s and 1950s. As I have already suggested, this embodiment was seen as many-sided and performative, but it was also suggestive of, if not commensurate with, a particular sexual 'body'. This was introduced to *Life*'s readers through the familiar figure of the 'double life'. The reference to Rivers's 'successful double life' as painter and jazz musician could be taken as signalling, albeit in a coded manner, the proximity of Rivers's (campy) body to a 'queer body'.[14] Conventionally apprehended through such a doubled interpretative frame, the queer body also figured significantly within Rivers's earliest artistic identifications. Indeed, it was a particular 'queer body' which appeared as commensurate in Rivers's cultural imaginary with that of the artist – a body which he therefore had to perform *as his own* in order that he might be appreciated as a truly 'modern' bohemian.

In speaking about the artist Nell Blaine, painter and one of the chief movers of the Jane Street Gallery artists in the late 1940s and early 1950s, Rivers has said:

> She was in a way the first artist I knew. She was fantastic, you know. On top of it, she was sort of queer. So I thought there was some connection between when you're in the art world or something like that, maybe you're queer – like you'd have to be queer.[15]

Blaine had a studio across from where Rivers lived on 21st Street in 1946 and, according to Rivers's own testimony, she had a tremendous impact on him at this time. She was the first 'real painter with a studio' whom Rivers had ever met, making her an extremely influential figure in forging his own ideas about what it meant to be an artist.[16] Rivers was drawn to her because 'not only was she a painter', she was also, in his own choice of words, 'abstract' and 'so out'.[17] If her production of semi-abstract canvases inspired by Arp and Léger could have easily earned her the appellation 'abstract', then it was Blaine's lesbianism, and her position within bohemian social circles which made her 'so out'. In 1946, being 'out' would have signified being part of a gay social scene and having gay friends, as much, if not more than, its current post-Stonewall meanings of being 'open' about one's sexuality and of being out of the closet.[18] In this regard, then, it was not only the 'fact' of Blaine's lesbianism, but also *her position within bohemian social circles* which Rivers took as a defining feature of 'being' a modern artist, that is, being 'in the life', being part of the 'gay' social world. Twenty-three years old and straight, Larry Rivers accepted this as the situation, and, consequently, for the next few years or so, he began to expand his gay social connections as part of his own bid to become an avant-garde artist.

But if it was not the 1940s (artistic) dyke who was most readily summoned by *Life*'s reference to the 'double life', then the gay *male* body, more powerfully figured within its semiotic orbit, soon loomed larger in Rivers's artistic imaginary. Later, around 1949 and 1950, Rivers powerfully identified with, and became part of, a largely gay male milieu which provided him with inspirational figures and intellectual associates, as well as with friends and lovers. These people included the poets Frank O'Hara and John Ashbery, his dealer, John Bernard Myers, and the gallerist Tibor De Nagy to name but a few. Rivers slept with both men and women including a brief liaison with Myers and a tempestuous relationship with O'Hara. Despite all of this, however, Rivers has always maintained his heterosexual orientation: 'I was in a rather conventional tradition of men who are mainly heterosexual, or have had mostly heterosexual experience, who when they get with men who are homosexual act as if they are allowing themselves to be had.'[19] This did not prevent Rivers from deriving a great deal of narcissistic joy from sleeping with and being desired by other men. He found that he was suddenly considered 'a dish' in gay circles, so much so that it sometimes led to bitchy in-fighting over his affections (there was much tension, for instance, between O'Hara and Myers about this).[20] However, I don't want to get into a debate about Rivers's sexual orientation – whether he was 'really' straight, or gay, or bisexual – but rather to consider how such queer artistic role models might have appealed to this, at least nominally, straight artist.[21] And it is certainly true that they did appeal to him; reading his autobiography *What Did I Do?* (1992) leaves you in no doubt about the fascination and admiration Rivers had for his homosexual fellows.[22] But what did gay society and culture mean to him in the late 1940s and 1950s? Upon what basis did Rivers identify with his gay peers, and how did these identifications determine the performances of his own artistic 'body'?

We cannot begin to answer these questions without first sketching in the changes that were afoot in bohemia at this time and in particular the emergence of the 'hipster' or 'beatnik' as the new paradigmatic bohemian type, which proved to be formative for Rivers's development as an artist. Such a figure was less concerned than his forebears with high culture and favoured instead various forms of 'street' and vernacular culture. The hipster typically shunned organized politics, rejecting the working class as the agent of history, and favouring instead a more romantic political attachment to the social outcast epitomized by the junkie, the negro, and the homosexual. Although the hipster was arguably to find its most articulate expression later on in the 1950s with the publication of the poetry and novels of the so-called 'beat generation' (Allen Ginsberg, Jack Kerouac, William Burroughs *et al.*), the beat 'attitude' was a much wider political and cultural performance adopted by a whole generation of mainly young Americans as early as the mid-1940s.[23] Many modelled themselves on the 'outlaw' image of the hipster, rejecting the consumerism and conservatism of American culture, and chose instead to drop out of mainstream life, quite literally, to 'find themselves' elsewhere – principally in an identification with the socially and culturally marginal. The hipster's primary identification was with the jazz scene – the music, the drugs, the 'hep' talk – all came to represent to the white hipster the transgressive essence of hip. Such a culture became hypostatized in the white hipster's mind as a kind of 'negro sensibility', famously elaborated by Norman Mailer in his 1957 essay 'The White Negro'.[24] Here Mailer discourses on the black man's 'existential' condition, idealizing his life of 'ever-threatening danger' brought about by racism as a life of vital experience, as a life 'on the edge'. This was a life supposedly ruled by a quasi-primitive instinct to survive, a life full of the pleasures and dangers of the body, as opposed to the supposedly mediated and reflective ones of the mind. Mailer goes on to argue that the white hipster, in his emulation of and identification with this 'primitivized' image of the black man, effectively became a 'white negro': a figure who 'drifted out at night looking for action with a black man's code to fit (his) facts'.[25] As Kobena Mercer has astutely argued, the process of identification here entailed a recoding of the meanings of blackness and of the debilitating effects of racism on black lives by constructing an 'inverted image of otherness'.[26] This is one 'in which the attributes devalorised by the dominant culture were simply revalorised or hypervalorised as emblems of alienation and outsiderness, a kind of strategic self-othering in relation to dominant cultural norms.'[27]

I would propose that Rivers performatively enacted himself through just such a hip construction of 'blackness' in the mid-1940s. Well in advance of becoming a painter, Rivers was already into drugs and was playing saxophone in various jazz combos in and around New York. He even went so far as erasing the Jewishness of his birth name 'Grossberg' and named himself instead after a black appellate court judge, Francis Rivers, in order to give himself black airs that might boost his hip standing.[28] However, if the dynamics of 'hipsterism' were instrumental in forging the young Rivers's artistic identifications with black music and culture, then a similar set of dynamics informed his foray into the art world – the difference being that this time the object of hip fascination was not 'blackness' but 'homosexuality'. What I want to argue is that, in becoming an artist, Rivers performs a further act of self-othering through his identification with the queer artistic community of which he also became part. This is to view him in the late 1940s and 1950s as a kind of queer-acting, or at least queer-identified, straight artist. That 'queerness', as well as 'blackness', could be coded as hip is less well documented in the literature on the beatnik, however it certainly had a similar transgressive aura in bohemian circles.[29] As Catharine R. Stimpson has written, given the beatnik's celebration of unfettered sexuality as a political ideal, the homosexual came to be seen, though not without some hesitations, as an agent of sexual freedom.[30] Sexuality, and in particular perverse or deviant sexuality, came to be valorized as an important form, if not the ur-form, of political and cultural transgression. Certainly, homosexuality was attractive to Rivers precisely because of its transgressive status and because it ran counter to the 'square' values of 1950s mainstream America. Frank O'Hara had astutely recognized the nature of Rivers's interest in homosexuality, and specifically in him, in a poem from 1953 which includes the line: 'to him my affection's as pleasing as an insult/ to a nun'.[31] And if we return to Rivers's well-nigh deification of Nell Blaine as artistic role model, then it becomes apparent that it is not only Blaine's lesbianism, but the fact that she is an active lesbian *who is married* that both attracts and fascinates Rivers, this making her a doubly transgressive figure:

> I thought being a lesbian and married was so fantastic it became a lighted gateway into art, the jazz, the parties, the banter that went on in her studio. If anything could be the relieving opposite of 'square', Nell's life of avant-garde sex, abstract art and a loft was it![32]

Blaine is held up by Rivers as representative of a 'hip' person with a 'hip' life-style. The fascination and attraction is for the 'Otherness' that she embodies. Her social, sexual, and artistic unconventionality are all seen to be part of the same bohemian equation as is demonstrated by the slippage Rivers effects between the transgressive values accorded to the avant-garde and those of Blaine's lesbianism in his reference to a 'life of avant-garde sex'.

'Avant-garde sex' is precisely what Rivers was interested in, and the more of it the better. Thus, his fascination with the largely gay male literary circles of John Ashbery and Frank O'Hara. Such men represented to him the 'beginning of another much more sexy, more groovy situation. They had more energy. They had more sexuality. They had more ego, drive. . . . They seemed to be more equal to my notion of what things should be about'.[33] They personified to him a sexuality that was all about *doing it*: 'You were sort of trying to make it everyday, wherever you were, that was the point'.[34] Even though, as Ashbery puts it, O'Hara was 'too hip for the squares and too square for the hips', it is primarily through his relationship with O'Hara that Rivers became part of gay bohemia, frequenting gay bars like the Blue Parrot and San Remo, as well as bohemian bars like Louis' where gay and straight would mix.[35] Rivers did frequent, along with O'Hara, the straight artistic bar scene comprising the Club and the Cedar Bar Tavern, but he tended to view the macho performances of Pollock *et al.* with more than a little disdain.[36] In this regard what becomes apparent is the degree to which queer bohemia provided Rivers with the imaginary and social matrix through which he was enabled to performatively enact his artistic body. 'Black bodies', 'lesbian bodies', and 'gay male bodies' – culturally devalorized bodies all – came to be revalorized and glossed as 'hip' in Rivers's performative (re-)enactment of them as the artist-beatnik. But it was the bodies of gay men – O'Hara, Ashbery, and Myers – which were the object of Rivers's particular fascination and identification as he began to perform himself anew in the world of art, as he began to make himself over into a 'perfect camper'.

THE REAL THING?

But how might such identifications, constitutive of Rivers's artistic identity, be seen to be played out in his work as a painter? How, if at all, can Rivers's painterly surfaces be understood as the site of queer identification and a performative self-othering of straight masculinity? Here a consideration of the relations between a campy gay vernacular and Rivers's painting is of particular relevance. In his autobiography, Rivers imaginatively reconstructs some snippets of gay male conversation that he routinely encountered at Nell Blaine's gatherings in the early 1950s incorporating the camp humour, the concern for what Rivers calls 'silly bits of information', and the 'pressure to exhibit a talent for the well-turned phrase'. His reconstruction is worth quoting at some length:

> 'My Dear, I've been reading Dostoyevsky's Raw Youth. It's marvellous. I found the spirit of the book to be –'
> 'Spirit, my ass,' someone interrupts. 'He filched it all from Dickens, who has everything Dostoyevsky has, plus being –'
> 'What, a social historian? How about the honourable Honoré? You're not telling me that Dickens had more balls than Balzac.'
> 'Ronald Firbank held more balls than Balzac.'
> 'Where?'
> 'In a ballroom, honey. Where do you hold balls?'
> 'I don't hold balls in a ballroom. I hold them in a bedroom.'
> 'I hold them in a men's room,' someone chirps up from the end of the couch.[37]

Hearing such exchanges like this for the first time, Rivers recalls that he 'began spinning in an ever-expanding reality'.[38] It may be that the cultured referencing of such conversation struck the budding artist from the lower-middle class Bronx as peculiarly Other – as 'classy' and sophisticated.[39] But what sent him spinning, I think, was the sliding of this performance of high cultural learnedness – an 'elevated' discussion about the great figures of literature – into a rather more 'trivializing' exchange of innuendoes about gay sex.[40] Rivers's imaginative recollection probably tells us as much about what he found impressive about camp conversation as it tells us about the kinds of things that were actually said. And, from this example at least, it seems that what impressed him most was the conjunction of a seeming high cultural sophistication with the debasing and banalizing effects of camp innuendo that made for a peculiar mixture of 'high' seriousness and 'low' triviality.

These features of a gay male vernacular can be seen to throw some interesting light on an interpretation of Rivers's 1953 painting *Washington Crossing the Delaware* (Plate 7.2). To set himself the task of doing a modern History Painting, with its attendant expectations of significant meaning and high grandeur, and to take as his subject a patriotic moment from American history, was to do something that 'no one in the New York art world would doubt was disgusting, dead, absurd' – that is, it was a deliberate attempt at painting the artistically and politically retrograde.[41] This is because 1953 was marked by the continuing dominance of Abstract Expressionism in the arts as well as being the high point of McCarthyism. Given the political sympathies of most of the New York art world, Rivers's choice of subject would have made him appear out of step with most of his avant-garde peers. Nothing could have been 'dopier', Rivers writes, than a painting 'dedicated to a national cliché.'[42] Thus the 'seriousness' of *Washington* was already compromised from the

Plate 7.2 Larry Rivers, *Washington Crossing the Delaware*, 1953. Oil, graphite, and charcoal on linen; 6ft 11⅝ in × 9ft 3⅝ in. Museum of Modern Art, New York. Photograph 1998, The Museum of Modern Art, New York

very outset. Further, Rivers's disidentification with the 'hand-on-chest heroics' of Emanuel Leutze's nineteenth-century painting of the same subject, which some critics see as important for a reading of Rivers's own, appears to have been rooted in one of those 'silly bits of information' characteristic of the gay chatter at Nell Blaine's parties. Apparently, Rivers thought that it just looked *too chilly* to be getting onto a river around Christmas time and to be putting on any kind of swaggering militaristic performance.[43]

But to assume from this that Rivers's intention was, therefore, to upstage the 'serious' by painting ironically – to suggest that *Washington* is a joke, perhaps with an anti-patriotic or anti-Republican message – is to go too far in the opposite direction and to miss the point of what I take to be Rivers's campy evocation of his subject. As recent theorists of camp have argued, to conflate camp with irony is to miss out on its wider potential for undermining conditions of meaning.[44] Irony works to shore up binary structures of signification by producing oppositional meanings to those stated or apparent. Camp, on the other hand, can be understood as a *performative* technology of subjectivity and meaning which denaturalizes the very process through which *any* determinate meaning is produced.[45] This does not mean, however, that 'serious' meaning is evacuated from camp discourse altogether, but rather that it is articulated as the object of a parodic pleasure which undermines its conventional signification. Rivers writes in *What Did I Do?* that the Leutze was not at the forefront of his mind while he was making the painting, nor was

Tolstoy's *War and Peace,* which had initially given him the idea to do a grand historical work. Rather, Rivers was thinking 'mainly about the patriotic grade school plays I sat through or participated in. I never took them seriously, even at seven or eight years old, but I enjoyed them and still have a pleasurable feeling remembering the experience.'[46] In this regard Rivers's campy attitude allowed him to endorse his 'pleasurable feeling' for serious culture – for Washington, for History Painting – while, at the same time, performatively undermining its naturalized significance and legitimacy. In this respect, by viewing *Washington* through a camp/performative lens, we can begin to approach it as a painting which neither affirms nor disaffirms patriotic meaning; which plays History Painting neither 'straight' nor as a joke, but rather as an occasion for camp pleasure which keeps the binary possibilities of its meaning in play. The undermining of the 'serious' in *Washington* might then be understood less as an ironic overturning and more as a performative destabilization of its naturalized signification.

In painterly terms, this 'campiness' appears to some critics as a kind of 'Broadway' or 'Hollywood' style painting where history is rendered as a kind of overblown, theatrical, performance, thereby making it 'too much' to be taken seriously.[47] Rivers himself can be seen to have contributed to such a view by saying that he was more concerned with what the subject could offer him in terms of painterly spectacle than anything else: 'there was plenty in *Washington Crossing the Delaware* to dazzle me – horses, water, soldiers, and so on.'[48] It is on this basis that Rivers has begun to suffer critically at the hands of the 'serious' discourses of art by being positioned as frivolous and superficial. When *Washington* was first shown in 1953 both the painting and its maker were attacked by artists Elaine de Kooning and Gandy Brody for their perceived *lack of authenticity*. De Kooning criticised Rivers's painting for its lack of drama and weak coloration, inviting comparison with the work of Bulgarian painter Jules Pascin by dubbing it 'Pascin Crossing the Delaware'. In criticizing its washy coloration, de Kooning appeared to be saying that Rivers's painting failed to match up to the 'real thing', that it was too much of a weak attempt or poor *substitute* for what *should be* a dramatic and powerful subject. Similarly, Brody called Rivers a 'phoney', denigrating him as a fake or an imposter and not a genuine artist. Such remarks resonate within a culture of art in which the heterosexual masculinity of Abstract Expressionism provided the dominant and 'authentic' model of art practice and subjectivity.[49] Indeed de Kooning's and Brody's comments could be construed as inflected with a homophobic thematics of the performative, with Brody's remark in particular seen as a slur on Rivers as something less than a 'proper' man.[50] Such responses, though, did not dismay Rivers, but rather gave him, in his own words, 'a rush of importance', presumably from the subversive impact of his camp performance on the 'serious' and 'authentic' world of Abstract Expressionism.[51]

ON THE SURFACE

This undermining of 'seriousness' and 'significant' meaning was a key feature of Frank O'Hara's poetry. Indeed O'Hara's work is crucial to my understanding of Rivers's paintings here because it would have offered to Rivers a way of deploying the features of a camp vernacular as a mode of artistic expression. O'Hara has often been criticized for his supposed superficiality as a poet, and derided for his inability to work earnestly and symbolically with subjects of great import. His poems are often taken to be too much like

115

chatty conversation or 'gossip', lacking in normative syntax and meaningfulness.[52] These features of O'Hara's work are the ones that O'Hara himself emphasizes in his mock 1959 manifesto for 'Personism': '(w)hile I was writing I was realising that if I wanted to I could use the telephone instead of writing the poem, and so Personism was born.'[53] In writing thus, O'Hara embraces the very characteristics of his poetry which some critics abhor: the emphasis on the poem as an intimate utterance between two people, and as a form of conversation where conversation means *chatting*, with no necessary intention, aim, or end-point. As Bruce Boone has argued, many of O'Hara's poems, such as *Lana Turner Has Collapsed* or *Second Avenue*, proceed paratactically by eschewing the proper connectives through which normal grammatical sense can be made.[54] This leaves the reader caught within the textual play of O'Hara's poetic narrative rather than being positioned as the addressee of any determinate or intentional 'message'.

Marjorie Perloff and Irving Sandler, among others, have argued that a similar structuring principle can be found at work in the organization of Rivers's painted surfaces, making them into a kind of painterly 'gossip'.[55] A number of paintings made by Rivers in the 1950s, such as *The Studio* (Plate 7.3), are made up of isolated, seemingly disconnected fragments of painterly detail. Looking at this painting is a 'roving, multiple, and episodic' experience, particularly because its sheer size – 6' 10" × 16' 1" – doesn't allow you to take it in at a glance.[56] Moreover, it is an image which engages its spectators in an unresolvable and *performative* interpretative play. Loosely based on Courbet's *The Painter's Studio* of 1855, which functioned as an allegory of the artist's life, Rivers's *Studio* mimics the composition and intent of Courbet's work. The painting contains (multiple) portraits of some of the key people in Rivers's life in 1956 – from left to right: Frank O'Hara, the artist's sons Joseph and Steven, his mother-in-law Berdie, as well as the centrally placed figure of the black muse. This latter figure has been read as the lynch-pin for a temporal reading of the painting's allegory, scrolling away to the left 'toward winter which includes the past and the stuffed hawk; and counter-actively to spring blossoming in, among other things, a nude and a tropical bird'.[57] However, just as *Washington* undermines the heroic patriotism that its subject and genre promise, Rivers's *Studio*, though appearing on some level to abide by the rules of grand allegory, frustrates attempts to fully recover or construct

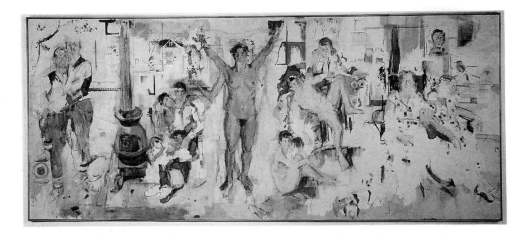

Plate 7.3 Larry Rivers, *The Studio*, 1956. Oil on canvas; 82 in × 193 in. Minneapolis Institute of Arts

any coherent allegorical meaningfulness for it. Any such attempt soon runs aground on the isolated fragments of painterly detail or 'incidents' that litter the surface of Rivers's canvas, for example, the free-floating patterning of Berdie's dress on the right, or the detailed modelling of Joseph's brown boot to the left. These freeze the spectator's gaze, isolating each fragment of surface *existentially*, as it were, within the viewer's field of vision. In this way, such fragments displace the whole architecture of allegorical meaning of which they are supposedly a constituent part. Hence, the painting structures our looking in terms of an amalgam of loosely related points of focus – a 'smorgasbord of the recognisable' as Rivers has described it.[58] As our eye wanders over the huge expanse of whiteness from incident to incident, unable to focus on the whole or take it in a single glance, we are kept at the level of surface as we flit from fragment to fragment, failing to make them cohere into a meaningful structure. Despite all of this, however, the painting resists being made over into pure surface. Instead what remains is an irresolvable tension between surface and at least the *potential* of determinate meaning.

This roving spectatorial and hermeneutic mode has echoes in the so-called 'vernacular glance' supposedly encoded in a Robert Rauschenberg painting such as *Rebus* of 1955 or even, perhaps, in one's attention to a Pollock (for example, *Full Fathom Five*, 1947) where one's gaze happens upon a cigarette butt or a paint-tube top, a nail, or a key embedded in its surface.[59] Making these comparisons begins to open up my camp/performative interpretative schema to the possibility of reading the *sexual* determination of such surfaces, and of surface *as such* in 1950s American art. This is a subject that I can only at best touch on here given both the constraints of space and the complexity of the issue. Needless to say, any such account would have to address the relations between poetry and painting, and a certain articulation of camp in 1950s culture. O'Hara's poems are very important for any such consideration since they were produced by someone deeply involved with the communities and languages of painting.[60] O'Hara's concern with the surface of his poetic narratives owed as much to the languages of modernist art as it did to the vernacular traditions of gay male camp. Short of any more detailed and thoroughgoing analysis of individual poems and paintings, it will have to suffice here to note how O'Hara wrote of his desire to keep the surface of a poem like *Second Avenue* 'high and dry . . . reflective and self-conscious' and to see the surface and the meaning of the poem as inextricable 'since the one is the other . . . and I hope the poem to *be* the subject, not just be about it.'[61] What I take this to mean is that the play of surface and meaning, of signifier and signified, is the subject of the poem and that there is nothing transcendental to be gleaned – nothing 'behind' or 'under' the textuality of O'Hara's work. In this regard, O'Hara's poems refuse any metaphysical 'bodying forth' of meaning. In so doing, they can be seen to perform a critique of the ontological condition of meaning ascribed to surface by at least some of its readers in New York's artistic culture in the 1950s.

It is precisely these features of O'Hara's poetry which have been taken by gay critics like Rudy Kikel and Bruce Boone as evidencing its camp/queer critique of dominant models of subjectivity and meaning.[62] His rejection of 'depth' models of meaning; his refusal to write 'seriously' about 'serious' subjects; his refusal to write in an autobiographical or confessional mode; his lack of any overt moral or political stance are read as a camp refusal of positionality. Or, more precisely, they are interpreted as an abdication of positionality as it is commonly constituted – one typically coded in terms of the straight male subject position. If one critic can say of O'Hara's work, 'what man could speak like this and still *be* a man?', then such a response only serves to underline the way in which O'Hara's poetry undermines the rhetorics of straight male masculinity that were historically specific to poetic utterance in the 1950s. In a similar way, it might also be possible to read Rivers's campy surfaces as proposing a different set of relations between surface, subject, and meaning from those commonly articulated, for example, by Harold Rosenberg for Abstract Expressionist painting.[63] Whereas the Abstract Expressionist surface is customarily seen as made up of the 'same metaphysical substance as the artist's existence' – which needless to say is the very 'being' of the heterosexual male artist – Rivers's surfaces, at least in my interpretation of them, appear to undermine any such metaphysical reading.[64] Rivers does not securely occupy any moral or political position in the *Washington* picture, nor is there any fully recoverable meaning to be read out of *The Studio*, and, as Thomas Hess has written of Rivers's work, even though you are invited to 'come . . . all the way into his painting . . . it must be understood (that) Rivers won't be there waiting for you . . . There are no shreds of tortured ego dangling from the edges of his forms'.[65]

READING CAMP

The hazards involved in making a reading of Rivers's paintings as camp are exacerbated by the ways in which art criticism has chosen to view the textualizing play of Rivers's painterly surfaces as a form of modernist self- or non-referentiality. In this light, camp becomes identical with modernism in a way that occludes its specific sex/gender meanings which I take to be its special sphere of effectivity. Camp did not pass into the art critical vocabulary until the 1960s, spurred on by the publication of Susan Sontag's 'Notes on Camp' published in *Partisan Review* in 1964. Only after this date, to my knowledge, do critics start to write about Rivers's work in terms of camp – Thomas Hess in 1965 and John Adkins Richardson in 1966.[66] Richardson tows Sontag's line on the relationship between camp and homosexuality allowing for a 'peculiar affinity and overlap' between them, while at the same time paving the way for the construction of a non-sexualized (read 'straightened-out') version of it. This notion of overlap he extends to his account of the relations between camp and Pop ('And in painting Camp also overlaps with Pop').[67] Rivers, he argues, is 'a precursor of the Camp sensibilities associated with it [Pop]':

> In his recent *The Second Greatest Homosexual*, a construction based on Jacques-Louis David's Napoleon (the famous pose of which struck him as unnatural and effete), Rivers would seem to be working very obviously within the mental set of Camp. And in *Dutch Masters and Cigars* of 1964 Rivers produced what amounts to a philosophical work expressing a Camp ideality.[68]

This 'Camp ideality' is expressed in terms of Rivers's approach to the 'great' and 'significant'. Based upon a billboard advertisement for cigars, Richardson reads *Dutch Masters and Cigars* as campy through its honouring of greatness, that is, Rembrandt's *The Syndics*, 'with levity', and through its monumentalizing of the trivial (the cigar box) – thus echoing Sontag's determination of camp as that which is frivolous about the serious, and serious about the frivolous. The painting's camp appeal also derives from the fact that the particular brand of cigars that Rivers paints enjoyed a certain prestige among intellectuals for their manufacturer's sponsorship of a television comedian called Ernie Kovaks, who was, according to Richardson, 'a somewhat camp character'.[69] What I find intriguing about this reading of Rivers's works is that Richardson reads not only a manifest campy attitude within them, but that for the first time in the critical reception of Rivers's work he also attaches gay or quasi-gay signifiers to them as well. The campiness of *The Second Greatest Homosexual*, for instance, is seen by him clearly to reside in its knowing jokiness about stereotypical forms of gay male deportment. In this respect Richardson's text is symptomatic of the *ambiguous* sexual meaning of mainstream camp in the 1960s. That is, while downplaying the relations between camp and homosexuality, just as Sontag does in 'Notes on Camp', Richardson does not extricate homosexuality fully from the horizon of camp's possible meanings – even when that camp is performed by a straight artist. The notion of camp as being somehow in excess of homosexuality can never be finally extricated from the notion of its *overlap* with it. This leads to an unstable interpretative horizon of trafficking meanings for camp in 1960s art. Richardson calls camp 'androgynous . . . delighting also in various kinds of inversions other than sexual ones'.[70] This not only serves to assign camp an indeterminate status, but also by adopting androgyny as a metaphor for *all* of camp's operations, reinscribes the 'overlap' and inextricability of its supposedly sexual and non-sexual meanings.

In making such a reading, Richardson highlights the aporetic dimension of Rivers's work as it impacts upon the performative field of interpretative desire. The constant sliding between 'being' and 'acting'; between 'the serious' and 'the frivolous'; between the 'straight' and the 'queer', is evidenced, I think, in a photo-portrait of Rivers in his New York studio in 1965 taken by Peter Moore (Plate 7.4). Rivers stands in his studio flanked by

Plate 7.4 Peter Moore, photograph of Larry Rivers in his studio, New York, 1965

119

the two paintings picked out for special consideration by Richardson in his consideration of Rivers's campness. On the right is *Dutch Masters with Cigars* and on the left his painting of 1964, *The Greatest Homosexual* (Plate 7.5), based on a portrait of Napoleon which struck Rivers as mincing and affected (hence the title). Rivers stands before the painting with his hands on his hips and a smile, I like to think, almost breaking out across his face, as he too adopts an affected, almost effeminate, pose. On one level, of course, this could be construed as a joke shared between artist and photographer as well as between artist and viewer, as he mimics the pose of the affected and painted Napoleon. However, on another level, this is more than an ironic performance and it can be seen instead as being continuous with the 'performative' being of Larry Rivers, who can no more stop posing than he can

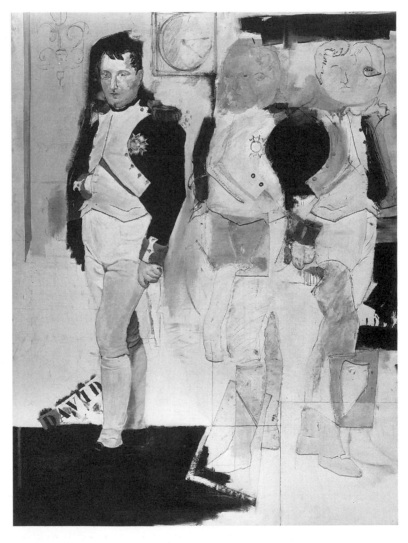

Plate 7.5 Larry Rivers, *The Greatest Homosexual*, 1964, oil and collage on canvas, 80 in. × 61 in., Hirshhorn Museum and Sculpture Garden, Smithsonian Institution, Washington, D.C. Gift of Joseph H. Hirshhorn, 1966. Photograph by Lee Stalsworth

stop being an artist since the very 'being' of his artistic self *is* the posing. To adopt an old adage, if this image is a lie, an affectation, then it is the lie that tells the truth, the truth, that is, of Rivers's queerly performative subjectivity – and the campy desire of this particular interpreter in bringing it to critical light.

NOTES

I would like to thank Jon Cairns, Andre Dombrowski, Amelia Jones, Kate Love, Adrian Rifkin, and Andrew Stephenson for their invaluable help and advice on this essay.

1 'Wonder Boy and His Many Sides', *Life*, 20 October, 1958, vol. 45, no. 16, pp. 100–1. All following references in my text are culled from here.

2 Rivers's construction of artistic identity differs substantially from the popular image of the brooding and centred masculinity of Jackson Pollock represented in *Life* some nine years earlier. See 'Jackson Pollock: Is He the Greatest Living Painter in the United States?', *Life*, 8 August 1949, vol. 27, no. 6, pp. 42–3, 45.

3 Indeed, the privileged position accorded to the painting within the photograph – as that which frames and unites Rivers's different poses within the image as a whole – may also belie its role as representational model for *Life*'s photo-portrait. The photo-shoot clearly appears to mimic or repeat some of the fragmented, multiple features of Rivers' painterly compositions. In this regard, *The Athlete's Dream* appears as a performative epistemological framework which, when reiterated as the *Life* photo-shoot, represents the performative dimensions of Rivers's own social and professional identity. The slippage enacted here between Rivers's 'art' and his 'life' should give us cause to rethink the habitual divisions that art history makes between the artist's 'life' and his/her 'work'. Rather than seeing 'the life' as ontologically prior to the performance of 'the work', to position it as origin or truth of the work, a performative hermeneutic might seek to view 'the life' as *enacted* through the reiteration of certain social and discursive norms, and indeed, within and through the work of art. I borrow here from the standard literature on the performative in signalling its critical potential, including Judith Butler, *Bodies That Matter: On the Discursive Limits of Sex*, London, Routledge, 1993 and Jacques Derrida, 'Signature Event Context', in *Margins of Philosophy*, Chicago, Harvester Press, 1982, pp. 307–30. However, it is the performative hermeneutic that I find photographically enacted in *Life* magazine which I attempt to extend in what follows.

4 My thinking about camp has been informed by a critical reading of Susan Sontag, 'Notes on Camp', *Partisan Review*, 1964, vol. 31, pp. 515–30; Jack Babuscio, 'Camp and the Gay Sensibility', in Richard Dyer (ed.), *Gays and Film*, London, British Film Institute, 1977, pp. 40–57; Dyer's 'It's Being So Camp As Keeps Us Going', in *Only Entertainment*, London, Routledge, 1992, pp. 135–47; Andrew Ross, 'Uses of Camp', in *No Respect: Intellectuals and Popular Culture*, London, Routledge, 1989, pp. 135–70; Moe Meyer (ed.), *The Politics and Poetics of Camp*, London, Routledge, 1994; Pamela Robertson, *Guilty Pleasures: Feminist Camp from Mae West to Madonna*, London, Duke University Press, 1996 and Andy Medhurst, 'Camp' in Andy Medhurst and Sally R. Munt (eds), *Lesbian and Gay Studies: An Introduction*, London, Cassell, 1997, pp. 274–93. It should quickly become apparent that what I am concerned to argue for is an understanding of camp that shares, to some degree, both Meyer's and Robertson's approach to camp as performative. However, I want to mark a difference from Meyer's construction of camp as that which can only be performed by a gay or lesbian subject (whereby one's aptitude for camp depends on who you sleep with) and the sometime tendency of Robertson to 'flatten out' what Richard Dyer calls camp's 'equivocality'. First, in my attention to a self-professed straight artist who 'camps', I want to rethink what happens to camp, and also to 'straightness', just before its entry into the mainstream. In some regard what I offer is a prehistory to Sontag's 'straightening out' of camp in her 1964 'Notes', making amenable to analysis a specific and different articulation of camp in the 1950s, which takes beat culture and the meanings attributed to 'the serious' in painting and poetry as its primary contexts. Second, in my attention to what I want to call camp's *aporetic* dimension, at least as it is articulated

within Rivers's artistic embodiment of it, I attempt to rethink camp through the aporia of the performative/constative binary set out in J. L. Austin's *How to Do Things with Words*, (ed. Marina Abisa and J. O. Urmson), Oxford, Oxford University Press, 2nd edn, 1975. This leads me to think camp outside of models which position it as simple irony or frivolity, or as simply and *purely* performative. Instead I consider camp's epistemological complexity which foregrounds its effect as that of the aporetic condition of the performative/constative distinction, of the undecidable play of the frivolous and the serious, etc. It is this aporetic movement which the camp consumer plays as pleasure and which the camp detractor finds undermining, often responding with ridicule and/or, as is the case in art historical writing on Rivers, with critical downgrading.

5   I deliberately use the metaphor of infection here to remind the reader of the parasitic abnormality that is ascribed to the theatrical performative in Austin, *How to Do Things with Words*, p. 22.

6   In this regard what *Life* stages as aporetic is the very Austinian distinction between constative and performative as it is played out across Rivers's life and work.

7   Rivers himself allows for the connection between the performative representation of the subjects in his paintings and the performative in life. In a typical campy expression, Rivers is quoted as saying: 'Most people have many facets and it's the same with life. I try to convey this multiplicity in my paintings. I want somehow to get the canvas full of things – full of shapes and colors exciting as a flower garden' (*Life*, 'Wonder Boy and His Many Sides', p. 100).

8   Irving Sandler, *The New York School: The Painters and Sculptors of the Fifties*, London, Harper & Row, 1978, pp. 103–11. Rivers takes his place alongside nine other artists in a chapter devoted to 'gestural realists' including Grace Hartigan, Robert Goodnough, Jan Muller, Lester Johnson, Fairfield Porter, Alex Katz, Philip Pearlstein, Richard Diebenkorn, and Leon Golub. Since the publication of Sandler's book, only Katz, Diebenkorn and Golub appear to have enhanced their critical and public profile, Golub in particular gaining widespread critical recognition in the 1980s for a series of large-scale paintings. Jasper Johns and Robert Rauschenberg are singled out for special attention by Sandler in a chapter dedicated to their work alone. In trying to account for Rivers's marginal position within the canon one might attend to the relatively interstitial status of his work in art historical terms, both marking a difference from the art of Pollock and de Kooning through his unapologetic deployment of naturalistic figuration, and at the same time retaining too much of a gestural look to make that difference over into the post-Abstract Expressionist 'new'. Rivers's work could be viewed as both too much like Abstract Expressionism and not enough like Pop art, or vice versa, to warrant him any special position in the history of postwar American art. One might make related observations, however, about the work of Jasper Johns and Robert Rauschenberg who, contrary to Rivers, occupy a pre-eminent position in most art historical narratives as progenitors of Pop art and the foremost artists of their generation. One need only compare the sheer volume of art historical monographs published on Johns with the few dedicated to Rivers, to be appraised of the discursive priorities of postwar art history (see note 9 below). As opposed to a purely formal or stylistic explanation, what follows attempts to find the peculiar condition of Rivers's camp *performativity* as a significant factor in determining his position within the art historical canon.

9   Sam Hunter, *Larry Rivers*, New York, Harry N. Abrams, 1970, p. 13. Hunter's book is still the most comprehensive text on the artist, revised and expanded as *Larry Rivers*, New York, Arthur A. Bartley, 1989. Other monographic studies include only Helen A. Harrison, *Larry Rivers*, New York, Harper & Row, 1984 and a sizable volume co-authored by Rivers himself with Carol Brightman, *Drawings and Digressions*, New York, Clarkson N. Potter, 1979. These few studies on Rivers contrast sharply with the wealth of material on Johns, which continues to expand. Such work includes, selectively, monographic studies by Max Kozloff (1968); Michael Crichton (1977); Richard Francis (1984); Mark Rosenthal (1988); Fred Orton (1996) and Kirk Varnedoe (1996).

10   Betty Kaufman, 'Rivers: Boy Painter', *Commonweal*, 24 June 1960, vol. 84, pp. 400–1. All following references are from this source.

11   For a useful account of the construction of the Abstract Expressionist artist see Caroline A. Jones, *Machine in the Studio. Constructing the Postwar American Artist*, London and Chicago, University of Chicago Press, 1996, pp. 1–59.

12 Hunter, *Larry Rivers*, p. 12.

13 'Jam Session', *Newsweek*, 26 April 1965, vol. 65, p. 56.

14 The 'queer body', as I invoke it here, is that social and discursive construct marked by the violence and pressures of homophobic culture. It is a body which is compelled to mutate across the strictly policed borders of private and public, a body spaced across the inside and the outside of 'the closet'. A similar figuring of the queer body is discussed by Peggy Phelan in 'Uncovered Rectums: Disinterring the Rose Theatre', in *Mourning Sex: Performing Public Memories*, London, Routledge, 1997, pp. 73–94.

15 Paul Cummings, interview with Larry Rivers, 2 November 1968, Washington, DC, Archives of American Art/Smithsonian Institution, microfilm no. 3949, p. 11.

16 Sam Hunter, interview with Larry Rivers, Sam Hunter Papers on Larry Rivers 1950–1969, Washington, DC, Archives of American Art/Smithsonian Institution, microfilm nos. 630 and 673, p. 5.

17 Ibid.

18 As Allan Bérubé writes, 'by 1941 gay men and women were using 'coming out' to mean that they had found gay friends and the gay life, and were saying that circumstances in their lives, not just their first sexual partner, had brought them out.' *Coming Out under Fire: The History of Gay Men and Women in World War Two*, New York, Plume, 1991, p. 6.

19 Brad Gooch, *City Poet: The Life and Times of Frank O'Hara*, New York, HarperPerennial, 1994, p. 229.

20 Upon seeing O'Hara and Rivers together at the City Center, John Myers remarked 'There they are, all covered with blood and semen!' – a remark originally uttered by Madame Verlaine upon seeing her husband with Rimbaud at the Opéra. See Brad Gooch, *City Poet*, p. 230.

21 I use the term 'queer' here to refer to both 'lesbian' and 'gay' since Rivers clearly took both Blaine and O'Hara as important embodiments of what it meant to 'be' an artist. However, as we shall see, by 1950/51 it was primarily gay *male* culture and society which fascinated and attracted Rivers, largely by dint of its transgressive performance of masculine sexual potency and the 'bewildering' argot of a camp vernacular.

22 'When I began playing saxophone and got hung up on jazz and it became clear who the greatest jazz musicians were, again I was envious, and at the same time madly attracted to blacks. The reasons for such adoration are not always appreciated by the adored, but I was not conscious then that my reasons could be regarded as an insult, and when life carried me into contact with yet another world, the world of homosexuals, which gave me such laughs and thrills and boundless joy, I developed the same unreserved admiration – at least for the hundred or so homosexuals I knew.' Quoted in Larry Rivers and Arnold Weinstein, *What Did I Do?: The Unauthorised Biography*, New York, HarperCollins, 1992, p. 223. Interestingly here, Rivers looks back somewhat ambivalently on the political character of his identifications with 'blackness' and 'homosexuality', which I explore below. What emerges as strikingly powerful, however, especially in the reference to a 'yet another world' of homosexuals, is how Rivers's fascination and attraction to O'Hara *et al.* appears to be driven by a quasi-colonialist 'pioneering' venture into uncharted and unknown territory – an investment similar in kind to the one that Rivers, and other hipsters around him, were making in black culture.

23 Harold Norse, for one, remembers as early as 1944 being a 'charter member' of the beat generation. See Norse, *Memoirs of a Bastard Angel*, London, Bloomsbury, 1990, p. 139. Also see Maria Damon, 'Victors of Catastrophe: Beat Occlusions', in Lisa Phillips (ed.), *Beat Culture and the New America 1950–1965*, New York, Whitney Museum of American Art, 1995, pp. 141–9, for a useful account of the less canonical manifestations of beat culture.

24 Norman Mailer, 'The White Negro: Superficial Reflections on the Hipster', in *Advertisements for Myself*, London, Panther, 1961, pp. 269–89.

25 Ibid., p. 273.

26 Kobena Mercer, 'Racial Difference and the Homoerotic Imaginary', in Bad Object Choices (ed.), *How Do I Look?: Queer Film & Video*, Seattle, Bay Press, 1991, pp. 207–8.

27 Ibid.

28 See Rivers and Weinstein, *What Did I Do?*, pp. 45–6. Rivers was later challenged by Clement Greenberg for attempting to disavow his Jewishness. When introduced some years later to Clement Greenberg as Larry Rivers, 'Greenberg's first words, before "Hello" were, "What was

your name before you changed it?" Meekly: "Grossberg." "Sounds like you're ashamed of being Jewish," he said, reminding me of my parents, who were hurt when I legally changed my name. I always feared I'd run into someone in my new world who would call me on this. I never dreamed it would be someone whose opinion about my work would be so important and whose feelings about an odious weakness of character would probably influence that opinion' (pp. 182–3). Rivers is revealingly candid here although his reference to his 'odious weakness of character' is perhaps best understood as common to others of his generation, some of whom, like the poet Harold Norse, resolved to settle his 'identity crisis', partly, in Norse's case, centred around his Jewishness, by aspiring to be 'American'. For both Norse and Rivers 'sorting out' their identity involved the erasure of Jewishness as a prerequisite for adopting their chosen cultural identities – be it as an 'American' or as a 'hipster.' See Norse, *Memoirs of a Bastard Angel*, p. 18.

29   As Maria Damon remarks, 'there is still much resistance to acknowledging the homoerotic art and dynamics of beat life.' Damon, 'Victors of Catastrophe', p. 144.

30   See Catharine R. Stimpson, 'The Beat Generation and the Trials of Homosexual Liberation', *Salmagundi*, Fall 1982–Winter 1983, nos. 58–59, pp. 373–92, for an excellent account of the problematic relationship of some of the straight(er) beats, principally Kerouac and Cassady, to homosexuality and their queer counterparts, Ginsberg and Burroughs. Also for a portrait of the queer beatnik, see Wallace de Ortega Maxey, 'The Homosexual and the Beat Generation', *One*, July 1959, vol. 7, no. 7, pp. 5–9. Sexual practice was a key way in which the beats elaborated their ethical and political vision of liberation. From their celebration of promiscuous and non-marital sex, perhaps most paradigmatically expressed in Kerouac's *On the Road*, to the hymn to transgressive homosexuality contained in Ginsberg's *Howl*, the beats laid claim to a politics of sexual libertarianism. However, beat culture was not, generally speaking, out to affirm the homosexual as a particular kind of *person*. Indeed beat's sexual politics entailed a working rejection of modern constructions of homosexual and heterosexual identity. As Allen Ginsberg is reported to have said: 'I sleep with men and women. I am neither queer nor not queer, nor am I bi-sexual. My name is Allen Ginsberg and I sleep with whoever I want' (cited in Maxey, p. 6). In this way, beat marshalled an individualist politics of sexuality which drew upon a pre-modern discourse of sexuality as an accumulation of *acts*, rather than as something which expressed the truth of a person's selfhood. In the context of heterosexist society, this view allowed for purveyors of homosexual acts to be valorized as rebels because they could be seen to be acting in the name of 'freedom', proclaiming 'the legitimacy of individual desire' (cited in Stimpson, p. 375). Or as Leslie Fiedler put it in 1958, homosexuality appeared as the 'purest and truest protest of the latest generation, not a burden merely, an affliction to be borne, but a politics to be flaunted' (cited in Robert J. Corber, *In the Name of National Security: Hitchcock, Homophobia, and the Political Construction of Gender in Postwar America*, London, Duke University Press, 1993, p. 166).

31   Cited in Gooch, *City Poet*, p. 240.

32   Rivers and Weinstein, *What Did I Do?*, p. 105.

33   Cummings, interview with Larry Rivers, op. cit., p. 12.

34   Cited in Gooch, *City Poet*, p. 249.

35   Cited in Bruce Boone, 'Gay Language as Political Praxis: The Poetry of Frank O'Hara', *Social Text*, 1979, no. 1, p. 67.

36   'Pollock? Socially, he was a real jerk . . . Very unpleasant to be around. Very stupid. He was always at the Cedar on Tuesdays – that was the day he came into town to see his analyst – and he always got completely drunk, and he made a point of behaving badly to everyone.' Larry Rivers cited in Andy Warhol and Pat Hackett, *POPism: The Warhol Sixties*, London, Harvest/Harcourt Brace Jovanovitch, 1980, p. 13.

37   Rivers and Weinstein, *What Did I Do?*, p. 109.

38   Ibid.

39   The class and racial dimensions of Rivers's identifications with camp talk here are worthy of further consideration. The painter Anne Tabachnick has written: 'Larry didn't have gay episodes to have sex but to improve himself. He thought that by hanging out in gay company he would learn to be classier . . . He really wanted to know how to dress and talk . . . No, it wasn't the homosexuality, it was upward mobility' (Rivers and Weinstein, *What Did I Do?*, p. 133). Rivers

himself refers to the 'delicate gait and matching limp wrist' which, he remarks, your 'average Joe would call a fairy but I would call "class"' (p. 47). So, for Rivers, camp conversation and camp demeanour signalled being 'artistic', being cultured and sophisticated. Such an identification with the 'classiness' of homosexuality on Rivers's part is productively understood in relation to his lower-middle class Jewish upbringing in the Bronx. Becoming an artist and getting involved in a largely homosexual network of artists and poets was a way to other himself from what he took to be the mundanity and supposed cultural paucity of his family's life. As Rivers recollects; '[my] parents were about as aware of culture, history, art, . . . as any Polish peasants. I mean, they really knew nothing' (cited in Hunter, interview with Larry Rivers, 'Jam Session', *Newsweek*, p. 1). In this way Rivers speaks dismissively of his immigrant family's (Russian) cultural heritage: 'the only thing in our house resembling art was a cheap tapestry with dark figures, a cross between a Fragonard and a Minsky stripper' (cited in *Newsweek*, 'Jam Session', op. cit., p. 56). Interestingly here, Rivers' identification with camp homosexuality masks a powerful disidentification with what he took to be culturally irredeemable about East European Jewish culture. Unlike 'blackness' and 'homosexuality', 'Jewishness', it seemed, was a cultural identity positioning incapable of being revalorized within the ideology of hipsterism.

40 This spinning response is also that of the critic of Rivers's painting, of Kaufman, as she is unable to finally secure a qualitative judgement or interpretation of his work.

41 Frank O'Hara (interview with Larry Rivers), 'Why I Paint As I Do', *Horizon*, September/October 1959, vol. 2, no. 1, p. 98.

42 Ibid.

43 'The last painting that dealt with George and the rebels is hanging in the Met and was painted by a coarse German nineteenth-century academician who really loved Napoleon more than anyone and thought that crossing a river on a late December afternoon was just another excuse for a general to assume a heroic, slightly tragic pose. . . . What could have inspired him I'll never know. What I saw in the crossing was quite different. I saw the moment as nerve-wracking and uncomfortable. I couldn't picture anyone getting into a chilly river around Christmas time with anything resembling hand-on-chest heroics' (ibid.).

44 Cynthia Morril, 'Revamping the Gay Sensibility: Queer Camp and Dyke Noir', in Meyer, *The Politics and Poetics of Camp*, pp. 110–29. However, despite its commendable repoliticizing of camp, this essay suffers from a highly problematic construction of it as that which can only be performed 'properly' by lesbian and gay subjects.

45 For more on camp as performative see Meyer, *The Politics and Poetics of Camp*, pp. 1–5; and Robertson, *Guilty Pleasures*, pp. 10–13.

46 Rivers and Weinstein, *What Did I Do?*, p. 312. In this regard Rivers echoes a character from Christopher Isherwood's 1954 novel *The World in the Evening* in elaborating camp's relationship to the serious: 'You can't camp about something you don't take seriously. You're not making fun of it; you're making fun out of it. You're expressing what's serious to you in terms of fun and artifice and elegance. Baroque art is largely camp about religion. The ballet is camp about love', *The World in the Evening*, (London, Methuen, 1984, p. 125).

47 Harold Rosenberg has written that 'Rivers' was "talent" in the Broadway or Hollywood sense of skill practiced to arouse an assortment of feelings.' In the same article, he argues that 'Rivers was prepared to renew art with the shady lyricism of the Sunday supplement.' Harold Rosenberg, 'Rivers' Commedia Dell' Arte', *Art News*, April 1965, vol. 64, p. 35.

48 Hunter, *Larry Rivers*, p. 24.

49 This was a culture in which, as Harold Rosenberg wrote in *Art News* in 1952, '(t)he test of any of the new paintings is its seriousness – and the test of its seriousness is the degree to which the act on the canvas is an extension of the artist's total effort to make over his experience' ('The American Action Painters', in *The Tradition of the New*, New York, Horizon, 1959, p. 33).

50 See Andrew Parker and Eve Kosofsky Sedgwick (eds), *Performativity and Performance*, London, Routledge, 1995, pp. 4–5 for a related discussion of the 'homophobic thematics' of the theatrical performative in Austin.

51 In an unpublished parodic play written in 1954, *Kenneth Koch: A Tragedy*, O'Hara and Rivers demonstrate their knowledge of how they were seen as 'inauthentic' or not-quite-men in Abstract Expressionist circles. They imagine a conversation undertaken by Pollock, Kline and others in their absence in the Cedar Tavern which was the Abstract Expressionists' chief social

haunt. The immediate mention of O'Hara's and Rivers' names is met by calls of 'phonies', 'fags' and 'cheapskates' (the play remains unpublished in its entirety but is printed in part in Rivers and Weinstein, *What Did I Do?*, pp. 277–80). For Rivers it seems it was the 'inauthentic' masculinity of O'Hara that becomes revalorized by his hip sensibility as, paradoxically, *the* authentic and transgressive form of artistic subjectivity. By parading an 'inauthentic' relation to gender and by drawing attention to the conventions of what passes as 'serious' culture, O'Hara's and Rivers's campiness can be seen to undermine the ontological condition of straight subjectivity and meaning as constituted within 1950s artistic culture.

52 See Boone, 'Gay Language as Political Praxis', pp. 59–63.

53 Frank O'Hara, 'Personism: A Manifesto', in Donald Allen (ed.), *The Collected Poems of Frank O'Hara*, Berkeley, University of California Press, 1995, p. 499.

54 See Boone, 'Gay Language as Political Praxis', pp. 80–86.

55 Marjorie Perloff, *Frank O'Hara: Poet Among Painters*, New York, George Braziller, 1977, pp. 92–6, 99–105. See also Irving Sandler, *The New York School*, p. 108. Rivers himself is quoted as saying that his painting is 'a kind of autobiography, even a visual gossip column' in Grace Glueck, 'Rivers Paints Himself into the Canvas', *New York Times Magazine*, 13 February, 1966, pp. 78–9.

56 Sandler, *The New York School*, p. 108.

57 Howard Griffin, 'Larry Rivers', *Art News*, December 1956, vol. 55, p. 9.

58 Cited in Sandler, *The New York School*, p. 108.

59 The term 'vernacular glance' is Brian O'Doherty's cited in Sandler, ibid., p. 179.

60 In 1955 O'Hara became an associate curator of painting and sculpture at the Museum of Modern Art. This presaged a more intensive engagement with art criticism thereafter, resulting in the writing of, among other things, a small monographic study of Pollock in 1959.

61 Frank O'Hara, 'Notes on Second Avenue', in Allen (ed.), *The Collected Poems of Frank O'Hara*, p. 497.

62 Boone, 'Gay Language as Political Praxis', pp. 75–86; and Rudy Kikel, 'The Gay Frank O'Hara', *Gay Sunshine*, 1978, no. 35, p. 8–9.

63 Rosenberg, 'The American Action Painters'.

64 Ibid., pp. 27–8. See Amelia Jones, *Postmodernism and the En-gendering of Marcel Duchamp*, New York, Cambridge University Press, 1994, p. 21 for some useful remarks on the gendering of Abstract Expressionist discourse.

65 Thomas B. Hess, 'Larry Rivers' History of the Russian Revolution', *Art News*, October 1965, p. 58. If this marks a difference between Rivers's and Pollock's articulation of surface then the same could be said of the performative undoing of the artistic ego in Rivers as opposed to Rauschenberg. As both Caroline Jones and Jonathan Katz have argued, the work of Rauschenberg and Jasper Johns can be viewed in terms of its performative absenting of the bodily ego of Abstract Expressionism. By contrast 'Ego' is written large in Rivers's life and work and yet it is simultaneously undermined by its campy articulation. The disarticulation of ego in Rauschenberg is different – distinctly more Cagean than camp in its orientation. See Caroline A. Jones, 'Finishing School: John Cage and the Abstract Expressionist Ego', *Critical Inquiry*, Summer 1993, vol. 19, pp. 628–65 and Katz in this volume.

66 Thomas B. Hess, 'Larry Rivers' History of the Russian Revolution' and John Adkins Richardson, 'Dada, Camp, and the Mode Called Pop', *Journal of Aesthetics and Art Criticism*, Summer 1966, vol. 24, no. 4, pp. 549–58.

67 Richardson, 'Dada, Camp, and the Mode called Pop', p. 552.

68 Ibid.

69 Ibid.

70 Ibid.

8

THE POLITICS OF FEMINIST
SPECTATORSHIP AND THE
DISRUPTIVE BODY
De Kooning's *Woman I* reconsidered

Fionna Barber

In 1953, Willem de Kooning first exhibited his most famous series of paintings on the theme of the female figure at the Sidney Janis Gallery. Entitled 'Paintings on the theme of the Woman', these have since been surrounded by a vast critical discourse, and have acquired a canonical status in histories of modernism. With the unsurprising exception of Clement Greenberg, who saw de Kooning's work at this time as an engagement with the spatial dialectic of late Cubism, many of their initial viewers already perceived their meanings in highly gendered terms.[1] One writer, Andrew Ritchie, who wrote the catalogue entry for de Kooning's showing at the 1954 Venice Bienniale, described them in terms that revealed a clear engagement with the Jungian archetypes so prevalent within 1950s constructions of gender, while simultaneously identifying the *Women* with violence and destruction: 'de Kooning's Eves, Clytemnestras, Whores of Babylon, call them what you will, have a universality, an apocalyptic presence that is rare in the art of any time or any country'.[2] This frame of reference was later reinforced by de Kooning's own comparisons of the *Women* to Mesopotamian statuary, and to his claim in 1956 that 'maybe I was painting the woman in *me*'.[3] The feminist art history which emerged subsequently in the 1970s was also to make specific links between these paintings and actual violence against women, an attribution which, in effect, set the limits of a discourse by identifying areas which were neither desirable nor indeed permissible for feminist spectatorship. What I want to do in this essay is to *challenge* these limits through the premise that, rather than being static or predetermined, meaning in visual culture is something continually enacted through the operations of art historians, critics, and other interested viewers. Interpretation, in this view, becomes an ongoing, performative process. In this case, my exploration initially takes the form of an investigation of a formative moment in the body of this criticism, before moving on to suggest other possible ways of reading images such as *Woman I*. (Plate 8.1).

The detailed reconstruction of the meanings attributed to these works at the moment of their reception has already been undertaken elsewhere. David Cateforis has provided a valuable historical overview of the critical reception of the 'Women' paintings, in addition to the arguments advanced by Michael Leja in his important text *Reframing Abstract Expressionism*, where the discussion of these works by de Kooning is used to contribute to

127

Plate 8.1 Willem de Kooning, *Woman I*, 1950–2. Courtesy of the Museum of Modern Art, New York

the development of his thesis of a highly significant 'Modern Man' discourse in the 1950s. [4] And within the field of feminist discourse the recent essay by Griselda Pollock, 'Killing Men and Dying Women: A Woman's Touch in the Cold Zone of American Painting in the 1950s', is of particular relevance. [5] Here the frame of sexual difference surrounding Abstract Expressionism is shifted through the necessity of explaining aspects of the work of female practitioners Lee Krasner and Helen Frankenthaler, an analysis that is situated against a discussion of two paintings by de Kooning, *Woman V* (1952–3), and *Marilyn Monroe* (1954). I am not taking issue with the importance of Pollock's essay in terms of its extension of a feminist understanding of the relationship between gendered subjectivity and the production of painting in the 1950s. But the construction of Pollock's argument is such that it only allows for the production of an all too familiar 'de Kooning', one whose images of women are, for example, 'viciously covered, strangled, trapped, or wrenched in or out of shape'. [6] My concern here is that there are other aspects of feminist spectatorship in the 1990s, whose interests are not advanced by the repetition of the existing critical discourse in this manner; rather, we need to begin to identify other ways of reading de Kooning's 'Women' paintings without necessarily reinstating their marginality to feminism. But apart from an interest in the ongoing critique of the operations of art history implicit in the notion of performativity as a critical strategy, as so often with these projects there is an autobiographical interest. I want to try to understand *my* pleasure in these paintings, a pleasure that is problematic by its very existence. As a feminist, I feel that I've been caught looking, caught speaking, in the territory of deviance in even wanting to name a desire capable of being triggered by these works.

The re-evaluation of questions of spectatorship in relation to de Kooning opens up the potential of readings by other marginalized subjects: what might, for instance, a critically positioned gay male spectatorship make of these paintings? The intention of this reassessment is not to privilege a unified and universalized female viewer with the sole right to reconsider a response to these works, but my focus on issues of specifically female spectatorship is largely generated by the fact that the body in the painting is *seen* to be female. This designation has for some time resulted in readings of a homology between perceptions of a violated painted body and a violated physical body: harm to the physical body is believed to be equated with – and legitimized by – the alleged harm done to the body on the canvas. And as such, the discursive shift that I'm proposing here has a parallel in another field of feminist political agency, one that is not unconnected. The integration within feminist politics since the 1970s of action against violence against women and pornography has had considerable consequences for the assessment of paintings such as *Woman I*: as some examples should make clear, the possibility of readings other than of violence and objectification has become hugely overdetermined, if not regarded as completely inadmissible, within feminist critical discourse.

However, in relation to pornography, feminist debates have shifted considerably since the arguments of the late 1970s encapsulated in Robin Morgan's slogan 'Pornography is the Theory, Rape is the Practice' and promoted within the writings of cultural feminists such as Andrea Dworkin or Susan Brownmiller .[7] Although frequently very persuasive through their use of highly emotive language, these were arguments which relied on a huge instrumental power being attributed to visual representation as responsible not just for the objectification of the female body, but for actual violence against women. [8] More recently however, there has been a discursive shift that would have been unthinkable in the feminist politics of the 1970s. That any degree of objectification in pornography will *inevitably* be harmful to women is itself open to question in the diversity of sexual identities which have emerged since the mid–1980s. And the notion of women as active spectators and consumers of the erotic calls into play a range of subject positions. Writing in 1991, for example, Feminists Against Censorship pointed out that objectification itself can play a role in the fantasies of individuals across a range of sexual identifications without necessarily having further consequences beyond the role of erotic play .[9] The recent work of Lorraine Gamman and Merja Makinen around notions of female fetishism, meanwhile, has helped to problematize this previously taboo area even further. [10] While not necessarily proposing a celebration of objectification in de Kooning's paintings of women, I am proposing that a similar shift needs to occur within the feminist discourse that surrounds them, to a point where a range of subject positions can be evoked, rather than just one. This is an issue bound up with the recognition of desires for the forbidden. As Carole S. Vance has argued, in writing retrospectively on the 1982 Barnard College conference 'Towards a Politics of Sexuality', a highly controversial exploration of the complex ambiguities of women's desires: 'Feminism must increase women's pleasure and joy, not just decrease women's misery.'[11]

Yet the meanings of a painting such as *Woman I* are determined by the nature of the discursive field which it encounters, and so before beginning to identify any new or revised positions, it is useful to map out the identifications attributed to these works within earlier feminist statements. Throughout the 1970s and 1980s, Carol Duncan's critique was the most fully formulated, reinforced by the accounts of other historians, critics, and practitioners who were part of the developing feminist consciousness within the United States. These need to be considered briefly before moving on to look at Duncan's arguments in more detail. Linda Nochlin, for example, has retrospectively described a course on Women and Art which she taught at Stanford College in 1971 as incorporating discussion of 'de Kooning's brutal tactics in his "Women".'[12] This was a view reiterated by Cindy Nemser in her 1975 publication *Art Talk* where, in interviewing Grace Hartigan, she suggested that the content of de Kooning's paintings of women embodied a misogynist violence. But Hartigan, herself an Abstract Expressionist painter, refused to play the game, replying that 'the violence is in the paint. De Kooning's women are very loving' – a view distinctly at odds with the dominant view of de Kooning currently under construction within feminist discourse. [13] Meanwhile, a major tendency emerging within feminist art practice was that represented by Judy Chicago. As she made clear in her highly confessional autobiography *Through the Flower* published in 1975, this was a practice involving an explicit language of sexual identity and naturalized femaleness based around a notion of biological difference – precisely the kind of reductive terms within which de Kooning's images of women could be seen to function as a trope of an aggressive masculine sexuality.[14] Significantly both Nochlin and the critic Lucy Lippard adopted positions which distanced them from such biological reductivism, Nochlin arguing famously in her 1971 essay 'Why Have There Been No Great Women Artists?' that 'the fault lies not in our stars, our hormones, our menstrual cycles, or our empty internal spaces, but in our institutions and our education'. [15] This degree of caution applied to explanations of the work of *women* as cultural practitioners was allied to the political imperatives of feminism, which at this point included a very real need to make visible and give serious consideration to previously overlooked work by women artists.

As a consequence it is easy to see why feminist art historians, critics, and practitioners have tended to see de Kooning's work as having little to offer the female viewer other than a means of evidencing the inequalities of gender difference. An important 1989 essay by Carol Duncan, for example, 'The MoMA's Hot Mamas', develops ideas which first appeared in two other locations, a 1977 article for the feminist publication *Heresies* and entitled 'The Esthetics of Power in Modern Erotic Art' and the essay 'MoMA: Ordeal and Triumph on 53rd Street' co-authored with Alan Wallach and published in its initial form in *Studio International* in 1978.[16] 'The MoMa's Hot Mamas' presents strong arguments about the function of paintings such as de Kooning's *Woman I* or Picasso's *Les Demoiselles d'Avignon* within the Museum of Modern Art, in terms of their ability to articulate and reinforce the construction of gender differentials within a significant cultural location through an emphasis on the 'monstrosity' of their female subject-matter. A key feature of this text is Duncan's claim that an effect of the prominent hanging of these two works is to 'assign . . . women to a visitor's gallery where they may watch but not enter the central arena of high culture'.[17] Within this argument *Woman I* thus becomes analogous to images of pornography signalled within public space, such as a billboard advertisement for *Penthouse* on a New York street and rephotographed by Duncan for inclusion in her essay; both have become instrumental in securing the marginalization of actual women. As Duncan concludes,

> [W]hat is true in the street may not be so untrue in the museum, even though different rules of decorum may make it seem so. Inside or outside, such images wield great authority, structuring and reinforcing the psychic codes that determine and differentiate the real possibilities of women and men.[18]

In this essay the comparison of the function of painting and pornography is highly significant, not least because one of the strengths of feminist interventions within art history has been to shift the terms of debate beyond that of iconographic identification or formalist explanation alone, and towards an awareness that visual images are themselves a site of struggle within which the social inequalities between men and women are both enacted and contested. Reclaiming access to sites of the formation of cultural power is obviously of great importance within a feminist political agenda; Duncan's discussion of the sources of de Kooning's imagery within mythical tropes of female monstrosity represents a valuable analysis of the visual means whereby gender difference is sustained and replicated. Yet beyond this necessary deconstruction there is a further question, and one which is perhaps more problematic for feminist critics or historians: Is there any possibility of a reinvestment of gendered signification in de Kooning's paintings? Or are these images so overdetermined that they deny any possibility of intervention?

As a critical project the reappraisal of gender issues within de Kooning's work is long overdue, with the consequence that the canonical power attributed to these images remains unchallenged. Duncan's argument for the effectivity of images such as *Woman I* as ritual objects, bound up with the materialization of psychical dramas around issues of identity, continues to retain a lot of explanatory power – and as Cateforis has argued, the terms of the feminist debate became a dominant feature of the more extensive discourse surrounding the Women paintings in the 1980s. One example of this is in Robert Rosenblum's essay entitled 'The Fatal Women of Picasso and de Kooning', published in *Artnews* in October 1985, in which he cites as a particular influence on de Kooning the retrospective exhibition of Chaim Soutine, held at MoMA in 1950. For Rosenblum, de Kooning's painting becomes an act of violence – he claims that the Soutine retrospective 'would have supported de Kooning's audacity in handling pink and red paint as if he were a wrestler or rapist attacking resistant flesh.'[19]

In tracking the construction of meaning for de Kooning's paintings of women across the different moments of their critical reception, Cateforis acknowledged the ability of feminist criticism to make connections between these paintings and cultural power relations between men and women. Yet he also denounced Duncan's critique of de Kooning's 'Women' paintings as 'unacceptably narrow' and as reliant ultimately on totalizing meanings similar to earlier formalist readings of the same works.[20] Rather than reduce this to a mere failure of criticism, as Cateforis appears to do, I would counter that Duncan's claim needs to be situated within a knowledge of the feminist politics around issues of visual representation which clearly informed the production of her argument. Otherwise feminism's explanatory power is thus relegated to a shadowy presence, the background to a foreground of an academic discourse of reification and classification. More importantly, the vital question of feminism and spectatorship is once again strangled at birth.

But there are further, more radical, implications if we regard the construction of gender in the existing feminist discourse on de Kooning within Judith Butler's terms of the 'performative' which she develops in *Gender Trouble: Feminism and the Subversion of Identity*.[21] Butler uses Foucault to investigate the increasing instability of the notion 'woman' as a category within feminist theory. A fundamental aspect of her argument is that the relationship between gender and identity is something that is actively constructed, in addition to being both variable and historically contingent. 'Woman', she argues, needs to be understood as a term subject to processes of regulation and restrained by structures of power. For a feminist critique, any attempt to comprehend how the category of 'women', the subject of feminism, is produced, and any desire to effect the emancipation of 'women' within such a framework, is always going to be problematic.[22] Gender is thus produced *performatively*, a term that, for Butler, involves some sense of it being framed or given stability by a further set of regulatory practices, so that it 'constitut[es] the identity it is purported to be'. Hence 'there is no gender identity behind the expressions of gender; ... identity is performatively constituted by the very 'expressions' that arc said to be its results'.[23]

Butler's arguments provide powerful ammunition for a view of 'woman' as no longer either universal or unified. The question remains, however, of the application of this position to issues of feminist art history and spectatorship and, more specifically, to the problems affecting a reading of paintings such as de Kooning's *Woman I*. I would argue that one example of Butler's regulatory practices could be a feminist politics of representation, if this is construed as one that both privileges some versions of female identity as acceptable for feminist spectatorship and denies others. As an alternative, I am suggesting that *Woman I* becomes the site of a gender identity that is enacted rather than pre-given, one whose *active* construction by feminist spectators has been given stability through the existing terms of feminist art history, and in relation to the category of feminist political activity – in this case around issues of pornography and violence against women. Such a recognition also allows for a further discursive shift: namely, the possibility of a feminist spectator's perception of a different kind of non-reductive or non-essentialist gender identity enacted within the painting. In keeping with Butler's proposals, this recognition in turn acquires its stability of meaning in relation to a feminist cultural politics which is itself engaged with the postmodern destabilization of identity, and with the recognition of desire as both perverse and ambiguous rather than as necessarily regulated within the channels of normative heterosexuality. This is a case of taking on board a revised viewing context, one that registers a shift within feminist theory and critical analysis towards an increasing fluidity of both sexual and gendered identities. It may be taken to a point where it may even be problematic to refer to '*the* female gaze' in a way that was possible in earlier versions of feminist cultural politics. Feminist spectators, whether art historians or other informed or professional subjects, can no longer be regarded as a single category who, in turn, will produce unified readings of 'woman' as subject-matter constituted through representation.

One position that emerges as capable of offering a more productive reading of paintings such as *Woman I* is Mary Russo's formulation of the female grotesque. [24] It is certainly not the only possible reading, but one that can offer a way out of the deadlock facing feminist spectatorship in this instance. Drawing on the work of both Bakhtin and Kristeva, Russo's notion of the grotesque is one that focuses on the transgressive aspects of the body's cultural significations – the excessive, the uncontained, a body that is both cavernous and oozing secretions from its orifices – and which names this body as female. As in Bakhtin, this is defined in opposition to the classical body – monumental, contained, and transcendent, but also primarily identified with the domain of masculinity. [25] Significantly, in a key work executed some ten years prior to *Woman I* de Kooning engaged with the representation of the classical body, which he specifically named as masculine. This was the painting *Seated Figure* (*Classic Male*) (1940) in which the upper torso of a seated figure becomes the site of articulations of masculinity (Plate 8.2). Here the readings of gender appear to be secured by de Kooning's use of a charcoal line to define a solid muscularity contained within an ordered format reminiscent of the protecting armature of a breastplate. Yet even within such an overt display of 'classical' masculinity, the signs of gender are unstable and heterogeneous. The same line, for example, also sweeps upwards to pick out delicate facial features more easily legible as signifiers of femininity. Although not fully identifiable (as yet) in terms of the grotesque, even here elements of the feminine appear to nudge the dominance of the masculine. Indeed, an instability of gendered readings of de Kooning's paintings and drawings of male subjects of the late 1930s and early 1940s was noted retrospectively by one of his main champions, Thomas Hess, who described them as 'men who can – and indeed will – turn into women'. [26] The secure identification of gender in de Kooning's figurative works would thus seem to be a more complex business than at first appears.

Significantly one of the key distinctions between Russo's and Bakhtin's categorization of the grotesque is that for Russo the grotesque as female is not something to be repressed. Rather it should be recognized as part of a discursive field across which female identities may be constituted; a field which evokes the inner space of fantasy as much as it transgresses the norms of the body as socially regulated. The focus on the construction of 'monstrosity' implicit within the notion of the grotesque is thus itself something that can be revalorized to suggest somewhat different readings from Duncan's earlier arguments concerning de Kooning's painting. But to what extent can a notion of the grotesque be taken further, to inform a reading of *Woman I*? It might help to consider how such an interpretation may be derived, within the tendency to read formal elements of the painting as signifying in gendered terms. The degree of disjuncture in the figure's twisted pose is often cited as the body dismembered and then reconstructed by the controlling brushstroke, as evidence of violence done to the body of the woman. My problem with this, as a feminist spectator, is that this explanation cannot accommodate my pleasure in seeing *Woman I* as constituting a

Plate 8.2 Willem de Kooning, *Seated Figure (Classic Male)*, 1940. Courtesy of Thomas Ammann Fine Art, Zurich

body in process: one that is embodied through the slow additive means of brushstroke onto canvas, but also one that departs from more normative representations of femininity. In the case of *Woman I* this cumulative process was extreme: de Kooning began work on the canvas in 1950 and worked on it for two years before it was finished. The process was documented in one of the earliest accounts of its production, Thomas Hess's essay 'De Kooning Paints a Picture', which appeared in *Artnews* prior to the painting's exhibition in 1953, accompanied by photographs by Rudolph Burckhardt tracking the slow emergence of the figure in its finished form. [27]

On examination, the dialectical relationship of order and disorder, with its implications of the relationship between masculine and feminine, continues to play a major role in the structure of this painting. The figure is contained within a play of horizontal and vertical brushstrokes, particularly visible at the bottom left and top right of the painting's background, and reinforced by the strip of relatively unworked canvas, which, according to Hess, only became visible at the right edge at a late stage in the painting's completion.[28] This is a grid format that emphasizes the displacement of the left shoulder - a consistent feature of de Kooning's figure paintings which also appeared in *Classic Male*. It contains the prominent breasts, and provides a compositional basis for the dislocation of the legs and lower torso. Despite its partial derivation from a window clearly visible at the top right in earlier stages of the painting, in the finished version the grid becomes the containing mechanism for the visceral qualities of paint out of which the grotesque body emerges. Indeed, it is precisely this contrast that permits this process of incarnation, not just in terms of a formal structure, but one that coalesces into highly gendered significations .[29] The cantilevered torso is one of the most striking features of this work, given structure and solidity through the degree of underpainting. Yet, as in the earlier *Classic Male*, this is also one of the key sites of the articulation of a gendered body; the masculine breastplate has become transformed into prominent breasts, unequivocal signs of a corporeal femininity that contrast with the lower part of the body, clothed and contained in skirt and platform shoes. Meanwhile, the grimacing smile and confrontational gaze which are so easily categorized as the mark of the castrating mother encourage psychoanalytic readings that are not necessarily productive in this context of the grotesque unless the castrating mother can be recognized as not necessarily 'bad'. A different possibility is that they may be read as signifiers capable of becoming legible within the terms of the grotesque: a point of identification beyond normative femininity and a representation which, although both threatening and deviant, is also empowering for its spectators. It is the subtle play of a range of disjunctures that add up to the sense of a body incapable of being regulated within more restrictive representations: formal structure and expressive handling of paint, order and disorder, masculine and feminine. The grotesque body, as represented in *Woman I*, becomes one that evokes Kristeva's claim that 'the grotesque is the undoer of narcissism' in its ability to destabilize categories of beauty and the normative female body.[30]

Obviously, shifting the painting into yet another set of critical terms of reference is not radical in itself, unless this is a move grounded within a feminist politics. But these are terms which involve a degree of risk-taking, messing with the established discourses that surround such a canonical painting as *Woman I*. No longer contained within the existing terms, she has become a disorderly woman behaving badly in public, but with full knowledge of her right to occupy that space.

NOTES

This is a revised version of a paper given at the Association of Art Historians conference, London, 1997.

1 C. Greenberg, 'American Type Painting' (1955), in J. O'Brian (ed.), *Clement Greenberg: The Collected Essays and Criticism*, vol. 3, Chicago, University of Chicago Press, 1995, pp. 221–2.

2 A. C. Ritchie, cited in D. Cateforis, *Willem de Kooning's 'Women of the 1950s': A Critical History of their Reception and Interpretation*, Ann Arbor, U.M.I. Press, 1993, p. 146.

3 W. de Kooning (1956), cited in M. Prather, *Willem de Kooning Paintings,* exhibition catalogue, Washington, National Gallery of Art and London, Tate Gallery, 1994, p. 132.

4 M. Leja, *Reframing Abstract Expressionism: Subjectivity and Painting in the 1950s*, New Haven, Yale University Press, 1993, pp. 203–74 .

5 G. Pollock, 'Killing Men and Dying Women: A Woman's Touch in the Cold Zone of American Painting', in F. Orton and G. Pollock, *Avant-gardes and Partisans Reviewed*, Manchester, Manchester University Press, 1997, pp. 219–94.

6 Pollock, op.cit., p. 258.

7 A. Dworkin, *Pornography: Men Possessing Women*, London, Women's Press, 1981; S. Brownmiller, *Against Our Will: Men, Women and Rape*, Harmondsworth, Penguin, 1976.

8 Dworkin, op. cit., pp. 129–32.

9 G. Rodgerson and E. Wilson (eds.), *Pornography and Feminism: The Case against Censorship*, London, Lawrence & Wishart, 1991, p. 54.

10 L. Gamman and M. Makinen, *Female Fetishism: A New Look*, London, Lawrence & Wishart, 1994.

11 C. Vance, 'Pleasure and Danger: Towards a Politics of Sexuality', in C. Vance (ed.), *Pleasure and Danger: Exploring Female Sexuality*, London, Pandora, 1992, p. 24.

12 L. Nochlin, 'Starting from Scratch', in N. Broude and M. D. Garrard (eds.), *The Power of Feminist Art: Emergence, Impact and Triumph of the American Feminist Art Movement*, London, Thames & Hudson, 1994, p. 135.

13 Hartigan, cited by C. Nemser, *Art Talk: Conversations with 15 Women Artists,* New York, Icon Editions, 1995, p. 136.

14 J. Chicago, *Through the Flower: My Struggle as a Woman Artist*, New York, Doubleday, 1977.

15 L. Nochlin, 'Why Have There Been No Great Women Artists?' (1971), in *Women, Art and Power and Other Essays*, London, Thames & Hudson, 1989, p. 150.

16 C. Duncan, 'The Esthetics of Power in Modern Erotic Art' (1977), reprinted in *The Aesthetics of Power: Essays in Critical Art History*, Cambridge, Cambridge University Press, 1993, pp. 109–20; C. Duncan and A. Wallach, 'MoMA: Ordeal and Triumph on 53rd Street', *Studio International,* 1978, no. 194, pp. 48–57. A revised version of this essay also appeared as 'The MoMA's Hot Mamas', in *Art Journal*, 1989, no. 48, pp. 171–8 and in Duncan *The Aesthetics of Power*, 1993, pp. 189–207.

17 Duncan, *The Aesthetics of Power*, p. 201.

18 *The Aesthetics of Power*, p. 206.

19 R. Rosenblum, 'The Fatal Women of Picasso and de Kooning', *Artnews,* October 1985, p. 100.

20 Cateforis, *Willem de Kooning's Women of the 1950s*, p. 318.

21 J. Butler, *Gender Trouble: Feminism and the Subversion of Identity*, London, Routledge, 1990.

22 Ibid., p. 2.

23 Ibid., p.25.

24 M. Russo, *The Female Grotesque: Risk, Excess and Modernity*, London, Routledge, 1994.

25 M. Bakhtin, *Rabelais and his World*, Bloomington, Indiana University Press, 1984; see also P. Stallybrass and A. White, *The Politics and Poetics of Transgression*, Ithaca, Cornell University Press, 1986.

26 T. Hess, *Willem de Kooning Drawings,* Greenwich, Conn., and London, Secker & Warburg, 1972, p. 25.

27 T. Hess, 'De Kooning Paints a Picture', *Artnews*, vol. 52, no. 1, 1953, pp. 30–33, 64–67.

28 Ibid.

29 The window is visible in most of the preliminary stages photographed by Burckhardt; in Hess, 'De Kooning Paints a Picture'.
30 J. Kristeva, cited in Russo, *The Female Grotesque*, p. 64.

9

'CATHOLIC TASTES'

Hurting and healing the body in Viennese Actionism in the 1960s[1]

Philip Ursprung

The actions of Günter Brus, Otto Mühl, Hermann Nitsch, and Rudolf Schwarzkogler in 1960s Vienna figure among the most spectacular events in recent art history. Nowhere else has such a comparably drastic and literal iconography of the body's violation and repair been developed. Performing shocking quasi-religious rituals of self-castration, rape, and slaughter using excrement, food, blood, and dead animals staged in secluded old coal-cellars and ruined castles, these artists combined subject-matter from an earlier Surrealist tradition with the shock tactics of a neo-avantgardist *épater le bourgeois*, while at the same time engaging with formalist issues raised by late modernist action painting. Because of this diverse heritage, the specific iconography of Actionism's use of the body and its relationship to painterly traditions has been studied in detail since the late 1980s.[2] Countless roots and references to ancient mythology,[3] Catholicism,[4] iconoclasm,[5] psychoanalysis,[6] national identity,[7] the trauma of 'Austro-fascism' during and after the Second World War,[8] and the history of styles, notably Tachism,[9] have been unearthed. However, while most historiographers, obsessed with the sheer quantity of data, have tended to get lost in the hermeneutical jungle of meaning cultivated by the contradictory and often vague rhetoric of Actionism itself, many artists have used Actionism as a rich, if decontextualized, source of formal reference.[10] Both historians and artists have also tended to reinforce the mythical structure of Actionism, thereby obscuring the phenomenon as a possible object of analysis.

By contrast, this essay proposes some historical and ideological references that might help to reopen the case of Actionism through an analysis that focuses on the last collective performance, *Art and Revolution*, in Vienna in 1968. I use the judicial/medical term 'case' because it refers to the German *Fall*, as commonly employed in the context of late nineteenth-century criticism after Nietzsche's *Der Fall Wagner* (1888). Unlike a legal or medical 'case', which calls for a closure, the *Fall* denotes an intellectual debate where various parties engage in an ongoing process of questioning and rewriting.

Therefore, I do not intend to foreclose the case of Actionism and provide any final, 'true' meaning. Neither do I intend to subscribe to an utopian 'openness' as an end in itself. I want rather, to articulate my own version of the case, while reflecting my own ambivalent standpoint as an art historian trained and based in the context of German-speaking academia (with its notorious neglect of the postwar period) and yet inclined towards the more innovative (and French-oriented) English-speaking academia. I mention this ambivalence to emphasize the difference between German-speaking and English-speaking art historical and art critical discourses, a difference echoing the hegemony of the postwar Anglo-American art world and the complex strategies within the German-speaking art world devised to cope with its relative marginality.

This difference (largely unnoticed on the English-speaking side and largely repressed on the German-speaking side) of course informs the topics and methodology of art historical discourses. This difference motivates my choice of Viennese Actionism as a particularly complex topic that challenges dominant interpretational models on either side of the Atlantic. And this difference is – to cite Peggy Phelan's characterization of performative writing – 'what I "wish all the same to say" (I want you to hear my wish as well as my miss).'[11]

On 7 June 1968, the Association of Socialist Students in Austria invited Günter Brus, Otto Mühl, Peter Weibel, Oswald Wiener, and Franz Kaltenbäck to participate in their event *Art and Revolution*[12] (Plate 9.1). A student opened the session with a paper on the possibilities of art in late-capitalist society. Mühl then gave a provocative, anti-American speech recalling the recent assassination of Robert Kennedy, and insulting members of the Kennedy clan. Weibel's contribution, a paper on the Minister of Finance and university professor, Dr Koren, dealt with the interrelatedness of media and discourse. The poet Wiener joined the speakers and gave another insulting diatribe. While the others were still speaking, Mühl entered the room with the members of his newly founded 'Direct Art Group' (Plate 9.2). As they undressed, each of them drank a bottle of beer. Then they performed a competition to see who could urinate furthest. The results were measured and written on the blackboard of the auditorium. After this competition, Mühl brought in a blindfolded masochist named Laurids whom he flagellated.

The most spectacular event, however, was the performance of Brus's *Action Number 33*. The artist, standing naked on a chair, slashed his chest and legs with a razor blade until the blood trickled down his body. Then, urinating into a glass and defecating onto the floor, he smeared his body with his own excrement, drank the urine, and stuck his fingers down his throat until he vomited. Finally, he proceeded to masturbate in front of the audience while singing the Austrian national anthem and the student's anthem, *Gaudeamus Igitur* (Plate 9.3).

This was not the first time such a performance had taken place. In a dry run for his piece, Brus had performed the action *Sheer Madness* four months before in February at the Reiffmuseum, at the invitation of the architecture school of the Aachen Institute of Technology (Plate 9.4). This event already contained the motifs of urinating and defecating. Furthermore, it was the first time that Brus had used razor blades to cut into his skin literally, thereby developing the motif of mutilating/slicing which he had employed in a metaphorical way in his earlier painterly actions such as *Self-Painting, First Hand-painting*, in December 1964.

Art and Revolution was meant to provoke – and it did. The public reaction was highly emotional. Although the majority of the 400 to 500 people in the audience were rather amused, the student activists immediately distanced themselves from the Actionists' performance. They had expected a debate, as announced on the posters, and felt let down by Weibel's and Wiener's mimicry of verbal protest. They probably saw themselves implicated within Brus's action and its use of masturbation as a critique of the intellectual narcissism and political neutrality of academia. Furthermore, Mühl's ironic homage to the favourite occupation of male students – namely, organizing laddish, macho beer-drinking

Plate 9.1 *Art and Revolution*, poster, 1968. Courtesy of *Schastrommel* and Günter Brus

Plate 9.2 *Art and Revolution*, action, University of Vienna, Neues Institutsgebäude, 7 June 1968. Courtesy of *Schastrommel* and Günter Brus

contests – probably did not serve the radical revolutionary image to which the student activists aspired.

A hostile press campaign ensued which defended the students and insisted that the 'university-swine'[13] were *not* students. This was probably the one and only time that the Austrian popular press supported students, but it reveals the closing of ranks against the Actionists' provocation. The Austrian state quickly mobilized its judicial system. Brus, Mühl, and Wiener were arrested, not for the first time in their careers, but this time the punishment was draconian. Mühl was sentenced to four weeks in prison for flagellating the masochist (the defamation of Robert Kennedy was never mentioned), and Brus received a six-month sentence for violating the Austrian flag and disturbing public order.

Viewed retrospectively, *Art and Revolution* can be seen as the climax and end-point of Austrian Actionism. After having worked together in various formations since the early 1960s, the group *de facto* dissolved soon afterwards.[14] Following his release from custody and the failure of an appeal, Brus fled to West Berlin with his family to evade imprisonment. After one last action in Munich – the infamous *Breaking Test* in June 1970 – he finally abandoned body performances and instead concentrated on drawing and poetry. He also instigated the historicization of his own oeuvre by founding the revue *Schastrommel* [The Farting Drum] ironically called the voice of the 'Austrian government-in-exile'.[15] He remained in Germany until the Austrian Chancellor Bruno Kreisky reduced his prison sentence to a fine in the late 1970s.

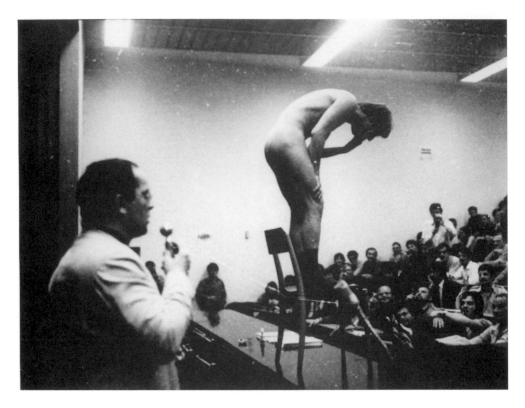

Plate 9.3 *Art and Revolution*, action, University of Vienna, Neues Institutsgebäude, 7 June 1968.
Courtesy of *Schastrommel*

Mühl, after leaving prison, effectively retired from the art world to found an alternative, free-living commune on an abandoned farm, Friedrichshof in Burgenland, where he established a large collection of Actionist art – especially his own.[16] Mühl's Action-Analytical Commune was forced to dissolve in 1990 and he served a six-and-a-half-year term after being convicted of child abuse. Nitsch, who had not participated in *Art and Revolution*, but who had been Mühl's closest collaborator in the mid-1960s, retired to his castle in Prinzendorf near the Czechoslovakian border, where, in his private grounds, he continues to work on the perfection of his six-day *Orgien Mysterien Theater* planned since the late 1950s. Rudolf Schwarzkogler, the youngest of the Viennese Actionists, died in 1969. His death, caused by either jumping or falling from the window of his apartment, was rapidly mystified, qualifying as a typical end for a self-destructive Actionist tendency.[17]

In terms of linear art history, Actionism led to a dead end. The location of the Viennese Actionists on the periphery of the international art world enforced an isolation that throughout the 1960s was only ameliorated by (mostly sensationalist) accounts in the popular press and reviews in newspapers. There were hardly any features in the established art magazines and so detailed information on the work of the Actionists was limited to publications by the artists themselves.[18] The only international event to which the Actionists were invited was the *Destruction in Art Symposium* in London in September 1966.[19] Unlike the American scene, where 'happeners' and performers such as Allan Kaprow, Carolee Schneemann, Yvonne Rainer, Dennis Oppenheim, Chris Burden, and Vito Acconci joined

Plate 9.4 Günter Brus, *Sheer Madness (Architecture of Sheer Madness)*, action, Aachen, Reiffmuseum, 6 February 1968. Courtesy of *Schastrommel* and Günter Brus

academic institutions, there is no such thing as an Actionist school and no consistent discursive model of interpretation.

Largely ignored in English-speaking discourse,[20] the historiography of Viennese Actionism is limited to the German-speaking sphere – where it is accounted for mainly by positioning the movement *ex post facto* into the linear evolution of an international mainstream. Thus, in various catalogue texts, Brus and Schwarzkogler are, on the basis of formal analogies, either declared to be 'forerunners' of international performance art, body art, and conceptual art or 'heirs' to Tachism and Art Informel.[21] These (often nationalistic) strategies of legitimization reinforce dominant formalistic and stylistic models of interpretation. Moreover, they tend to discourage any attempt to review Actionism's case and its marginal positioning using the tools of recent art historical revisionism.

Since I am interested in the differences between the English-speaking and the German-speaking discourses, my reading of the work of the Actionists, especially that of Brus, concentrates on questions of art politics and historical references and on actions in public spaces, namely the performance of the artists' bodies outside the studio or gallery.[22] But this raises a number of questions: Is it legitimate to neglect the (hostile) reception by the mass media, in search of 'the authentic Viennese Actionism', as Peter Gorsen, the closest observer and theoretician of Actionism since the mid-1960s, suggests?[23] Or does the 'meaning' of Actionism itself reside precisely in the process of fragmentation, distortion, and (mis)understanding of an ephemeral event in the spectator's and historian's memories? Was the Actionists' reference to the (artist's own) body and their symbolic rather than indexical use of it an expression of a reactionary attitude, perhaps motivated by the feeling of frustration and loss in the midst of a fast-moving (art)world – not to mention the feeling of loss after the *Zusammenbruch*, the lost war? Or was it a short-lived revelation of subversive, anarchic action that the establishment was unable to appropriate?

With these questions in mind, there are striking parallels between the Actionists' position and artists' roles as defined within the *fin de siècle* German-speaking concept of *Kultur*.[24] As Norbert Elias shows in his *Studien über die Deutschen*,[25] *Kultur* promised by means of aesthetics to compensate for the political frustration, social alienation, class struggle, and rapid changes imposed by modernity in the late nineteenth century. The economically powerful but politically disadvantaged middle class claimed a monopoly of this field since it promised to distinguish them as *Bildungsbürger* not only from the aristocracy but from the proletariat as well. *Kultur*, 'apolitical or even anti-political',[26] promised in principle to be more 'direct' than parliamentarism, relatively more 'popular' than aristocratic elitism, more 'humane' than capitalism, and more 'nationalistic' than socialism. From such a perspective, *Kultur* can be seen as a Utopian field open for the inscription of changing collective desires for the sublimation of anxieties and for the symbolic performance of political struggles. *Kultur* – approached through Herbert Marcuse's concept of 'affirmative culture'[27] – functioned as a 'better world' and as the last bastion against the brutal dynamics of modernity (although, paradoxically, it had also to be 'modern' and to articulate the *Zeitgeist*).

By the late nineteenth century, the German cultural field consisted of rapidly growing sectors such as museums, concert halls, journalism, and universities. Various interest groups struggled to increase their control over these infrastructures. The situation grew particularly complicated for the newly established German-speaking art world in the late nineteenth century after an 'invasion' of French art, especially Impressionism and post-Impressionism, buoyed by the growing success and rising prices of French works on the international art market.

As a result, the 'deficiencies' of German and Austrian art when compared to French art (namely the technical inferiority of German painters and the less sophisticated critical discourse) had to be turned into positive 'qualities' with clear signifiers of national difference. In the *feuilletons* of the German and Austrian press, the notion of *l'art pour l'art* became synonymous with the 'superficiality' of French art. By comparison, modern German art, exemplified by the highly praised allegorical paintings of the Swiss painter Arnold Böcklin, was considered 'deep' and intellectually demanding, democratic in its appeal. In a series of negative antinomies, French 'wit' as perceived in the prints of Henri de Toulouse-Lautrec was opposed to the Germanic 'humour' of the paintings of Franz von Stuck. Pierre Puvis de Chavannes's 'cold virtuosity' was compared unfavorably to German painter Hans Thoma's 'sympathetic clumsiness'.[28]

Unlike in France, where avant-garde artists radically opposed bourgeois values and keenly articulated the discontinuities of 'modern life', the leading German and Austrian artists of the 1890s were positioned as being largely 'apolitical' and 'anti-modern' yet advocating a Utopian social community which promised a better life inherent within the realm of *Kultur*.

Julius Langbehn's *Rembrandt als Erzieher*, published in 1890 and often reprinted throughout the first half of the twentieth century, contributed to this trend of disseminating the ideology of cultural internalization and reinforcing the status of the artist as a cultural hero.[29] Critics and historians similarly proposed the artist's 'personality' with its inflated notions of 'originality' as exemplary for the middle-class intelligentsia. Throughout the last two decades of the nineteenth century, artists such as Giovanni Segantini, Gustav Klimt, or Arnold Böcklin were literally worshipped by an increasing number of admirers alongside the ranks of established cultural heroes of the *Bildungsbürgertum* such as Luther, Rembrandt, Goethe, Beethoven, Nietzsche, and Wagner. By the turn of the century – to take one example – the *Böcklin-Kult* was sustained by innumerable publications, adulatory ceremonies, and the wide distribution of affordable reproductions of his paintings. Equally, by 1908, it was credible for Klimt to proclaim that 'for us, artisthood signifies the ideal community of artistic creators and beholders.'[30]

This unique yet contradictory 'crystal' of 'affirmative culture' with its various facets, some progressive and some reactionary, disintegrated with the end of the German and Austrian empires in 1918, some of its fragments to be appropriated by fascism in the 1930s. Yet, certain aspects survived late into the twentieth century, notably the function/projection of the 'artist as cultural hero', be it as a nostalgic evocation of the past or as a Utopian evocation of the future.

For my argument, it is noteworthy that the beginning of the Actionists' careers in the late 1950s corresponded exactly to the nostalgic revival of *fin de siècle* Vienna, which recycled as positive the ambivalent image of the artist as hero/martyr.[31] As a result, this stance was cultivated and criticized by the Actionists as a pastiche of the role-models offered by their predecessors.

It can be argued that such an ideological grounding in the notion of a crisis within a specifically 'Viennese' cultural past was urgently needed around 1960, for, as in 1900, the emergence of a powerful, highly sophisticated and theoretically well-armed artistic system was represented as a threat to the provincial, postwar status quo. This time the invasion of the German-speaking art world did not come from Paris but from New York in the form of Abstract Expressionism, Happenings, Pop art, and Minimalism. Once again the old enemy was back: *l'art pour l'art* – the self-referential, *brilliant*, elitist, successful, and exclusive companion of modernity. Arnulf Rainer, closely related to the Actionists, responded polemically in a 1962 article entitled 'L'art contre l'art'.[32]

With these cultural dynamics in mind, I propose to read the violent strain of Actionism as a specific formulation of a basically anti-modern impulse drawing on the earlier notion of 'affirmative culture'. The first collective action was Mühl's, Nitsch's, and Adolf Frohner's *The Blood Organ* in 1962. The Action started in a cellar rented by Mühl. The artists announced that they would wall up the cellar and stay there for three days without eating or sleeping. In reality, the back entry remained open so that the artists could come and go. When the action was announced, Nitsch declared that 'I shall disembowel, tear and pull to pieces a dead lamb.[. . .]'[33] The opening up of the cellar three days later was performed by a young woman, especially hired for the event, in evening dress and high-heeled shoes, who ceremoniously kicked in the wall. The assemblages by Mühl and Frohner and the remains of Nitsch's 'lamb action' were exposed to the flashlights of reporters, gaining publicity that led to the exhibit being closed by the police after a couple of hours.

Nitsch's use of the slaughtered and crucified lamb can, of course, be seen as referring to religious iconography and to the cruelty of war. But his performance of the endless repetition of violence through the mutilating, hammering, slicing, and chewing of the lamb can be understood as a symbolic re-enactment of the brutalities of modernism (namely its erosion of the organic coherence of art within the context provided by German 'affirmative culture'). The same goes for Brus's symbolic mutilation of his own body with a razor blade. One is even tempted to read Brus's consumption of his own excrement as a somewhat bitter allusion to the closed circuits of modernism and as a performance of an 'organic' counterpart to the 'cold', alienated self-referentiality common to avant-garde modernist art.

In this context, it is important to note that the actions were hardly ever 'real' in the sense of actually slaughtering live animals or endangering the health of the participants. The animals were usually bought already slaughtered and Nitsch admitted using red paint for his actions because it 'looked more bloodlike than blood.'[34] The majority of the actions were performed without an audience present and were staged exclusively for the camera; even the seemingly dangerous actions of Brus were at no time life-threatening.[35]

I therefore cannot subscribe to Peter Gorsen's essentialist reading of the Actionists' Artaudian 'directness', or to his interpretation that the Actionists embody an 'art which returns to sensuality and life and transcends the crisis of language'[36]. Gorsen opposes the suppression of the 'real' body in the international, modernist mainstream of happenings in the 1950s and 1960s and the re-appropriation of the body by the Viennese Actionists and writes: 'The Viennese Actionists concretely and biographically experienced the [. . .] theory of 'art=life', and the theory of Happenings in general, as an unreal, *academic play*, contradicting their own life and work in Austria' (emphasis added).[37]

By shifting between contradictory active and passive roles, the Actionists were performing their own ambivalence to modernity. Within this context, Schwarzkogler's photographic tableaux of the artist as blind, lame, impotent, and as an irrational author *and* helpless victim of endless experiments are particularly evocative. And I propose to read Mühl's and Laurids's performance in *Art and Revolution* as one representative of the ambivalent situation of the artist as a sadist *and* a blindfolded masochist.

Nevertheless, as mentioned earlier, this contradictory attitude towards dominant modernist art is just one component of a complex *fin de siècle* artistic heritage. The other part concerns the compensatory substitution of political inadequacy through 'affirmative culture'. With this in mind, it is important to recall the context in which the actions were performed. Most of them, like *The Blood Organ*, originated in private places, such as apartments, studios or alternative galleries, and then revealingly transferred to public venues. The act of kicking in the wall (in *The Blood Organ*), and the moment of reception marked by the flashlights of public interest are more important than the artworks produced in the cellar during the actions.

The motif of the artist's body as place for the encounter of public and private, crucial to *Art and Revolution*, was first used in Brus's *Vienna Walk* (1965), two days before the opening of an exhibition of his paintings in the Galerie Junge Generation. *Vienna Walk* consisted of his walking around the centre of Vienna painted all in white with a black line over face and body (Plate 9.5). As a consequence, Brus was stopped by the police, sent home in a taxi and later fined. Nevertheless, the action was documented by a professional photographer and achieved widespread notoriety.

What such actions underscore is the fact that the public sphere in the highly oppressive society of postwar Austria was largely controlled by the state. In order to highlight this aspect, the Actionists had to expose and transgress the boundaries of the art world. In fact, since the state was the main addressee of Austrian Actionist politics, the police were the 'ideal' audience. After all, they really 'saw' and 'reacted' to the transgression. Their

Plate 9.5 Günter Brus, *Vienna Walk*, action, Vienna, 5 July 1965 (photograph: L. Hoffenreich). Courtesy of *Schastrommel* and Günter Brus

response was amplified by the hysterical overreaction of the mass media that made visible the authoritarian infrastructure of the postwar democracy. In fact, the documentary photographs of the arrests often show Mühl, Nitsch, and Brus surrounded by police officers; with the artists looking like actors enjoying the applause. In an odd way, the very moment of imprisonment can be read as a compensation for the lack of official recognition by museums.

Seen from such a perspective, *Art and Revolution* assumes particular significance because of its site specificity. It is the first and only one of the actions to have take place in an Austrian state institution, namely, the university;[38] and it is unique in that it included a large number of spectators. Insofar as it tested the viability of Actionism on a national level, it ultimately failed. However, the question remains, Did it also fail on an art historical level? From the perspective of performativity, I would argue that it was a success since in its failure it marked out an art historical shift. What *Art and Revolution* made clear was that there was not one public, but various publics. While the state audience – the judicial system and the popular press – reacted hysterically, the wider student audience just laughed. The student body could not be mobilized by the reactivation of that old chestnut of the artist as a mediator between social and political functions. The students did not want art *as* revolution nor art *instead* of revolution since they considered the two as separate domains.

For their part, the student activists were embittered by the artists' negative stances, by their lack of dialogue, and by their refusal to subscribe to the activists' political agenda. Equally, the Actionists' mimicry of the 'real' student revolution going on in Paris, Berlin, and the United States was considered offensive. In blurring the distinction between aggressor and victim, the Actionists openly subverted received political and moral agendas. Because of this, the Austrian Left saw Actionism as politically compromised and could never forgive their performance in the university. Subsequently, they were banned throughout the 1970s and 1980s and labelled neo-fascists.

What is most revealing from my perspective, however, is the response of the art critical and historical audiences who successfully repressed the topic. To take two examples. First, Gorson regrets the 'nihilism' of Actionism which he sees as 'forwarding its own execution' through the 'impotent and hateful gestures of protest' during the 'university action under the slogan "Art and Revolution"'.[39] Gorsen derogatively labels *Art and Revolution* a slogan rather than a title, thereby denigrating its historical importance. He seems *not* to consider *Art and Revolution* a work of art at all. In Gorsen's disappointment about a missing 'political concept of social transformation'[40] we can trace, I would argue, the remains of the *fin de siècle* ideology of the artist embodying the potential for politial transformation. Equally, Werner Hofmann, framing *Art and Revolution* within the context of artistic iconoclasm, condemns their fascist intentions stating that 'they performed methods of physical intimidation, submission, [...] comparable to fascist methods of terror.'[41]

Taken together, Hofmann's and Gorsen's refusal to acknowledge *Art and Revolution* as legitimately within the realm of art reflects their own *angst* as art historians. Faced with the possibility that artists might literally enter into the sphere of radical political action (as opposed to symbolically embodying a 'political concept of social transformation') they write them out of their histories.

Such an erasure is in marked contrast to the ways in which other 'political' art from the 1970s and 1980s has been interpreted by German-speaking art historians. Perhaps the best example is the treatment of Joseph Beuys. He became Germany's most controversial artist during the 1970s and his vague but striking idea of the 'expanded notion of art' (*erweiterter Kunstbegriff*) entered colloquial language. His gesture of 'expanding' the notion of art was welcomed by art historians and art critics because it promised cultural hegemony. Beuys, by veiling his own artistic strategies behind the imagery of disinterested collectivity ('social plastic'), perpetuated the mystery of art as a realm open to anyone ('everyone is an artist'). By contrast, the Actionists overtly displayed their collective authorship and revealed the location of their art in society. And whereas Beuys (with big impact in the art world and with virtually no impact on politics) performed the image of the omnipotent/universal artist and provided utopian models of social practice, the Actionists (with some impact in politics and virtually no impact in the art world) performed the very impotence/marginality of art.

The main art historical scandal of *Art and Revolution* was, I would argue, the ways in which it disclosed the futility of a utopian aspiration for art. Performing their bodies as contaminated and corrupted, the Actionists dramatically conveyed the impossibility of cultural autonomy.[42] By refusing to express identifiable, reproduceable 'meaning', by refusing to endorse the aesthetic mystification of art, and by systematically violating accepted cultural borderlines, *Art and Revolution* struck at the very *raison d'être* of art history and art criticism. It challenged the extraction and transfer of 'meaning' from the realm of culture to other spheres of society and questioned the viability of the very notion of 'communication'. In Brus's words:

> I reject the often sought incorporation of the audience into the action of the play. The results of such an experience are superficial (at the most, dance/music-related activity brings halfway valuable results). I don't reject such efforts totally, but feel however that one cannot do without more deep-going means. This is not, however, to be expected from those interested in furthering the development of the theater. Useful results are not a conglomerate made up of tomfoolery, post-dadaism and public participation in willy-nilly street theater socialism. Useful results have proven themselves first class. The action moves for the most part outside language or such - at least outside the speech and language normally used.[43]

Brus's polemic notion of 'willy-nilly street theater socialism' can, of course, be read as a critique of the practices of artistic 'Activism' emerging in Germany, France, and the United States in the late 1960s. More interesting for our purpose is Brus's proposal that the 'action' moves 'for the *most part* outside language *or some such*' (emphasis added), an idea comparable to Derrida's questioning of the univocality of the meaning of the term 'communication' in his paper 'Signature événement contexte' presented in 1971.[44] Addressing the art world, Brus's critique undermines the model of a disinterested exchange of meaning. Rather than refusing 'communication' or 'language' altogether, he stressed the fact that communication is not neutral but open to be (ab)used as an instrument of power.

For Hofmann and Gorsen, as for most other interpreters of Actionism, its 'nihilism' was and is unbearable. The 'true' meaning of Actionism, therefore, was and still is sought for elsewhere – either in the stylistic heritage of the Actionists' tangible works of art or in the 'expression' of certain ideas, but not in the performativity of the actions as such, nor in the random imprint of those actions in the mass media and the public memory, nor in the critique of the power of communication.

I do not know the 'true' meaning of *Art and Revolution*. In my view, its very resistance to participation by its beholders and by historians and the fact that the 'work of art' and the 'context' cannot be described separately are, at the present moment, a challenge to art historical practices of narrative description. In the particular 'balance' of expectation and frustration, of short-term preparation (the event was planned very rapidly after the student activists accepted the participation of the Viennese Actionists) and long-term effect, of irreproduceability and mass reproduction, lies, in my view, the 'beauty' of *Art and Revolution*. For art history it remains a legacy yet to be negotiated.

NOTES

1 I am very grateful for the excellent suggestions of Amelia Jones, Andrew Stephenson, Peter Friedl, Olav Westphalen, and Lynnette Widder when revising the essay. Special thanks go to Linda Cassens and Antonina Bevan Zlatar for their invaluable help in correcting my English, to Dieter Schwarz for providing unfindable source material, and to Günter Brus for his information and for kindly allowing me to reproduce the photographs of his work. I would also like to express my gratitude to the Institut für Geschichte und Theorie der Architektur at the

Swiss Federal Institute of Technology for enabling the completion of this essay.

2 See *From Action Painting to Actionism, Vienna 1960–1965. Günter Brus, Adolf Frohner, Otto Mühl, Hermann Nitsch, Alfons Schilling, Rudolf Schwarzkogler*, Museum Fridericianum, Kassel, Kunstmuseum Winterthur and Scottish National Gallery of Modern Art, Edinburgh (eds), Klagenfurt, Ritter Verlag, 1988, vol. 1; *Viennese Actionism. 1960–1971*, H. Klocker (ed.) in co-operation with Graphische Sammlung Albertina, Vienna and Museum Ludwig, Cologne, Klagenfurt, Ritter Verlag, 1989, vol. 2. Since Mühl insisted on manipulating the chronology and on the elimination of two articles from the first volume, an important addition is the chronology *Aktionsmalerei–Aktionismus. Wien 1960–1965*, Dieter Schwarz, Zurich, Seedorn Verlag, 1988. Recent surveys of Actionism include Peter Gorsen, 'Der Wiener Aktionismus: Begriff und Theorie', in P. Werkner (ed.), *Kunst in Österreich 1945–1995. Ein Symposium der Hochschule für angewandte Kunst in Wien*, Vienna, Wuv Universitätsverlag, 1996, pp. 140–54; R. Fleck, 'L'actionnisme viennoise', in *L'art au corps. Le corps exposé de Man Ray à nos jours*, Musées de Marseille, Réunion des Musées Nationaux, 1996, pp. 73–87; J. Hoffmann, *Destruktionskunst. Der Mythos der Zerstörung in der Kunst der frühen sechziger Jahre*, Munich, Verlag Silke Schreiber, 1995, pp. 25–36, 130–44; G. Berghaus, 'Happenings in Europe', in M. R. Sandford (ed.), *Happenings and Other Acts*, London, Routledge, 1995, pp. 362–8. Earlier surveys include P. Weibel with co-operation of V. Export (eds), *Wien. Bildkompendium Wiener Aktionismus und Film*, Frankfurt a. M., Kohlkunstverlag, 1970.

3 E. Stärk, *Hermann Nitsch's 'Orgien Mysterien Theater' und die 'Hysterie der Griechen'. Quellen und Traditionen im Wiener Antikenbild seit 1900*, Munich, Wilhelm Fink Verlag, 1987.

4 See W. Schmied, 'Hermann Nitsch', in *Gegenwart Ewigkeit. Spuren des Transzendenten in der Kunst unserer Zeit*, W. Schmied in co-operation with J. Schilling (eds), Berlin, Martin-Gropius-Bau and Stuttgart, Cantz, 1990, pp. 252–7.

5 W. Hofmann, 'Die Wiener Aktionisten', in *Luther und die Folgen für die Kunst*, W. Hofmann (ed.), Hamburg, Kunsthalle and Munich, Prestel Verlag, 1983, pp. 641–7.

6 Psychoanalysis is used in many art historical approaches as a key to the Actionists' intrinsic content. Considering the fact that Brus, Nitsch, and Mühl have a more or less professional background in psychology and therapy and that their rhetoric is based on psychoanalysis, I would argue that this kind of *key* applies to doors that are not locked at all.

7 See D. Ronte, 'Günter Brus', in *Günter Brus. Der Überblick*, H. Amanshauser and D. Ronte (eds), Vienna, Museum Moderner Kunst, and Salzburg, Residenz Verlag, 1986, pp. 5–9.

8 The references to war in Actionism have yet to be studied. Mühl, Nitsch, and Brus themselves constantly refer to their cathartic function as artists. The chronology by Dieter Schwarz, in *From Action Painting to Actionism, Vienna 1960–1965* (see note 1), p. 91, is extremely valuable with listing of traumatic experiences of the Actionists. Nitsch's and Schwarzkogler's fathers died in the war; Mühl, somewhat older than the others, held the rank of lieutenant and was imprisoned.

9 See R. Fleck, *Avantgarde in Wien: Die Geschichte der Galerie nächst St. Stephan 1954–1982, Kunst und Kunstbetrieb in Österreich, vol. 1, Die Chronik*, Vienna, Galerie nächst St Stephan and Locker Verlag, 1982, pp. 186–96.

10 The title of this essay refers to *Mike Kelley: Catholic Tastes*, E. Sussman (ed.), New York, Whitney Museum of American Art and Harry N. Abrams, 1993. Kelley's interest in Viennese Actionism is mentioned in the introduction by E. Sussmann, p. 17.

11 P. Phelan, *Mourning Sex: Performing Public Memories*, London, Routledge, 1997, p. 12.

12 Documentation can be found in P. Weibel, with co-operation of V. Export (eds) (1970) (see note 2), pp. 202–23, 262–4, 292; *Happening & Fluxus*, Cologne, Kölnischer Kunstverein, 1970, n.p.; *Die Schastrommel*, vol. 8b, Bolzano, 1972, pp. 98-140.

13 'Endlich die Uni-Ferkel verhaftet!' ['University swine arrested at last!'] and 'Polizei sagt: Uni-Ferkel sind keine Studenten' ['Police say: university swine are not students'] were the headlines in *Die Neue Zeitung*, 14 June 1968. 'Anklage gegen die Uni-Ferkel wurde sehr rasch erhoben' ['University swine quickly accused'] was the headline of *Kronen Zeitung*, 26 June 1968.

14 Although the participants came from different backgrounds and did not form a homogeneous group, they proclaimed on various occasions that their artistic aims were comparable and they regularly worked and performed together. The only manifesto-like publication was the review *Le Marais* published in July 1965 by Brus, Mühl, Nitsch, and Schwarzkogler, where Brus defines the group as the 'Wiener Aktionsgruppe'.

15 Starting in 1969 (no. 1) and ending in 1977 (no. 17), *Die Schastrommel* was published by Günter Brus in an edition of 500, first in Bolzano and, after 1975, in Berlin. Brus's own 'actions' are documented in: *Die Schastrommel*, no. 8a, 'Brus-Aktionen 1964–1966', no. 8b, 'Brus-Aktionen 1967–68', and no. 8c, 'Brus-Aktionen 1969–1970', Bolzano, 1972.

16 See R. Ohrt, '"Wiener Aktionismus"', *Texte zur Kunst*, vol. 2, no. 7, October 1992, pp. 77–87.

17 See, for a critical revision K. Stiles, 'Notes on Rudolf Schwarzkogler's Images of Healing', *White Walls*, vol. 25, Spring 1990, pp. 11-26.

18 One exception is the inclusion of Mühl and Nitsch in J. Becker and W. Vostell (eds), *Happenings. Fluxus, Pop Art, Nouveau Réalisme*, Reinbek, Rowohlt, 1965.

19 See the chapter on the Destruction in Art Symposium in J. Hoffmann, *Destruktionskunst* (see note 2), pp. 147–62. See also K. Stiles, 'Synopsis of the Destruction in Art Symposium (DIAS) and Its Theoretical Significance', *The Act: Performance Art*, vol. 1, no. 2, 1987, pp. 22–31.

20 K. Stiles is an exception. See note 17.

21 See P. Weibel, 'Zur Aktionskunst von Günter Brus', in *Günter Brus. Der Überblick* (see note 7), pp. 33–47, especially p. 47. Schwarzkogler as well is declared a 'forerunner of Body Art and Conceptual Art' in E. Badura-Triska's and H. Klocker's introduction to *Rudolf Schwarzkogler. Leben und Werk*, Vienna, Museum Moderner Kunst, Klagenfurt, Ritter Verlag, 1992, p. 8.

22 Amelia Jones's essay on the dis/playing of the phallus offers a variety of analytical tools that, applied to Viennese Actionism, promises a radically new reading of the performance of masculinity in the specific context of Catholicism. See A. Jones, 'Dis/playing the Phallus: Male Artists Perform their Masculinities', *Art History*, vol. 17, no. 4, December 1994, pp. 546–84.

23 Gorsen, 'Der Wiener Aktionismus' (see note 2), p. 151.

24 See the chapter 'Die Kategorien der Kunstkritik im "Atelier"', in my *Kritik und Secession. 'Das Atelier' – Kunstkritik in Berlin zwischen 1890 und 1897*, Basel, Schwabe Verlag, 1996, pp. 139–65.

25 N. Elias, *Studien über die Deutschen. Machtkampf und Habitusentwicklung im 19. und 20. Jahrhundert*, Frankfurt a. M., Suhrkamp, 1993. pp. 161–73; see also N. Elias, 'Zur Soziogenese der Begriffe "Kultur" und "Zivilisation,"' in N. Elias, *Über den Prozeß der Zivilisation*, Frankfurt a. M., Suhrkamp, 1976, pp. 1–64.

26 Elias, *Ein Exkurs über den Nationalismus* (see note 25), p.165.

27 H. Marcuse, 'Über den affirmativen Charakter der Kultur', *Zeitschrift für Sozialforschung*, VI/1, Paris, 1937.

28 An echo of this ideology, I would argue, can be heard in American anti-formalist criticism in the 1950s and 1960s. See Leo Steinberg's (ironic) remark, 'All honest work, from hammering to engineering, is preferable to facture and cuisine, or whatever it is the French put in their painting', in 'Other Criteria', in L. Steinberg, *Other Criteria: Confrontations with Twentieth-century Art*, New York, Oxford University Press, 1972, p. 60.

29 J. Langbehn, *Rembrandt als Erzieher*, Von einem Deutschen Leipzig, Hirschfeld, 1890.

30 C. Nebehay, *Gustav Klimt, Dokumentation*, Vienna, Verlag der Galerie Nebehav 1969, p. 394; see my '"Wir wollen eure Herolde sein!" Gustav Klimt und die secessionistisch Kunstkritik', in *Gustav Klimt*, Zurich, Kunsthaus and Stuttgart, Gerd Hatje, 1992, pp. 315–21.

31 Exhibitions of Alfred Kubin (1959), Edvard Munch (1959) and Gustav Klimt (1962) focused on anti-modernist heroes. In *Gustav Klimt, 1862–1918, Zeichnungen, Albertina Gedächtnisausstellung*, Vienna: Albertina, 1962, Alice Strobl recalls the fate of Klimt's *Fakultätsbilder*. Designed for the University of Vienna, the exhibition of the paintings in 1901–3 provoked a political scandal. Strobl, in her text, emphasizes that the refusal of an artist by his contemporary public is a sign of the artist's historical importance (p. 4). Her mentioning that such a scandal would be impossible in the context of the 1960s Vienna may have inspired the Actionists to test their public. The parallels of the public's reaction to *Art and Revolution* and Klimt's *Fakultätsbilder* are in fact striking.

32 Cited after A. Zweite, '"Eigentlich habe ich alles nur von oben bis unten beschüttet und besudelt"', in *Nitsch, Das bildnerische Werk*, Vienna, Museum Moderner Kunst, Munich, Lenbachhaus, Salzburg, Residenz Verlag, 1988, p. 23, note 41.

33 H. Nitsch, *The O.M. Theater* (1962), reprinted in *Orgien Mysterien Theater*, Darmstadt, März Verlag, 1969, pp. 35–40, reprinted in K. Stiles and P. Selz (eds), *Theories and Documents of Contemporary Art: A Sourcebook of Artists' Writings*, Berkeley, University of California Press, 1996, p. 747.

34 H. Nitsch, unpublished lecture, University of Vienna, 1987.

35 The pathologization of Actionism represses the highly professional structure of their work. See, for example, Günter Berghaus: 'The masochistic element employed in these performances became increasingly dangerous. [. . .] Brus came so close to self-destruction that he was forced to abandon all further performance work.' G. Berghaus, 'Happenings in Europe', in M. Sandford (ed.), *Happenings and Other Acts*, London, Routledge, 1995, p. 366.

36 Gorsen, *Der Wiener Aktionismus* (see note 2), p. 147.

37 Ibid., pp. 148-9. Gorsen's distrust for 'academic play' echoes, I would argue, the *fin de siècle* distrust of 'French wit'.

38 Originally the artists had planned to occupy the Viennese Burgtheater and thus to follow the model of the students of Paris who, in May 1968, had not only occupied the Sorbonne, but also the theatre. But the socialist student activists refused to support the artists' plan.

39 Gorsen, *Der Wiener Aktionismus* (see note 2), p. 150.

40 Ibid., p. 149.

41 W. Hofmann, 'Die Wiener Aktionisten', (see note 5, p. 642). Hofmann's blindness concerning *Art and Revolution* is a perfect example of the ambivalent ideological legacy of affirmative culture. In his book *Gustav Klimt und die Wiener Jahrhundertwende*, Salzburg, Verlag Galerie Welz 1970, he mentions Klimt's *Fakultätsbilder* and concludes: 'Only the work of art [. . .] is capable of enabling the blind to see' (p. 22). Hofmann, founding director of the Viennese Museum des 20 Jahrhunderts and instrumental in (re)connecting the Viennese art world to the international mainstream, organised, in September 1968, an exhibition of press photography covering the Paris student revolution of May 1968. The institutional protection of the realm of high art could not be made clearer.

42 Twenty years earlier, I should add, than Fredric Jameson's idea of the dissolution of an 'autonomous sphere of culture' as the price for the 'explosion' of the cultural sphere. See F. Jameson, *Postmodernism, or the Cultural Logic of Late Capitalism*, Durham, Duke University Press, 1991, p. 48.

43 G. Brus, 'Notes on the Action: Zerreissprobe' (1971), in *Aktionsraum I oder 57 Blindenhunde*, Munich, Aktionsraum, 1971; reprinted in an extended version in *Die Schastrommel*, 8c, 1972, p. 161; reprinted in Stiles and Selz (eds), *Theories and Documents on Contemporary Art* (see note 33) p. 754.

44 J. Derrida, 'Signature événement contexte', in *Marges de la philosophie*, Paris, Éditions de Minuit, 1972, pp. 365–93.

10

CONTESTS FOR MEANING IN BODY POLITICS AND FEMINIST CONCEPTUAL ART

Revisioning the 1970s through the work of Eleanor Antin

Lisa Bloom

Why, after so many years of relative neglect, write on questions of gender, assimilation, geographies, nationalisms, and jewish identities[1] in the 1970s California art world? What provides the privileged ground of the 'return' of an interest in 1970s feminist performance art practices along such lines now in the 1990s? To what extent does the legacy of that moment in feminist activity continue to inflect artistic practice and historical writing?[2]

In order to trace the intersection of questions of identities with 1970s artistic practice, it may be helpful to consider a major publication edited by Norma Broude and Mary Garrard in 1994 titled *The Power of Feminist Art: The American Movement of the 1970s, History and Impact.*[3] The anthology presents a wide array of works from this period including the work of Adrian Piper, Faith Ringgold, Ana Mendieta, and other women of color who were active at the time. The anthology is also the first in recent years to begin to bring back to scholarly attention the work of many jewish artists from the period – such as Judy Chicago, Miriam Schapiro, Carolee Schneemann, Joyce Kozloff, and others who have otherwise been neglected. Strong and refreshing a revisionist history as this collection represents, I will argue that it is nonetheless structured by the terms of exclusion that still presuppose a feminist sisterhood that cannot account for racial and white ethnic differences. I will point out how the relative invisibility of ethnicity as a category in the book, and of jewishness in particular, over and against the visibility of African-Americans and Latina artists (identified as 'women of color'), is quite striking and points to the limits of this kind of revisionist project. While the book attempts new inclusions, it thus also reinstates longstanding values (visibilities and invisibilities) dating from the very period it chooses to study.

The difficulties current feminist art historians have confronted in dealing with racial, ethnic, and generational differences from the 1970s has led me to revisit the work of Eleanor Antin, who stands out as one of the few artists who has actually foregrounded in her work these intractable differences. Providing a critical account of the different kinds of ethnically marked practices in Antin's work is part of a larger book project that I am currently working on. Entitled *Ghosts of Ethnicity: Rethinking the Relation between*

Ethnicity, Nationalism and Feminist Art Practices in the U.S., the book looks at a range of US feminist artists to consider the contested history and meanings of artistic practices from the 1970s in a different light from the way that the authors of *The Power of Feminist Art* themselves conceived of the project.[4] In this book I aim to give a more complex portrait of 1970s white ethnic feminist artistic practices in the United States.[5] This is an important topic since many well-known feminist artists, poets, and critics who were prominent during that period in California, such as Eleanor Antin, Kathy Acker, Martha Rosler, Judy Chicago, Joyce Kozloff, Lynn Hershman, Miriam Schapiro, among others, emerged out of households in communities in New York and Chicago which were heavily marked in ethnic, racial, religious, and class terms before they made the move to California (some permanently, others temporarily) in the 1960s.

Since spectators are also ethnically, racially, and generationally constituted, such a study is significant also in that it attests to the difference and diversity among feminists along these axes of identification. A younger feminist community shaped by feminist visual cultural studies, post-colonial discourse, queer theory, postmodernism, and the burgeoning field of jewish cultural studies within the academy might be especially alert to certain ethnic references in Antin's work, especially given the recent studies by theorists such as Sander Gilman, Richard Dyer, and Ann Pellegrini, among others – studies that examine how ethnicity, gender, sexuality, and race have signified different relations between the body and society at various historical moments. [6]

Another generational change in the last twenty-five years has been a redefinition of priorities around identities and a reconceptualization of feminism informed by the shift in consciousness prompted in part by recent poststructuralist philosophies and theories of representation as well as the shift in feminist art practices prompted by the concerns of lesbian women, women of color, and white women.[7] How I situate myself as a feminist has been in part shaped by such debates. Though I am of a younger generation than the women artist I write about here, my own jewish family's trajectory – immigration to the United States from eastern Europe and Russia, and then from New York to California, and finally (in my case) from California to Japan – shapes the contingencies of how I perceive myself in relation to American culture. In rethinking Antin's work along such lines I am interested in setting up a different historical trajectory of feminist work from the 1970s – one that allows space for other divergent and competing histories of jewish immigration which both inflected and were shaped by the models and life-styles that influenced the norms of a dominant southern Californian feminism of the period.

Though the concerns and passions that shape Norma Broude and Mary Garrard's history are different from my own, their project alerted me to some of the specific directions and priorities of their generation. In the introduction to the anthology, they provocatively write:

> How then do we situate the Feminist Art Movement on the broader stage, conceptually and historically? Is it merely another phase of avant-garde? Or is it not, rather, to borrow a phrase that has been used to describe the cultural climate of the 1960s, 'one of those deep-seated shifts of sensibilities that alter the whole terrain?' The feminist critic Lucy R. Lippard argued persuasively in 1980 that feminist art was 'neither a style nor a movement,' but instead 'a value system, a revolutionary strategy, a way of life,' like Dada and Surrealism and other nonstyles that have 'continued to pervade all movements and styles ever since.' What was

revolutionary in feminist art, Lippard explained, was not its form but its content. Feminist artists' insistence on prioritizing experience and meaning over form and style was itself a challenge to the modernist valorization of 'progress' and style development. [8]

Because women of my generation no longer face the same kinds of highly structured resistances from patriarchal institutions, it is easy to forget the force that feminism had at that moment when women were engaged in activist movements and aimed to alter dramatically their personal lives as well as their art practices and teaching. The feminist commitment to revolutionary socialist ideals was an important part of the idealism of the 1970s.

If we are to have a greater understanding of generational differences within feminism now, some of these older histories and antagonisms in the past need to be re-encountered, revisited, and rethought. Given the paramount importance in the last twenty-five years of work theorizing differences, it seems that one of the key strategies in revisiting this period would be to examine how race and ethnicity have operated within the US feminist art movement. Responding to such a concern, Moira Roth and Yolanda M. López, in *The Power of Feminist Art*, write:

> There is a dramatic inequality of information on women of color as opposed to Euro-American women. The feminist art movement . . . . suggests an identity prioritized by gender not race. For women artists of color – despite their concern with women's issues – ethnicity more than gender has shaped their primary identities, loyalties, and often the content of their art. Also from the start the women's art movement has been dominated by Euro-American leadership. [9]

López and Roth's critique is a significant intervention in the book, since their essay, 'Social Protest: Racism and Sexism,' provides a way to describe the larger cultural issues that have conditioned the development of North American feminist art up to our current historical moment. Their emphasis on the need for a complex understanding of the way in which the categories of gender and ethnicity are interarticulated is important, but I would extend their categories to include not only women of color but white ethnic women who might have also had an uneasy allegiance to a feminism that would erase a consideration of other differences beyond gender. Thus, there still remains a great need for an examination of how different Jewish women's identities are tied to other social identities and mediated through institutional discourses of art history and modernism. Furthermore, it would be a mistake to believe that ethnicities could be understood in isolation, without considering the ways in which they are part of a complex matrix of differences among women.

Eleanor Antin's work is particularly suggestive for such purposes since it highlights the inadequacy of a unitary history of US feminism in which gender is the sole emphasis. For example, her photo-piece *Carving: A Traditional Sculpture* (1972) was seen at the time and continues to be interpreted as the work of a white woman making an ironic comment on how the ideal of the generic nude is gendered in the history of art (Plate 10.1). Emphasizing its feminist importance, a 1975 essay by art critic Cindy Nemser claims that *Carving* is about 'how women are always concerned with the need to improve their bodies.'[10] Here Nemser is referencing all women and focusing on how female desire in general is courted with the promise of future perfection through the lure of the feminine

Plate 10.1 Eleanor Antin, *Carving: A Traditional Sculpture*, 1972. One hundred and forty-four photographs depicting weight loss over 36 days. Courtesy of the Art Institute of Chicago

ideal – whether it be that of the Greek nude or that of a thin female body, achieved through dieting. According to Nemser, Antin shows that the ideals on offer don't actually exist for women, not even as the end product of photographic techniques. Similarly, Joanna Frueh writes on *Carving* in the *Power of Feminist Art* that, 'just as the Classical Greek nude occludes women's bodies in this kind of aesthetically rigid form, so the socially correct beautiful body disciplines and punishes women, through frustration, guilt, anxiety, and competitiveness with other women.'[11]

However, despite the considerable critical attention given to *Carving*, much of what makes it a specific work that doesn't conform to such a generic feminist reading is the ethnic subtext to the project – the fact that her photographic self-portrait depicts an attractive, but short/jewish woman; readings of *Carving* have largely ignored this subtext. It is significant that Antin's body is not the generic body of any woman. Antin's use of her own body as the subject thus reveals that she starts from the notion of what it means to be both an embodied female and ethnic subject. In this regard Antin's attempt to exert formal control over her own body in order to achieve the aesthetic ideal required has also a great deal to do with societal constructions built upon body differences, a legacy not only of art history but also the physiognomically based racial theories of the last century. It is significant in this respect that *Carving* references police or medical photographic and cinematic practices of the early twentieth century in which discourses of physiognomy, photographic science, and aesthetics coincided and overlapped.

This connection between her work and earlier medical and scientific photographic and cinematic discourse is established through Antin's use of a sequence of photo-

156

graphs that appear almost as film stills: the stills present her isolated body, which changes slightly from frame to frame, standing in four different poses against a stark white background. It is in this sense that we can view Antin as playing off of these early traditions in order to mark herself as jewish. The cultural critic Sander Gilman writes on the difference of the jewish body in relation to medical theories of the nineteenth century, and explains how these theories included a theory of adaptability: 'one form of that difference was their [jews'] uncanny ability to look like everyone else (that is, to look like the idealization of those who wanted to see themselves as different from the Jew).' [12] In this sense Antin's project can also be seen in terms of her willful 'failure' to adapt to the 'ideal' feminist subject and thus to assimilate as an unmarked subject. In this regard, Antin doesn't offer an easy solution to the dilemma of being both jewish and female. Rather, she points to the limits of fitting in, by presenting a series of anti-aesthetic photographic self-portraits that refuse to offer a neutral and non-disturbing aesthetic experience.

Though less well-known than *Carving*, Antin's 1971 *Domestic Peace: An Exhibition of Drawings* (Plate 10.2) operates in a similar way, offering no easy closure to the problem of marked identities. Moreover, unlike other renowned works from the period, such as Judy Chicago's *Dinner Party* (1979), which frames women within the normative spaces of dominant cultural aesthetic practices and its religious Christian iconography, *Domestic Peace* allows Antin to explore the equally taboo subject of conflict in mother-daughter relations within the context of her own jewish family. Given its unusual focus and the fact that art historical discourses tend to privilege references to the history of art and high culture over the popular and the everyday, it is not surprising that the project has received little attention by both the art world and the feminist community in comparison to the other works discussed so far. According to Cindy Nemser, 'the art world did not like it because it disrupted the whole romantic myth of the artist as someone who doesn't have the same everyday family connections as everyone else.'[13]

If avant-garde artists felt uneasy with it at the time because it dealt with the taboo topic of what was seen as bourgeois jewish familial relations, feminists also kept their distance because the piece was at odds at that time with accepted white feminist notions of the mother–daughter bond as a non-contested category. In relation to this conceptual work, Antin's description of her mother is significant in that it highlights the fact that generational differences between jewish women are not so conflict-free and, indeed, that the kind of independence that feminism offers women artists can become a divisive force separating certain mothers and daughters:

I live in California and from Nov. 29–Dec. 15, 1971 – a period of 17 days – I planned to visit NYC with my husband and small child. It would serve our economic and domestic convenience but was also an opportunity for me to discharge familial obligations. However, though my mother insists upon her claim to the familial she is not at all interested in my actual life but rather in what she considers an appropriate life. No matter what kind of life a person leads he can always, by careful selection, produce an image corresponding to anyone else's view of appropriateness. By madly ransacking my life for all the details that suited my mother's theory of appropriateness and by carefully suppressing almost all the others, I was able to offer her an image of myself that produced in her 'a feeling of closeness.' It should be kept in mind that this 'closeness' was a 'closeness' to her

MAP CODE

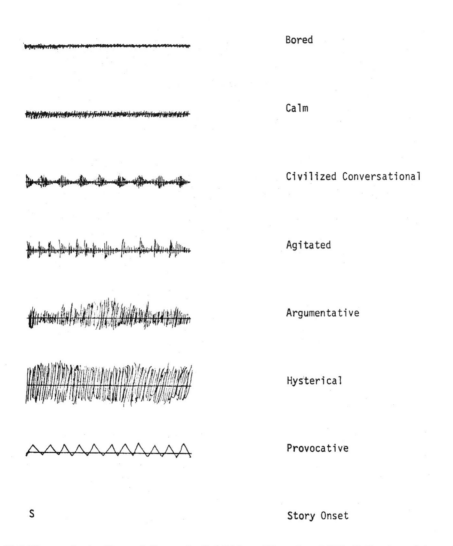

Bored

Calm

Civilized Conversational

Agitated

Argumentative

Hysterical

Provocative

S Story Onset

Plate 10.2 Eleanor Antin, *Domestic Peace: An Exhibition of Drawings*, 1971. Collection of the artist

theory rather than to her life but appeal to her didacticism was the only way to give her sufficient satisfaction to ensure the domestic peace necessary to free me for my own affairs. I planned a daily set of conversational openers consisting of carefully chosen stories. Several of these stories contained a slightly abrasive element which might be expected to mitigate peace. I considered these to be alternates for use only on 'good' days. For those hectic times when I would be forced to remain in the apartment for fairly long periods, I kept a set of reserves I could throw in to hold the line. Hopefully, these stories would act as gambits leading to natural and friendly conversation. [14]

158

Antin's desired 'domestic peace' could never be on her own terms nor could it ever conform to nostalgic feminist notions of harmony between mothers and daughters. Neither does it follow the more conservative, mythic script of the gifted (male) artist who does not need 'domestic peace' since he is seen as separate from economic, social, familial, sexual, and social relations. Antin casts mother–daughter relationships as the private sites of warfare, in which female conflict is expected as the norm. Thus, in order to achieve 'peace' during the periods in which she was forced to remain in the house for long periods of time, Antin would stage a set of conversations that would best coincide with 'what her mother considered revealing of an appropriate middle-class life,' such as a sixty-minute discussion of the artist's purchase of a green velvet love-seat.

These conversations specifying a white jewish ethnicity situated in middle-class affluence were short and peaceful by comparison to others that posited the possibility of enjoying a different form of consumption deviating from her mother's notion of middle-class success. The latter type of conversation is exemplified by a seven-hour agitated interaction between mother and daughter; they were most likely engaged in this interaction while doing other things around the house. The story included in the piece is a half-hour of calm from that longer conversation in which Antin discourages her mother from shopping at Good Will stores in California because the 'stuff is low-class.' In trying to gain her mother's acceptance, she says 'even if they had bargains you wouldn't want them.' Those conversations that explored ideological conflicts in the workplace between middle-class eastern European jews and African-Americans (her mother was working as a clerk in a state office at the time) and delved into class and even racial tensions within the jewish community created the strongest disagreements and conflicts between mother and daughter, as evidenced by the way that Antin satirizes her mother's hypocritical racial politics in one of the charts in the piece (Plate 10.3).

What is so suggestive about *Domestic Peace* is the way it reveals how harmony and calm between mother and daughter come only at the price of the artist's own silence. Yet, the parodic form of the project – the exaggerated way it meticulously records in a pseudo-scientific manner the reactions to various conversations – enables Antin to lighten the oppressiveness of these relations, since the satirical mode of discourse renders explicit the points of tension. In this respect, *Domestic Peace* has a lot in common with her *4 Transactions* (1972–5) *Encounter and Withdrawal* pieces, which also deal with the problematic bonds between women but in a setting that ordinarily would not allow much space for the examination of their differences – a feminist group of working women artists in San Diego in 1972 and 1975. The performances consisted of four declarations that were officially signed and stamped in advance of the meeting by a notary. *Encounter # 1* (Plate 10.4) provides an example:

> At the February 20th meeting, I shall take on the job of ombudsman. This will necessitate my pointing out to each member of the group, and in any manner I choose, a particular failing she displays in relation to the others. These may be of an ephemeral sort such as personal bugginess taken out on someone else or of a more serious nature like, say, a rip-off of the entire group. I must always keep in mind that my statements are intended to bring about more satisfactory behavior from the others and are never used for egotistical purposes of my own. I must complete these 8 tasks before the group normally disperses, otherwise I must keep the session going by whatever means I can until I do complete them.[15]

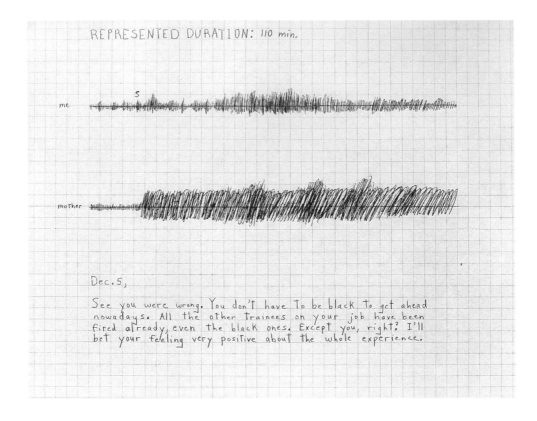

Plate 10.3 Eleanor Antin, *Domestic Peace: An Exhibition of Drawings*, 1971. Collection of the artist

What makes this piece unusual is the way in which Antin perversely performs the problem that she claims to identify and to remedy. At first glance the use of the official rhetoric of the notary document itself, with its seal and signature, seems to suggest what might appear to be female authoritarian behavior since it references a legal discourse that opens the women in the group to unexpected scrutiny and observation. However, on closer inspection, Antin's use of such a device is performative in that it dislodges the women from the pretense of a safe Utopian environment and puts them back within a context that recreates the more complex pressures the art world and academia present for feminists such as Antin (a university professor at the time): hierarchy, competition, and distrust on the one hand, coalition, mentorship, and respect on the other. Moving beyond simple Utopian feminist art projects of the period, Antin's piece stages the complex relations of betrayal, knowledge, and power among women and reminds the viewer of the more unsightly side of feminism. The fact that the pieces were produced in secret and have never been publicly exhibited is important since it suggests that, even within a progressive social movement such as feminism, many issues were left at the time unexamined. Despite the rhetoric of openness that seemingly prevailed, problems and imbalances within the group were not addressed and thus the artist was not willing to risk being misunderstood or perceived as disloyal to the feminists in the group.

Antin's work called *Portraits of 8 New York Women* (1970), which consists of biographies of some well-known New York women involved in the arts at the time

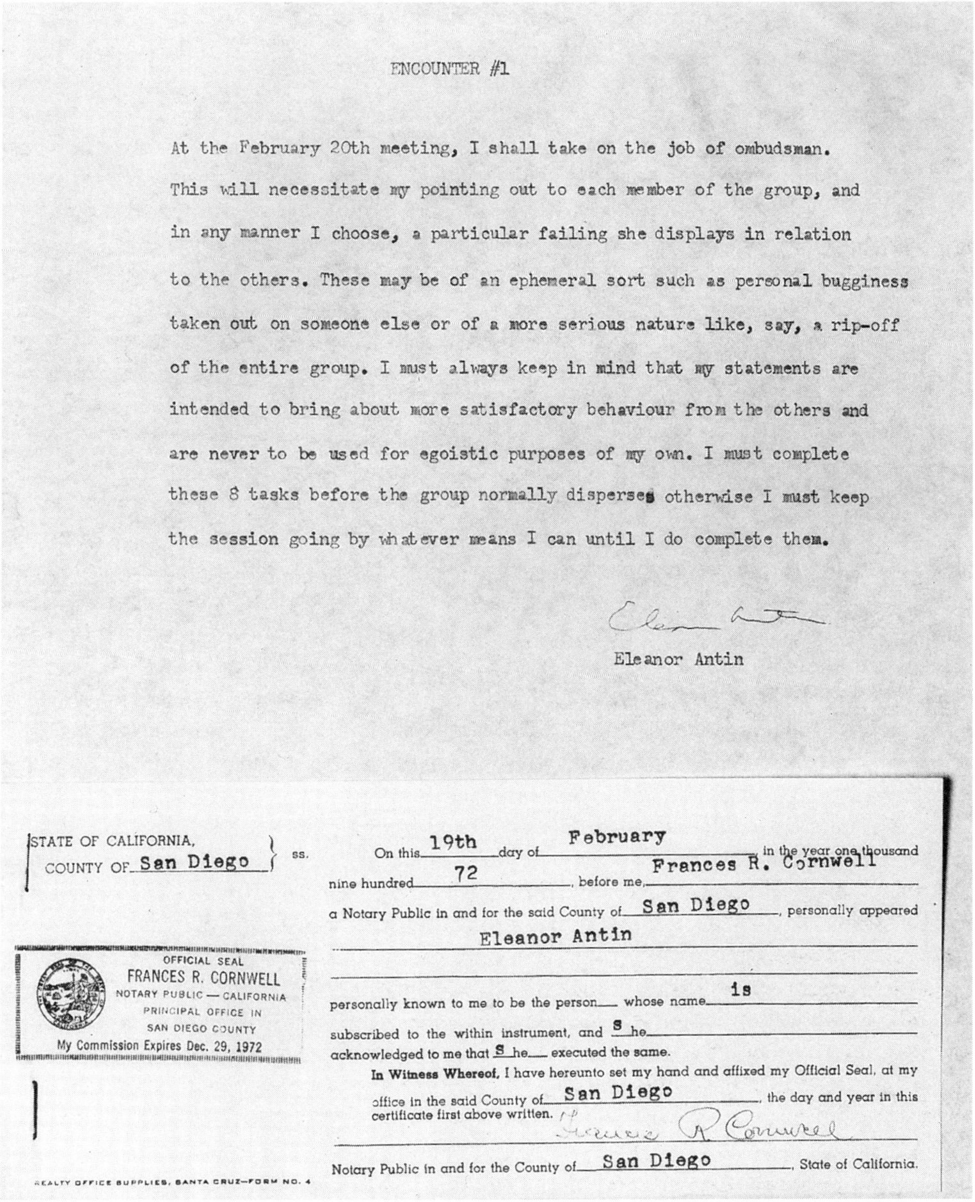

ENCOUNTER #1

At the February 20th meeting, I shall take on the job of ombudsman. This will necessitate my pointing out to each member of the group, and in any manner I choose, a particular failing she displays in relation to the others. These may be of an ephemeral sort such as personal bugginess taken out on someone else or of a more serious nature like, say, a rip-off of the entire group. I must always keep in mind that my statements are intended to bring about more satisfactory behaviour from the others and are never to be used for egoistic purposes of my own. I must complete these 8 tasks before the group normally disperses otherwise I must keep the session going by whatever means I can until I do complete them.

Eleanor Antin

STATE OF CALIFORNIA,
COUNTY OF San Diego } ss.

On this 19th day of February in the year one thousand nine hundred 72, before me, Frances R. Cornwell a Notary Public in and for the said County of San Diego, personally appeared Eleanor Antin

OFFICIAL SEAL
FRANCES R. CORNWELL
NOTARY PUBLIC — CALIFORNIA
PRINCIPAL OFFICE IN
SAN DIEGO COUNTY
My Commission Expires Dec. 29, 1972

personally known to me to be the person whose name is subscribed to the within instrument, and S he acknowledged to me that S he executed the same.

In Witness Whereof, I have hereunto set my hand and affixed my Official Seal, at my office in the said County of San Diego, the day and year in this certificate first above written.

Notary Public in and for the County of San Diego, State of California.

REALTY OFFICE SUPPLIES, SANTA CRUZ—FORM NO. 4

Plate 10.4 Eleanor Antin, *Encounter # 1*, from the series *4 Transactions*, 1972–5. Collection of the artist

(including Yvonne Rainer, Carolee Schneemann, and Amy Goldin), also confronts one of the seemingly insoluble dilemmas presented by women's relations with other women: that is, how the ethical problems of using other women as the subject of portraiture itself can become a source of tension.[16] These portraits bring Antin directly up against the way in which women are confronted by dual, if not multiple, allegiances. On one hand, for women to take feminism seriously, they must be committed to a transformative politics of representation. On the other hand, given the male-dominated New York art world, and the fact that Antin was teaching at the University of California, San Diego at the time, it is clear that Antin was obligated to please her mostly male reviewers and exhibition curators, even if her art projects to a certain extent entailed the transformation of those very institutions and galleries on which she depended for her success.

Writing on *Portraits of 8 New York Women* in *Art News* in 1971, Antin gives us some insight into her process. Antin does not insist on a sisterhood grounded in a common oppression; rather, her interest lies in the different and complex activities and functions generated out of women's lives:

> I am determined to present women without pathos or helplessness. Since a life style is the ability to recognize in the morning the same person who went to bed at night, it can be said to be a person's most important decision. My women had all chosen life styles independent of men's. It is true that some life styles proved more successful in practice than others, but they were all interesting and complex enough to be worth the try. [17]

Citing Linda Nochlin's path-breaking essay 'Why Have There Been No Great Women Artists?' (1971), written in the same year Antin wrote her own piece 'Women without Pathos' from which I just cited, Antin writes 'I agree with Linda Nochlin that the question "Why have there been no great women artists?" is a useless one and that there are very real questions to be considered about the relation of women to the arts.'[18] Though these questions include for Antin the ones that concerned most female artists of the period, such as how to present women differently so as to challenge their construction in canonical histories of art, what made her work especially unusual for the period was its ethnic inflection and insistence on presenting women 'without pathos or helplessness.' In her exhibit *8 New York Women* Antin wants to tell a different tale of women from that period, one that directly deals with the influence the US media had on issues of assimilation, glamour, Americanness, and ideals of female beauty. For this exhibit, she writes,

> I deliberately chose expensive, shiny, glamorous objects. I chose bright colors, reds, and pinks. And as much chrome as possible. I didn't want the viewer to come too close. We women have had enough love. Frank O'Hara said once that he loved Marilyn Monroe. Protect us from such love![19]

Antin's comment about Marilyn Monroe is significant because it also evokes the ethnic subtext of her project, and the ambiguous boundaries between Marilyn, the American sex symbol of the early 1960s, and the more marginal mostly jewish white women artists, gallery workers, and critics she mostly represents in the piece (Carolee Schneemann, Lynn Traiger, Hannah Weiner, Amy Goldin, and Yvonne Rainer). Building up images of these women from appropriately chosen 'brand new American manufactured goods,'[20] Antin also referenced the influence that the US mass media had had in its attempt to secure white, American middle-class values and traditional familial norms through its marketing of model homes and new consumer goods in the formative years of the post-Second World War era.

What is significant in Antin's piece is how she ironicizes the process through which a generic home and its shiny objects become accepted sites of national and familial identity as well as of female beauty and proper behavior, a process through which dining rooms and bathroom materials alone are the stuff of dreams of assimilation, national belonging, and female desirability. Since most of the women in this project were single, urban white ethnic women pursuing independent careers in the arts at the time and living in mostly New York apartments with little room and often very few modern conveniences, it is particularly striking how Antin uses these consumer objects to signify the complex lives of women who pursued their own careers rather than supporting the careers of men. Though the kinds of consumer objects with which Antin identified these women might be similar to the ones most typically associated with more traditional women, Antin's interest is in showing how the women in her biographical portraits use these otherwise mute objects in unexpected ways. For example, though Antin chooses for her portrait of Yvonne Rainer a new chrome exercise bicycle that might otherwise exist in a traditional family suburban basement or garage, such a stationary object – especially one with a superfluous basket and horn – takes on a completely different meaning in its connection to Rainer, who was at the time a dancer with the Judson Dance Theater and was known for her early experiments with repetition as a means to breakdown the traditional vocabulary of classical modern dance.

Antin's portraits are unusual for the period also in that she renders the likenesses among women but does not necessarily propose their experiences or modes of living as identical, in kind or degree. Moreover, her portraits tend not to focus either on women's oppression or on women's heroic and exemplary qualities. Rather, they are more everyday. What distinguishes them are their differences: Antin does not generalize from one example to another. In several of the more disturbing portraits (of Hannah Weiner and Lynne Traiger) Antin presents women who are less armored against the difficulties connected with trying to create interesting independent lives for themselves. In one piece, Weiner, a publicist at the time for the Museum of Modern Art in New York, is represented by a perfect little breakfast nook with striped upholstered chairs, a tea pot, and an elegant wrought-iron gate of flowers outside the window. Antin emphasizes Weiner's vulnerability and repressed anger by placing a large stylish hammer on the empty breakfast table, introducing a disturbing flaw in the otherwise perfectly appointed and spare interior.[21] By contrast, Antin's portrait of Naomi Dash, a gallery worker at Gain Ground, New York City's first alternative gallery space, is somewhat lighter than the Weiner portrait, in that it represents a less repressive and fraught subject but again a less than ideal interior – the objects selected by Antin suggest that Dash might have lived alone with her cat in a cold water New York flat (Plate 10.5).

In certain ways Antin's work reveals her interest in addressing the discourse of modernism, if only to critique and occasionally reference it as she does in the 1970s construction of an invented autobiography of the black ballerina Eleanora Antinova from Diaghilev's Ballets Russes. Moreover, there is a tendency in Antin's work to mime and parody whiteness, as in the perfectly immaculate, bright but empty spaces of her portrait of Hannah Weiner in *Portraits of 8 New York Women* and, in this respect, her work complexifies the relations between the universalizing discourses of feminism and modernism within which she is in part situated.

Besides the content of Antin's conceptual pieces discussed so far, the spareness and coolness of her work is also extremely suggestive in the way that it formally suggests a distance from the typically cluttered interiors and traditional melodramatic theatrical gestures of an immigrant eastern European jewish culture and the presumed highly emotional content of jewish ethnic relationships. Conflict, anger, and disagreement between

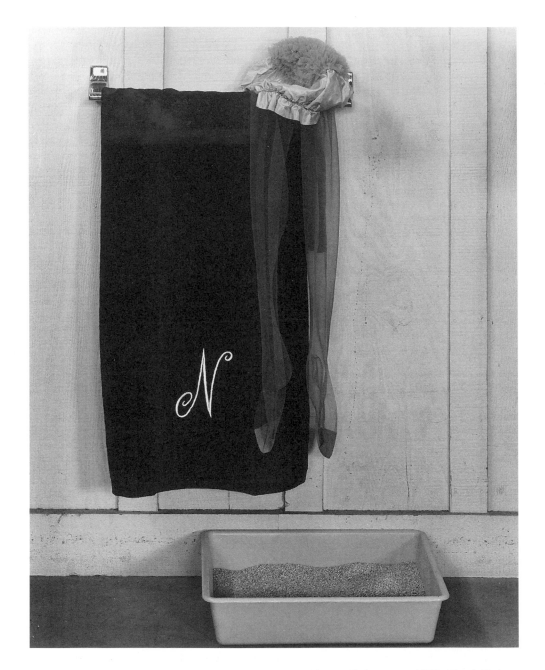

Plate 10.5 Eleanor Antin, *Naomi Dash*, from *Portraits of 8 New York Women*, 1971. Hotel Chelsea, New York. Collection of the artist

and among women get mapped literally by codes, graphs, a notarized document, or by the perfectly cool interiors and objects in *8 New York Women*. Official documents and stereotypical domestic interiors stand in for the pressure to assimilate and adopt the relatively more controlled body-language of Anglo-American northern European culture, which has stigmatized expressive gestures and clutter as signs of backward and uncultivated societies. What is also striking about all of Antin's projects is how each satirizes bourgeois codes of American etiquette, of privacy, politeness, and good manners in a way that reduces these codes to their hypocritical core. Even the US women's movement does not escape Antin's critical scrutiny in this regard.

The intersections of race, ethnicity and culture not surprisingly do not yet appear in the projects of Antin's discussed so far, since even in *Encounter # 1* Antin speaks about differences between women in a feminist space occupied exclusively by white ethnic, Euro-American, middle-class women. It is only in her invented autobiographies, each of which experientially recreates a character and a history, that she deals directly with other kinds of difference – though she mostly references other models of difference in Europe and Russia instead of in the United States. In many of Antin's performances she deliberately situates herself in the margins and plays British or European roles – The Seventeenth-Century French King, Eleanor Nightingale, or in the case of the piece that I will discuss, a black Russian prima ballerina from the Ballets Russes, Eleanora Antinova. Before dealing with the specifics of Antin's blackface, however, it worth citing Richard Dyer's description of the ballerina as the epitome of whiteness in his book *White*:

> The white woman as angel was . . . both the symbol of white virtuousness and the last word in the claim that [what] made whites special as a race was their non-physical, spiritual, indeed ethereal qualities. It held up an image of [what] white women should be, could be [,] essentially were, an image that had attractions and drawbacks for actual white people...
>
> The ambiguity of the image is caught in the figure of the ballerina in the Romantic ballet (and the related genres of féerie, pantomime, and burlesque), where the soft, flaring gaslight caught and was diffused up by the fluffed up, multiple layers of the tutu, introduced in the mid-nineteenth century. Together with scenarios about sprites and the use of pointe work (ballerinas seeming to dance on the tips of their toes and thus to be weightless), the Romantic ballet constructed a translucent, incorporeal image. [22]

What is striking is how Dyer connects nineteenth-century representations of the ballerina to notions of femininity, virtuousness, whiteness, and disembodiment. Antin seems to be working out of similar assumptions, making connections between representations of ballet as a 'white machine' but then attempting to translate herself across racial boundaries by constructing herself as 'black' in order not to conform to an image of what an unmarked white woman performer should be:

> I have a curved spine, my breasts are too large, my legs too short, my feet are weak, they bleed after *pointe* work, my skin is too dark to be a ballerina. Ballet is, after all, a white machine. There's very little room for life in it. I was a black face in a snow bank.'[23]

By presenting herself as 'black' – rather than simply as white and jewish – Antin seems to suggest that jews like herself who have assimilated to the point that they are now indistinguishable in appearance from dominant white Americans could not be imagined as having parents or grandparents who were seen in terms of arbitrary racialist distinctions.

Thus Antin dresses up in 'blackface' to treat stereotypes of, and discrimination against, jews as ideologically akin to such treatment of blacks.

Though Antin's black ballerina, Antinova, is from Diaghilev's Ballets Russes, she descends from both the world of modernist dance as well as a whole tradition of US vaudeville and theatre in which jewish women as well as black women were seen as exotic and erotic spectacles. Antin both references and disrupts such spectacles in her work. Thus, Antin's affinity with Antinova goes beyond an interest in producing her merely as spectacle; Antinova's memoirs, penned by Antin, present a complex commentary on the marginalization of both jewish women and black women in exoticized modernist dance and performance productions, such as those Diaghilev's Russian ballet company helped shape and create. In this respect the piece shares affinities with her earlier piece *Encounter # 1* in its perverse performance of the racial and ethnic stereotypes she claims to identify and to remedy. For example, each dance Antin creates for Antinova is a parody of the kinds of dance an African-American or European jewish ballerina might have been forced to perform by a European dance company: Antinova as a slave girl in a ballet where she doesn't move her feet; or as Pocahontas; or as choreographer of *The Hebrews* (Plate 10.6). These dances thus comment on the exoticization of jews and blacks within European modernist ballet. Yet Antin's critique also challenges whiteness itself and its class system as defining a set of normative high cultural practices against which all are measured and into which all are expected to fit. For example, her parodic performance as Marie Antoinette, the shepherdess (the queen dressed as working-class Other), ironicizes an older form of appropriating otherness and thus disrupts any notion of a transcendent position of whiteness that can be easily occupied.

If the power of the works by Antin that I have shown seems somewhat contingent on their ethnic, racial, and gendered subtext, it is important to note that Antin is currently constructing herself more self-consciously as white and jewish in her recent work, such as her wonderful 1991 film *The Man without a World*, a simulation of a silent era Yiddish film.[24] However, in this more recent project there is a certain consistency with some of her earlier works; Antin returns to the rich cultural *schtetl* life in Poland in a satirical way and this strategy is linked to that of presenting the heterogeneity of identities among women in her earlier projects on women. Here, she emphasizes the heterogeneity of identities among jews to reveal that the shift that has taken place in the United States towards jewish assimilation has been anything but uniformly even.

It is significant that the situation now, which has shifted towards questions of immigration, is quite different from that earlier situation referenced in Antin's work. Indeed, Antin's work provides a rare example of a white woman dealing with questions of feminism, assimilation, and jewishness during the 1970s. Through her use of performativity as a critical strategy, one of the recurring pleasures of her work is the way in which she turns what otherwise might be considered demeaning roles and complicated relationships into resistant performances. At the same time, her notion of the performative also highlights the open-endedness of questions connected to identities, since it acknowledges her ambivalence at positioning herself or others in terms of fixed, stable identities that can be fully knowable or controlled.

In historicizing the position and perspective of Antin's work in terms of gender and ethnicity, I have attempted here to come to a better understanding of the work as well as the struggles of an older jewish feminist artist who is part of a generation that created the fields and markets that have allowed my generation of feminists to flourish. To my mind,

Plate 10.6 Eleanor Antinova, *The Hebrews*, from *Recollections of My Life with Diaghilev*, 1970s.
Courtesy of the Ronald Feldman Gallery, New York

women working and writing on the arts today should continue to re-examine and rethink our relationship to previous generations of feminists and to challenge the increasingly entrenched perception of generational differences. Generational affinities as well as conflicts need to be further theorized now; such a dialogue is crucial for our collective feminist futures.

NOTES

1 The term 'jewish' is in lower case to emphasize the changing set of historically diverse experiences rather than a unified and monolithic notion of jewishness. Even though this paper focuses exclusively on a jewish-American woman of eastern European descent, it is important to emphasize the diversity of the jewish diasporic community, especially the marked differences between the German and eastern European jews (many of whom did not speak English in the mid 1940s), or, say, the complicated status of a jewish Iraqi in the United States today.

2 For an example of how one recent excellent anthology on the topic of 1970s art practice (in particular the work of Judy Chicago's *Dinner Party*) sets up a trajectory for contemporary feminist art practice in Los Angeles now rooted in feminist debates around the representation of the female body and pleasure, see Amelia Jones (ed.), *Sexual Politics: Judy Chicago's* Dinner Party *in Feminist Art History*, Berkeley and Los Angeles, University of California Press, 1996.

3 Norma Broude and Mary Garrard (eds), *The Power of Feminist Art: The American Movement of the 1970s, History and Impact*, New York, Abrams, 1994.

4 Works related to this project include: *With Other Eyes: Looking at Race and Gender Politics in Visual Culture*, Minneapolis, University of Minnesota Press, forthcoming (1999); 'Ghosts of Ethnicity: Rethinking Art Discourses of the 1940s and 1980s,' *Socialist Review*, Winter/Spring, 1995, vol. 94, nos. 1–2, pp. 129–64; 'Ethnic Notions and Feminist Strategies of the 1970s: The Work of Eleanor Antin and Judy Chicago,' in Catherine Soussloff (ed.), *Jewish Identity and Art History*, Berkeley and Los Angeles, University of California Press, 1999; 'Gender, Jewish Identity and Representation: US Photographer and Feminist Martha Rosler Reconsidered,' *The Bulletin of the Graduate School of Josai International University*, Chiba-ken, Japan, 1998, no. 2, pp. 31–44; 'Rewriting the Script: Eleanor Antin's Feminist Art,' Howard Becker (ed.), *Eleanor Antin*, Los Angeles County Museum of Art, 1999.

5 This includes historical research on the different ways in which jewishness and feminism were marked at that time in various northern and southern Californian artistic communities versus urban centers such as New York and Chicago, and the wider impact of anti-Semitic policies on the way that jewishness distinguished itself from a more assimilated notion of Americanness during that period. The project includes, among other things, oral interviews with artists from that period as well as historical research on both official and tacit convenants that prevented jews from owning land in affluent areas in southern California (La Jolla, for example) or from sitting on the board of trustees of California museums, such as the Pasadena Art Museum. For an analysis of how deeply entrenched anti-Semitic policies were at the Pasadena Art Museum (now the Norton Simon Museum), see the Walter Hopps oral history transcript at the Department of Special Collections, University Library, University of California, Los Angeles.

6 See Sander Gilman, *The Jew's Body*, New York and London, Routledge, 1991; A. Pelligrini, *Performance Anxieties*, New York and London, Routledge, 1997; and Richard Dyer, *White*, New York and London, Routledge, 1997.

7 For further discussions on this generational shift in feminist art history, see: Griselda Pollock (ed.), *Generations and Geographies in the Visual Arts: Feminist Readings*, London and New York, Routledge, 1996; Griselda Pollock, 'The Politics of Theory: Generations and Geographies: Feminist Theory and the Histories of Art Histories,' *Genders*, Fall 1993, no. 17 ; Janet Wolff, 'The Artist, the Critic and the Academic: Feminism's problematic relationship with "Theory",' in Katy Deepwell (ed.), *New Feminist Art Criticism*, New York: Manchester University Press, 1995, pp. 14–19; Thalia Gouma-Peterson and Patricia Mathews, 'The Feminist Critique of Art History,' *Art Bulletin* 69, September 1987, pp. 326–57; and Amelia

Jones, 'Postfeminism, Feminist Pleasures, and Embodied Theories of Art,' in *New Feminist Criticism: Art, Identity, Action*, Joanna Frueh, Cassandra Langer, and Arlene Raven (eds), New York, Harper Collins, 1994, pp. 25–9.

8 Broude and Garrard, 'Introduction: Feminism and Art in the Twentieth Century,' *The Power of Feminist Art*, p. 10.

9 Yolanda M. López and Moira Roth, 'Social Protest: Racism and Sexism,' *The Power of Feminist Art*, p. 140.

10 Cindy Nemser, 'Eleanor Antin,' *Art Talk*, New York, Scribners, 1975, p. 281.

11 Joanna Frueh, 'The Body through Women's Eyes,' *The Power of Feminist Art*, p. 195.

12 Sander Gilman, 'The Jew's Body: Thoughts on Jewish Physical Difference,' in Norman Kleeblatt (ed.), *Too Jewish: Challenging Traditional Identities*, New Brunswick, Rutgers University Press, 1996, p. 70.

13 Nemser, 'Eleanor Antin,' p. 282.

14 Text from artist's archives.

15 This series by Eleanor Antin has never been exhibited or published; collection of the artist.

16 The portraits of Naomi Dash, Yvonne Rainer, and Carolee Schneemann from *Portraits of 8 New York Women* are reprinted in the exhibition catalogue, *Ghosts*, Winston-Salem, North Carolina, Southeastern Center for Contemporary Art, 1996. The original exhibition was represented in its entirety at the Ronald Feldman Gallery, New York, May, 1998.

17 Eleanor Antin, 'Women without Pathos,' *Art News*, January 1971, nos. 3–4; reprinted in Thomas Hess and Elizabeth Baker (ed.), *Art and Sexual Politics*, New York, Collier Books, 1973, pp. 86–7.

18 Ibid.

19 Ibid.

20 Ibid.

21 In many ways, this project recalls the recent work of Elaine Reichek's *Post-colonial Kinderhood* from 1993, displayed at the Jewish Museum, New York City; both are ironical portraits that deal simultaneously with questions of ethnic assimilation, domestic interiors, and white ethnic female lives.

22 Dyer, *White*, pp. 130–31.

23 Cited by Henry Sayre in 'Introduction,' *Eleanora Antinova Plays*, Los Angeles, Sun and Moon Press, 1994, p. 13.

24 For an excellent review of the film, see Jeffrey Skoller, 'The Shadows of Catastrophe: Eleanor Antin's *The Man Without a World*,' *Film Quarterly*, Fall 1995, vol. 49, no. 1, pp. 28–32; Ellen Zweig, 'Constructing Loss: Film and Presence in the Work of Eleanor Antin,' *Millennium Film Journal*, Fall 1996, vol. 29, pp. 34–41.

11

DISMEMBERSHIP

Jasper Johns and the body politic

Jonathan Katz

> Perhaps it will become clear that disclaiming, which is no simple activity, will
> be what I have to offer as a form of affirmative resistance to a certain
> regulatory operation of homophobia.
>
> (Judith Butler[1])

Premised on a simple polarity of body and mind, Western Cartesian logic seems strikingly insufficient when looking at the plaster echoes of the human form which crown Jasper Johns's *Target with Plaster Casts*, 1955. Here the opposition flesh and the not-flesh, surely one of the simplest, most self-evident binaries we have, collapses. These casts are both bodily and not, and we register that knowledge in a manner both bodily and not. What, exactly, is a plaster cast's relationship to the body and what makes us think of it in the way we do?

> One thing made/ of another. One thing used/as another. *an arrogant object./*
> Something to/ be folded or/bent or stretched./(SKIN)/ Beware of the body &
> the mind. Avoid a polar situation. Think of the edge of the city and the traffic
> there.
>
> (Jasper Johns[2])

A Johnsian riddle: When is a body not a body? Answer: When it's a cast of a body. Neither purely assimilable to the phenomenology of flesh, nor purely to that interpretive capacity we call mind, a plaster cast of the body somehow partakes of aspects of both. We think *and* we feel, employing knowledge that is simultaneously visceral and intellected, simultaneously of body and mind. It is, as Johns puts it above, 'One thing made of another,' a body turned plaster – or is that a plaster cast turned body?

In this essay I'm going to concentrate on two 1955 paintings with plaster casts: *Target with Four Faces* and *Target With Plaster Casts* (reproduced in Plates 16.6 and 16.7 on pages 262 and 263). These are isolated in Johns's oeuvre of the period, and are the only works explicitly to feature the body amidst manifold images of flags, numbers, targets, and other iconic sign-based imagery. As a consequence of their distinctiveness, critics like Fred Orton have understood these paintings as marking a direction not taken by Johns, an autobiographical mode ultimately deemed too dangerous within the policed consensus of the 1950s for its connection to the artist's sexuality. Johns began the two cast paintings during the first year of what would prove to be a defining six-year relationship with Robert Rauschenberg. Tellingly, Johns would not take up a body-based imagery again until 1962, the year after they split up.

Orton writes that, after these two target paintings with casts, Johns was 'withdrawing from the dangers, real or imagined, of self-exposure which could be identified in the *Targets with Plaster Casts.*'[3] But my point is, rather, that Johns's 1955 plaster cast paintings are important precisely because they engage the body in a way that is not premised on self-exposure (which I take to be a central premise of body art, particularly from its heyday of the 1970s) but in a sense on its very opposite: on disclaiming the meanings which inhere in the body. And, I will argue that such disclaiming, as Butler reminds us in the above quotation, can nonetheless function as a powerful form of what she terms 'affirmative resistance.'

Johns's invocation following the mention of '(SKIN)' in his sketchbook notes above – 'Beware of the body & the mind' – might be read as a warning to himself against one of our habitual cognitive dualities, as if somehow the simple idea of body demands its fraternal twin – in a binary oppositional relation. In an attempt to avoid such a 'polar situation,' Johns adopts a metaphor which supplants such body/mind dualism with a new form of knowing modeled on 'the edge of the city and the traffic there.' Like the permeable boundary between city and surrounding countryside, not all borders are necessarily sharp.

I am struck by a previously unnoticed similarity between Johns's discussion of the edge of the city and certain passages from Wittgenstein's *Philosophical Investigations.* Left unfinished at Wittgenstein's death in 1949 and translated by his colleague G. E. M. Anscombe into English in 1953, the *Investigations* were, Johns has told us, enormously important to his thinking.[4] Indeed, he may have borrowed the metaphor of the edge of the city directly from this Wittgenstein text.[5] That Johns did not encounter the text until 1961, six years after the plaster cast paintings, is evidence of the fact that Wittgenstein did not influence Johns's art but rather served as a confirmation for the artist's own intuitions. But it is nonetheless telling that Johns chose to articulate those intuitions through a metaphor borrowed from Wittgenstein. In one passage, Wittgenstein describes the experience of going for a walk in the environs of the city:

> As we talk it comes out that I am imagining the city to lie on our right . . . Not only have I *no* conscious reason for this assumption . . . I had *no reason* to think it. But though I see no reason still I seem to see certain psychological causes for it. In particular certain associations and memories . . . 'But what is this queer experience?' – Of course, it is not queerer than any other; it simply differs in kind from those experiences which we regard as the most fundamental ones, our sense impressions for instance.'[6]

What I think Johns (and Wittgenstein) suggest through this metaphor is the possibility of many different kinds of knowing beyond the rational. We can know what we see. But we can also know what we feel – through association, memory, the whole complex of causes Wittgenstein calls psychological. It is this part of knowledge, uncredited, even un-recognized, before the hegemony of the sense world that Wittgenstein calls 'queer.'[7] It is 'queer' knowledge because it's entirely individuated, untraceable, illogical, without pattern, shifting from person to person – and for all that no less real. It is 'queer,' too, because it is an unauthorized knowledge, in the sense that it evades the communal usage with the track record behind it that commands obedience, conditions responses and delimits the knowable. We may feel the city is on our right, but a map announces its place in very authoritative terms on our left. 'Queer' knowledge, because it is felt more than thought, cannot be communicated to another except through metaphors or other approximations. It divides us from one another – unlike most other forms of knowing, such as language, which unite us.

Because 'queer' meaning is conditional on our individuated responses, it is thus a very different kind of meaning than we usually acknowledge when, for example, we invoke the notion of a 'city.' A city is thought to be simply and self-evidently a city. Indeed, 'city' engenders a set of generalized cognitive expectations so powerful that it causes us to lose the fact that the relationship between our concept 'city' and the actual city is, in one sense, purely arbitrary. What makes this city seem to be, naturally and self-evidently, a city is a history of usage, a convention whose power is proportional to the degree it can deny its governing presence. To *know* that city is precisely not to need to think about it.

Wittgenstein 'queers' our experience of the city; he textures the experience of knowing it such that it loses some of its transparency. He invites in other forms of knowing with their potential for disruption. In the process he destructures a regime of knowledge whose authoritativeness precludes these other forms. Paradoxically, the more we know about what we know, what we know becomes less sure, less self-evident.

What is true of cities is equally true of bodies – if not more so. (Try this exercise: Go back to the previous paragraph and substitute the word 'body' for the word 'city.') And while we have no association with the notion of a queer city, a queer body is another issue entirely. To queer a body in the Wittgensteinian and Johnsian sense is to invite in (even seduce) all these other kinds of meanings in order to query authoritative usage. It is to refuse boundaries and borders and delimited knowledges.

In his first published statement in 1959, Johns wrote that one of '[t]hree academic ideas which have been of interest to me . . . [is] Leonardo's idea ("Therefore, O painter, do not surround your bodies with lines . . .") that the boundary of a body is neither a part of the enclosed body nor a part of the surrounding atmosphere.'[8] The body here is quite specifically not demarcated, but rather extends as a concept and a presence beyond the limits of flesh or physicality into its surroundings.[9] Later Johns wrote in one of his sketchbooks:

Leonardo
Meeting of figure
& ground in (?)
Dimensions – silence (Cage)
The mind makes marks, language, measurements.[10]

Here Johns has no language for this meeting of figure and ground without benefit of boundary lines, for convention demands the delimitedness of bodies. Yet he equally notes that it is the mind alone that makes our markings, that seeks before the flux of all that is potentially knowable to carve out the limited field of the known. We are all, like Leonardo's figure, embedded in our surroundings. Though we may imagine ourselves separate, that is a fiction. We speak and measure what has been spoken and measured before us; we mark and label our world through a form of discrimination, selecting out that which was always already known to us as that which we may know. This is what queer theorist Judith Butler means when she characterizes knowledge as demarcation:

Or are we perhaps referring ... to an inevitable practice of signification, of demarcating and delimiting that to which we then 'refer,' such that our 'references' always presuppose – and often conceal – this prior delimitation?... And insofar as the extra-discursive is delimited, it is formed by the very discourse from which it seeks to free itself. This delimitation ... marks a boundary that includes and excludes, that decides, as it were, what will and will not be the stuff of the object to which we then refer. This marking off will have some normative force, and, indeed, some violence, for it can construct only through erasing; it can bound a thing only through enforcing a certain criterion, a principle of selectivity.[11]

Thus to know the body is in some sense to cite an already extant series of definitional criteria that mark body off as body: a body built of a series of exclusions. What Butler names 'extra-discursive' (which is to say that which cannot be spoken), Johns calls '(?),' an unnamed, and unnameable meeting-place, and Wittgenstein designates 'queer.' This extra-discursive knowledge constitutes the ground out of which the body emerges, like a chimera materializing out of the dust. Butler further argues that if the body is constructed through a series of exclusions, certain bodies will fail to materialize properly precisely because they stand outside the criteria of selection. These bodies, deformed and abjected, constitute the ground against which the normative body becomes itself.[12]

Chief among these deformed and abjected bodies are gay bodies, but I am getting ahead of myself here. At this point, it is important only to point out that 'unqueered' knowing is accordingly an identification with power, and a complicity with that series of exclusions which mark the known as knowable. How then to resist this complicity and open oneself to other forms of knowing? In his sketchbook notes Johns invokes Cage and his advocacy of silence.[13] In silence, Cage argues, other voices can be heard, and other, unauthoritative, extra-discursive possibilities can emerge. Silence engenders the possibility of other forms of knowing beyond the authorized: 'queer' knowing, body knowing. If reference is demarcating, then silence definitionally refuses such strategies of exclusion. It is literally the unmarked, the unsaid, refusing the boundary between the known and and the excluded. But how to actualize Leonardo's prescription for a similarly 'silent' meeting of figure and ground? It is one thing simply not to surround the body with lines in drawing, but quite another to achieve the same effect in three dimensions. Yet plaster casts of the body in a sense answer Leonardo's terms. Neither body nor, exactly, not body, they can be seen as precisely the refusal of boundary lines advocated by Leonardo and Johns (and, in a slightly different sense, by Wittgenstein and Butler).

Jasper Johns first began making and storing plaster casts of the body in 1953. Among the earliest surviving works to deploy them is the 1954 *Untitled* (Plate 11.1), which includes a cast of his friend Rachel Rosenthal's head ranging from ear to ear. The head is placed in a cavity below a rather Rauschenberg-like collaged panel. Apparently, Johns found this work and others like it problematic, for he sought to disavow and even destroy such images, along with all the other pre-flag works in his possession in 1954. As an attempt to integrate into a singular pictorial entity a cast of the body and a more traditional two-dimensional collaged surface, it is less than successful. Here two seemingly incommensurable systems of representation stand in uneasy proximity, and the cast head wins, trumping the collaged surface, wearing it like a hat.

Plate 11.1 Jasper Johns, *Untitled*, 1954. Hirshhorn Museum and Sculpture Garden, Smithsonian Institution, Washington, DC. Photograph by Ricardo Blanc

This head, somehow more tangible, makes a lie of the rest. Yet that authoritatively natural-looking head, molded over a human face, is surely no less a representation than the collage surface above it. If anything, the collage materials are more natural in that they are clippings – not a representation but the actual thing itself – one generation less removed from an existence in the world. So if this cast head seems more capable of compelling conviction than actual collage, perhaps it is because of the status of its subject, the human form. After all, bodies have an arrogance about them in Western art; they tend to consign everything else in the image to the status of background or filler.

Or does the head seem somehow more natural because a casting is an index of the real, in the Piercian sense, a sign which points us inevitably back towards an originating referent in a way that other pictorial elements cannot? Or, perhaps it seems more natural because of the way the head has been cast, such that it seems an orthodox recitation of what we recognize as 'head' in sculptural terms (white, modeled in rich relief, fully three-dimensional, like a precious fragment of a Greek statue)? We know that head as soon as we see it; it quotes our understanding of what a sculptural head should look like.

My point is that the ability of this image to dominate its representational field – whether as body, as cast, or as sculpture – is a product of its familiarity; it cites a series of pre-existing criteria in a chain of significations, conforming to a (transparent) principle of selectivity. What makes the head seems 'real,' then, is precisely its complicity within an orthodox quotation of what we take to be normative 'headness.' What is 'real' is what is familiar; in comparison to such sure recognition, the collaged field offers mere background static.

In 1955, only a year later, Johns completed another work involving casts of the body. *Target with Four Faces*, 1955, (see Plate 16.7, p. 263) is, however, very different from *Untitled*. The nearly three-quarter head of *Untitled* is now just a face, but a face cut off above the chin and below the eyes, rendered four times in similar poses. The faces are recessed in lidded frames that flatten them even further and are placed above rather than below the two-dimensional field of a target. The four faces, which have been tinted the same color as their wooden frame, are thus rendered fragmentary, genderless, and decorporealized. Each is no longer a face but a plaster fragment of a face whose relationship to the human body is distanced and made distinctly pictorial. This is no longer an authoritative citation of the body *in* art – a familiar quotation of the human form as was the head in *Untitled* – but rather a distinctly unsettling amalgam of the body and art. Here the human body is more fully domesticated to the pictorial surface, its relationship to living flesh attenuated – literally bound within the painting and circumscribed by a frame. Whereas the cast head trumped the picture in *Untitled* now, a year later, picture trumps plaster.

The resulting image conforms to Johns's definition of an *'an arrogant object'* ('One thing made/of another. One thing used/as another'). It is arrogant, I would argue, in the sense that the target now arrogates to itself the conditions of meaning and reference, forcing the assimilation of the casts into the terms of a painting of a target. Targets are especially 'arrogant' objects, even more arrogant than bodies, for they have the power to affect the ontology of things. Any representation of a target becomes an instantiation of it – since any drawing of a series of concentric circles in alternating colors is perforce, definitionally, a target. Moreover that power to control representation is, in a sense, mobile, allowing a target even to subsume its host – whatever its ontology or status, and however much resistance the host might put up – into itself becoming part of the target.

In *Target with Four Faces*, body becomes intertwined with targetness, its seamless participation in a web of pre-existing significations disrupted, even stymied.[14] Assimilated into the target, body meaning is now linked with the non-body below. For all its arrogance, the body has been, in Wittgenstein's terms, 'queered.' Its boundary lines have been erased, made subject to 'other' forms of knowledge beyond the conventional.

Target with Plaster Casts (see Plate 16.6, p. 262), its sister painting of the same year, takes similar fragments of the human form, and does similar things with them. Each body part is again segregated from its natural anatomical context, sheared off idiosyncratically, then painted monochromatically in a range of different colors and hung in a box behind a door. A green penis is conjoined with an orange ear, their part-by-part arrangement now exclusively lateral; one box is entirely empty. Here, too, Johns queers the body, twists it away from its pre-authorized meanings and leaves it hanging – framed, subsumed, dominated. Wrested from the chain of conventional significations which surround bodies and through which they come to mean, a habitual citational litany has been silenced.[15]

But a silencing does not imply a silence, as Cage's famous composition *4' 33'* of silence makes clear. Indeed, what silence permits is the emergence of other meanings and readings that evade the grip of orthodoxy or authority. Silence opens up the process of artistic signification to alternative or 'other' purposes, permitting the re-articulation of a discourse of control. In that sense, silence is the precondition of a queering.

The problem with queering the body away from its authoritative citations, however, is the degree to which that silence is read not as silence, but as violation. So authoritative are our iterations of the body that a silenced body risks appearing mutilated or dead, rather than simply open to re-articulation. It has been repeatedly noted that Johns's plaster casts in these paintings are psychologically loaded not only in their evocation of the human anatomy in general, but quite specifically due to their perverse fragmentation of the body. In the face of the presumptive wholeness of the human form, Johns's casts appear as body parts, ossified remains dug up at the scene of a crime. As such, they betray an unsettling mix of violence and torpor – the now silenced record of a once fraught encounter. Of course, the body is widely understood as a collection of parts, but our division of the body into its constituitive elements has a certain normative logic of its own. A foot is taken to include the heel, a face, the eyes. But Johns's mummified fragments lack even this coherence, violating the sanctity not only of the human form, but of its part-by-part relationships as well.

In short, there is a history even of the fragmentations of the human body which precedes and conditions our readings of it. Certain partitions of the body are themselves normative, but Johns's fragmentation of the body seems precisely resistant to this history.[16] Body parts are hacked, painted, boxed in ways unlike anything we've seen before. To be sure, Johns recognized the inherent psychological force of this body in pieces. He originally intended to make the body parts in *Target with Plaster Casts* produce noises when touched. As he later told an interviewer:

> I thought that what one saw would change as one moved toward the painting, and that one might notice the change and be aware of moving and touching and causing sound or changing what was visible. In such a complex of activity, the painting becomes something other than a simplified image. I don't want to say that I didn't understand thoughts that could be triggered by casts of body parts, but I hoped to neutralize, at least for myself, their more obvious psychological impact.[17]

While Johns obviously understood these body parts as loaded, he tells us he wanted to neutralize 'thoughts that could be triggered by casts of body parts.' I take it that what he means here is the orthodox reading of body fragments as traumatic, what he calls 'their more obvious psychological impact.' As he described it,

> [t]here's a kind of automatic poignancy connected to the experience of such a thing. Any broken representation of the human physique is touching in some way; it's upsetting or provokes reactions that one can't quite account for. Maybe because one's image of one's own body is disturbed by it.[18]

Before fragments of the body, in place of this passive replication of an extant iteration (much less ponderously signaled by Johns's use of the term 'automatic'), Johns had originally hoped to thematize the viewer's active involvement in the construction of meaning in the work. Viewers changing the image, generating sounds, and so on could be made aware of their role in the constitution of its meaning, engendering a seduction away from authorized significations towards an otherness which is the precondition of liberatory readings. Before such an active, 'empowered' viewer, dismemberment and death would presumably be merely one of many available understandings of the fragmented body. But even in the current, more delimited context, Johns's placement of these casts in their closets behind doors makes the viewer (now the art institution or its represenative the curator) choose what the image is going to look like; concretizing this process of the active construction of meaning.[19] The viewer has to do some work in order to see.

Because body parts are psychologically 'disturbing' and targets are not, Orton and many others have argued for a fundamental difference between these two pictorial modes. I want to argue the opposite, and suggest a radical consanguinity, a coming together of the two.[20] Perhaps Johns sought to neutralize the psychological impact of these body parts because he had a different purpose for them in mind, not as metonymy – as parts standing in for a normative whole – but as opacity. Perhaps this is an attempt at a body deliberately separated from its traditional social context and functionality, and hence from its traditional meanings.

The point is that in these two 1955 paintings both targets and body parts are abstractions made flesh through the workings of a social semiotic; it is only through the social that they come to mean what they do. The body is every bit as much a sign system as is the target; both constitute citations or iterations of an always already chain of significations which allow us to make intelligible the thing itself as a body or target. But while we can recognize that an abstraction is converted into a target by a social creed – though we do not often do so – the body has a kind of presence. It possesses an authoritative signification that is able to transcend delimiting context and conditions. Furthermore, there is no social investment in obscuring the sign-nature of a target; bodies are a different story entirely.[21] Targets may be 'arrogant' in their meaning-making, but bodies are authoritative. Bodies, we believe, simply *mean* – though of course they mean differentially: female bodies mean differently than male, black than white, old than young, and so on. In this context, these plaster casts, defleshed, decontextualized, made artifact, strip the body of any 'inherent' corporeal meanings. Instead, the body – just like a target – conspicuously awaits its use by the viewer. Here the body is played just as surely, albeit more subtlety, than if sounds were to emanate from the body parts when touched.

Tellingly, in his drawings of *Target with Plaster Casts* and *Target with Four Faces*, both from 1955, the year of the paintings, Johns drew the boxes which contained the casts, but left them empty. Perhaps he feared that if he simply drew in the casts, they would be too easily assimilated into the body's extant chain of significations, giving it a presence that casting it in this way denies. In other words, drawings of the body tend to dissimulate the historicity of the body as a citational system; at the same time, they can be said to have contributed to the constitution of that system. In order to problematize such an extant signifying system, something much more resistant to assimilation like casting would be required.[22] A cast body like this is tentative in a way the human form rarely is. Manifestly constructed, denaturalized, contingent, it stands in direct opposition to the more traditional understanding of the body as ur-form.

Ultimately, Johns found a way to draw that succeeded in maintaining a complicated alterity – a queerness – before the chains of binding convention that exceed and control any the representation of the body. Essentially merging drawing and casting, in the early 1960s Johns took to using his own body as imprint. This resulted in a two-dimensional imagery that, given its self-evident indexical relation to the real, was nonetheless unassimilable to simple drawing or picturing. In *Folly Beach* of 1962, for example, Johns includes his own handprint emerging out of the left-hand margin. The ephemeral and shadowy, even fugitive handprint is easy to overlook. The same handprints reappear more centrally in the drawing *Study for Skin 1* (see Plate 16.10, page 267) of the same year.

To make the skin drawings, Johns covered his head and hands with mineral oil and pressed his skin to the paper. He then covered the oily residue left on the paper in charcoal, yielding what looks like an imprint of a charcoal covered body. Originally, Johns had hoped to cast a head in plaster, fashion a mold around it, make a rubber mask from the mold, slice the mask into strips, lay these out flat on a canvas, and then cast the entire thing in bronze.[23] *Study for Skin 1* was made as one study (there are four) for this bronze image, which was never to be completed.[24] While Johns had hoped in this unrealized piece to turn the body itself into pictorial surface, the irreducible associations with flayed skin blocked that approach.

In *Study for Skin 1*, as in *Folly Beach*, Johns abandoned the use of another's skin and instead chose his own, producing a work that technically falls under the category of self-portrait. But this is a self-portrait in negative, the head and hands appearing as a patchy black field. Like the target paintings with casts, this image stands unmarked by traditional indices of an easy, legible positionality – race, class, even, sometimes, gender are simply not to be found. As an unreadable self-portrait, it maintains the same evocative alterity – the same queerness (in Wittgenstein's use of the term) – as did the earlier plaster casts, for both evoke the figure through the fossilized traces it has left behind. Before *Study for Skin 1*, I am reminded of Rothko's claim that, '[p]aintings are skins that are shed and hung on the wall.' But whereas Rothko's phrase meant that the expressive potential of his painting was so extreme it was as if it were the artist's shed skin, Johns's *Study for Skin 1* is made from his real skin, yet with no clear self-expression. The body is here present but unaccounted for, which is to say undemarcated or unboundaried within the extra-discursive miasma out of which 'body' sediments into being. Like the cast paintings, *Study for Skin 1* bears the mark of a literal presence without the 'presentness' – the immediate citational virtuosity – to which the flesh is traditionally heir.

It is Johns's peculiar insight – amid an Abstract Expressionist culture that cited (sighted) the body as the guarantor of that particular form of artistic expression achieved through gesture – that here the body emerges as feint, open and ready to receive significations from the viewer. Through an imprint or cast of the actual body, 'body' paradoxically begins to relax its grip on nature and instead stands increasingly revealed as a product of naturalization, in itself a historical process. This is, in other words, a postmodernist body, calibrated to the viewer's critical investments, in distinct contrast to the explicitly authorial modernist body apotheosized in Abstract Expressionism, the consolidation and material-ization of a whole range of white heterosexual male prerogatives. Whereas the Abstract Expressionist body was known – which is to say it assumed a widely legible positionality within the culture of its time – the Johnsian body affects a productive silence.

For example, in *Number 1, 1948* (Plate 11.2), Jackson Pollock lays claim to his painting with a border of his handprints, not unlike Johns's handprint in *Folly Beach*. In the Pollock, however, the body is present both through its literal mark-making and as indexed through the pyrotechnic application of paint. Pollock's skeins of gestural paint stand authenticated by the autographic imprint of his hand; visually intertwined, they seem very much the same thing. Here, as in so much Abstract Expressionism, the body is logos, the natural locus of an expressivity made manifest through gesture, the material embodiment of that high modernist premium on the self. The artist, his body, and his self-expression (I use the male pronoun advisedly) are unproblematically one; they refer back to one another. As a

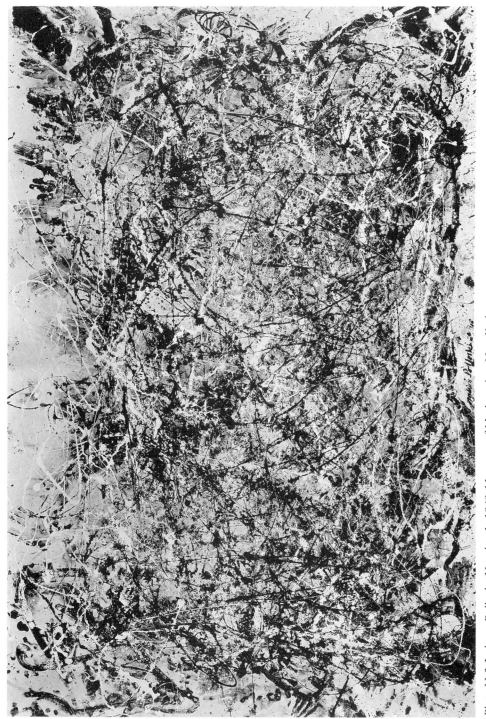

Plate 11.2 Jackson Pollock, *Number 1, 1948*. Museum of Modern Art, New York

consequence, despite the fact that we only have Pollock's hand prints here, it is his body that is indexed – expression turned automatically and immediately into flesh, into the spilling, pouring, gesturing artist and then, just as immediately, returning from flesh back to paint. Through gesture, the body's literal absence is transubstantiated into a secure and transcendent sign of presence – that deracinated presence so much feminist body art subsequently sought to confront. Like the gold in Fort Knox, the value of Pollock's body stands in obverse relationship to its material visibility.

My point is that Pollock's gestural traces can be taken as an index of his body, securing meaning through the citation of his authorial presence. This is an example of what Hal Foster has termed 'the expressive fallacy.'[25] In brief, Foster argues that 'expressionism' sought to convince the viewer that pictorial terms such as gesture were coterminous with the natural, unmediated self of its maker, rather than a specific, culturally endorsed language of *signs* of emotional engagement and immediacy. Expressionists sought to obscure the rhetorical figures that always intervene between self and signification, even in the most 'expressionist' or automatic of pictorial terms. Thus expressionism, like the authoritative body itself, depends on the projection of a confluence between a reading and the real, such that it can erase the conditions of its own production in a dehistoricized present. Body and expressive gesture merge, reifying one another as the material embodiment of that which is authentic and unmediated.[26]

Thus we have the entire discourse in Abstract Expressionism of artist bodies – as in Hans Namuth's famous photos of Pollock pouring, dripping, splashing, gesturing in paint – or tested in battle at the Cedar, or stupefied in alcoholic slumber. We peer up through the clear glass canvas at Pollock's powerful form in Namuth's classic film or we see de Kooning slash at the canvas with huge brushes in Emile De Antonio's 1972 film *Painter's Painting* – and it is all so unlike the non-gesture of Johns in that same film in which he simply sits, folded into himself and talks.[27]

In Johns's work, the body functions neither as a site for identification with a specific, authorized reading (as in much Abstract Expressionism), nor as the manifestation of an oppositional identity (as in much feminist body art of the 1970s). Rather, the body in Johns is a mark of an epistemological resistance, an emblem of unknowing – despite, as here, the often literal figuring of the body on canvas. Since the conditions of knowing the body precede it and, in making it intelligible, bind the viewer within a set of imperatives mediated by power and authority, a disidentification with that knowing is also an anti-authoritative act. In being quite specifically unreadable, Johns's body breaks a narrative chain that, Kafka-like, writes its judgments onto the body the minute it comes into focus. Instead, in Johns's art of the 1950s and 1960s, the body is always cast or imprinted; paradoxically Johns dematerializes the body through the indexing of a literal bodily absence at the very moment it is figured. Fugitive, desubjugated, here the body evades pre-ordained signification, which is to say citation; the body is produced as a silent screen. As Fairfield Porter inquired of Johns early in his career, 'What does he love, what does he hate?'[28]

Johns declared this process of disclaiming or negating citation as a 'positive' creative act: 'if you can avoid everything you know about that situation, and still make an action . . . you must be making a positive action, even though your means are negative. You say 'not' to this and 'no' to that, and so forth, and you get somewhere.'[29] This is not to suggest that through such serial negation, a casting of the body operates outside the citational system that produces 'body,' for there is effectively no such outside. Indeed, anything that stands outside only serves to enhance the binary that allows a normative 'body' to cohere through reference to delegitimated bodies. In other words, it is only through the citation of the conventional body that resistant bodies – in terms of gender, race, class, sexuality, and so on – are produced, bodies that then promptly echo and reinscribe that system of domination and its margins. The point, then, is not to produce an oppositional body – an outsider body – which is itself but another species of authoritative citation, but rather to disrupt the citational system itself. This is what I mean by queering the body, which is simply to offer a body that evades immediate citational reinscription. To queer the body is to refuse to write either its authoritative citation or its equally authoritative oppositional one, but to make reference to that 'queer' form of knowledge Wittgenstein described when he thought the city was on his right. It is to engage the body against the grain of our knowledges, redeploy it against the process of reinscription by opening it to fugitive thoughts born of a citational silence.

Johns has explicitly remarked on the anti-binaristic cast of his thinking:

> It is the gray zone between these two extremes that I'm interested in – the area that is neither a flag nor a painting. It can be both and still be neither. You can have a certain view of a thing at one time and a different view of it at another. This phenomenon interests me.
>
> It may be too simplistic to divide a thing into two opposing poles (ie., into the picture and its title, as was the case with the flag) but let me do so for the sake of simplicity and easy understanding. Then mightn't I say this: suppose there are two portions, one is external and the other one is internal.
>
> Let's try to consider the reverse case, too. Now even if you take up the external portion and draw it into a picture, the internal portion continues to exist all the while. I think this fact should be kept in mind.[30]

Fred Orton was the first to relate Johns's embrace of what he here calls a 'gray zone' to the Derridian notion of 'indecidables,' arguing that such destabilizing mechanisms operated against binary systems of knowing in ways similar to deconstruction.[31] Derrida has argued that the only exit from the binaries that structure and enable systems of knowing like the body is through the use of 'indecidables.'[32] He named them indecidables because they operate like ball-bearings in a binary system, overturning first in this direction, then in that, so as to keep the binary itself from being re-established. Indecidables do not constitute or construct a third term in a traditional Hegelian dialectic, for that would only produce yet another binary logos. Instead they subject the binarism itself to scrutiny. The irritating indigestibility of indecidables to the polarizing either/or of our habitual epistemology is what makes them so effective in deconstruction.

But what Derrida and Orton call indecidable, I want to specifically correlate to a queering.

Queering, too, engenders disruption without polarity, producing an unstable and always fluid hermeneutic opacity that denies the recolonizing force of the binary. But queering also implies a specific social-historical precedent for this particular hermeneutic in Johns's art. I am of course referencing the closeted queer, the subject of what Chantal Mouffe has termed in another context 'contradictory interpellation.'[33] Gay artists like Johns experienced themselves as subordinated subjects under one set of discourses (heterosexist) but equally could generally elect to be interpellated under another as equals or even dominant (since they were, after all, professional white men) – so long as they remained in the closet. Mouffe argues that it is specifically this kind of contradictory interpellation that provides the tools, and motive, for a destructuring critique – one that does not simply reproduce the structure of domination through reference to a privileged inside and an excluded outside.[34] As a quality both inside and outside the structures of authority, queerness occupies precisely that gray zone that Johns characterizes when he says, '[t]hen mightn't I say this: suppose there are two portions, one is external and the other one is internal. Let's try to consider the reverse case, too.' At once inside and outside the authoritative binary structure which produce difference, queerness offers a privileged position for sowing the disruptive subject.

Johns' body-based imagery thus stands in an obverse relation to much of what propelled the use of the body in the art of the 1970s. Where others sought to materialize, he sought to dematerialize; where others sought identification, he sought disidentification; and where others sought to distinguish, he sought to generalize. In employing the body, much body-oriented art of the 1970s hoped to register the specificities of a social existence, to elucidate and map out a body politics.[35] These subsequent artists lay claim to the body as tool for both opposing the avant-garde dematerialization of power relations, and for specifying important and heretofore ignored social differences. But the very opacity of Johns's bodily reference – some fifteen years before the heyday of 'body art' – consequently inverts the traditional reading of body art as a call to social situatedness.

Rather than situate the body, we have seen that Johns instead defamiliarized it. Through casts that mime the body, but can never be mistaken for it, Johns navigates the gap between seeing and meaning. And why this extraordinary non-self-identical bodily practice, this mutilation or a dismembering of what was once unproblematically whole? In part, we can see that marking the body off from our normative expectations requires a literal violence, but it is also tempting to link Johns's imagery here to that 1950s' pseudoscientific practice whereby the queer body was in a manner of speaking dismembered and read for signs of perverse difference – gay men were studied for effeminized genitals, lesbians for masculinized breasts, and the lot. Surely, these so-called 'studies' came about in part because homosexuals disturbed, at least as far as dominant culture was concerned, 'one's image of one's own body.' Homosexual difference had instead to be located bodily in order to assert an essentialized otherness. Difference – social, sexual, racial, and so on – is thus mapped all over the body, clear evidence, if we needed it, of the social construction of what was once thought of – much more simply – as a brute fact of nature. Like a target, the body is in fact a sensitive field for registering our social differences, produced as it is through relations of power.

Thus to dismember the body is to enact a dismembership – of us from Johns, and Johns from us.

Standing before these targets with their casts, there is no orthodox or authorized position from which to view and thus make sense of Johns's art. They proffer no privileged or even shared perspective, no prerogatives of membership, no rewards of belonging, no promise of inclusion. There is no community referenced, no code to crack. It is, if you will, every body for her/himself – alone, alienated. And it is a powerfully queer sensation to be so alienated from the meanings carried in one's own body.[36]

Johns thus succeeds in shifting the representation of the body from a position of consonance with authoritative readings to one of dissonance. Johns enacts a seduction away from our normative understandings of the body to an otherness, a queerness, which is in essence a state of possibility. As we, the people, make targets or flags, so too have we made bodies – all abstraction made real through the working of the social.

Johns's bodily indices are not available for use by authority; they point neither to Abstract Expressionism's transcendent presence through the hypostasized male body, nor to body art's response through a situated corporeality but rather to simple absence itself – a body present but unaccounted for, an imprint of a citation. Johns's bodies are, in short, unusable material resistances, unassimilable to any hegemonic discourse.

In this period of the early 1960s when sexual orientation was yet to be mobilized as a marker of a new cultural politics, queerness was still unrepresentable except through a queering. I would argue that it is thus only through absence that the gay body politic could be realized in Johns's art.

NOTES

1   Judith Butler, 'Imitation and Gender Insubordination,' in *Inside/Out: Lesbian Theories, Gay Theories*, Diana Fuss (ed.), New York: Routledge, 1991, p. 14.
2   Jasper Johns, *Sketchbook A*, 1964, quoted in *Jasper Johns: Writings, Sketchbook Notes, Interviews*, Kirk Varnedoe (ed.), New York, Museum of Modern Art, 1996, p. 34.
3   Fred Orton, 'Present, the Scene of . . . Selves, the Occasion of . . . Ruses,' in *Foirades/Fizzles: Echo and Allusion in the Art of Jasper Johns*, exhibition catalogue, Los Angeles, Grunwald Center for the Graphic Arts, Wight Art Gallery, UCLA, 1987, p. 177.
4   Johns had read the *Investigations* carefully by 1964, and his language in his sketchbook notes echoes a Wittgensteinian approach. See Kirk Varnedoe, *Jasper Johns: A Retrospective*, 'Chronology and Plates' compiled by Lillian Tone, exhibition catalogue, New York, Museum of Modern Art, 1996, footnote 30, p. 195, for a discussion of the literature on Johns and Wittgenstein.
5   'Our language can be seen as an ancient city: a maze of little streets and squares, of old and new houses, and of houses with additions from various periods; and this surrounded by a multitude of new boroughs with straight regular streets and uniform houses.' Ludwig Wittgenstein, *Philosophical Investigations, Part 1*, tr. G. E. M. Anscombe, New York, Macmillan, 1953, section 18, p. 8.
6   Wittgenstein, *Investigations*, Part 2, p. 215 (italics in original).
7   Recently, some scholars have speculated that Wittgenstein's use of the word 'queer' is a coded aside to fellow queer – in the sense of homosexual – readers. I would further speculate that this term and its deployment may have been of particular interest to one specific queer reader, Jasper Johns.
8   Jasper Johns, artist's statement, in Dorothy Miller, *Sixteen Americans*, New York, Museum of Modern Art, 1959, p. 22.
9   It may prove useful to problematize our traditional notion of skin as surface and reconceptualize it as core, the point of genesis of a set of social relations through which our bodies come to mean. In this sense, Johns's casting of the body mimetically replicates the larger social dynamic whereby skin originates a process of signification.
10 Johns, *Jasper Johns: Writings, Sketchbook A*, p. 52.
11 Judith Butler, *Bodies that Matter: On the Discursive Limits of Sex*, New York, Routledge, 1993, p. 11.
12 Butler writes, 'The process of that sedimentation or what we might call materialization will be a kind of citationality, the acquisition of being through the citing of power, a citing that establishes an originary complicity with power in the formation of the "I",' in *Bodies that Matter*, p. 15.
13 For a fuller discussion of the politics of silence in the work of John Cage, see my 'John Cage's Queer Silence or How to Avoid Making Matters Worse,' in *John Cage*, ed. David Bernstein, Chicago, University of Chicago Press, 1999.

14 In this context, it is interesting to speculate whether any other representation besides a target would have the 'arrogance' to be able to subsume the body so readily – and indeed, in early Johns, body casts are placed in conjunction only with targets.

15 Johns recognizes such silencings as a willful, even affirmative act. In another sketchbook note he writes, 'Judd spoke of a "neutral" surface but what is meant? Neutrality must involve some relationship (to other ways of painting, thinking)? He would have to include these in his work to establish the neutrality of that surface. He also said "non" or "not" expressive. This is an early problem/a negative solution or/expression of new sense/which can help one into/ what one has not known. "Neutral" expresses an intention.' *Jasper Johns: Writings, Sketchbook A,* c. 1963, p. 52.

16 As Butler reminds us, the legitimation of the body entails a violent marking off from the extra-discursive – the erasure or abjection of that which constitutes the delegitimated outside, allowing the inside to cohere. So, too, then, does the disruption of this process invoke violence, breaking with discursive norms through their violation. See Butler, *Bodies that Matter,* pp. 221–42.

17 Jasper Johns, in Roberta Bernstein, 'An Interview with Jasper Johns', in Lawrence D. Krizman (ed.), *Fragments: Incompletion and Discontinuity,* New York, New York Literary Forum, 1981, p. 287.

18 Ibid.

19 Indeed, Alfred Barr, chief curator of the Museum of Modern Art, had hoped to purchase *Target with Plaster Casts* out of the artist's first one-person show, but ultimately decided against it when Johns informed him that he could not agree to Barr's permanently closing the door over the cast of the penis.

20 In a typical formulation, Richard Francis writes, '[s]ince they are human, these parts – some "private" in the conventional definition, all private in this context – suggest an emotional quality at odds with the "cool" target below them.' Richard Francis, *Jasper Johns,* New York, Abbeville Press, 1984, p. 24.

21 See Butler, *Bodies that Matter,* pp. 223–42.

22 That Johns was aware of drawing as a particular form of citational utterance is evident in his fondness for Wittgenstein's famous rabbit/duck problem, a drawing that from one perspective looks like a rabbit, and from another a duck. In his *Sketchbook B* he writes:

> 'Something' can be either one thing or another
> (without turning the rabbit on its side).
> This requires the idea of representation (or 'picture').
> A rabbit (a real rabbit) on its side is not a duck.
> Johns, *Jasper Johns: Writings,* p. 62.

So a picture is not to be confused with a cast, any more than a rabbit (a real rabbit) can be with a duck, but in pictures, well, anything can happen.

23 As Johns writes in *Sketchbook A,* c. 1960:

> Make a Plaster Negative of whole head.
> Make a thin rubber positive of this.
> Cut this so it can be (stretched) laid on a board fairly flatly. Have it cast in bronze and title it *Skin* . . .
> Johns, *Jasper Johns: Writings,* p. 50

24 Michael Crichton, *Jasper Johns,* New York, Harry N. Abrams, 1977, p. 49.

25 Hal Foster, 'The Expressive Fallacy,' *Art in America* (January, 1983), reprinted in *Recodings: Art, Spectacle, Cultural Politics,* Seattle, University of Washington, 1985, pp. 59–77.

26 Thus, Harold Rosenberg in *The American Action Painters* not only describes the new art 'as an arena in which to act – rather than a space in which to reproduce, re-design, analyze or 'express' an object, actual or imagined,' but furthermore repeats the denunciation: '"B – is not modern," one of the leaders of this mode said to me. "He works from sketches. That makes him Renaissance."' Harold Rosenberg, 'The American Action Painters,' reprinted in *The Tradition of the New,* Chicago, University of Chicago Press, 1982, p. 25.

27 See Caroline Jones's discussion of *Painters Painting* in her *Machine in the Studio*, Chicago, University of Chicago Press, 1996, pp. 98–105.

28 Fairfield Porter, 'The Education of Jasper Johns,' *Art News*, February 1964, vol. 62, p. 44.

29 Jasper Johns, on the record of interviews accompanying the show *The Popular Image*, recorded and edited by Billy Klüver, March 1963.

30 Jasper Johns in an interview with Yoshiaki Tono, 'I Want Images to Free Themselves from Me,' in *Getijutsu Shincho* (Tokyo), August 1964, vol., 15 no. 8, pp. 54–7; quoted in *Jasper Johns: Writings*, p. 98.

31 Fred Orton, 'On Being Bent "Blue" (Second State): An Introduction to Jacques Derrida/ A Footnote on Jasper Johns,' *Oxford Art Journal*, 1989, vol. 12, no. 1, pp. 35–46.

32 Gayatri Spivak, 'Translator's Preface' to Jacques Derrida, *Of Grammatology*, tr. Gayatri Spivak, Baltimore, Johns Hopkins University Press, 1974, pp. xiii–xx.

33 Chantal Mouffe, 'Hegemony and New Political Subjects: Towards a New Concept of Democracy,' tr. Stanley Gray, *Marxism and the Interpretation of Culture*, ed. Lawrence Grossberg and Cary Nelson, Urbana, University of Illinois Press, 1988, pp. 89–104. Mouffe's point is that the postwar discourse of democratic equality coupled with the fact of subordination produced contradictory interpellations that spawned many of the new social movements. Although I think this reading elides the important differences between discursive or symbolic interpellation and the lived experience of the same (since racial minorities experienced discrimination at all points from dominant culture despite its claims of equality), I have borrowed her argument because I think it is particularly well suited to the white gay male culture of the time, wherein both contradictory terms were fully experiential.

34 Mouffe points to the false promises of democratic equality as the motive force behind what she calls 'new social movements' like feminism. Foucault's project is in part to describe the processes through which subordination is naturalized and even reinforced by the subordinated. See Michel Foucault, *The Order of Things: An Archaeology of the Human Sciences*, London, Tavistock, 1970.

35 Performing the body carried with it certain implicit assumptions of commonality and community. There had to be a common or shared cultural context in which these bodies could be understood as meaningful, a logos of the body. Johns in 1955, a closeted gay man in a violently homophobic culture, had no such logos. Indeed, he remains unwilling to discuss his sexuality today, and, through his considerable art world power, continues to restrain institutions and publishers against any mention, much less analysis, of his sexuality.

36 This sentiment is standard in Johns literature; thus Michael Crichton writes, '[a] person looking at Johns' work often feels *alone* in an odd way,' in *Jasper Johns*, p. 74.

12

PERFORMING CLITS AND OTHER LESBIAN TRICKS

Speculations on an aesthetics of lack[1]

B. J. Wray

Holly Hughes is a lesbian and her work is very heavily of that genre.
  (John Frohnmayer, former National Endownment for the Arts chairman)

Both the clitoris and the penis being anatomical entities, their capacity to signify desire depends on their representation.

(Teresa De Lauretis)

I see myself as a political artist, and I think that making more people wrap their mouths around the word, if not the thing itself, is precisely the kind of political goal one can hope to realize through the theater.

(Holly Hughes)

The materialization of the lesbian subject within the official discourse of late nineteenth-century sexology figured forth a characteristically unnatural body.[2] Lesbian historians such as Lillian Faderman have persuasively documented the ways in which the emergence of lesbian identity as a legal, social, and political reality was coterminous with the denaturalization of her bodily appearance.[3] More often than not, sexual deviance was written on the body in order to visually demarcate an otherwise unmarked identity category. Broad shoulders, narrow hips, and a deep voice marked the lesbian body as an improper female form and simultaneously reiterated the contours of a normative feminine physique.[4] Indeed, the continual invocation of a sexual inversion discourse in which the female homosexual was understood as a man trapped in a woman's body (hence, the inevitable display of 'masculine' traits) worked to codify how the lesbian could appear in representational forms. These nineteenth-century anatomical performatives produced a recognizably lesbian body, and ensured that the circulation of lesbian identity was predicated on the concomitant invocation of a degenerate female body. The masculinization of the lesbian through the textual performatives of sexology secured her ontological placement within a phallocentric visual logic that regulated how and in what form bodies may appear.

Lesbian identity, then, entered the domain of cultural intelligibility insofar as it was attached to a visibly 'Other' body. This impulse to mark difference by inscribing anatomical irregularities points both toward the materializing power of discourse as well as to the centrality of visual culture in the making of identities. Nowhere is this dual function of marking more evident than in psychoanalytic accounts of identity formation. Freudian and Lacanian narratives of sexual difference underscore the primacy of the visible realm in terms of structuring (hetero)normative relations. Freud's essay on 'Femininity' outlines how the castration complex arises in boys 'after they have learnt from the *sight* of the female genitals that the organ which they value so highly need not necessarily accompany the body'[5] and for girls, 'the sight of the genitals of the other sex'[6] provokes a recognition of difference based on deference to 'the boy's far superior equipment.'[7] The 'inferior clitoris'[8] simply cannot measure up to the boy's protruding presence within the visible realm. Just as the girl's clitoris disappears from view in the development of heteronormative relations so, too, does the pleasure she derives from clitoral stimulation: 'she loses her enjoyment in her phallic sexuality . . . she renounces her masturbatory satisfaction from her clitoris.'[9] The visibility of the penis and relative invisibility of the clitoris structure proper gender and sexual identities, and, as with the sexologists, Freud differentiates 'normal femininity'[10] from lesbian tendencies or 'masculinity complex'[11] by naturalizing certain anatomical performances. Only the female homosexual 'clings to her clitoridal activity'[12] as she attempts to take up a phallic identification. This clitoral phallic identification is, however, always already lacking in stature and remains relegated to the position of stunted penis.[13] In 'Femininity' Freud discursively constructs the female form, and this textual performance endows particular body parts with performative significance.[14]

Similarly, Lacan's articulation of the privileged status of the phallic signifier in 'The Signification of the Phallus' tends, perhaps unwittingly, to reinforce the importance of visibility in determining symbolic power. Although Lacan goes to great lengths to deny a necessary link between the penis and the phallus ('It is even less the organ, penis or clitoris, that it symbolizes'[15]), and to point out the unreliability of the visible realm, his reiteratation of the prominence of the penis ensures that visibility delineates sexual difference: 'It can be said that this signifier is chosen because it is the most tangible element in the real of sexual copulation.'[16] The conflation of the phallus with the penis adheres around a visual economy that privileges presence. Lacan says as much when he comments, 'Of what cannot be seen, of what is hidden, there is no possible symbolic use.'[17] The clitoris, for the most part hidden from view, cannot signify presence and, therefore, cannot attain privileged status within a phallocentric visual logic. Femininity, then, is characterized in the domain of signification by an absence or lack that appears invariably linked to the lack inherent in the female sexual organ. In her assessment of 'The Signification of the Phallus,'[18] Rosalind Minsky succinctly describes this relationship between discursive and anatomical power:

> It is because it is so easy to confuse the most obvious sign of difference for the child – the visible, physical penis – with the phallus, the cultural sign of power that the construction of femininity can never be on the basis of anything other than lack, of 'not having' and therefore 'not being.'[19]

In both Lacanian and Freudian accounts of subjectivity, the intimate connection between bodies and texts is made explicit by the fact that, as Jacqueline Rose explains, 'anatomical difference comes to *figure* sexual difference.'[20] This figuration takes place discursively and elevates the phallus to its role as the central organizing principle of signification. It is crucial to remember, however, that Lacan discerns the fraudulent basis of phallic power. The phallus is, indeed, valued as a signifier, but signifiers are arbitrary and lack any intrinsic value. The precarious foundation of this phallic signifier must be covered over by incessant repetitions and recitations of its privileged status.[21] It is precisely this tenuous hold on signification that performance artists such as Holly Hughes often exploit in order to shift the relationship between textual and bodily performances. Hughes's interventions occur, though, within an already existing framework of feminist and lesbian opposition to phallic dominance, and it is to this context that I will now briefly direct my attention.

Given that nineteenth-century sexology and conventional psychoanalytic narratives of sexual difference tend to subsume lesbian identity into a phallocentric representational matrix by materializing a particular lesbian body,[22] it should come as no surprise that challenges to this imperative have frequently coalesced around the (dis)appearance of female genitalia in representational forms. Key to phallocentric paradigms of sexual difference is the paradoxical status of 'proper,' that is, heteronormative, female genitalia within the realm of the visible; the 'sight' of these parts is, more accurately, characterized as an absence of sight, a lack, an invisible presence. Lesbian and feminist artists and theorists alike have sought repeatedly to rework this notion of female 'lack' and the control that it wields over the terms of women's appearance in traditional visual economies. As Rosalind Minsky's aforementioned comments indicate, 'lack' is one of the primary concepts that has structured female identification and desire, and as such, 'lack' has consistently haunted women's attempts to enter a representational economy in which our only mandated positions are either invisibility, or object rather than subject of the gaze. This dilemma becomes particularly accute in the realm of lesbian representation where the only possible sites of identification and desire are doubly bound within both phallocentric and heterocentric pre-scripted narratives.

It is no wonder then, that pyschoanalytic notions of 'lack' and their subsequent regulation of representation have been soundly denounced in lesbian and feminist texts for several decades.[23] More often than not, these oppositional texts have enlarged the signification of the clitoris to phallic proportions in the hopes of replacing invisibility with visibility and absence with presence. To this end, literary critic Paula Bennett concludes her article on 'Critical Clitoridectomy: Female Sexual Imagery and Feminist Psychoanalytic Theory' in praise of the little lacking organ: 'With the clitoris, theorists can construct female sexuality in such a way that women become sexual subjects in their own right, taking their sexual, social, creative, and political power into their own hands.'[24] Bennett's transformation of the clitoris into a positively signifying entity counters head-on the assumptions concerning clitoral (non)status in traditional psychoanalytic accounts of female subjectivity. In a similar gesture, lesbian writer Celeste West endows the clit with almost mythical proportions in *The Lesbian Love Advisor*,[25] her guidebook to lesbian courtship. Through the character of Lady Clitoressa, West not only personifies this 'inferior organ' into a regal figure, but also exaggerates the Freudian narrative of lesbian clitoral fixation in order to ascribe delight rather than deviance to this anatomical site.

Both of these recent examples of clitoral re-valuation take to task the naturalization of phallic lack through recourse to the depiction of so-called 'positive images.' Foregrounding clitoral visibility, these revisionist texts attempt to alter the signifying power of female anatomy.[26] This recourse to the realm of the visible as the site of identity-making and identity-empowerment is, of course, precisely the tactic employed by identity politics of all leanings in the hope of expanding the limits of what can and cannot be represented.

The difficulty with such tactics is that they are necessarily predicated on the very system of representation that they seek to undermine and are heavily invested in maintaining the parameters of the binaries they take up. In *Unmarked: The Politics of Performance*, Peggy Phelan (via Lacan) discerns the problematics associated with such an investment:

> Visibility is a trap ('In this matter of the visible, everything is a trap': Lacan, *Four Fundamental Concepts*. . .); it summons surveillance and the law; it provokes voyeurism, fetishism, the colonialist/imperialist appetite for possession. Yet it retains a certain political appeal.[27]

This tyranny of the visible in terms of constructing and disseminating truths (seeing is believing), coupled with the long history that lesbian subjects have had with visibly marked anatomical difference, has frequently meant that counter-representations unquestioningly take up the notion of the body as pure essence, the body as uncompromised site of identity constitution. The Australian performance artist and writer Anna Munster makes precisely this point in her comment that 'queer performance is literally saturated by a desire to understand and pose the body unmediated by the form and consumption of spectacle.'[28] Although the notion of an 'unmediated' performance has been substantially critiqued by postmodernist understandings of representation, Munster touches on the seemingly unassailable drive toward visibility and recognition that permeates gay and lesbian identity politics. Or, as Lynda Hart describes it in her 1995 piece on 'The Queer Real,' there is still 'an overwhelming urge (is it indeed a "drive," something like an instinct?) to mark a stationary place, to appeal to a referent, to have recourse to a/the "real thing."'[29] This recourse to the 'real thing' requires that we perpetuate existing divisions between representation and the real and that we set aside what Munster terms the 'form and consumption of spectacle.' In doing so, oppositional strategies of representation must ignore their own complicity with taken-for-granted paradigms and proceed as if the transformation from invisibility to visibility is a seamless one that is open to all bodies equally.

To return, then, to my earlier invocation of the performance art of Holly Hughes, I am interested in how her work radically destabilizes this seamless substitution by making use of representational tactics that consistently foreground their paradoxical relationship to visual and discursive economies. Since 1983, Hughes has written and performed plays and monologues that incisively critique heteronormative imperatives. In tandem with Phelan, Hughes insists on a 'much more nuanced relationship to the power of visibility'[30] and her performance art remains highly attentive to the ways in which the body itself, especially the lesbian body, is materialized in and through textual performances. By this, I mean that her performance pieces (most notably 'World Without End' [1989] and 'Clit Notes' [1994], both of which are extended monologues and require minimal staging) re-cite phallocentric configurations of lesbian bodies, as well as feminist revisions of those representations, in order to gesture towards the performative power of anatomy itself. In doing so, Hughes takes to task the notion of an unmediated performance of the body, and fashions a politics of performance at the site(s) where discourses and bodies intertwine.

I have termed this representational tactic an 'aesthetics of lack.' It is an attentiveness to, even an absolute reliance on, paradox that characterizes the performance of lack in Hughes's 'Clit Notes.' Clearly, resignifications of lack can only occur within the paradoxical situation of inhabiting a construction in order to critique it. The seemingly

Plate 12.1 Holly Hughes, *Clit Notes*, book jacket photograph, 1996. Courtesy of Holly Hughes.
© John Lovett

impossible display of lack hinges, in her text, on the spectacular focus on sites of female
lack. The hyperbolization of existing modes of knowing and the representational forms
that they generate is crucial as a marker of the parodic interventions that Hughes initiates.
Marking the performance as a performance seems crucial to any discussion of the campy
refigurations of female lack that she plays with. As signifiers of the tensions inherent in any
articulation of subjectivity that is mindful of contradictions, the parodic performances of
lack in these pieces foreground the complex relationship between 'real' lesbian bodies and
their entry into a phallic representational economy. Whether or not lack may be successfully
recuperated from its historical baggage of oppression is perhaps a less useful consideration
than how, precisely, lack is used as a strategic disruption of what Donald Morton has
termed the 'easy trafficking of meaning in culture.'[31] I am hesitant to link 'Clit Notes' or
the notion of an aesthetics of lack to a renewed lesbian-feminist revisionist project and am
more concerned with exploring the necessary tensions inherent in any resignification. In

what ways does 'Clit Notes,' in the words of Teresa de Lauretis, 'produce modes of representing that effectively alter the standard frame of reference and visibility, the conditions of the visible, what *can* be seen and represented?'[32] How does an aesthetics of lack represent the problem of representation?

Lynda Hart, in the aforementioned article on the queer real, postulates that the way out of narratives 'haunted by the father,' out of 'the endlessly repetitive Oedipal drama ... is not through accumulating testimonials about the 'truth' of our illusions. Rather, it must be through performing the illusions, producing, multiplying, and traversing them.'[33] In 'Clit Notes,' Hughes refuses to play properly conventional scenes of female lack and insists, instead, on framing the disjunctions that are made possible and plausible through the process of resignification. I would suggest that Hughes's performance in 'Clit Notes' functions to shift the Oedipal drama precisely through the multiplications and traversals that Hart advocates. 'Clit Notes' moves deftly through and across psychoanalytic narratives of sexuality, family, disease, and passion as a means of creating a space for lesbian representation somewhere in the interstices of provisionality and pathology. Hughes insists on maintaining a complicated relationship to dominant narratives by exploiting their authoritative significance as a citation device for lesbian desire. Shortened to the more colloquial 'clit' and the less structured 'notes' (surely a playful recuperation of the clitoris's inferior status as well as the penchant of psychoanalysis to transform notes into epic studies), even Hughes' title re-marks axiomatic sites of sexual difference. In her performance across various discursive registers, Hughes provokes a productive tension within the already established matrices of identification and forces her viewers and readers to negotiate the critical layers of notations. Perhaps the most blatant example of this refigured citation in 'Clit Notes' is demonstrated by sections in which Hughes elbows her way into the case histories. Performing the role of 'a distinguished professor giving a lecture at the Famous Performance Artist Correspondence School,' Hughes proceeds to outline her topic: 'Performance Art: What Causes It? Where it comes from and what can be done about it.'[34] What follows are three performances (perhaps talking cures) that offer no explicit reflection on the topic at hand and refuse to replicate the psychoanalytic process of observation, analysis, and conclusion. Occupying the sites of both patient and analyst, Hughes facilitates a shift in the pathologizing of lesbianism by imbricating the traditional position of observation within the narrative itself. If lesbian is a genre, as the epigraph from John Frohnmeyer suggests, than perhaps this re-occupation of psychoanalytic narratives typifies the genre.

Re-citing these case histories functions as the method of infiltration that mimetically displaces the system it critiques. Butler describes this process of citation 'not as enslavement or simple reiteration of the original, but as an insubordination that appears to take place within the very terms of the original, and which calls into question the power of origination.'[35] Hughes relies on the 'knowingness' of her audience and our investment in the conventional psychoanalytic paradigms of lesbian sexuality in order parodically to replay these scenarios. This knowing parody is, of course, the site of humour in 'Clit Notes' but, even more crucially, it is frequently the location of conservative wrath. To give a brief example, Hughes's performance incited one magazine reviewer to whip his conservative audience into a frenzy by literalizing her parodic mode within the confines of his column:

Ms Hughes complained that gay men had far more support and publicity than lesbians. Her whimsical solution: convene 'the National Woman-Girl Love

Association,' modelled after the notorious New York-based homosexual pedophile network, the North American Man-Boy Love Association. This suggestion roused the crowd to cheers.[36]

Dismissing Hughes's narrative as 'whimsical' and, thereby, attempting to disempower her re-citation, this reviewer seeks to contain the operations of parody by 'playing it straight.' That is, he invokes his own knowing rendition of NAMBLA's activities and makes a simplistic correlation between representation and the real. Terrified by the audience's reaction (clearly, they 'got it' and he didn't), he desires to restabilize the process of signification that Hughes perverts to her own ends. I provide this example not as a warning label that should be attached to a politics of parody, but as an instance of the multivalent ways in which parodic provocation unsettles viewers. The proximity of a parodic representation to an 'original' text means that a close resemblence may be (mis)read, as in the example above, for its verisimilitude. It seems to me that it is precisely this 'failure' of interpretation and its impulse to re-cite the performance event according to a morality discourse that highlights the very arbitrariness of signification. This review, in its desire to straighten out Hughes's bent musings, exposes the ways in which textual or discursive performances of all ideological leanings work reiteratively to materialize identities. As I note later in this article, the conservative backlash to Hughes's earlier work unwittingly hieghtened the performative significance of her monologues by re-citing their illicit passages on the floor of the US Senate.

Throughout 'Clit Notes' Hughes exploits perversion to interrogate an ontology of lack – it's when she fucks up that she realizes she has a life. 'Clit Notes' terrorizes with a spectacle of lack as Hughes forces this traditionally diminutive four-letter word into the mouths of her audiences, sending her reviewers into a flurry of symbolic re-alignment. In the introduction to her text *Clit Notes*, Hughes outlines the reaction her piece generated in the popular press:

> The *New York Times*, for example, wouldn't print the title, which was described as containing 'a slang term for the word "clitoris".' Before going on the air on some National Public Radio Station, I was told I could use the word only if I was talking about myself. Under no circumstances, I was warned, could I call someone else a clitoris on the air.'[37]

Clearly, Hughes understands the performative power that this 'little, lacking' organ wields as she tells her readers 'that making people wrap their mouths around the word, if not the thing itself, is precisely the kind of political goal one can hope to realize through the theater.'[38] Politics and performance mingle in 'Clit Notes' as co-conspirators plotting momentary ruptures in identificatory coherence. (My favorite example of the pandemonium initiated by these ruptures is the section in 'Clit Notes' that describes the chaos created by the Alpine sets falling down during a school production of *The Sound of Music*. As the mountains topple over the audience sees that the nuns and the Nazis are the same people.)

Hughes's strategy of spinning the trajectories of culturally enforced paradigms in unpredictable directions is further exemplified by the ways in which she propels the sign system through a dizzying course of twisted significations. She comments in the intro-duction to *Clit Notes* that, '[i]f a broken kitchen chair could be transformed into a castle, then why not use secondhand language the same way: take it apart, paint it, glue it, pervert its meanings.'[39] In the opening segment of 'Clit Notes' we follow Hughes along the seamless (yet, entirely convoluted) pathway of radically diverse signifiers – during the course of this piece a linkage is established between Republicans and freed slaves; lesbians, prostitution, and Democrats; homosexuals and 'their compulsive erotic relationship to household appliances;'[40] and between lesbian sexuality and the prized animals on display at the Saginaw County Fair that are hand-raised by Four-H kids. The disparate relationship of signifier to signified in 'Clit Notes' not only deconstructs coherent articulations of meaning, but these signifiers, in their multiple significations, point to the possibilities that the lack of a stable referent holds for reconfiguring lesbian representations. Kate Davy, in her article on Hughes's performance art observes that 'when signals are crossed in every dimension, increased effort and attention are required on the part of spectators to "read" the performance, scanning and rescanning the production's visual and narrative fields.'[41] That lesbians do not appear within Hughes's reference book 'Dr David Reuben's *Everything You Always Wanted to Know about Sex*'[42] is the necessary precondition for the imaginative possibilities generated in 'Clit Notes.' The presence of lesbian sexuality in this section of the performance flows from the absence of the lesbian in Reuben's standard historical reference. Conversely, the appearance of lesbian sexuality also occurs within this unstable context and is subjected to the same process of mutation and transformation that all of the signs in 'Clit Notes' must endure. For Hughes, as she comments in a 1993 interview with C. Carr, 'The question is about what you give up when you become visible. And who you are becoming visible to.'[43] To become visible is, as I have noted, to risk succumbing to the operations of a phallocentric visual culture whose ideology 'erases the power of the unmarked, unspoken, and unseen.'[44]

Reverberating around this presence/absence dialectic, the appearance of the lesbian within the representational space of 'Clit Notes' is necessarily provisional and highly contingent.[45] She is constantly caught in the ambiguous space between Utopian desires for full, unrestricted access to the symbolic *and* the power of erasure that is always already embedded within those appearances. Phelan outlines this dilemma in her chapter on the 'ontology of performance' in *Unmarked* : 'Since the female body and the female character cannot be "staged" or "seen" within representational mediums without challenging the hegemony of male desire, it can be effective politically and aesthetically to deny representing the female body.'[46] This denial foregrounds, in Phelan's words, 'the suspension of the female body between the polarities of presence and absence.'[47] This suspension is acutely invoked near the end of 'Clit Notes' when Hughes, the performer, relates the story of kissing her girlfriend in front of a Ukrainian meat market. At the height of this blissful kiss a 'a man whips out of the store . . . cradling a newborn baby ham' (a lovely comment on the piggishly patriarchal law of the Father) and calls them '"Shameless!"'[48] The moment of the spectacle of the lesbian kiss, and by extension the appearance of lesbian desire, is simultaneously the moment that the wrath of the symbolic is incited.

The onlooker's anger briefly plunges Hughes into the history of her shame and a discussion of the ways in which these memories infiltrate queer existence: 'I have seen shame work its backward alchemy overnight. I've seen people who've gone to bed perfectly respectable bull daggers, only to wake up the next morning claiming to be somebody's wife, a stray Republican, their own mother.'[49] Hughes counters the erasure of the lesbian under the regulatory force of shame within the Symbolic *not* by resorting to the liberationist frame of 'lesbian pride' but, instead, by playing out two distinct performances. First, the recounting of this meat market experience ensures that we are witnesses to the scene and shifts our gaze from the kiss to the objectification of the Father. The Father does not remain an unmarked arbiter of shame but, in the retelling, becomes a spectacle for our consumption. Second, Hughes privileges the *performance* of shamelessness in her narrative as a counter-hegemonic strategy when she comments: 'What my girlfriend and I are good at is acting shameless.'[50] This 'acting shameless' manifests itself as either 'kissing like there's no tomorrow'[51] or, conversely, 'kissing as if there were no past.'[52] Each of these perform-ances, through a recourse to the discourse of fantasy, desires to provoke a crisis in the temporal order as a means of representing desire. That they must lack a past and a future is paradoxically exemplary of both the regulation of lesbian bodies within the symbolic and the radical potential that a performative present holds for the appearance of lesbian desire.

Phelan argues that 'performance uses the body to frame the lack of Being promised by and through the body – that which cannot appear without a supplement.'[53] Perhaps the kiss in 'Clit Notes' signals this lack of Being as a means of suspending any Utopian claims for the purity of lesbian desire, or its existence outside of phallic representational systems. Indeed, perhaps this lack is what allows the kiss to exist at all, and the addition of shame and the subsequent performance of shamelessness is what identifies this as lesbian desire. If so, what are the implications for lesbian representation? At the very least, Hughes's extended dialogue with the various guises of shame that occur and recur throughout 'Clit Notes' gestures toward the seemingly inescapable situation of lesbian desire in the interstice between shame and shamelessness. This gesture complicates the ways in which lesbian pride and other similar liberationist projects tend to propel identity politics along a trajectory that moves from a past existence of humiliation and shame to a future world of acceptance and celebration. As the kiss collapses the space between these two spheres, Hughes foregrounds not only the pervasive and enduring threat that heterosexist judgment poses to performative acts of lesbian desire. She also points toward the constituting power that shame wields in these acts of desire and, in doing so, implicitly rejects a positive images style of representation/politics that heavily relies on the elision of negative effects.

Perhaps it is at this point of binary collapse in 'Clit Notes' that the possible impact of performance on real-world politics becomes glaringly evident. Right-wing morality stances often invoke the spectre of shame in order to censor or regulate the appearance of non-normative desire in the public arena. The 1990 National Endowment for the Arts (NEA) controversy over Holly Hughes was meant to demonstrate, among other things, that lesbian artists, if they wish to be heard/seen at all, must exhibit a proper amount of sexual shame.[54] That Hughes talks back to these critics in 'Clit Notes' not simply by refusing a position of shame but by recasting that shame as integral to lesbian desire is, as I have argued, a laudable and forceful re-articulation of the law against itself. Ultimately, as RoseLee Goldberg rather cynically observes, the NEA defunding garnered a degree of attention for Hughes's work that Jesse Helmes surely never anticipated: 'no one could invent a better trailblazer for their work than the lurid, tale-telling media that finds evil in the things artists say, rather than in the things congressmen do.'[55] Simultaneously a literal and textual act of survival, Hughes's piece recuperates shame, taking it back from the purview of authoritative discourses by invading that narrative with a vengeance.

The complex and frequently paradoxical relationship of 'Clit Notes' to conventional representational systems is further underscored by the fact that five of Hughes's performance pieces are anthologized in her book *Clit Notes: A Sapphic Sampler*.[56] If '[p]erformance's only life is in the present,'[57] then documenting her performances in such a tangible production as a book means that Hughes must contend with the tendency of print form to stabilize signification. Again, to invoke Phelan, '[p]erformance cannot be saved, recored, documented, or otherwise participate in the circulation of representations *of* representations: once it does so, it becomes something other than performance. . . . Performance's being . . . becomes itself through disappearance.'[58] The provisional subjectivity circulating in 'Clit Notes' is in danger of solidifying into a knowable, concrete presence whose form is fixed by the limitations of punctuation, typeface, and numbered pages. My critical analysis of 'Clit Notes' ironically, yet necessarily, also participates in the process of articulating a fully recognizable and coherent subject. Although I had the good fortune to see Hughes perform 'Clit Notes,'[59] I am primarily reliant upon the published text for my assessment of her work. This reliance obviously influences my interpretation to the extent that the performing body (no matter how many photographs are included!) materializes *only* through discourse. Inevitably, as Phelan comments, any 'attempt to write about the undocumentable event of performance is to invoke the rules of the written document and thereby alter the event itself.'[60] Rather than see this alteration as a limitation, I am enticed by the possibility of performing a further reiteration of Hughes's reiterations. As Amelia Jones and Andrew Stephenson make clear in their introduction to this collection, it is crucial to understand 'interpretation as a definitively *invested* kind of performance' (see page 3). That is, perhaps my critical performance and its situation within the parameters of queer theory materializes the body in/of 'Clit Notes' through yet another series of performatives. Certainly, marking the layers of representations at work in this article (Hughes re-citing pyschoanalysis, the book *Clit Notes* representing the performance piece 'Clit Notes,' Hughes as performer reiterating autobiographical moments, my own critique of the textual 'Clit Notes,' and so on) points towards the highly mediated nature of the performing body and disallows any simplistic exploration of identity configurations. More importantly, however, these reiterations send us on a labyrinthine journey through the maze of presences and absences that are at the heart of representations of lesbian identity and desire.

Deconstruction has taught us that no counter-hegemonic strategy can be radically outside the system it seeks to oppose and, indeed, an aesthetics of lack must perpetuate what Lacan has called the 'misrecognition' of the power of the phallus if the most radical effects of this aesthetics are to emerge. On the other hand, according to Carole Anne Tyler via Slavoj Zizek no ideology is totalizing because 'there is always something (real) which exceeds it, which slips through the signifying net as its "outside",'[61] which exists as the possible politicization of *dis*-identification. As the exaggeration of a pre-scripted narrative, 'lack' exists in the interstices of identification and dis-identification, and it is this rich paradox that potentially unravels the dichotomies of presence/absence and visibility/invisibility and further takes up the Butlerian task of 'making the signifier into a site for a set of rearticulations that cannot be predicted or controlled.'[62] I would hope that an aesthetics of lack, with its attentiveness to spectacular modes of performance, occasions a displacement of conventional paradigms and with renewed vigor interferes in existing representational forms.

NOTES

1   A version of this article was presented at the 1997 'Unnatural Acts' conference at the University of California, Riverside.

2   The conceptual base for this introduction is drawn from my forthcoming article 'Structure, Size and Play: The Case of the Talking Vulva' to be published in the second *Unnatural Acts* anthology, Phillip Brett, Sue-Ellen Case, and Susan Foster (eds), Bloomington, Indiana, University of Indiana Press, forthcoming.

3   For a comprehensive analysis of the influence of sexology on the emergence of lesbian identities see Faderman's *Odd Girls and Twilight Lovers: A History of Lesbian Life in Twentieth-Century America*, New York, Columbia University Press, 1991; see especially pp. 37–61.

4   Richard von Krafft-Ebing's 1888 description of the the female homosexual typifies the ways in which the lesbian body was discursively materialized: 'She had coarse male features, a rough and rather deep voice, and with the exception of the bosom and female contour of the pelvis, looked more like man in woman's clothing than like a woman.' ('Perversion of the Sexual Instinct – Report of Cases,' *Alienist and Neurologist*, October 1888).

5   Sigmund Freud, *The Standard Edition*, vol. XXII, ed. James Strachey, London, Hogarth, 1964, p. 125.

6   Ibid.

7   Ibid, p. 126.

8   Ibid, p. 127.

9   Ibid, p. 126.

10 Ibid.

11 Ibid.

12 Ibid.

13 Freud infamously announces in his 1927 essay on fetishism that 'the normal prototype of all fetishes is the penis of the man, just as the normal prototype of an organ felt to be inferior is the real little penis of the woman, the clitoris'; Freud, "Fetishism," tr. Joan Riviere in *Sexuality and the Psychology of Love*, ed. Philip Rieff, New York, Collier Books, 1963, 219. The inferiority of smallness is given axiomatic status in Freud's work as it is in Western culture as a whole.

14 Of course 'Femininity' is but one example of an essay in which Freud outlines normative anatomical roles and discusses deviance in anatomical terms. For a more extended discussion of the relationship between sexuality and anatomy see, among others, 'Three Essays on the Theory of Sexuality,' and 'Some Psychical Consequences of the Anatomical Distinction Between the Sexes.'

15 Jacques Lacan, *Écrits: A Selection*, New York, Norton, 1977, p. 285.

16 Ibid, p. 287.

17 Ibid, p. 286.

18 Rosalind Minsky, 'Commentary on "The Signification of the Phallus",' *Psychoanalysis and Gender*, New York, Routledge, 1996, pp. 137–177.

19 Ibid, p. 154.

20 Jacqueline Rose, *Sexuality in the Field of Vision*, London, Verso, 1986, p. 66.

21 The notion that phallic power is dependent on reiteration for its effects is at the heart of Judith Butler's highly nuanced discussion of a potentially retooled phallic signifier in 'The Lesbian Phallus' chapter of *Bodies That Matter*, New York, Routledge, 1993, pp. 57–92. Rather than simply repudiate Lacan's notion of the phallus as a privileged signifier within the realm of the symbolic, Butler conceives of a specifically lesbian phallus which disrupts Lacan's privileging schema. According to Butler, a space is opened up for the insubordination of a lesbian phallus precisely because the phallus itself is an idealization, a construct that anxiously governs the description of its own origins in order to conceal its non-originary status.

22 I use the term 'materialization' in accordance with Butler's discussion of the ways in which bodies ('sex') are materialized through discourse: '"sex" is a regulatory ideal whose material-ization is compelled, and this materialization takes place (or fails to take place) through certain highly regulated practices. In other words, "sex" is an ideal construct which is forcibly materialized through time' (Butler, *Bodies That Matter*, p. 1). I extend this analysis to suggest that the sexuality of particular bodies (in this case, lesbian bodies) is marked through anatomical

performatives that give a literal shape to the construction of lesbian identity. That is, the emergence of the female homosexual as a discursive subject occurs in tandem with the demarcation of her bodily appearance. The re-citation of certain anatomical characteristics has established stereotypical identificatory traits for the lesbian body.

23 Among the many theorists who have critiqued the notion of 'lack' and suggested alternative models are: Hélène Cixous, especially in 'The Laugh of the Medusa,' *The Signs Reader*, ed. Elizabeth Abel and Emily K. Abel, Chicago, University of Chicago Press, 1983, pp. 279-97; Jane Gallop, *The Daughter's Seduction: Feminism and Psychoanalysis*, Ithaca, NY, Cornell University Press, 1982; Luce Irigaray, especially in *This Sex Which Is Not One*, tr. Catherine Porter, Ithaca, NY, Cornell University Press, 1985; Elizabeth Meese, *(Sem)Erotics: theorizing lesbian: writing*, New York, New York University Press, 1992; Monique Wittig, *The Straight Mind and Other Essays*, Boston, Beacon Press, 1992. This list only highlights a few of the major texts written in opposition to female lack. It would require several pages to give a comprehensive ennumeration of all the counter-arguments.

24 Paula Bennett, 'Critical Clitoridectomy: Female Sexual Imagery and Feminist Psychoanalytic Theory,' *Signs*, Winter, 1993, vol. 18, n. 2, p. 257.

25 Celeste West, *A Lesbian Love Advisor*, San Francisco, Cleis Press, 1989.

26 West and Bennett are but two examples in a long line of feminist writers and artists who have sought to re-value female anatomy by using clitoral images to depict female power and subjectivity. I think immediately of Judy Chicago's attempts to represent women's often invisible place in history through her clitoral and vulvic place settings in her installation piece *The Dinner Party*. In Chicago's words: 'The incorporation of vulval iconography was certainly intended to challenge the pervasive definitions of women and of female sexuality as passive. But, more significant, in the context of this work of art, it implies that the various women represented – though separated by culture, time, geography, experience, and individual choices . . . – are unified primarily by their gender, which in my opinion, is the main reason that so many were and are unknown'; in Chicago, *The Dinner Party*, New York, Penguin, 1996, p. 6.

27 Peggy Phelan, *Unmarked: The Politics of Performance*, New York, Routledge, 1993, p. 6.

28 Anna Munster is quoted in Lynda Hart, 'Blood, piss, tears: the queer real,' *Textual Practice*, 1995, vol. 9, n. 1, p. 57.

29 Ibid, p. 58.

30 Phelan, *Unmarked*, p. 7.

31 Donald Morton, 'The Politics of Queer Theory in the (Post)Modern Moment,' *Genders* Fall 1993, vol. 17, p. 124.

32 Teresa De Lauretis, 'Film and the Visible,' in *How Do I Look? Queer Film and Video*, ed. Bad Object-Choices, Seattle, Bay Press, 1991, p. 224.

33 Hart, 'Blood, piss, tears,' p. 63.

34 Holly Hughes, 'Clit Notes,' *Clit Notes: A Sapphic Sampler*, New York, Grove Press, 1996, p. 196.

35 Butler, *Bodies that Matter*, p. 45.

36 Ezra Levant, 'A special performance for Gary Mar,' *Alberta Report*, 20 June 1994, p. 34.

37 Hughes, 'Clit Notes,' p. 184.

38 Ibid.

39 Ibid, p. 18.

40 Ibid, p. 186.

41 Kate Davy, 'Reading Past the Heterosexual Imperative,' *TDR* (The Drama Review), 1989, vol. 33, n. 1, p. 166.

42 Hughes, 'Clit Notes,' p. 186.

43 C. Carr, 'No Trace of the Bland: An Interview With Holly Hughes,' *Theater*, 1993, vol. 24, n. 2, p. 68.

44 Phelan, *Unmarked*, p. 7.

45 Hughes' performance art has been criticized by lesbian theorists such as Sue-Ellen Case for the ways in which the lesbian subject disappears under this postmodernist rubric of identity: 'Postmodern slippage is one thing and lesbian sexuality on a banana peel is another' ('A Case Concerning Hughes,' *TDR*, 1989, vol. 33, n. 4, p. 11. I find this need to limit postmodern slippage and, thereby, fix the parameters of lesbian sexuality dangerous in its tendency to once again outline 'proper' identity configurations.

46 Phelan, *Unmarked*, p. 164.
47 Ibid.
48 Hughes, 'Clit Notes,' p. 205.
49 Ibid, p. 206.
50 Ibid.
51 Ibid.
52 Ibid.
53 Phelan, *Unmarked*, p. 151.
54 In the summer of 1990 Hughes received national attention in America when she became part of the controversial 'NEA four.' Hughes, along with Karen Finley, Tim Miller, and John Fleck were de-funded by the Bush-appointed Chairman of the National Endowment for the Arts, John Frohnmayer. Yeilding to pressure from the religious Right, Frohnmayer denied grants to these performance artists who had already been approved by peer panels. Hughes was vilified as a pornographer on the floor of the US Senate by Jesse Helms. The performance piece 'Clit Notes' earned Hughes her second Obie award. Hughes has, in fact, received numerous awards, commissions, and grants. Notably the New York Shakespeare Festival, Yellow Springs Institute, National Performance Network, the Walker Art Center, Performance Space 122, the New York Foundation for the Arts, the New York State Council, the Aestrea, Jerome, Ford, Zellerbach, and Rockefeller Foundations, and the Franklin Furnace Fund for Performance Art.
55 RoseLee Goldberg, 'Holly Hughes,' *ArtForum*, 1990, vol. 29, n. 4, p. 142.
56 *Clit Notes: A Sapphic Sampler*, N.Y., Grove Press, 1996, contains 'The Well of Horniness' (1984); 'The Lady Dick' (1985); 'Dress Suits to Hire' (1987); 'World Without End' (1984); 'Clit Notes' (1994).
57 Phelan, *Unmarked*, p. 146.
58 Ibid.
59 Hughes performed 'Clit Notes' in 1994 at The Engineered Air Theatre, Calgary, Alberta, Canada.
60 Phelan, *Unmarked*, p. 148.
61 Carole-Anne Tyler, 'Passing, Narcissism, Identity, and Difference,' *Differences*, Summer-Fall 1994, vol. 6, n. 2–3, p. 232.
62 Butler, *Bodies that Matter*, p. 219.

13

RENAMING *UNTITLED FLESH*

Marking the politics of marginality

Meiling Cheng

NAMING THE IDENTITY

In a narrative about their company history, Sacred Naked Nature Girls, four women artists who have formed a triracial and multi-ethnic ensemble in Los Angeles, describe an incident that may endure as the mythic origin of their collaboration: 'The women officially christened their group one morning at Zuma Beach, CA, when they spontaneously shed their clothes during an improvisation at the water's edge.' The artists frame the incident as the primal scene for their ensemble. Suddenly, as if by magic, their individual bodies were reborn into one mobile, sentient, and tactile organism, which bore the name of their newly emerged collective identity: Sacred Naked Nature Girls (Plate 13.1).[1]

If somewhat terse, all elements present in this unabashedly embellished account about the genesis of an artistic team feed into a well-designed nativity ritual. The birthing takes place in a natural surrounding – 'at the water's edge' – a liminal space between water and earth, between a moist environment and the loose flesh of the sand. The line that tortuously delineates 'the edge' stretches like an umbilical cord. The throes of reproductive labors assume a dramatic ease; they are pleasures from improvised movements. The artists who are at once their own mothers and daughters select a most 'spontaneous' costume for their collective body: 'Naked came I out of my mother's womb.'[2] After the birth comes the naming: the birth of a name. The women act as midwives to deliver their nominal quadruplets: Sacred Naked Nature Girls, a name composed of four words, four loaded concepts, four refashioned and conjoined signifiers that anticipate new significations. Now that their 'christening' procedures are nearly completed, the women might have culled another phrase from the Bible to be their culminating chant: 'My name is Legion: for we are many.'[3]

The four artists who name themselves Sacred Naked Nature Girls (SNNG) came from diverse ethnic and artistic backgrounds: Danielle Brazell, an Irish-Polish, ex-Catholic, third-generation American artist who teaches performance workshops for women at Highways in Santa Monica; Laura Meyers, a Polish Catholic, Russian-Jewish American body artist who has studied with Leo Shapiro and John Malpede; Akilah Oliver, an African-American poet, teacher, and performance artist who had worked with the Los Angeles Poverty Department led by Malpede; and Denise Uyehara, a Japanese-American solo performer and writer whose play, *Hiro*, has been produced by various regional theatres (Plate 13.2).[4] The artists' cultural diversity is further compounded by their diverse

Plate 13.1 Sacred Naked Nature Girls, 1996. Photo design Joe Notaro; photograph by Jerry Browning. Courtesy of SNNG

Plate 13.2 Sacred Naked Nature Girls, 1995. Photograph by Linda Kliewer. Courtesy of SNNG

sexualities (homosexual, heterosexual, and bisexual). The four performing together thus amass the interests of intersecting audience communities. Their usual spectators include artists, gays, lesbians, bisexuals, HIV-positive people, Caucasian, Asian-American, and African-American men and women.

Sacred Naked Nature Girls have to date produced three collaborative projects. They internationally toured the first piece, *Untitled Flesh*, an all-nude performance first presented in Boulder, Colorado, in April 1994.[5] Their second piece, *Home. The Last Place I Ran to Just About Killed Me*, premiered at Highways in August 1996.[6] SNNG presented its third piece, *The Party* – which the ensemble co-created with an outside director, Elia Arce – for five evenings in October 1997, also at Highways.

Although the three pieces deal with different issues of sexuality, ethnicity, identity, and culture, they share a common feminist foundation. The first two pieces feature the multifaceted experiences of women in society as their themes. The third piece is autobiographical, built upon SNNG members' relationships as artists and women working together in an ensemble for the past five years. This latest piece, infused with a self-reflexive honesty, exposes many of the difficulties confronting the women as artistic colleagues. It heralds their joint decision that SNNG will go into hiatus, in order for members to pursue their individual goals. In the past, however, a shared concern for women's interests had prompted the company to designate at least one show during each tour exclusively for an audience of women. SNNG had also instituted a pedagogical component in its company practice, offering workshops with women from diverse social, ethnic, and economic strata. This commitment to empower women demonstrates the ensemble's proactive, feminist tendency.

If gender politics manifested as a proclaimed love for women has motivated SNNG's company praxis, a racial politics embodied by the collective's multicultural makeup inspires SNNG's most conscientious experiment. A concrete result of this multicultural experiment can be seen in the dialectic tension between unity and diversity which characterizes the group's spirit and ethos. Both in their work and in the ways they represent their work in interviews, publicity materials, and post-show discussions, Sacred Naked Nature Girls repeatedly stress the differences *and* commonalities among individual members. Such a double emphasis on disparity and collectivity finds its best example in the wide range of labels available for them to identify their group: they are 'Sacred Naked Nature Girls,' or, in its various shortened forms, 'Sacred Nature Girls,' 'Sacred Girls,' 'Nature Girls,' etc.; they also call their company by its four-letter acronym, SNNG. As a writer on the group's work, I have to use a plural verb when referring to 'Sacred Naked Nature Girls' or 'the Girls' as a grammatical subject, but I might use a singular verb to follow 'SNNG,' the collective, as a single entity. This indicates an interesting yet far from unique linguistic problem that a commentator has to resolve before writing about the ensemble. More pertinently, it suggests that the Girls have succeeded in signifying their work's complex dialectics with an act of naming.

VOICE AND SIGHT

Naming as an act of explication offers a theoretical angle to view SNNG's work. Yet, even more crucial than this hermeneutic function is the generative function that it serves for the group. I shall return to the 'primal scene' constructed by the Sacred Girls as the ceremony that both celebrates their union and defines their collaboration. My reading has attempted to establish that the artists are reborn in their union into one flesh and their collaboration formally begins with the birth of their ensemble name. The scene therefore involves a double birth. The initial birth envisions the artists' intent to collaborate as one body/unit when they disrobe in front of one another, symbolically ripping off the boundaries that prevent their union. Witnessed by one another and by the surrounding landscape, their union now exists as a novel sight – an assemblage of figures made of many colors – but the sight remains anonymous. Without a name that declares their emotional and spatial relationships to one another and to the world, the sight of their union yields no special meaning and is therefore ontologically indistinguishable from any sight of animate or inanimate objects that happen to occupy their present fields of vision. Their union, for lack of a proclaimable identity, is at this instant continuous with the visible natural milieu, possessing no autonomous status. To acquire a sense of independence for their artistic matrimony/nativity requires that the artists match their physical visibility with linguistic visibility; they have to annul their anonymity to announce their union. Hence, the subsequent birth of their shared name: Sacred Naked Nature Girls. Only through naming could their collaboration as SNNG begin to claim its being, identify its image, and pronounce its entrance into the symbolic order, one maintained by textual memories.

Naming as a performative action coordinates SNNG's self-enacted memory of its own advent; it is a performance that consists of giving voice to a hitherto silent sight. The artists represent their self-naming as a christening ceremony, yet they baptize themselves solely by the sanctity of their joint agency. Their rite of naming appropriates and modifies both pagan and Christian motifs, simulating the hallowed gesture of creativity in a setting brimming over with the hints of animistic spirits. They evoke the vision of a covenant of witches, partaking sacraments in high tides, holding communion with the teeming cosmos. SNNG, their newly-found body/identity, emerges like the many-headed Hydra who has evolved the ability to split its monstrous body into four separate bodies that move about in adjacent, contiguous, or intersecting spheres. The moving bodies, when they so desire, re-merge into one. An anachronistic tonality of earnestness characterizes these pantheistic visions. The artists seem to have de-gravitated away from the weight of fin de siècle cynicism, but have also remained rooted against the levity of postmodernist parody.

Just as earnestness is defined by the agreement between surface and interior, the Sacred Girls approach the Christian thematics which they mis/quote with a similar level of piety that sustains belief. SNNG's modulation of the Christian theology centers around the power of naming. The Christian God enunciates Himself as the Word in the image of the Trinity, thereby linking the (speech) act of naming with creating. His word renders visible the myriad sights that populate the earth; His voice coincides with the created sight. As a well-established, almighty Subject, the Christian God owns the font of originality, buttressed by His scripturally ordained omniscience, omnipotence, and omnipresence. Read against this context, the performative naming employed by the Sacred Girls is strictly an act of re-creation. Their union first registers as a sight – as it were – on the tablet of Nature, before they find words to name it. Their voice articulates the significance of their collective being as sight: their voice reinforces the sight, but it neither precedes nor coincides with the sight. Regarded as *marginalized*, hence *anomalous subjects* within the Judeo-Christian, patriarchal structure, the Sacred Girls cannot possibly claim 'the font of originality' reserved for the long-standing, authoritative Father. What they can do instead is to intervene, inserting their presence as visual information onto the premises of the powers that be and, by sheer insistence, begin inscribing/naming their own versions of truth in the Holy Book.

So goes SNNG's performance score: Sight. Voice. Text. Then perhaps the harvesting of anticipated yields: Recognition. Power. History. The force of such a score is primarily self-confirmed, validated by a community of viewers who cohere because of shared belief. The Sacred Girls are sacred first of all to one another; they constitute their own basic witnessing community. Their community has the potential to expand as they offer performances to other spectators, who may or may not experience the gracious violence of conversion. The spectators who gather to form nomadic communities for the Sacred Girls could extend or withhold their beliefs in the performance, contingent upon the degree to which they respond to the promise of the SNNG 'salvation.'

Since they borrow the magic of naming as a point of inception for their ensemble, the Sacred Girls necessarily assume the biblical model for spiritual efficacy in conceptualizing their potential public appeal. What I have extracted from their self-witnessed ritual of naming as their *performance score* and *anticipated yields* follows the theological design for religious conversion and confirmation of faith/belief: manifestation of miracles (*sight*); dissemination of gospels (*voice/text*); bearing witness (*recognition*); holding communion with fellow believers (*power*); repeated affirmation of believed 'Truth' (*history*). The artists nevertheless depart radically from the orthodox code of conduct that governs both sight and voice in the Bible. They critique the theological formation of Christianity by exercising a feminist exegesis of the Scripture. Their exegesis proceeds simultaneously with two interpretive strategies: *literalization* of metaphors and *inversion* of values. They take to task, in particular, the gender-specific metaphors which the Bible uses to convey heavenly/spiritual matters in worldly/sexual terms.

The Christian Scripture narrativizes the relationship between God and man as that between man and woman; the metaphors of sexual difference establish a hierarchy of spiritual difference. A parable from the Book of Ezekiel expresses such sexual/spiritual hierarchy in no uncertain terms. The parable compares Jerusalem to an exposed infant girl. The Lord takes pity on her, washes off her blood, raises her up to become a jewel. As her breasts are formed and her hair grows, the Lord sees that she is 'old enough for love.'[7] He covers her nakedness with His garment and makes her His wife. But, prideful of her own beauty, the wife willingly becomes 'a prostitute,' sharing her body promiscuously with other lovers. The Lord condemns His adulterous wife:

> Therefore, you prostitute, hear the word of the LORD! This is what the Sovereign LORD says: Because you poured out your wealth and exposed your nakedness in your promiscuity with your lovers, and because of your detestable idols . . . therefore I am going to gather all your lovers, with whom you found pleasure, those you loved as well as those you hated. I will gather them against you from all around and will strip you in front of them, and they will see all your nakedness. I will sentence you to the punishment of women who commit adultery; . . . I will bring upon you the blood vengeance of my wrath and jealous anger. Then I will hand you over to your lovers . . . . They will strip you of your clothes and take your fine jewelry and leave you naked and bare.[8]

'Naked female body' is the pivotal image in this parable. The thematic connotations for this image, like the scarlet letter 'A' dangling from Hester Prynne's neck in Hawthorne's novel, change through time and circumstances. The deserted baby girl's nakedness indicates vulnerability; it bears the sign of parental neglect and social disdain. The nakedness of a woman 'old enough for love' might suggest the maturity and allure of her virgin body, the proof of her eligibility for matrimony and for biblical knowledge. Made wife, the woman takes pleasure in her own body and shares her naked beauty with other lovers; she violates her vow to be in eternal possession by the one Lord who was first her adopted Father, then her true/legitimate Husband. Her 'sin' of adultery arises from her *re*-possession of her naked body as her own. Consequently, the Lord punishes her by turning her nakedness into her shame, a sign of her *dis*-possession: she is stripped bare and stripped off all the rewards for her gratitude and fidelity to the Lord.

The woman, almost identical to her naked body, is perceived by the Lord as an object or a sign throughout the parable. Her image remains visible to her Watcher, but her voice is not heard. In contrast, the Lord shields His body in a 'garment' and exerts His presence primarily as a narrative voice. The woman, a sight without a voice, is under constant surveillance by the narrative voice. The narrative voice establishes its power not only by representing the Author, but also by its freedom from being watched; its authority increases when it pronounces the Author's jealous will to punish His adulterous subordinate. But how does the woman begin to sin? She 'sins' the minute she collapses her subjective will with her own body object; she decides to 'become a prostitute,' exposing her nakedness in promiscuity. In the eyes of the Lord, the woman has sinned because she has infused the sight of her body with her own determination. The invisible markings of the woman's will on her own body animates her in erotic actions. Her actions, be them motivated by pride or by pleasure, are then the physical manifestations of her voice. She has given a voice to her naked body as sight.

204

Inverting the terms of this parable would bring us back to the moment when four women artists 'spontaneously shed their clothes' and name themselves Sacred Naked Nature Girls. The parable uses 'nakedness' as a metaphor for the condition of human original sin. The Naked Girls, however, take *nakedness* literally as being *unclothed*. In their first piece, *Untitled Flesh*, the artists turn nakedness into a performance condition, confronting its pejorative connotations to examine its complexity. The sight of 'naked female body' recurs as a visual subtext for the performance concepts listed by the Girls: 'multiple layers of nakedness,' 'flesh memory,' 'the construction and appropriation of desire,' 'the mythos of cultural identification,' 'the gaze,' 'power,' 'erotica and pornography.'[9] SNNG's work then inspects the social, mythical, or historical traces left on, remembered or appropriated by the female bodies on display. In making public their nakedness, the Naked Girls have rendered their own bodies 'promiscuous.' The crux of their investigation therefore lies in provoking the spectators' self-conscious responses to their own viewing of the 'impure' bodies in performance.

What most fascinates me about the Girls' naked actions is that they perform in a collective comprising women of diverse racial and ethnic origins and of multiple sexual orientations. In other words, I *perceive* their bodies as uncompromisingly different from one another because of both *visible* and *invisible* markings; no matter how partial and deceptive my perceptions are, I discern their divergences as both skin-deep and hidden in libidinal compulsions barred from my sight. Sacred Nature Girls' performances consciously take stock of their acknowledged differences, making the dynamics between their unity and disparity a conceptual and performative issue. To me, SNNG's collective art, at least during the duration of performance, presents the actual image of a utopian dream, a glimpse of a possible global ethos advocating forbearance for differences. Their feminist, multicultural coalition promises me – an anomalous subject myself, a foreign-born Asian female immigrant – *a politics of marginality*, a force of anomalous identification that may disrupt the Anglo-American, masculocentric status quo. Notably, this politics of marginality is invested in what Peggy Phelan terms 'an ideology of the visible,'[10] tackling one of the questions that Amelia Jones and Andrew Stephenson raise in this anthology: whether becoming (in)visible in performance could lead to liberation. I shall bracket this question for the moment to consider the most obvious effect of women self-producing 'promiscuous' sights and sounds in front of a congregated crowd.

From the media-milked case of Karen Finley, whose 1989 piece *We Keep Our Victims Ready* was involved in the National Endowment of the Arts censorship furor, we know that a solitary woman's disrobed figure engaged in public action can still be seen by a large segment of population as transgressive, as working against 'appropriate' gender behavior. How much more so then it is for four women of different colors to protest their love and lust for one another by forming a post-Rodin flesh sculpture of *The Kiss* on stage! (Plate 13.3). While a single female body displaying herself in performance could be construed as 'essentialist' or 'universal,' at once reduced and inflated to be a stand-in for all women, the less familiar – arguably harder to be contained or recuperated – sight of four female subjects divulging their pain and pleasure in public deflates the myth of universality with their perceived visible and audible specificities.[11] Such an accent on specificity invites the viewers' attention to the immediate and the localized, compelling them to heed, in Jon Cruz's terms, 'the nuances of flesh-and-blood subjects who must negotiate through sensuous knowledge-making the conditions of everyday life.'[12]

The multiethnic and transgendered particularities among the Girls create a distinct

Plate 13.3 Sacred Naked Nature Girls. *Untitled Flesh*, 1996. Courtesy of SNNG

chemistry and a tangle of conundrums that bring home a thorny dilemma confronting the dominant culture of United States in the 1990s: namely, the struggles of disenfranchised subjects to reach 'moral solidarity'[13] and obtain intellectual, political, and economic equality. While maintaining feminism as their united front, the Girls identify that 'thorny dilemma' as 'multiculturalism.' As the artists themselves state, they wonder if there is 'a feminist investigation of multiculturalism.'[14] To pursue an answer, they survey the existence of 'psychic, physical, cultural, gender and imagined borders'[15] in search of 'a language that does not deny or erase differences.'[16] By creating works together as 'people of varying class, cultural, and sexual identities,'[17] the Girls wish to inspire dialogues with and among their diverse audience members. While they stress that performance is a transformative process shared by the artists and spectators, they also deliberately play up the interactions among the performing women themselves. For they endeavor to find how women construct their identities, how their bodies are appropriated or abused, and how they relate to one another as women, be they lesbian, straight, or bisexual.[18] Consequently, Sacred Naked Nature Girls turn their own bodies into both their experiments and laboratories. They proffer a visible, audible, tangible, and mobile monument of flesh to render their artistic union an embodiment of multiculturalism.

MARKED AND HEARD

In an attempt to 'revalue a belief in subjectivity and identity which is not visibly representable,' Peggy Phelan launches a brilliant critique against 'the ideology of the visible' in her 1993 book *Unmarked: The Politics of Performance*.[19] Phelan interrogates the ironically similar assumption held by progressives and conservatives alike concerning the equation between representational visibility and political efficacy. Because of a mistaken judgment about 'the relation between the real and the representational,' Phelan diagnoses, both groups believe that 'greater visibility of the hitherto under-represented leads to enhanced political power.'[20] Thus, progressives promote a greater circulation of visibility for the racial, ethnic, and sexual others in the representational economy, whereas conservatives dedicate themselves to defaming or censoring such a circulation. Phelan maintains that the tactics used by both groups reflect insufficient understanding 'of the relationship between visibility, power, identity, and liberation.'[21] 'If representational visibility equals power,' Phelan comments wryly, 'then almost-naked young white women should be running Western culture. The ubiquity of their image, however, has hardly brought them political or economic power.'[22]

Phelan expresses a strong suspicion of the purported political benefits of increased representational visibility, as illustrated humorously by her example of scantily dressed young white women. Casting her vote for the 'real power in remaining unmarked,' Phelan's challenge to the ideology of the visible consists in reversing what she calls 'the binary between the power of visibility and the impotence of invisibility.'[23] According to her, visibility is 'a trap'[24] because the represented image – the given to be seen – is placed under surveillance and regulation. 'In framing more and more images of the hitherto under-represented other, contemporary culture finds a way to name, and thus to arrest and fix, the image of that other,' argues Phelan.[25] She further observes that visibility provokes 'voyeurism, fetishism, the colonial/imperial appetite for possession.'[26] Although she admits that there is certain political appeal to the idea of attaining a more inclusive representational landscape, she resists conceding more theoretical virtues to the power of visibility because of undesirable consequences.

Phelan's caution against an over-investment in the merits of obtaining visibility is highly compelling. As I demonstrate in my reading of the parable from the Book of Ezekiel, the woman is quite visible as an image, but she enjoys neither freedom, nor power. Instead, she is confined by the constant vigil of her Keeper. In contrast, the Lord's almighty power is hardly abated by affirming his presence primarily as a voice. Voice, rather than sight, then, is the key element in defining who has the real power in this parable. Voice has the ability to empower and authenticate the truth effects of sight. This crucial linkage between voice and sight indicates a limit in Phelan's conception of the unmarked, 'a configuration of subjectivity'[27] which secures the subject's power and freedom by evading being sighted. The problem with Phelan's politics of invisibility is that there is often no distinction between her tactic of '*active* vanishing'[28] and the actual result expressed by the truism: out of sight, out of mind. It is also hard to tell the difference between the subliminal policy of invisibility administered by the dominant culture to absent its 'abnormal' members and the invisibility politics adopted by the 'abnormal' members themselves to induce the implosion of the dominant culture. It is unfortunate but likely that the ideology of the invisible would result in the erasure of 'abnormality' from the privileged norm. As a sight unseen and a voice unheard, the abnormal, anomalous subject would then become a negligible deposit conveniently kept on the margin as a lost memory, lost to the norm – out of seeing, out of hearing, out of mind!

I suggest that presence – defined as representational visibility – still offers more possibility than absence – secured by representational invisibility – for the subject to achieve momentary liberation and exercise individual will. As marginalized subjects, we must *reclaim the corporeal attributes of presence.* Michele Wallace observes in *Invisibility Blues* that 'black women are more often visualized in mainstream American culture – most prominently as fashion models or as performers in music videos – than they are allowed to speak their own words.'[29] Hence, black women suffer from the problem of 'high *visibility,*' a problem that is aggravated by their 'total lack of *voice.*'[30] In other words, black women are unable to make their presence felt because their existence in vision does not ensure the coexistence of their voice. The best way for these over-visualized but mostly muted individuals to redress this problem, I believe, is not voluntarily to disappear from view but to become *a speaking sight.*

While there is no direct connection between representational visibility and political power, there is at best a dubious correlation between invisibility and freedom; the link is even more precarious between invisibility and power. Visibility may be turned into a surveillance mechanism by the Establishment to enforce control over anomalous subjects, who are 'undesirable elements' in relation to mainstream culture. Indeed, allowing oneself to be watched subjects one to the disadvantage of being scrutinized, co-opted, and misread. But these drawbacks might be the price that disenfranchised and marginalized subjects have to pay in order to contest, even to upend *the norm of their invisibility.* From the perspective of the always already invisible, the privacy of movement in the dark must be sacrificed for the risks entailed by the exposure under the light. This is the reasoning that makes the sight of four nude women of different skin colors, body sizes, and physiognomic features moving and talking together on stage such a liberating presence to my eyes. As an interpreter who consumes SNNG's art for my textual performance, I have *named, framed, and transfixed* as if on a memory wall SNNG's *naming rite* as the ensemble's discursive genesis. *To name is to mark*; to be named is to be *remarked*; to name again is to ensure – if provisionally – that the originary naming is *heard.* Sacred Naked Nature Girls have *named themselves* in order to *mark* their new presence. I exert the verbal violence of *renaming their name* in the service of my *performing words,* but I do so also to extend *a paper stage* for their name to live, sing and dance. Have I empowered myself as critic or empowered the subject of my critical gaze and hearing? Or perhaps I and my artists and you, our reader, have simply consented to our imaginary conspiracy so as to *mark the exchange* of our representational currencies.

There is admittedly an uncertain correspondence between the power of self-generated naming and the public-elected political power; the former is performative while the latter is legislative. But I question whether such incommensurability between performative and political power is a difference in kind or in degree. Performative power lasts for the duration of its witnessed enactment. It may or may not have a lasting impact on the performer and the spectator. But does political power last forever? I suspect great uncertainty even for spiritual power's hold on eternity, although spiritual engagement allegedly occupies a deeper space – the event horizon – in the human psyche: the Law of the Father may be challenged or would grow infirm yet.

Thus consider the opening tableau from *Untitled Flesh*:

In the beginning there are random sounds in the dark. The sounds progress gradually in accelerated intervals, thumping out a rhythm like a fist hitting a sand bag. The sudden intrusion of an on-again, off-again strobe light fleshes out the phantom sounds with illuminated parts of female bodies. A litany of repeated questions burst from the now ruptured darkness: 'I am falling,' announces a woman's voice. Another quickly replies, 'I'll catch you.' 'I'm falling.' 'I got you.' Bluish strobe flashes disclose the sources of these refrains: a carousel of naked flesh made of three women with outstretched arms, cradling a woman who keeps falling in their midst. As often as the refrains warn of her falling, the free-falling woman is caught in the safety net formed by her companions' magnanimous bodies.

A woman cries out a varied motif, 'She said, "I'm falling. Will you catch me?"' The cry leads to a chorus of catechism that tests the boundary of unconditional love, confirmed by the voice, 'Yes, I'll catch you.' The reassurances seem to urge the falling woman not to stop falling. The velocity of her falls is matched only by the degree of her physical abandon, and the certainty of her being caught in mid-air, by some woman's bosom as their naked bodies clash. This performance segment ends, ironically, when the spinning body crashes to the floor: a heavy date with gravity. Does it suggest abandonment, accident, or death?

The ambiguity of this last suspense, however, cannot neutralize the tremendous tenderness released in the segment. Significantly, the Girls have chosen this paradigmatic scene to announce their emotional engagements as women in their first public appearance. Their acrobatics of love therefore establishes the basic tone of their performance, mapping out an autonomous realm of female desire independent of male presence. Sexuality in its manifold manifestations, especially when it involves *female bodies*, is a priority in SNNG's representational system, the top item on its performance to-do list. The Girls show off their fleshy, colored torsos, adorned with birthing scars, stretch marks, some tattoos, and traces of aging. By simply exposing themselves, the artists make no comment on the 'constructedness' associated with popular images of the 'female body.' The sight of their corporeal peculiarities, however, construct more possibilities for the inventory of gender and sexual representations. For they exhibit sights and voices of women that subvert the norms produced, endorsed, and commodified by commercial idealization. Their nude performance hence controverts the 'most wanted' models of 'female body,' who are predominantly white, young, thin, smooth, proportioned, and alluringly positioned – Phelan's 'almost naked, young white women.' (By the way, these ubiquitous models of 'beauty' may not have political power; notwithstanding, by virtue of their commodifiability, some do possess immense economic power.)

It is worth noting that the Girls engage in this task of diversifying the representations of 'femaleness' by interacting among themselves as diverse females. They propose 'sexuality' or 'eroticism' as an important aspect of female relationships, but they want also to include other possibilities. The Girls posit their unconditional trust for one another – demonstrated by the image of a woman's unconstrained falling and the choral refrains, 'I'll catch you' – as the principal support of their artistic union. By extension, their collaborative art pursues an all-embracing sisterhood. The amorous tension ignited by flesh contact, nonetheless,

209

complicates and diversifies what Susan Gubar has analyzed as 'the monolithic ideal of sisterhood.'[31] Instead, the scene casts a wide net of female liaisons that espouse lesbian sexuality without precluding other permutations of bonding among women.

MARKED, REMARKED, BUT UNTITLED

Although Phelan is 'carefully blind'[32] to the limitations of invisibility and to the inadequacy of any dualistic schema (visibility vs. invisibility), her privileging the force of the unmarked in identity formation is seductive. Phelan's argument persuades because it highlights the negatives in our self-produced films of subjectivity. For in the terrain where my identity forms, the invisible conditions the visible. The invisible engine of my psyche propels me to tilt my head when I think without my knowing why. Fragments of my subjectivity might have coalesced into a namable mass from the angle of my tilted head without me ever noticing such etiologic episodes. Or as Phelan expresses it, 'Identity emerges in the failure of the body to express being fully and the failure of the signifier to convey meaning exactly.'[33] Phelan cites Adrian Piper's performance of the problematics of 'race' to exemplify the arbitrary relation between the body's visible markings and the self's choice of identity. A visual artist and philosopher, Piper identifies herself as an African-American, but she has pale skin and could 'pass as white.' In her 1989 performance piece, *Cornered*, Piper proposes her individual 'racial' situation as a common scenario for her spectators, given the history of enforced or voluntary miscegenation resulting from the trauma of slavery in the United States. Piper unmoors the fixity of racial identification from the visible signifier of skin color. She asks her 'white' spectators who happen to carry ancestral 'black' genes if they would identify themselves as 'black' or 'white.'

In Phelan's analysis, *Cornered* demonstrates the unreliability of visible body features in grounding one's choice and perceptions of self-identity. For Phelan, Piper's question to her spectators exposes the relativity of racial designations: 'The same physical features of a person's body may be read as "black" in England, "white" in Haiti, "colored" in South Africa, and "mulatto" in Brazil.'[34] Since the link is entirely artificial between the signifier for racial identification (that is, physical markings) and its signified cross-culturally, Phelan deconstructs the myth of skin color intrinsic to the dominant ideology of race. As she states, 'Race-identity involves recognizing something other than skin and physical inscriptions. One cannot simply "read" race as skin-color.'[35]

Sympathetic as I am to Phelan's analysis, I nevertheless find an aporia in her rejection of the probable, if partial, visual foundation that informs racial identification and rationalizes the ideology of race. The aporia comes from the basis of Phelan's critique against racialization: Adrian Piper's *Cornered*. The major crisis of meaning established by Piper's performance of identity involves a corporeal detail particular to the artist herself: Piper can 'pass as white.' That is to say, Piper has barely discernible skin features that would mark her as non-white; this visual factor contributes to her particular dilemma and to the privilege that she explores as her performance theme. Therefore, it is actually a *superficial* physiological trait – the *skin color* near-white or white – that enables Piper, and, for that matter, Phelan to begin contemplating the artificiality of racial designation. I join Phelan and Piper in their protest against the simplistic equation between race and skin color, but I wish to point out that skin color *does* register visual information and implies social and psychic consequences. As the color white is naturalized to be the norm in this society, Piper is 'liberated' by her pale skin color to become unmarked, thereby enjoying the freedom to intervene from within her ostensible position of privilege. If she wants to, Piper can choose to appear as white, or, as she says, 'to pass as white.'

I ask, then, what kind of freedom or self-agency can I enjoy if I happen to have Piper's opposite dilemma: a visible *non-white* skin color? What questions should I raise or challenges would I face if I take pride in Piper's opposite privilege: a beautiful and readily discernible non-white skin color? To ask these questions is not to deny the insights of Phelan's commentary or of Piper's performance, but to refocus our attention on the corporeal sources of social constructions. For social constructions such as race and gender acquire their truth-effects precisely because they enlist our body's external features as evidence and grounding. Our admittedly incomplete perceptions of the body serve to reinforce the plausibility of those constructed ideas that regulate human typologies. If we desire to induce an implosion of the status quo so as to emancipate the oppressed values and the eclipsed human resources, we would do better not to dismiss the solidity of the Establishment, but to reconceptualize the anima and corpus of that solidity. In my own partially blind view, there is a perceptible animus working in the solid body of dominant ideologies: the logic of the visible, the abhorrence for incongruous sights, which become harder to digest but also harder to overlook when they are paired with incredible voices. We must, then, acknowledge that, just as the invisible conditions the visible, the visible also guides and thus constricts the invisible. There is, in Michele Wallace's phrase, 'a "Harlem" of the mind.'[36] We could of course pronounce that both Harlem and the mind are fabrications, but we could also join in the fabrication assembly line to manufacture our own discursive and imagistic cartographies of 'Harlem' and of 'the mind.' Let us note the potential power of the visible as it exists in a continuum with the aural and the textual.[37] To *mark* the norms, we have to *remark* and begin *remarking on* the surface – the plainly to be seen – taking Oscar Wilde's witty remark about the profundity of surface earnestly.

An all-nude performance enacted by four distinct bodies, SNNG's *Untitled Flesh* provides me with a paragon to examine the surfaces of various soft-tissue containers. But the work's contribution to my current pet ideology – the politics of marginality – does not end with the visible. *Untitled Flesh* begins with the exposure of the plainly to be seen – the naked skin; the performers frankly champion a return to the body as an art material, brushing elbows with Michelangelo's paint-dripped sleeves. In their visible diversity, however, the performing women disturb the blank but unified tranquillity of the vanishing point, and multiply the ideal Renaissance body into 'promiscuous' female bodies. By the principle of inclusive multiplicity, absorbing both the positive and negative values, the 'promiscuous' artists insist that there is more to the 'eye/I' – borrowing from Phelan's conflation.[38] SNNG's project is one of reclamation and excavation. In either case, the focus on multiplicity provides the theoretical foundation. The Girls maintain that they investigate 'multiple layers of nakedness,' implying that there are various ways to perceive 'nakedness' – physiological materiality, historicized nudity, and internalized nakedness are all included. Their performing naked is tantamount to a *reclamation* of their rights as women artists to be seen without clothing in a theatrical context. Such reclamation is concurrently a confrontation with the many problems and controversies aroused by their naked situation, provoking the performers to *excavate* deeper and deeper layers of their own nakedness. Finding performative expressions for these multiple layers is then SNNG's self-assigned task. The Girls have to scan the visible and render visible and audible the anatomy of the invisible.

ARCHAEOLOGY OF THE VISIBLE

A subsequent scene from *Untitled Flesh*: four naked women walk freely on a largely bare floor occupied by multiple sites of symbolic and functional objects like personal altars. This is an environment subdued in coloration, minimal in its architectural arrangement. Conversely, the performers and their naked bodies now roaming the space provide the colors, from the shades of their different skin and hair, which comprise a range of mixed pigments irreducible to the uniform black, white, or yellow essential to established racial identifications. Observed at close range, these colored masses appear as a lush variety of pinkish white, olive black, pale and bright orange, gold with matte finish, grayish blond, jet black tinged with auburn red. The women's uncovered flesh moving in space displays mobile sculptures, fluid or tensed at various moments, intricate in their carnal plasticity.

At this juncture, the Girls are experimenting with the first and the most rudimentary layer of nakedness, shameless and without history. The naked bodies placed in performance are the artists, the paintings, and the canvases. As paintings, the artists mock the reductiveness of racial designations with the complexity of their hues. If their flesh and hair of mixed-tints be the truth that claims visual attention, then the prime-color categories of *Homo sapiens* must be a myth. As canvases, the artists invite the gazing spectators to fantasize about their bodies – with wonder, with lust, with awe, or with surreptitious conscience. But these canvases are equipped with eyes that don't hesitate to gaze back at the gazers. These are canvases that hold paintings well-crafted with revenge schemes: 'An eye for an eye,' decrees the Hebrew Bible.

Voyeurism is a game tested by such revenge schemes, recalling one of the dangers of visibility identified by Phelan. Linda Williams in *Hard Core* defines voyeurism as 'unauthorized spying, the ability to be everywhere and to see all that is forbidden, hidden.'[39] The Girls, however, not only authorize but expose the spying. They allow no illusionistic screen to stand between the naked spectacles and their implicated watchers. As much as the Naked Girls invite fantasies with unveiled bodies, they also make the fantasizers self-conscious about their own acts of fantasy-genic spying. Between the gazers and the performers being gazed upon and gazing back, there is a double-lane optical highway, rather than the (stereotypical) cul-de-sac which captivates the voyeuristic object. The gazers are made to earn their vicarious pleasure or guilt in their watching by witnessing not only the women's own pleasures, but their erasure of historical traces from their naked – hence untitled – flesh. Moreover, they are obligated to receive the women's counter-gaze. In this state of mutual surveillance, the spectators' voyeuristic license is suspended, if not revoked.

In *Alice Doesn't*, Teresa De Lauretis suggests that concepts such as voyeurism and fetishism 'are directly implicated in a discourse which circumscribes woman in the sexual, binds her (in) sexuality, makes her the absolute representation, the phallic scenario.'[40] Under such a patriarchal lens, 'woman' is perceived by the presumed male-identified spectator as a sign, 'as scene, rather than subject, of sexuality.'[41] She is a lustworthy object in 'a drama of vision, a memory spectacle, an image of woman as beauty – desired and untouchable, desired *as* remembered.'[42] According to the above analysis, 'woman' as voyeuristic and fetishistic target is characterized by her lack of subjectivity, lack of self-willed desire, and lack of material presence. A passive receptacle of the proprietary gaze, she is destined to be a sexual and beautiful spectacle, rather than an aggressive spectacle-maker.

Judging from De Lauretis's formulation, I contend that the Naked Girls have managed to present a feminist spectacle of transgression which derides the 'phallic scenario.' They withhold the colonizing force of male spectatorial desire by making the relationships among themselves their foremost performance condition. They both act and interact as eroticized female subjects. They *have chosen* to utilize their naked flesh as their respective and collaborative art object/substance, basking in its sensorial gratification without the shadow of social taboos. They have turned their theatre into a moving museum, which curates their female bodies as exhibits of corporeal diversity. Since these Naked Girls do not hesitate to view one another as potential companions or sex partners, their performance boldly solicits the interests of female spectators, heterosexual, bisexual, and lesbian alike, who are no longer excluded from the implications of voyeuristic desire. While the performers stare straight into their spectators, they entice, challenge, and interrogate the actions of both men and women who stare at them.

MEMORIALS TO THE INVISIBLE

Another section in *Untitled Flesh* consists of numerous collaged, independent actions: A nude brunette (Brazell) crawls slowly on the floor, spitting out obscenities interlaced with Biblical phrases. Her crawling is occasionally intercepted by an African-American dominatrix (Oliver) who belts out recollected horrors from the history of slavery, while hitting the floor with a whip. The brunette climbs up to a cage made of wire-mesh and becomes an exotic dancer, her torso bathed under an eerie red light. Another nude (Meyers) poses as a body-builder, flexing her muscles.

The performance configurations gradually shift in tone. The exotic dancer, now wasted, squats in a stupor. The body-builder repeatedly throws herself against the floor. To the side, a mixed-race, lesbian couple (Uyehara and Oliver) are engaged in a sadomasochistic ritual: the African-American dominatrix is chased by her kneeling Asian American partner, who spanks her with a whip and pursues her up a ladder raised from a circle of stones and withered leaves. The image presents a distorted amalgam of Biblical parables: a mock crucifixion by 'Jacob's ladder.' The defiant martyr portrayed by Oliver does not call upon her Father for mercy; rather, she chants her own apotheosis: 'I decide to call myself Jezebel. I decide to change my name. I call myself Jezebel Pussy.'[43]

With the overlaid presentations of various probable scenarios, the cacophonous quartet challenges the totalizing force of stereotypes. The interactive S/M drama and the two solo actions encompass an array of emotional ramifications concerning women's experiences. The episodes are vaguely related to one another, creating a sense of disorder similar to Michel Foucault's analysis of the disturbing 'Heterotopias':

> the disorder in which a large number of possible orders glitter separately, in the lawless and uncharted dimension of the *heteroclite*; and that word should be taken in its most literal etymological sense; in such a state, things are 'laid,' 'placed,' 'arranged' in sites so very different from one another that it is impossible to find a common place beneath them all.[44]

The 'common place' lost in the disparate episodes of *Untitled Flesh* is the ultimate sanctified 'universal truth' about female sexuality. The manifested disorder coming out of

213

these coexisting incompatible scenes serves to affirm one message: Variety is the rule rather than the exception in the province of desire.

Thematically, these collaged actions tackle the multifarious structures of relations that women have with their internal and external worlds. Such feminist themes, combined with the method of juxtaposition, allude to a particular strain of 1970s feminist performance art in California. *Ablutions* (1972), for example, a collective piece from that era, was also made by four women artists: Judy Chicago, Suzanne Lacy, Sandra Orgel, and Aviva Rahmani.[45] It likewise included a duet – a woman methodically winding gauze on another's body – and two solos – a woman nailing beef kidneys on the rear wall; another taking a bath in three consecutive tubs filled with egg yolk, blood, and clay. In the meantime, a tape recording was playing women's rape incidents. Toward the end of their heterogeneous actions, the performers were bound by a mess of ropes into immobility (Plate 13.4).

Despite the similarities in their performance methods, what distinguishes SNNG's work from its feminist predecessors is the aspiration to diversity. SNNG's heterogeneity is biographically reflected by its members' divergent sexual identities. SNNG has further complicated its feminist politics to incorporate diverse ideological positions. In *Ablutions*, the women are united by their joined protests against victimization; the possible differences among themselves are downplayed. The raw beef kidneys, the blood-drenched female body, and the cocooned figure all condemn patriarchal society's abusive sexism – the vicious violence of rape. There is no such clearcut alliance by victimization in *Untitled Flesh*.

Plate 13.4 Scene from *Ablutions*. © Judy Chicago, 1972. Courtesy of *Through the Flower*

The sadomasochistic ritual played out between Oliver and Uyehara most overtly transgresses the pre-existing mode of feminist collective art. The two women, divided by their ethnicities and sexual roles, adopt the prey/predator dynamics in their sexual games, consciously alternating between aggressive and passive positions. Although their erotic rituals might not be endorsed by all, theirs is a carnal partnership sanctified by individual resolve and mutual contract. Given our present social circumstances, however, such personal sanctity could be tolerated as long as the practitioners keep their erotic role-playing within the private realm. Once the S/M act appears in public, the intimation of perversity immediately 'scandalizes' the occasion, making it a public health or ethics hazard. By representing an S/M rite in performance, Sacred Naked Girls deliberately provoke the audience's reactions. The spectators who witness the rite might feel the instant urge to judge. Their moral judgments could go at least three ways: to understand, to reserve disapproval, or to condemn. But they cannot remain sedated.

Through the 'outrageous' ritual enacted by a mixed-race, minority couple, *Untitled Flesh* forces open a space of ambivalence unavailable to a piece like *Ablutions*. *Ablutions* demands social justice as an appropriate response to its performance. *Untitled Flesh*, conversely, solicits diverse and very likely conflicting audience responses. It aims for both a larger variety and a greater scope in the freedom accessible to women for satisfying their desires. The Girls' advocacy is, here and elsewhere, tolerance for diversity.

These performance segments examine an interior layer of nakedness: nakedness as cultural memory, or, in Oliver's insightful term, as 'flesh memory.' According to her,

> There is a text, a language, a mythology, a truth, a reality, an invented reality as well as a literal translation of everything that we've ever experienced and known, whether we know it directly or know it through some type of genetic memory, whether through osmosis or our environment. Our body holds its own truth and its own reality that may or may not correspond directly with what actually transpired in any given situation. We are trying to tap into the multiplicity of languages and realities that our flesh holds.[46]

This definition of 'flesh memory' is informed by an inclusive philosophy. For Oliver, 'flesh' refers to the body as an open receptor of all experiences – 'the multiplicity of languages and realities' – that pass through its sensory field. As she identifies these experiences with 'memory,' she places them in an elusive realm permeable by factual and fictitious information, cerebral and somatic knowledge. She packs the two words together and coins a neologistic term, 'flesh memory.' The term conflates the conventional distinctions between 'flesh' as a physical property and 'memory' as a mental attribute. 'Flesh memory' is a major concept for SNNG's work. It also provides the ensemble with an improvisational method. SNNG's discipline, then, lies in sensitizing the artists' 'imaginary bodies,' to quote the illuminating notion from Moira Gatens.[47] Through rehearsals and performances, Sacred Naked Girls strive to heighten the elastic capacities of the mind-flesh-body-heart that remembers, ad-libs, alludes, appropriates, and freely associates.

Oliver's references to 'genetic memory,' 'osmosis,' and 'environment' are ideas culled from natural science disciplines such as biology, chemistry, and ecology. Her statement sketches out a conceptual framework supported by metaphors, loose analogies, and the theme-oriented accumulation of ideas. Her eclectic methodology enthralls me because of the assertion that she can acquire any idea floating in the cultural ether merely by self-permission. The right to property, she seems to aver, comes with the very fact of residence. Her location and participation in contemporary culture gives her the legitimacy to formulate any theoretical system for her art.

This sequence of reasoning becomes especially poignant considering that Oliver is African-American. Her claim to ownership by participation significantly evokes the history of African-Americans' enslavement. Her ability to assume intellectual authority contrasts with the lack of freedom suffered by her ancestors who, being 'American residents' forcefully imported from Africa, were not even allowed to own literacy. Within this context, the hegemonic intent implied by Oliver's act of universal appropriation becomes a strategy of resistance against the Anglo-American cultural hegemony. When she performs the S/M ritual, her theorization explodes with the rage of direct accusation. As Marianne Dresser points out, 'the erotics of bondage and domination' treated in the scene quickly 'transmuted into an examination of the historical roots of S/M paraphernalia in chattel slavery.'[48] Oliver has clinched the two references by spewing memories of slavery with a whip in her hand.

Both the site and source of flesh memory, the naked bodies enlisted by performance generate their own creative energies. Oliver explains further, 'Flesh memory is more than just memory, it's the way we re-invent scenarios and worlds and languages and images to transcribe what we see, what we feel, what we think. It's a language that's activated in our bodies.'[49] Flesh memory implies, then, an active agent who selects cultural experiences and programs them into art, as opposed to a receptacle of inert information. The body where flesh memories lodge digests experiential data to fabricate story-truth, if not true stories. In this light, the notion of flesh memory echoes what Antonin Artaud has proposed as the 'sempiternal' self: 'that is, a self that moves and creates itself at every instant.'[50] The Girls' choice of improvisations in their training and performance suggests more than a stylistic preference; it is a methodology that – ideally – compels them to evolve 'sempiternally' during every collaborative encounter.

In one aspect, the 'sacredness' conjured up by Sacred Naked Girls' untitled flesh arises from this very desire for instantaneous creativity embodied by their sempiternal being. In another aspect, their sacredness comes from self-affirmation. A striking example of the latter is what I have described as Oliver's 'mock crucifixion by Jacob's ladder.' Oliver conducts her martyrdom-cum-apotheosis by chanting a litany that both condemns the misogyny of Christian theology and renames herself. Up on that phallic ladder, she experiences the passion induced by the ongoing S/M rite. Oliver's Passion, then, springs from carnal sensations made spiritual by the 'sacred' situation. There is no need for her to peep into Heaven's Gate above; she has pulled down Heaven to house her.

TEMPORARY LIBERATION

Through story-telling, chanting, and body-painting ritual, the last movement of *Untitled Flesh* treats the theme of sacredhood-by-self-affirmation, a motif which echoes Oliver's Ladder rhapsody. The Girls attempt to reach a holy fellowship with their audience by the act of naming. Their moving symphony of utopian affirmation pays homage to a mosaic of myths/histories from ancient Greece to the United States in the 1970s. SNNG's storyland floats between the island of Lesbos where the poet Sappho once lived to the kingdom of the Amazons whose warriors traded one of their breasts for archery.[51] The Girls' body-painting and scarification echo two extraordinary performances in New York, 1975: Carolee Schneemann's *Interior Scroll,* in which the artist applied paint-marks to her nude body and extracted a winding parchment from her vagina; and Hannah Wilke's *Starification Object Series* (*S.O.S.*), for which the artist scarred her own nude body with vagina-shaped chewing-gum remains.[52]

The Girls' construction of the sacred links their efforts, in particular, with the feminist foremothers whose performances of the late 1970s featured the Great Goddess archetypes. According to Gloria Orenstein, artists such as Schneemann, Mary Beth Edelson, Ana Mendieta, and Betsy Damon regarded the use of Goddess motifs in their works as the catalyst for an 'Earth Alchemy,' through which a women's culture would be reborn. The means of effecting this rebirth include the assumption of a 'holistic mind-body totality' that reflects the Goddess-consciousness; 'the repossession of the female visionary faculties' through 'intuitive body-knowledge'; the restoration of 'the spirit already inherent in the natural world'; and the 'exaltation of natural energies' as the power of the Goddess.[53]

The 'Goddess archetypes' practitioners adopt a literal understanding of 'Nature,' taking it to be the embodiment of Earth Goddess. In their exuberant celebration of Mother Nature's sacred beauty, the artists approach their bodies as a natural element and aim to retrieve natural splendors with their art. Sacred Nature Girls, with their performance quilt of feminist legends, pay homage to this Goddess heritage, but they differ from their 'sacred' precursors in their interpretation of 'Nature.' *Untitled Flesh* submits a less innocent or exuberant view of 'Nature' than that implied by Earth Alchemy. The Girls have expanded the corpus of 'Nature' by the same principle with which they have multiplied every other concept: 'Naked' – 'Girls' – [playing in] – 'Nature' – [and acting/being] – 'Sacred' (Plate 13.5). The Girls' interpretation of 'Nature' appears to have swallowed up the line slashed between Nature/Culture, together with the body of Culture itself. They have managed to elude feminist debates about essentialism by refusing to acknowledge that there is a dichotomy between nature and culture. Their refusal to identify a female essence with a single ideological front has in effect nullified the 'anti-essentialist' critique.[54] In its approach to the tremulous explosion of desire, to the internalized bruises of history, and to the capacities of the flesh/consciousness to remember and rejuvenate, SNNG has marked Culture as the scars of Nature.

The above chain of signifying sequences leads us to the culmination of the Girls' pilgrimage to the sacred. As Oliver states, 'I like to try to marry the sacred and the profane. What I call the profane is life with its ugliness, scars, all of that. There is a sacredness in the profane, a spirit in material, and they intermarry, they don't separate from one another.'[55] SNNG's methodological rigor lies in its insistence on 'intermarrying' radically varied concepts. It is a rigor earned by the Girls' consistent repudiation of monolithic uniformity and by their advocacy of the beneficial unification of differences. To phrase it in a more 'culturally scarred' terminology, to *intermarry* is to perform the act of *miscegenation.* SNNG's social vision, in this sense, proposes a literal writing of multiculturalism on the natural body of contemporary culture. My reading suggests that the multiethnic constitution of SNNG has a more *embodied* (imbued in flesh) reason than the superficial (skin-deep) pursuit of the fashion called Los Angeles multiculturalism. They perform the invisible from the visible and journey deeper into the invisible to section multiple terrains from surface to core.

For this feminist quartet, 'sacredness' initially comes with the ceremony of inter-marrying among its multiethnic members. The health of SNNG as a collaborative unit

Plate 13.5 Promotional composite photograph for the Sacred Naked Nature Girls, *Untitled Flesh*, 1996. Showing the Girls rejoicing in 'cultured' Nature. Photo design Joe Notaro; photograph by Jerry Browning. Courtesy of SNNG

depends upon its partners' continuous emotional and physical commitments to their artistic miscegenation. Constant effort is required to sustain the original sacredness. Meyers has emphasized the interpersonal engagement among the Girls as the cohesive force: We 'learn to trust, that's where our magic comes from and that's what's most sacred.'[56]

At this moment, however, when the Girls have decided unanimously to separate from their 'intermarriage' for an indefinite period, Meyers's comment has unwittingly taken on the quality of an epitaph. The register of sentiments struck by her note shifts from the ardor of proclamation to the irony of presentiment. Do the Girls split because they 'trust' that their 'sacred' 'magic' has dwindled? Or has their 'magic' vanished because they could no longer 'trust' the 'sacredness' that had bound them together? Has their claim for individual sanctity proved to be finally incompatible with the pain that is needed to maintain collective sanctity? Is their theory of intermarrying divergent values – individuality and community, differences and unification, the sacred and the profane – challenged by life's own convoluted logic, which defeats all theorization? Has the SNNG ensemble ceased to be an organism that liberates the members' artistic potentials, and become a constraining institution? Could the suspension of SNNG's miscegenistic intermarriage indicate a dilemma larger than the fate of a particular group? Could the problems experienced by the Girls as collaborators indicate the difficulties inherent in this multiracial society that its contemporary culture seeks to understand, negotiate, and express? Does the sense of sacredness proposed by SNNG exist, at best, only as an immediate historical memory?

The last action in *Untitled Flesh* adds a physical footnote to Meyers's statement. It also demonstrates performatively what I have called the many-headed, newly evolved Hydra/ SNNG.

Sacred Naked Nature Girls now stand in various corners of their performance field. Disorienting lights flash in darkness, illuminating parts of the women's bodies alternately and intermittently. The frequency of the flashes creates an optical illusion that these women are more than four bodies; they are a multitude. They chant the opening refrain, 'Will you catch me?' Their increasingly intense polyphony of overlapping monologic calls creates an auditory illusion that they are really of one giant body. There is a seamless coextension between the air, the light and darkness, the edges of their personal altars, and the fluent skin of their flesh.

The sacredness of unifying diverse multitudes arises from the balance between intersubjectivity and composite subjectivity. Such balance, nevertheless, subsists tenuously and fleetingly, in a state of transport, manifested as a mutable, performative utopia.

NOTES

1 I would like to acknowledge the support of a Junior Faculty Grant offered by the Southern California Studies Center at the University of Southern California for the writing of this essay. Special thanks to Amelia Jones, Kristine Stiles, Vincent Cheng, Ted Shank, David James, Toti Mercadante O'Brien, Mariellen R. Sandford of *TDR*, and Nonchi Wang for their comments on my previous drafts. I offer a more extensive study of Sacred Naked Nature Girls and *Untitled Flesh* in an article entitled '*Les Demoiselles d' L.A.*: Sacred Naked Nature Girls' *Untitled Flesh*,' published in *TDR: The Journal of Performance Studies*, Summer 1998, vol. 42, no. 2, pp. 70–97. Parts of this essay are from that article, but the current version has a different theme and structure of argument.

2   I am citing the biblical phrase out of its original context of Job's meek endurance for his sufferings. I take the phrase as a *literal* description of an existential condition. The original reference appears in Job 1: 21: 'When Job heard of the destruction of his animals and of his sons, he said, "Naked came I out of my mother's womb, and naked shall I return thither: the Lord gave, and the Lord hath taken away; blessed by the name of the Lord",' in W. B. Fulghum, Jr, *A Dictionary of Biblical Allusions in English Literature*, New York, Holt, Rinehart & Winston, 1965, p. 181.

3   In the original biblical context, 'Legion' is one of the names the devils call themselves. I intend to *invert* the terms of this parable here. The reason for such inversion will become clear later. The original parable from Mark 5: 9 and Luke 8: 30 cited in *A Dictionary of Biblical Allusions in English Literature* goes as follows: 'When Jesus met the man possessed with devils, in the country of the Gadarenes, he asked him his name. The maniac replied, "My name is Legion: for we are many,"' meaning possessed by many devils. Jesus permitted the devils to enter a herd of [Gadarene swine], and the man was cured,' in Fulghum, Jr, p. 152.

4   I conducted an interview with Brazell, Meyers, and Uyehara on 28 March 1997 and another interview with Brazell, Meyers, Uyehara, Oliver, and Elia Arce on 13 October 1997. Both interviews took place in Los Angeles. Unless otherwise indicated, my information about the Sacred Girls and their comments on their work are based on these two interviews. I cite the reference to these interviews only when I make direct quotations. When I inquired about each SNNG member's ethnic background, noticeably Meyers replied that she prefers to identify herself with Texas. For her, Texas is an ethnicity.

5   SNNG presented an experimental performance later named *Untitled Flesh* in Boulder, Colorado, in April 1994. The relatively finished version of *Untitled Flesh* premiered at Highways in August 1994, and toured to the following places: the Institute of Contemporary Art, London; Randolph Street Gallery, Chicago; Sushi Performance and Visual Arts, San Diego; Echo Theatre, Portland, Oregon; Luna Sea Women's Performance Project, San Francisco.

6   See my article, 'Sacred Naked Nature Girls,' which covers SNNG's second piece, *Home. The Last Place I Ran to Just About Killed Me*, in *Theatre Forum*, Summer/Fall 1997, pp. 5–13.

7   The parable appears in Ezekiel 16: 1–47. I quote this phrase and the following passage from a Bible Study Internet Site concerning 'Spiritual Adultery,' @ http://www.acts 17-11.com/sa.html.

8   Ibid. See also *The Holy Bible: The Authorized or King James Version of 1611*, New York, Random House, 1963, pp. 630–33. *The Oxford Annotated Bible: Revised Standard Version Containing the Old and New Testaments*, New York, Oxford University Press, 1962, pp. 1015–17.

9   Sacred Naked Nature Girls, 'Artistic Statement,' Los Angeles, SNNG, 1996.

10 P. Phelan, *Unmarked: The Politics of Performance*, New York and London, Routledge, 1993, p. 1.

11 Amelia Jones argues that corporeal and identificatory particularities evinced in a performing body have the potential to expose the normative prejudices inherent in modernist/formalist art history and criticism. In Jones's words, 'when the body in performance is female, obviously queer, non-white, exaggeratedly (hyper)masculine, or otherwise enacted against the grain of the normative subject (the straight, white, upper-middle-class, male subject coincident with the category "artist" in western culture) the hidden logic of exclusionism underlying modernist art history and criticism is exposed' (*Body Art/Performing the Subject*, Minneapolis, University of Minnesota Press, 1998, pp. 8–9).

12 Jon Cruz suggests that 'essentialism' could be avoided by 'a retreat from systems and histories to the present and the local.' He believes such an epistemological move to the specific 'has restored the problem of meaning, retrieved the value of hermeneutics, and brought social and cultural analysis back to an appreciation' for the individual subjects. 'From Farce to Tragedy: Reflections on the Reification of Race at Century's End,' in *Mapping Multiculturalism*, ed. Avery F. Gordon and Christopher Newfield, Minneapolis, University of Minnesota Press, 1996, pp. 19-39.

13 As Cruz phrases it, 'multiculturalism is, in part, about groups struggling to achieve moral solidarity, a precious good in an era of profound transformation and instability' (ibid., p. 31.

14 Sacred Naked Nature Girls, 'Company Activities,' Los Angeles, SNNG, 1996.

15 Ibid.

16 SNNG, 'Artistic Statement.'
17 Ibid.
18 Ibid.
19 Phelan, *Unmarked*, p. 1.
20 Ibid., p. 2.
21 Ibid., p. 2.
22 Ibid., p. 10.
23 Ibid., p. 6.
24 Ibid., p. 7.
25 Ibid., p. 2.
26 Ibid., p. 9.
27 Ibid., p. 27.
28 Ibid., p. 19.
29 M. Wallace, *Invisibility Blues: From Pop to Theory*, New York, Verso, 1990.
30 Ibid., p. 5.
31 S. Gubar, 'Sapphistries,' *Signs*, Autumn 1984, vol. 10.1., no. 1, pp. 43–62.
32 This phrase alludes to Phelan's superb remark on vision and blindness in *Unmarked*: 'Taking the visual world in is a process of loss: learning to see is training careful blindness. To apprehend and recognize the visible is to eliminate as well as absorb visual data' (p. 13).
33 Ibid., p. 13.
34 Ibid., p. 8.
35 Ibid., p. 8.
36 Wallace, *Invisibility Blues*, p. 6.
37 I would like to thank Amelia Jones here for her contribution to this important insight.
38 Phelan uses the conflation, 'I/eye,' to analyze the intricate relations between subjectivity (I) and the visual faculty (eye) discussed by Lacan (*Unmarked*, p. 20). I understand that many other scholars have used such a conflation, but I am alluding specifically to Phelan's usage here.
39 L. Williams, *Hard Core: Power, Pleasure, and the 'Frenzy of the Visible,'* Berkeley and Los Angeles, University of California Press, 1989, p. 44.
40 T. de Lauretis, *Alice Doesn't: Feminism Semiotics Cinema*, Bloomington, Indiana University Press, 1984, pp. 25–6.
41 Ibid., p. 27.
42 Ibid., p. 27.
43 Again a reference to the Bible. The Hebrew prophets denounce Jezebel, the daughter of the King of Tyre and wife of King Ahab, because she introduces different types of worship to the Israelites. Like Medea, Jezebel commits murder to help her husband, King Ahab. Later King Jehu orders that Jezebel be thrown out of the window as a punishment for her flirtation with him. Her body is eaten by dogs. See Fulghum, Jr., *A Dictionary of Biblical Allusions in English Literature*, pp. 129-30.
44 M. Foucault, *The Order of Things: An Archaeology of the Human Sciences*, a translation of *Les mots et les choses*, New York, Vintage Books, 1970, p. 48.
45 I base my description on Moira Roth's documentation in *The Amazing Decade: Women and Performance Art in America 1970-1980*, Los Angeles, Astro Artz, 1983, p. 86.
46 C. Fusco, 'Sacred Naked Nature Girls: An Interview,' *Bomb*, Summer 1995, p. 21.
47 M. Gatens, *Imaginary Bodies: Ethics, Power and Corporeality*, New York and London, Routledge, 1996.
48 M. Dresser, 'Working Girls: The Sacred Naked Nature Girls at Luna Sea,' *Bay Area Reporter*, 20 April 1995, p. 34.
49 Fusco, 'Sacred Naked Nature Girls: An Interview,' p. 21.
50 A. Artaud, *Selected Writings*, ed. Susan Sontag, Berkeley and Los Angeles, University of California Press, 1988, p. 465.
51 Gubar mentioned Sappho and the island of Lesbos in her article, 'Sapphistries,' p. 44; an account about the Amazons can be found in E. Hamilton, *Mythology: Timeless Tales of Gods and Heroes*, New York, Menton Books, 1942, p. 287.
52 Schneemann performed *Interior Scroll* twice: in 1975 and 1977. In the second performance, she painted her body with mud. See Schneemann, *More Than Meat Joy: Complete Performance Works*

and Selected Writings, B. McPherson (ed.), New York, Documentext (1979), 1997, pp. 234–9. A description of Wilke's *Starification Object Series* (*S.O.S.*) appears in Roth, *The Amazing Decade*, p. 146. See also Amelia Jones's excellent studies of Schneemann and Wilke in 'Interpreting Feminist Bodies: The Unframeability of Desire,' *The Rhetoric of the Frame*, P. Duro (ed.), Cambridge, England, Cambridge University Press, 1996, pp. 223-41; 'Postfeminism, Feminist Pleasures, and Embodied Theories of Art,' *New Feminist Criticism: Art-Identity-Action*, J. Frueh, C. L. Langer, and A. Raven (eds), New York, HarperCollins, 1994, pp. 16-41; and 'The Rhetoric of the Pose: Hannah Wilke and the Radical Narcissism of Feminist Body Art,' in Jones, *Body Art/Performing the Subject*, pp. 151–95. For the most recent exhibitions of the two artists' work, see *Intra-Venus: Hannah Wilke*, New York, Ronald Feldman Fine Arts, 1995; *Carolee Schneemann: Up To and Including Her Limits*, New York, New Museum of Contemporary Art, 1997.

53   Gloria Feman Orenstein, 'The Reemergence of the Archetype of the Great Goddess in Art by Contemporary Women,' in *Feminist Art Criticism: An Anthology*, A. Raven, C. L. Langer, J. Frueh, Ann Arbor (eds), Michigan, UMI Research Press, 1988, pp. 72–73.

54   See J. Barry and S. Flitterman-Lewis, 'Textual Strategies: The Politics of Art-Making,' for an epitome of the anti-essentialist argument, in ibid., pp. 87–97.

55   Fusco, 'Sacred Naked Nature Girls: An Interview,' p. 22.

56   Ibid., p. 22.

14

ANDY WARHOL

Performances of *Death in America*

Peggy Phelan

Within the critical literature about his work, *Death in America* refers to an exhibition Andy Warhol was planning to do in Paris in 1964: 'My show in Paris is going to be called *Death in America*. I'll show the electric-chair pictures and the dogs in Birmingham and car wrecks and some suicide pictures.'[1] *Death in America* is also the title Warhol gave to a collection of UPI photographs of suicide attempts he had purchased in the late 1950s and early 1960s. Not all of these photographs were published, but they all were composed as if they might be. *Death in America* (1963) is now exhibited in the Warhol Museum in Pittsburgh, and has the status of a posthumous publication. As a collection, it signals the great themes of Warhol's best work. Composed as a meditation on seriality, *Death in America* asks: What kind of act is death and how might it best be framed, represented, received, circulated, sold? If death is a 'once in a lifetime' occurrence, how come its representations look so similar? If US culture encourages us to render death an event always to be deferred, how come so many people fly toward it, lunge after it, gun for it, and swallow it in pills and water?

While Warhol's own fear of death has been much remarked, it has not been seriously pondered. Many commentators take note of the preponderance of attention Warhol paid to death as a subject, but there has been little attempt to understand what made his interest in death so vital to his creative output, especially in the early 1960s when he was moving from commercial art to fine art. There has been a critical effort to define and contain, indeed to arrest and fix, Warhol's disturbing fascination with death, but that effort has been unsuccessful in part because this fascination is the least comprehensible aspect of Warhol's oeuvre. Warhol's attraction to death as subject cannot be explained adequately by either autobiography or poststructuralist theory (and it is worth emphasizing that much of this theory is indebted to Warhol's work, rather than an explanation of it). Rather, Warhol's use of death invites us to return to some old-fashioned philosophical concepts such as the distinction between mortality and immortality, creation and destruction, and performance and performativity. Warhol was the son of immigrants who seems to have had a simple belief in 'the American dream.' He was an uncomplicated capitalist who lived a good portion of his adult life with his mother and attended Catholic mass regularly. Since the discourse about Warhol's work continually associates him with 'the new,' these more conventional aspects of his life have rarely been noticed as influences on his work. Even the more successful attempts to address Warhol's difficult, even ambiguous pattern of thought and desire in regard to death tend to leave unspoken what animated the link between creativity and death for him.[2]

Bradford Collins, for example, argues that Warhol's career between 1960 and 1968 is best understood as an effort to 'commit emotional suicide.' As part of the evidence he assembles to justify this claim, Collins employs Henry Geldzahler's remark, "'Sometimes he would say that he was scared of dying if he went to sleep. So he'd lie in bed and listen to his heart beat. And finally he'd call me . . . That was it – a cry for help of some kind'." But surely this comment reveals more about Geldzahler's sense of his own importance to Warhol than it reveals about what kept Warhol up at night. For Collins, the 'cool industrial character of [Warhol's] '60s art was antithetical to the warmly personal quality of both his advertising and artistic production of the preceding years.'[3] One of the implications of Collins's argument is that both the man and the art were better when they were more emotional. Leaving aside the psychoanalytic and aesthetic assumptions embedded in Collins's argument, we must nonetheless contend with the possibility that Warhol changed his work because it made him a better artist and he recognized this. To notice the renunciation of emotion in the content of Warhol's work does not logically lead to the conclusion that he 'commit[ed] emotional suicide.'[4] Warhol's libidinal and emotional investment in his work was enormous. But rather than making a direct transfer from his 'inner-emotional' self to his work, Warhol attempted to transfer this transference from the work to the viewer.[5] Part of this ambition came from his own sense of being riveted by images. Warhol was as interested in the reception as in the production of art and, as Collins points out, his background in business led him to survey many people about their responses to his work. But even if Collins is correct and Warhol committed emotional suicide, it leaves unanswered the larger problem of why Warhol produced so much after his (emotional) death. What is the appeal of making an image after its source and inspiration, its model and maker, have 'departed'? Surely it must have something to do with staging an encounter between the living and the dead.

In order to free the stage for the observer's reception, Warhol tried to renounce the trace of himself as maker. What he came to discover, however, was the impossibility of this renunciation, and he gradually learned to renounce this renunciation too. For in erasing his 'emotion' from the content of his work, he invariably created a smudge, a blur, indeed, as Hal Foster points out, a 'pop,' that marked the effort of that erasure.[6] The spectator confronts Warhol's expression of his desire to disappear, to be as dead, which is the backbeat to his equally intense effort to create the art work itself.

Warhol's best work, remarkably, issues an invitation to his spectators to imagine themselves as simultaneously dead and alive. This invitation is a mimetic one: Warhol inhabits that double space in the production of his work and thereby rehearses the spectator's performance of observation of it. Warhol's early work is the result of both his audacious presence and his provocative disappearance, his precise necessity and his utter dispensability. Thus, this work operates in a liminal space between life and death, a space we might call the tension of the present tense. The duality of Warhol's work, the transfer of the transference and the renunciation of renunciation, has been difficult to articulate in part because Warhol's visual art is more theatrical and performative than it is 'art historical.' Before turning to a more direct engagement with this work, I want to dwell for a moment longer on some of the critical tangles his work has produced.

While Collins argues that Warhol's work is the result of an emotional suicide, Thomas Crow argues that Warhol's celebrity portraits are actually exercises in mourning, disciplined illustrations of the Freudian concept of 'working through.'[7] Objecting to Crow's 'humanistic view of early Warhol' in his reading of the *Marilyn* series, Thierry de Duve suggests that the series expresses 'an extraordinarily strong desire on the side of the death drive. He is touching on the pleasure that people derive from what makes other people suffer. Marilyn kills herself, and Warhol derives that strange pleasure out of it.'[8] But when I look at the *Marilyn* series I can find neither pleasure nor mourning. On the contrary, for me, part of the riveting fascination of the series is its ability to renounce resolutely and theatrically an affective response. The staged renunciation of affect is the work's aspiration and achievement. For in making us conscious both of the expectation of affect and its withholding, Warhol's *Marilyn* series invites its observer to remake her image as a personal and private phantasm while participating in what is both a collective and personal hallucination of celebrity. Warhol's representation of the representation of her image is provocation and incitement rather than statement and conclusion. 'It confused me,' Warhol lamented about misreadings of his work, 'that people expect Pop art to make a comment.'[9]

What compels Warhol in the *Marilyn* series is how the image performs after the death of its subject, how it remains alive long after its inspiration is dead. His alterations of her image are not only expressions of a 'ghastly cosmetology,' or an elaborated ghostly death mask, but, more importantly, incitements to continue to dance with the image of the dead.[10] It is here that we begin to see one of the more radical insights of Warhol's project: the dead do not actually die but through death become recognized as the always already living. That the recognition of this 'life' is necessarily a phantasm, a creation, links it to the essential purpose of art itself. Moreover, it suggests that this art-work, the keeping-alive of the dead, is the work of everyone who has ever had an encounter with the dead.[11] And it is this idea that helps Warhol sustain his belief that 'art is for everyone.'

In Warhol's conviction that art helps us live more intimately with the dead, he resembles T. S. Eliot's ideal poet who 'is not likely to know what is to be done unless he lives in what is not merely the present, but the present moment of the past, unless he is conscious, not of what is dead, but of what is already living.'[12] What is 'already living' in us is both the fear of and attraction to death. To render that oscillation vital Warhol had, quite literally, to put his work on the line. That is, he had to imagine again the way the line, ink-blotted, traced, silk-screened and drawn, allows us to trace the ink-blotted, shakily screened and endlessly projected attempt to draw a line between life and death, a line that both sutures and bisects that relationship.

Sam Rosenberg, Warhol's painting professor at the Carnegie Institute of Technology, assigned his students Paul Klee's *Pedagogical Sketchbook*, and Klee's relationship to the line was crucial for Warhol's own.[13] As is well known, Klee conceived of the line as a dot going out for a walk. That is, he thought of the line as something that moves, as something that refuses to stay still. In Klee's view, the line creates 'symbols in the form of motion.'[14] In thinking about the motion toward and away from death, one can see a link with Klee's diagrammatic discussion of the spiral:

> Shortening of the radius narrows the curve more and more, till the lovely spectacle dies suddenly in the static center. Motion here is no longer finite, and the question of direction regains new importance. The direction determines either a gradual liberation from the center through freer and freer motions, or an increasing dependence on an eventually destructive center. This is the question of life and death; and the decision rests with the small arrow.[15]

The small arrow refers to the line at the base of the spiral pointing in two opposite directions labeled 'either' 'or.' In Warhol's silk-screen *Suicide* from 1962, a figure captured in a black and white photograph leaps from a building whose representational shadow is bisected by a startling horizontal white line that fades as it comes closer to the gray space of the jumper's free fall (Plate 14.1). This horizontal line interrupts the trajectory of the vertical line established by the motion of the leap and suggests that the fall will actually be 'caught' by a net we cannot see, but can hallucinate because the horizontal line seems at once to underline and stop the fall.

This white horizontal line, what Foster calls a 'pop,' prohibits the possibility of viewing *Suicide* as a transparent documentary.[16] The line accents the impossibility of Warhol's renunciation of artistic presence, which is to say, of life. To silk-screen, massage, or treat an image that records death is also necessarily to insist on the image's afterlife and the life of the one to whom the record is addressed. Suicide as an act that is documented presupposes an exchange that survives death.

POSTHUMOUS PHOTOGRAPHS

Death in America provides an intriguing point of entry into Warhol's overdetermined interest in death, America, and art. The photos and captions adhere to strict rules of the genre; the

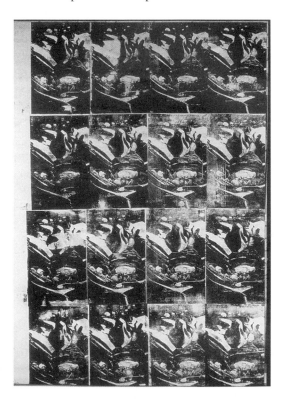

Plate 14.1 Andy Warhol, *Suicide*, 1964. Collection Adelaide de Menil, New York. Courtesy of Andy Warhol Foundation for the Visual Arts/ARS, New York (1998)

photos are all the same size and follow the aesthetic codes of newspaper portraits; they are framed so that the exact center of the composition is the actor undertaking the approach to death. The captions are uniformly terse and have the neutral 'no comment' tone of 'just the facts, ma'am.' Taken together, the photographs and captions suggest that death is an ongoing theatre that has no beginning and no end. The similarity of the stories and aesthetic codes raises the disturbing question of whether or not anyone is alive to death at all, or if death is produced in the same way newspapers are – mechanically. The affectless reporting of the caption and the macabre but precisely contained and skillfully cropped events that the photographs document encourage an indifferent response on the part of the viewer. And yet, there is nonetheless a strange fascination provoked by these image-texts.

These 'action photos' document the final moments of a life attempting to become still. The photographic shutter, the click of death's pseudo-mechanical shudder, delivers that stillness and arrests the actor in pursuit of the aggressive, often violent, desire 'to have been.' As has been frequently demonstrated, all photographic portraiture touches death.[17] Photographic portraits of suicide attempts, whether successful or failed (and perhaps especially rejected photographs of suicide attempts), occupy a somewhat different ontological category. For, in addition to carrying the association with death that all photographic portraits carry, photographs of attempted suicides participate in, rather than merely record, the race between the desire to live and the desire to die. In active pursuit of death, these photographs do not hide or repress the fascination with 'that which has been,' but in mimetic homage to their actor-subjects seek strenuously to embrace it. As photographs composed in order to be sold to tabloids (or to collectors such as Warhol) they also pass beyond the outcome of the act in the moment and seek a life-as-image after death. That is, they aspire to move from the 'present tense' of the performative (speech) act to the constative description of an act that once was. In this sense, the photographs and captions aspire to be both news and history, to be both arresting drama and sober documentary.

The captions function as stage directions and brief synopses that illustrate plots that are in every way 'larger' than the scene that the photograph captures. Each text cites a reason for the suicide attempt. 'Nagging husband' is listed beneath the photo of a black woman attempting to jump off a bridge; a white woman teacher takes an overdose of pills because she does not believe she can offer her third-grade students all they really need. A white man in his fifties jumps off a hotel roof because he suffers from asthma in an act that seems at once an exhilarating rush and a suffocating collapse. Another man jumps out of a building that the caption notes is a psychiatric hospital. The illuminated neon sign yelling 'Emergency' frames his fall.

There is something very personal about each of the cited reasons and yet the effect of reading each in a row in Warhol's collection drains the reasons of their particularity; the overwhelming regularity of the genre renders each explanation of the reasons for the suicide attempt empty, hollow, a cliché. The captions are footnotes to visual texts that render captions insufficient. As a collection, *Death in America* provokes a movement from the particular to the general, from the personal narrative to the structural imperative. Why must we document these suicide attempts and sell them? Who cares? And why? Or as Warhol liked to put it, 'so what?' What are the consequences of turning death into an act, an image, that can be repeated, circulated, sold? What does it do to this 'once-in-a-lifetime' event to see it all around us?

Death in America suggests that what shapes 'national character' is not the outcome of the plays the actors find themselves in, but rather how we respond to the structural imperative to encounter death, our own and others'. The documentation of death in tabloids and television is also part of the American experience of death, in a way that it simply is not in, say, the Australian outback of the late 1950s and early 1960s. (The 'International' in United Press International is an appeal to a market that it is trying to create.) Rather than being a once-in-a-lifetime experience, death in America is an act we absorb repeatedly before we fall into our final one. As an act, death demands an image, and that image is both an aesthetic and commodity fetish. Warhol's famous observation that Nancy Reagan's and Liz Taylor's can of Coke is the same as the can of Coke you and I drink, applies as well to death. How we arrive at its lip will differ, but death is the sip of the same carbon for each of us. Moreover, just as we need Coke advertisements to help us learn how to recognize 'the real thing,' so too do we need documentary photographs of suicides, car crashes, and other disasters to help us learn how to die and how to view the deaths of others. But despite the density of the circulation of images of death in America, one cannot actually imagine the image of one's own death. Death excites an enormous anticipation, and yet its actual image is somehow curiously vacant, without content (not unlike Warhol's 'presence' in this work). Our comprehension of death oscillates, in short, between the recognition of it as a singular event, a unique performance, and a massive, historical, highly coded, and ongoing drama. That is, death and its representations oscillate between performance and performativity.

THE POLITICS OF PERFORMANCE AND PERFORMATIVITY

While Warhol was producing his *Death and Disasters* paintings in 1963, Gene Swenson asked him why he choose death as a theme.

> I guess it was the big plane crash picture. The front page of a newspaper: 129 DIE. I was also painting the *Marilyns*. I realized everything I was doing must have been Death. It was Christmas or Labor Day – a holiday – and every time you turned on the radio they said something like '4 million are going to die.' That started it. But when you see a gruesome picture over and over again, it doesn't really have any effect.[18]

It is here that Warhol comes to connect 'doing Death' with iteration, repetition, and citation. This insight is at the heart of Warhol's art. What is misleading about his statement, however, is the last clause. It is not that multiple experiences of encountering death drain death of its 'effect.' Rather, it is that the individual story of death becomes insignificant (after fifteen minutes) and the structural logic of the ongoing continuity of death as repetition comes to the fore. And it is the latter that provides Warhol with his most important subject. As Warhol creates and sees the same 'gruesome picture over and over again' he reminds us of the force of the accumulation and repetition. Part of what 'has an effect' is the density of death's repetitions.

In short, Warhol's work on death pivots around the distinction between performance and performativity. That distinction might, at least initially, be understood as the movement between singular presence – performance is the effort to achieve a vivid connection between the actor and the role, between the spectator and the image in the act of being made on the stage or the screen – and collective inevitability – performativity signals the iteration of the act that precedes the one that the spectator apprehends in the present tense. Thus each singular experience of death is apprehended and interpreted through the iterative force of the collective history and future of death. The performativity of death renders it banal (just as one cannot escape with only one image of Marilyn, neither can one escape with only one image of death); the singular performance of one's own death (or the death of the beloved) makes vivid, however briefly, the loss of language, narrative systematicity, and iteration in which death as a unique act might be understood and communicated. It is this impossibility that renders death an event that is simultaneously dreaded and desired. Thus, in *The Philosophy of Andy Warhol*, Warhol claims: 'I don't believe in [death] because you're not around to know it's happened.'[19] Death is an act that can only achieve meaning in and through the observation of the other, the spectator-witness. In this sense, death is the moment in which doubt – 'I don't believe in it' – triumphs over one's submission to the logic of the collective, iterable 'real' – to that collective fantasy that insists that the real is that which is observable and capable of being apprehended. The specificity of individual death ruptures the flow of death's collective performativity. The observer of that death, perhaps temporarily, falls out of the meaning-machine and hallucinates another real, while the actor dies only to be newly recognized as the already living.

'Where Is Your Rupture?' ask two of Warhol's early paintings. In one, *Advertisement* (1960), the question cannot be fully formulated, cannot be completely legible within the alphabet of the real. Warhol's painting actually reads 'wher Y Rupture?' In the other, *Where Is Your Rupture?* (1960), the question sits on top of a bold line that extends past the position of the sentence's subject: 'Where Is <u>Yo</u> Rupture?' The fading of the letters in mid-breath collapse on top of the line that carries on without filling in the subject's letters. The lines multiply as the image of the outlined body becomes pierced with entry and exit points (Plate 14.2). The 'rupture' is enacted at the level of the signifier and at the level of the visual surface.

From the silk screen to the silver screen, Warhol's art insisted on underlining the imperative of the loss of the artist's 'self,' in an artistic enterprise that had hitherto been dedicated to the valorization, indeed reification, of both the artist and the art object as a sublime stage for the play of Being. By producing screen upon screen and exposing the performativity of collective iteration in the place where 'singular presence' and 'originality' had previously stood, Warhol's work returns us to Heidegger's sharp observation that humans are 'the place holder of nothingness.'[20] It is in our capacity to hold this place while resisting the desire to fill it that the radical nature of Being most fully emerges. For the German Heidegger, that radical nature was expressed as Being-Towards-Death. But for the American Warhol, that radicality held a more difficult-to-assimilate-form of emancipation from depth, presence, and interiority that had been celebrated as the ultimate trajectory of high art. Warhol's particular genius was to initiate a thoroughly American idea of death as an act, a piece of theater, that sits beside us and behind us rather than in front of us. 'I realized everything that I was doing must have been Death,' because precisely 'doing death' is what we have already done.

Such a notion of having already done death initiates an ethical challenge for both the artist and the viewer. For Warhol, part of the fascination of the photographs that comprise *Death in America* must have had to do with the strange theater they created: for what the photograph reveals is the moment at which the photographer chooses to be on the side of

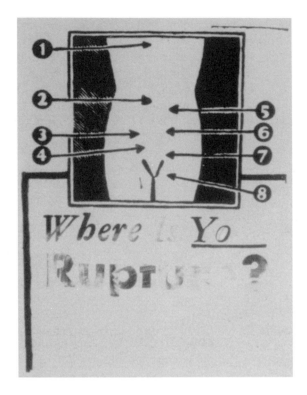

Plate 14.2 Andy Warhol, *Where Is Your Rupture?*, 1960. Private collection. Courtesy of Andy Warhol Foundation for the Visual Arts/ARS, New York (1998)

the recording machine, the passive registering camera, as opposed to an actively engaged combatant in death. The photographs then reveal a kind of double death: the death of the person who chooses suicide (regardless of whether or not the actor is 'rescued' from this choice) and the death of a conventional (and peculiarly Catholic) notion of ethics, that the spectator of the theater of death must intervene to forestall death. When Warhol said he wanted to be a machine he meant in part that he wanted to have the courage to observe without intervening in the drama of someone else's pursuit of and escape from death. But as the last four decades in the United States have shown, machines themselves have been created to take over the part of the unreliably intervening spectator – medical technology, especially the mechanical ventilator, has been assigned the role of forestalling death.

Warhol, like Heidegger, knew that the essence of technology was ambiguous and that it was intimately involved both with art and with death. '[T]he more questioningly we ponder the essence of technology, the more mysterious the essence of art becomes.'[21] In turning over our deaths to the saving power of machines, we transform the art of dying. For Warhol, the art of dying, like the other arts, requires rehearsals of both the past and the future. Death is an act, a performance, a script that, if we are lucky, might hold the attention of its witnesses for at least fifteen minutes (although the dead won't be here to enjoy the (after)glow). After that illumination and Heideggerean 'enframing,' each death will pass into the machinery of silence. Part of what it means, then, to enframe death is to learn how to respond to the imperative of SILENCE that death also dramatizes. On the one hand, the silence of death ruptures iteration and renders us wordless witnesses; on the other, our silence in the face of death's images helps us become dead to death.

Warhol's famous disdain for originality, for the etiolating spirals of the line as a means of expressing 'inner depth,' moves us closer to the heart of the technology of art and further from the effects of autobiography, interiority, originality and other post-Enlightenment tropes that had been propped up as 'the truth' of art itself. Warhol's work is a technology that illustrates the vast reach of the machinery of representation, a machinery capable of eroding the distinction between life and death which allows the dead to be always already a figment in the creative life of the living. The serialized Marilyns, Jackies, and Elvises are illustrations of the way in which repetition and 'cloning' create a reproductive technology that ensures the maintenance of art, memory, celebrity, and money.[22] The closer the subjects come to death – a biological death and also the death-like fading integral to celebrity-making – the more available their images become for the creative projections of the living. For Derrida, one way to know if a set of codes is a language is to ask if it can be decoded after the death of those who use it. If the code can continue after the death of its users then it is a language.[23] The space of the act that occurs after death is what Warhol's work continually enframes. And as such, it can usefully be described as a speech act.

Performativity is, of course, a term that derives from linguistics, and most coherently from J. L. Austin's potent book, *How to Do Things with Words*.[24] Although Austin was British, in his pragmatism he might be said to have had a North American habit of mind. *How to Do Things with Words* (1975) is one of the finest 'how to' books ever written, and like Warhol's dance diagrams and do-it-yourself flowers, there is an almost naive tone of instruction that runs throughout the argument. In an effort to understand what he calls 'ordinary language' (oh would there were such a thing!), Austin proposes that speech acts be divided into two groups: constatives and performatives. Constatives describe things as they are, or were, or will be. Performatives make something happen in the act of being uttered; they occur only in the present tense of their utterance. Warhol helps us see that part of the appeal of the performative speech act is its compatibility with a peculiarly 'American' ethos:

> The President, the news magazines, television – they only want to capture America's mood at the moment, reflect it back, and tell anyone who's not in the same mood to get over it and start feeling American just like everyone else. So if following your own moods makes you feel like everything's just up in the air, you can just listen to the media and the President and just go along with whatever they say. You can talk yourself into their moods, what they think the rest of the country is thinking.[25]

It is easy in America to forget one's feelings, to change one's mood, to think like everyone else, because there is an ever-present representational reflection of 'what everyone else' is feeling, thinking, doing. That this reflection is itself a reflection of a reflection only serves to secure its power.

Warhol suggests that the energy and distorting intelligence of 'America' is related to its constant shuttling back and forth between performance and performativity. The iterative, collective constative speech act that says, 'We are alive, we are Americans,' becomes performative as individuals, quite literally, buy it. High art in America, Warhol's work argues, has overemphasized individual artists' performances and ignored the much more pervasive and vast trajectory of the performativity of a democratic, indeed phantasmatic, art object. This art object gathers more power because its death is also a collective phantasm, something that is projected and screened, rehearsed for and survived, rather than experienced as a singular image or event that 'ends.'[26]

I am trying to emphasize that Warhol's renunciation of emotion in the content of his work did not derive from a desire to 'commit emotional suicide,' but rather was a form of radical artistic and ethical discipline. In order to achieve this renunciation, the artist had to render himself a blank, a mirror, a machine. This is readily, perhaps even too easily, acknowledged as the heart of Warhol's ambition. But it is not in any sense an easy claim to assimilate. In the effort to arrive at the speech act, 'I want to be a machine,' perhaps the axiom of all of Warhol's work, one must conceive of oneself as simultaneously dead and alive – alive to the desire to become mechanical, to become indifferent to wanting to be.[27] This is an aspiration of a different order than wanting to resemble a machine, which is almost always how Warhol's statement is interpreted. Warhol wanted his work to participate in the external iterative structure of performativity, for he trusted this logic more than he believed in his own performances. He also understood, like the good business man he was, that such a seamless participation would ensure that both his art and his image (his celebrity-ness) would survive his death. The renunciation of affect on the surface of his work was a consequence of this ambition, not its central aspiration. He learned that his art got better – sold more, made more money, fitted more congenially into the logic of capital, but also became more aesthetically, ethically, and philosophically substantial – the more he removed his 'affect' from it. 'Neutrality' was something he achieved in his work after an act of will and discipline, after a quite startling submission to the iterative structure and logic of performativity.

Warhol's *Death in America* and *Death and Disasters* series collect and preserve encounters with death that have already happened. To save and collect the photographic documents of those moments of plunging, lunging, gripping, flying toward death is also to prepare, to rehearse, for their return in the act of observation. The encounter with death, for Warhol, is best understood as a performance that requires practice, rehearsal, repetition, revision. To encounter death is to enter into the technology of performativity, it is, in other words, to re-encounter it as phantasm, memory, and projected anticipation. For just as humans have a capacity for speaking, so too do we have a capacity for dying. Warhol shows us that this capacity comes to be seen as 'extraordinary' because it is thoroughly theatrical.

POP POP POP

In his series of electric chairs Warhol's meditation on death reached its most coherent expression. An image he began to work with in 1963, the electric chair returns and is recited again in a series he did in 1965, 1967, and again in 1980. (In 1985, he added monochromes to some of the earlier screens to make diptychs.) The iteration of the electric chair in Warhol's corpus is a repetition that spatializes death as an event that is simultaneously behind us and in front of us. In repeating it and returning to it in different colors and cropped in various ways, Warhol used the electric chair as a way to measure both the accretion of his own machine-like mastery of art-making, and the evacuation of the 'personal object' from the signifying chain of that work. For the electric chair gains its force only as an expression of collective will. The electric jolt of death flickers in and out of the political and ideological scene. Capital punishment is at once an idea associated with 'deterrence' – the prevention of projected phantasmatic acts – and the guarantee that no future acts will be undertaken by its inhabitant. The electric chair is a signifier that always exceeds, by design, the actors it ensnares in its drama.

In Warhol's work with the electric chair he moved most definitively into the abstraction that death as event and force exerts on living actors. In other words, rather than contemplating the death of Marilyn Monroe, Warhol used the electric chair as a way to frame both the recollection and anticipation of death itself. By not restricting death to the autobiography of a singular character, Warhol dramatizes death's universal quality, even while insisting on the particular political-historical implications of its form. The emptiness of the chair, the lack of the specificity of an embodied subject in the act of dying, suggests that death, like all technologies according to Heidegger, becomes itself precisely as 'stored reserve.' Political power in the United States in the past four decades has been consolidated precisely on the performative promise of that stored reserve. From Ronald Reagan's Strategic Defense Initiative to the coffers of the Federal Reserve, America's performative force in the world is executed as stored reserve. Forever on call and available as a kind of eternal return, the electric chair juices through the cultural body as image, whether or not its seat is inhabited, whether or not it sizzles and pops.

The image of the electric chair makes literal death as theater. Executing art, like executing death, presupposes a spectator, a witness, a reader. In the corner of Warhol's image, the word SILENCE blinks (Plate 14.3). The state asks the witnesses of execution to

Plate 14.3 Andy Warhol, *Silver Disaster*, 1963. The Sonnabend Collection, on extended loan to the Baltimore Museum of Art. Courtesy of the Andy Warhol Foundation for the Visual Arts/ARS, New York (1998)

be silent, to allow the machine to do its work without comment. The state anticipates and encourages what it seeks to assure will be the silence that issues from the grave. Warhol's steady massaging of the word across his serial screens, however, continually changes the volume, the color, and the legibility of that SILENCE. Death is perhaps not so quiet, not so still, not so colorless, as the state would command it to be.

Pop, pop, went Valerie Solanis's gun: 'When I got shot, two bullets went through my stomach, liver, spleen, esophagus, left lung and right lung. The doctors and everyone else, including me, was sure I was going to die, so we all got ready, and then I didn't do it. But I always wished I had died, and I still wish that, because I could have gotten the whole thing over with.'[28] For Warhol, the certainty of death – 'sure I was going to die' – opens up onto a radical uncertainty – suppose there is no death after all? Suppose death is just another performance, another image to circulate? Suppose that the collectively of death makes it impossible for any one person to get 'the whole thing over with'? As Eliot reminds us, the artist-poet 'is not likely to know what to do' unless he lives 'in the present moment of the past.' Surviving an attempted murder rendered Warhol's previous work on death eerily prophetic and oddly literal. The assassination attempt performed another radical encounter with the aim of his work: to visualize Being as 'the place holder of nothingness,' to make dramatic the space between life and death in all its radical blankness and unknowability. 'I always thought I'd like my own tombstone to be blank. No epitaph, and no name. Well, actually, I'd like it to say figment.'[29] To read the words for death as they issue from the state's chair, 'SILENCE,' or to imagine the chiseled line of his gravestone spelling out 'FIGMENT,' is to recognize that death, like all acts, initiates a specific reading practice. One that takes practice.

To become a figment of the phantasmatic imagination of one's reader and witness is a huge ambition indeed. Andy Warhol tried to be a filament in the light bulb of the machinery we call art. Pop pop pop goes the gun; pop pop pop goes the flashing camera – and the empty seat of the soon-to-be-sizzling or just-now-turned-off electric chair holds all these pops. Walt Whitman, the poet who helped define an American sensibility more precisely than any other artist of his generation, wanted to sing the body electric. Warhol wanted to declare the state's control of that body a 'disaster.' His almost obsessive return to the image of the performativity of death, made literal by the circulation of electricity commanded by the state, and to his and our own quiescent silence in the face of that disaster implicates both actor and spectator in the theater of death. Red, yellow, lavender disasters: communism – Vietnam, gay pride: Warhol put a line under and through and across the things that the state would like to kill. As we attach and detach ourselves from the theater that both illuminates and obscures the history of death, the state continues to perform its sizzling operations.

Warhol often said he never wanted to paint; he claimed he wanted to be a tap dancer. The electric chair gave him his best stage and he kept tapping on it and across it until there was nothing left to lose. Sizzle, pop, tap, a figment, a ghost, a shadow rhyme. A skull, a screen, a silence. A filament flickering in the recess of our imagination, a figment, a silver ghost that comes and goes both before and after his deaths, and before and after our own.

NOTES

I am grateful to the Open Society Institute, Project on 'Death in America,' for research funding for this essay.

1   Gene Swenson, 'What Is Pop Art?,' originally published in *Art News*, 1963; reprinted in *Pop Art: The Critical Dialogue*, ed. Carol Anne Mahsun, Ann Arbor, Michigan, UMI Research Press, 1989, pp. 118–21.

2   See Trevor Fairbrother's important piece, 'Skulls,' in *The Work of Andy Warhol*, ed. Gary Garrels, Seattle, Bay Press, 1989, and Hal Foster's excellent, 'Death in America', *October*, Winter 1996, vol. 75, pp. 36–59. Both essays have strongly informed my own sense of the centrality of death in Warhol's work.

3   Bradford Collins, 'The Metaphysical Nosejob: The Remaking of Warhol, 1960–68,' *Arts Magazine*, February 1988, vol. 62, pp. 52, 47; Geldzahler is cited on p. 52.

4   Ibid., p. 52.

5   The phrase 'transfer the transference' comes from John Guillory's discussion of Paul de Man's work. See his chapter, 'Literature after Theory: The Lesson of Paul de Man', in *Cultural Capital: The Problem of Literary Formation*, Chicago, University of Chicago Press, 1993, pp. 176–268. I am grateful to Mary Poovey for this reference.

6   Foster, 'Death in America,' p. 43.

7   Crow points out that Warhol began the *Marilyn* portraits 'within weeks of her suicide in August 1962' and he traces the *Liz* series to her 'famous catastrophic illness in 1961.' Crow, 'Saturday Disasters: Trace and Reference in Early Warhol,' in *Reconstructing Modernism: Art in New York, Paris, and Montreal 1945–1964*, ed. Serge Guilbaut, Cambridge, Mass., MIT Press, 1990, pp. 311–32.

8   Thierry de Duve's comment follows a presentation of Crow's lecture at the University of British Columbia in September 1986. The dialogue is published in *Reconstructing Modernism: Art in New York, Paris, and Montreal 1945–1964*, pp. 311–32.

9   Quoted in Collins, 'The Metaphysical Nosejob,' p. 52.

10   The phrase 'ghastly cosmetology' comes from Mary Josephson's 'Warhol: The Medium as Cultural Artifact,' *Art in America*, May–June 1971, vol. 59, pp. 40–46, quotation on p. 43.

11   In this regard I think Crow is correct to alert us to the intensity of the creative act of mourning that suffuses Warhol's work.

12   T. S. Eliot, 'Tradition and the Individual Talent,' in *The Sacred Wood: Essays on Poetry and Criticism*, London, Methuen, 1960, pp. 47–59, quotation on p. 59.

13   See Donna M. De Salvo, ed., *'Success is a job in New York': The Early Art and Business of Andy Warhol*, New York, Grey Art Gallery and Study Center and Pittsburgh, Carnegie Museum of Art, 1989, p. 28. The best discussion I have seen of Warhol's apprenticeship with the line is Ellen Lupton and J. Abbot Miller's 'Line Art: Andy Warhol and the Commercial Art World of the 1950s,' which appears in this catalog on pp. 29–43. See also Benjamin Buchloh, 'The Andy Warhol Line,' in *The Work of Andy Warhol*, ed. Gary Garrels, Seattle, Bay Press, 1989, pp. 52–69.

14   Paul Klee, *Pedagogical Sketchbook*, trans. Sybil Moholy-Nagy, New York and Washington, Frederick A. Praeger, 1953, p. 51.

15   Ibid., p. 53.

16   Foster, 'Death in America.'

17   The best discussion of the connection between photography and death occurs in Roland Barthes' *Camera Lucida*, tr. Richard Howard, New York, Hill & Wang, 1981.

18   Swenson, 'What Is Pop Art?,' pp. 120–21.

19   Warhol, *The Philosophy of Andy Warhol*, New York, Harcourt Brace Jovanovich: 1975, p. 123. Foster offers a different interpretation of this claim in 'Death in America,' p. 37.

20   Martin Heidegger, 'The Question Concerning Technology,' in *The Question Concerning Technology and Other Essays*, tr. William Lovitt, New York, Harper Torchbooks, 1977, pp. 3–52.

21   Ibid.

22   For a provocative discussion of the erotic trajectory of repetition, recycling, and cloning, see Richard Meyer, 'Warhol's Clones,' *The Yale Journal of Criticism*, Spring 1994, vol. 7, no. 1, pp. 79–111.

23 This claim is iterated throughout Derrida's work, but his essay, 'Signature, Event, Context,' offers an important assessment of performance and performativity as well. In *Glyph*, 1977, vols. 1–2, pp. 172–97.

24 Austin, *How to Do Things with Words*, 2nd edn, Cambridge, Mass., Harvard University Press, 1975.

25 Andy Warhol, *America Really Is The Beautiful*, New York, Harper & Row, 1985, p. 152.

26 In this sense, Princess Diana might be said to be the central Warholian art object of our time. Her death continues to live in tabloids, magazines, lawsuits, and other places of collective distortion.

27 Compare 'I want to be a machine,' with Warhol's other axiom: 'As soon as you stop wanting something you get it. I've found that to be absolutely axiomatic,' quoted in Collins, 'The Metaphysical Nosejob,' p. 53. This helps us see how active and alive the desire to be a machine, to pursue indifference and death, must remain.

28 Warhol, *America Really Is The Beautiful*, pp. 126–7.

29 Ibid., p. 129.

15

STUFF

A Performance

Coco Fusco and Nao Bustamante

INTRODUCTION

In 1996, we decided to create a performance that dealt with Latin women, food, and sex. We started from our own stories. Nao is from an immigrant farm worker family that was involved in the Chicano political struggles of the 1960s and 1970s. She grew up in the San Joaquin Valley of California, a region that at one time produced more fruit and vegetables than any other in the world. Coco's family is from Cuba, a country that gained a reputation in the 1950s as an international whorehouse and which, in response to its present economic crisis, has reverted to sex tourism as a strategy of survival. In the course of writing *STUFF* Coco traveled to Cuba to interview women in this burgeoning industry. Then we both went to Chiapas, the center of indigenist culture tourism in Mexico, and the site of the 1994 Zapatista insurrection. We spent several weeks in conversation with women and children whose livelihoods are linked to their daily contact with foreigners.

 STUFF is our look at the cultural myths that link Latin women and food to the erotic in the Western popular imagination. We weave our way through multilingual sex guides, fast food menus, bawdy border humor, and much more. In the course of the performance, we mingle with audience members, treating them to a meal, a host of rituals and exotic legends, an occasional rumba and at least one Spanish lesson as part of our satirical look at relations between North and South. Our spoof, however, is not without a serious side. Latin American literature is full of references to cannibalism: in terms of the European colonial's fear of the indigenous 'other' as a cannibal; cannibalism as a trope for Europe and America's ravaging of Latin America's resources; and finally, cannibalism as the symbolic revenge of the colonized who feed off the colonial. If food here serves as a metaphor for sex, then eating represents consumption in its crudest form. We are dealing with how cultural consumption in our current moment involves the trafficking of that which is most dear to us all – our identities, our myths, and our bodies. *STUFF* is our commentary on how globalization and its accompanying versions of 'cultural tourism' are actually affecting women of color both in the Third World, and in Europe and North America, where hundreds of thousands of Latin women are currently migrating to satisfy consumer desires for 'a bit of the other.'

Plate 15.1 Nao Bustamante and Coco Fusco, STUFF, 1996–7

STUFF

by Coco Fusco and Nao Bustamante
(© 1996, Fusco and Bustamante)

Cast

Blanca	Coco Fusco
Rosa	Nao Bustamante
EEE Jones (on video)	Adam Bresnick
Travel Tasters	various

Scene 1

Intro: The audience has received with their tickets a colored slip of paper. There are four colors (red, blue, yellow and green), and an equal number of audience members have received stubs of each color.
Pre-show music
Music: intro music tape #1
Lights: preset
Top of show lights and music fade to black
Coco and Nao take their places on stage at the small dressing tables, stage left and right.
Lights 1: lights up over the two tables
Coco and Nao are sitting at the table in their street clothes, writing postcards.

COCO: [*Picks one up and reads from it*] March 15, New York – Dear Liz, I finally had that meeting about my piece on Cuban hookers. First, the editor was disappointed that I didn't want to say that Cuban women turned tricks because of the US blockade. Then the editor says to me – you know if I go to a bar here to pick up a guy it's for my enjoyment, but if a girl there does it, she has to give the guy what he wants. Imagine a bunch of overeducated women sitting in an office on Madison Avenue, saying things to me like – 'I mean, if a guy says put my cock in your mouth, those girls just have to do it. How could that possibly be pleasurable?'

NAO: [*Reading from a postcard*] April 4th, Copenhagen: Dearest D.L. Last night I was walking home at 3 00 a.m. when a young guy started following me. He asked me to go home with him, and said he just wanted to make me feel good. At one point he noticed that I had dark hair sticking out from under my cap and that made him very excited. He wanted to know if I was Mexican. When we got to the house where I was staying and I started to go inside, he made one last attempt to win my affections. And then he said, with a smile on his face as if it were some big turn on, I have chips and salsa at my place and if you can have some if you come home with me. That asshole thought I was some little chihuahua or something, desperate for mama's home cooking.

COCO: [*Picks up another postcard*] November 20, Toronto: Dear Kim, I really ticked off some people at the film festival when I joked about how the documentary on Zapatista women looked like a rerun of films about Sandinistas, Salvadoran guerrilleras, and Cuban milicianas. It's not that I don't agree with the Zapatistas. I mean come on, those woman are saying they want to marry the men they choose, and they're enjoying getting free condoms when they're in combat. Who wouldn't sympathize with someone who says they'd rather wash clothes in a machine than on a riverbank? It's just that I'm not that crazy about seeing yet another movie about women getting off on guns.

NAO: [*Picks up another postcard*] May 10, Hamburg: Hello my sweet Suzy, I just can't seem to get away from sex! I'm staying in St. Pauli, the bizarre sex district of this city. The working girls here dress like aerobics intructors. I guess it's more practical than the usual puta-wear. Well, the locals and the tourists are eating it up. They are really crazy about the Brazilian girls. Ooh la la, the Brazileñas are beautiful and I guess it's cheaper for the men to have them here than to go to Brazil. Dark-skinned women drive the Germans wild! Everywhere I go there is a lingerie ad staring me in the face that features a gorgeous black girl with huge breasts. I see

239

the ad all over the place, but I can't seem to remember which company I'm supposed to buy from. The girl is oh oh oh-so-distracting.

COCO: [*Picks up another postcard*] July 14, San Cristobal de las Casas, Chiapas. Dear Consuelo, Last night we had dinner with Marieta. She told us about how the fighting between the mestizos and Indians here goes way way back. The Indians don't really believe that anyone else has the right to live on this land, and the mestizos are afraid of the prophecies that say they'll have to leave one day. Marieta said that one thing people don't talk much about is that the mestizos in San Cristobal rape Indian women from the countryside all the time. She told us about one Indian woman from the market who was raped and got pregnant. When the baby was born the guy went and took it away from her. That woman went mad. From then on, she would only go out with her face covered with mud so that no one would ever go near her again.

Lights 2: fade out on table, stage left
Nao exits.
Video 1: video on
Music 1: tape 2 track 1 (Jorge Reyes)
Level: start high and lower as voice begins
A large video screen (or TV set) is lowered in front of stage with dim lights, and if possible, drawn curtains. Weird, New Age music tunes in and then out, slowly. A man's face fills the screen. He is wearing a conservative dark-colored suit and a carnation in his lapel. His hair is slicked back and he has a moustache. He smiles in a geekish way and holds his smile a little too long.

SCENE 1

EEE JONES: Good evening and welcome. I am your host, Elizardo Eduardo Encarnación Jones, (also known as triple E). I am the director of the Institute for Southern Hemispheric Wholeness. Please allow me to ask you this – Have you thought about what are you going to do on your next vacation? Would you like to try something . . . different?

Most of my clients have endured the pain of waiting all year long for their holiday trip to someplace warm and inviting. They long to bask in the sensual beauty and ancient wonders that my part of the world offers up so willingly. Then, much to their chagrin, they come back irritated by all the tropical storms, masked bandits, parasites, and poverty. They find themselves saying, 'Why not stay home, get some of that spicy take-out food and fondle some crystals instead?'

To them, and to you, I say, objects are not enough. You need complete nutrition for the spirit, and only people can provide that. Why not have the best without suffering the worst? I have devised a service that will bring you heat without sweat, ritual without revolution, and delicacies without dysentery. And you don't have to go anywhere – we deliver it to you. In just a few moments you'll begin to sample the delights of post-spacial travel as we approach the third millenium.

Music 2: fades out

[*Triple E still speaking*] For our first session, we will need four members of our audience.

Lights: house lights up anticipate Blanca

My agency representative, Blanca [*Pause*], [*she stops abruptly and poses like stewardess*] will escort each post-spatial traveller into our *studio*. (Lights on here)

Lights 3: on dining table and a soft general wash

Would all those with red tickets please raise your hand? [*Pause*]
Blanquita, please escort a male with a red ticket on stage.

Video 2: video pause

240

Blanca picks male and escorts him on stage.
Video 3: video play

For this evening's first event, you are going to be an economist in search of authentic pre-Colombian food and music. Your name is François. [*Male sits down at table*]
Good. Now would all those with yellow tickets, please raise your hand? [*pause*] Blanquita, please escort a woman with a yellow ticket on stage.

Video 4: video pause
Blanca picks woman and escorts her on stage.
Video 5: video play

You were orphaned at birth and you just found out that you're Cher's cousin. You want to train as a medicine woman. Your name is Wanda Desert Flower. [*Woman sits at table.*]
Wonderful. Now would all those with blue tickets, please raise your hand? [*Pause*] Blanquita, be a dear and find a man with a blue ticket please.

Video 6: video pause
Blanca picks male and escorts him on stage.
Video 7: video play

You've been wanting to quit smoking for ages and are ready to try anything. Your name is . . . um, Bert.[*Man sits at table.*]
Marvelous. Only one more. This time, those with green tickets, please raise your hand. [*Pause*]
You know what to do, Blanca darling. Female again.

Video 8: video pause
Blanca picks woman and escorts her on stage.
Video 9: video play

You're a creative consultant for the Body Shop and you're eavesdropping on my seminar. Your name is Tippy O'Toole. [*Woman sits at table.*]
I'm sure you're all comfortable. Please notice that you each have a spiritual guidebook in front of you, which you will be asked to read from occasionally. You have entered a new realm and will be known from now on as travel tasters. Are you ready?
BLANCA: All travel tasters nod your heads.
EEE JONES: Marvelous, marvelous. Let the program begin.
Course number 1.

Video 10: EEE strikes a pose, then video fades to black, then video off
Stage action: begin to lower book slowly
Lights 4: overhead special comes up, general wash brought lower and reveals a large book being lowered from the ceiling. It stops at chest level.
Music 3: tape #3 track 1 (Jorge Reyes #2)
All the while, Blanca is playing the rainstick and praying to the heavens.

BLANCA [*going off at moments and not remembering she's on stage reading*]: A long, long time ago, before the times of our mothers, our grandmothers, and our great-grandmothers, before credit-card debt, toxic waste and computer viruses, life was good. The sun shone, the rain was light, and it was never cold. No one had to make decisions about anything because the gods decided everything. Adults and children alike frolicked all day long, since the land bore fruit without any need of human effort. Corn, yucca, potatoes, papaya, tomato, chile, and cacao sprang forth from the soil in abundance. [*Pause*] Recognizing their extreme good fortune, the people occasionally ceased their playing to give thanks. Travel tasters, you give thanks too.

Music 4: music fades out

TASTERS [*in unison*]: We give thanks and praise that the dead once ate.
BLANCA: At the end of each lunar cycle, the people prepared a homage to their most revered

Plate 15.2 Nao Bustamante and Coco Fusco, STUFF, performance, 1996–7. Photograph by Hugo Glendinning

Plate 15.3 Nao Bustamante and Coco Fusco, STUFF, performance, 1996–7. Photograph by Hugo Glendinning

goddess, Cuxtamali, keeper of the earth, the mother of all things. Travel tasters repeat –
TRAVEL TASTERS: The keeper of the earth, the mother of all things.

Blanca moves rain stick as . . .
Lights 5: floor light, downstage left comes up on Rosa
Rosita appears with a small food cart on wheels from stage right. She starts to dance towards downstage center, pounding her feet in a rhythm complementary to Blanca's reading.
Rosa faces audience standing behind her cart.
Lights 6: front light for Rosa, cross fade out floor light

BLANCA: Cuxtamali not only provided for the world, but she was wise enough to provide for herself. Being somewhat insatiable, she kept three lovers. One of them was water [*Rosa spits to the side*] the second one was the wind [*Rosa yawns*] and the last one was fire [*Rosa lights her cigarette and takes a drag.*] Cuxtamali needed all three of them to fulfill her needs. When she took up with the wind, together they spread seeds. [*From her apron pocket Rosa throws seeds at audience.*] When she embraced water, they increased the land's bounty. [*Rosa serves drinks to tasters.*] And when she fought with fire, the world shook and spat forth its insides. [*Rosa looks at Blanca and shrugs.*] To satisfy herself, she rotated her sessions with her three lovers on a regular basis. Tasters –
TRAVEL TASTERS: The goddess is wise.
ROSA: You betcha she's wise.
BLANCA: In honor of this wise and lustful goddess, the people would make a feast at the end of each lunar cycle, and would eat and eat and eat and eat . . .
ROSA [*getting corn from cart*]: I've been serving up this corn mush for three thousand years and boy am I fed up. [*Rosa moves around table, spooning corn mush (or tamales) onto each taster's plate.*]
BLANCA: Oh priestess, please tell the tasters what you are about to serve them.
ROSA [*serving – says very casually*]: Oh . . . yeah. The feast would begin and end with corn, because corn is the beginning and end of all things.
BLANCA: Yes, this is true. Most of the people would be given corn to eat. Filling themselves with the wealth of the earth, they celebrated the generosity of their great goddess. When they had filled themselves with corn, they would begin to eat potatoes. And when there were no more potatoes, the people would eat papaya. Then tomatoes, and then avocados, and then chiles, which were, of course, seeded and finely chopped in advance. [*Meanwhile Rosa takes each type of food off the cart and puts it on the table.*]
ROSA: Don't look at me! I ain't no prep cook and I'm not doing the dishes either! Tasters repeat after me, The goddess does not do dishes!
TASTERS: The goddess does not do dishes!
BLANCA: Let us continue. Between each course the people would commemorate the rise and fall of the great goddess's love affairs with the wind, water, and fire. They sprinkled water on their food, burned incense, and blew sanctified melodies with horns made of giant shells. Tasters, raise your horns and blow!
TASTERS: With this, we honor the goddess. [*They blow on paper horns.*]
BLANCA: Then, the priestesses of the people would take corn, the potatoes, the papaya, and tomatoes, the cacao and the avocado, and they would begin to make an offering to the great sensual goddess Cuxtamali with them.
[*Rosa scrambles to pick up each fruit as it is being named.*]
ROSA: Actually, the priestesses had the feeling at one point that the goddess was getting a little sick of her three boyfriends . . .
BLANCA: Excuse me?
ROSA: Yeah, over it. Cuxtamali had had enough. One day, she decided that she was going to make the perfect mate for herself and dump those machos.
BLANCA: Uh, well yes, let us praise the goddess for being an independent spirit! Tasters! Raise your cups! Que puta madre!
TASTERS: [*they raise their cups*]: Que puta madre!
ROSA: She decided to make her mate out of the stuff she loved the most – food!
BLANCA: You must have gotten a revised version of the legend . . .

ROSA: She started with corn, figuring that since corn is the beginning and the end of all things, why not make it the middle too?
BLANCA: And so with that, she made the torso.
ROSA: [*piecing together the figure*]: Then she took the yucca and fashioned it into delectable arms and legs. The potato became the head. And from the tomato she created her lover's soft and tender heart. When that was done, she took a nice, big banana and –
BLANCA: Uh yes, well, and then the dancing to the goddess, mother of all things and keeper of the earth, would begin.
ROSA: The dance?
BLANCA: Yes, the dance of the blade. For on the occasion of the twelfth lunar cycle, the ceremonies included a knife dance that would be led by the priestesses. [*She pulls out knife.*]
ROSA: Could I have some ritual blade dance music with drums, flutes and horns please?

Music 5: tape #3 track 2 (Tribu)
Start high and fade down quickly
Rosa starts 'the dance.'

BLANCA: The dance was a particularly sacred element of the celebration of the great goddess. All the people would sway back and forth while the priestesses surrounded them. Tasters, please sway! [*The sculpture lies on the table. Rosa is circling the table sensually with the knife.*] And then, the priestesses would reach the climax of their dance. At that point there would have to be a blood sacrifice –
ROSA: [*turns the knife on herself then stops abruptly*] Are you kidding or something?
BLANCA: No. No. Not at all. Blood sacrifice was needed to satisfy the great, lustful, and all-powerful goddess. By order of the goddess the priestess must self-sacrifice.
ROSA: Oh for Christ's sake!

Music 6: music fades out

BLANCA: I beg your pardon, priestess, there was no Christ in those times.
Tasters, repeat after me, self-sacrifice!
TASTERS: Self-sacrifice! Self-sacrifice!
ROSA [*staring at the knife*]: OK, OK, listen to this. The priestess did sacrifice a part of herself . . .
BLANCA: Oh really?
ROSA: Yes. The fruits they had used for their offerings were born of the earth, of the goddess herself. Hence it was flesh of her flesh.
BLANCA: Oh. I hadn't thought of that.
ROSA: [*turning her knife on her food sculptpure*] Die, Mr. Potato Head! Die!
BLANCA: Tasters, please move back and give the priestess enough space for her to carry out her blood-letting ritual. And so, they would first baptize their creations and then begin to draw and quarter them, crying tears of blood as they completed their sacrifice. [*Rosa is tearing away at the food in a frenzy.*]
BLANCA: Rosa, you'd better get a hold of yourself!
ROSA: [*ranting*] The priestess cried tears of blood! Tears of blood!
BLANCA: Tasters, please don't worry, I'm sure the priestess will be finished shortly. And so, according the legend left to us by our mothers, our grandmothers and our great-grandmothers, the priestesses would reach a state of ectasy in the course of their sacrifice, while the people stood witness. Their wild state was said to symbolize the goddess's happiness at having a new lover who was more pleasing to her than those she had had before. And then, as night fell on them and the people grew weary, they would begin their return to their cute little grass-roofed huts.
[*Rosa is still pounding away at the sculpture.*]
Tasters, please rise and return to your seats in the audience. I'm sure this has been an enriching experience for you. I thank you for your participation. [*Tasters rise and file off stage with Blanca assisting them.*]

Lights: house lights brought in until audience participants are seated
Stage action: book is lifted out

Lights 7: book specials cross fade to colored light on screen
Rosa keeps on cutting up the sculpture and is now groaning.

BLANCA: Rosa, the session is over. You can stop now. [*Rosa ignores her.*]
BLANCA: OK. I'm going to call Triple E. [*Blanca points remote control towards screen.*]

Video 11: video on
Lights 8: video screen light out
The screen comes down with EEE's face on it, smiling. Blanca starts sweeping up the mess.

EEE JONES: Well, my friends, wasn't this wonderful? The energy circulating in this room is so powerful it makes my soul jump for joy. I am so glad to see how well our first session with you has gone and how satiated and spiritually satisfied you all look.
BLANCA: Wait a second, Triple E, we've gotta problem. I don't know if you noticed, but Rosa has made a mess of everything. First, she wrecked the ritual, then she wents nuts on me and . . . .
EEE JONES: Do you feel as cleansed and fortified as I feel that you are?
BLANCA: Triple E, we're in trouble. Rosa blew it. Can't you see that things aren't turning out the way they were supposed to . . . .
EEE JONES: Isn't it simply marvelous to move in and out of a distant time and place at the flick of a switch?
BLANCA: Alright, let's stop things right here.

Blanca points remote control towards screen.
Video 12: video pause

ROSA: What do you mean, I blew it? That was a great finale!
BLANCA: Come on, Rosa, you're not supposed to make a mess of everything and groan like some weird extraterrestrial.
ROSA: I thought our ancestors were extraterrestrials, and besides whose idea was this blood-spilling business? Gimme that control!

Blanca and Rosa start a cat fight for the control. Rosa wrestles it away and 'turns on the video'.
Video 13: video play
Blanca pulls off Rosa's wig. Rosa turns to Blanca and pulls off her wig.
Lights 9: general lights fade out, leaving only spots at dressing tables

EEE JONES: It is at this stage of our sessions that our guests feel so spiritually renewed that they are ready to embrace the world anew. But first they must embrace one and other. So, now, turn and hold out your arms to your neighbor. Share with one and other the richness you carry inside yourselves! Thank you. And thank you, my beloved initiates, for being part of this occasion. You have received a taste, only a taste of what we'll be offering to you via satellite in the very near future. So keep tuned in and turned on. [*Triple E poses in a smile, video fades to black.*]

Video 14: video off
Lights out
Center spotlight goes on again
Nao comes on stage.

ROSA: Hi, I'm Nao. I need to get some information about your experience of our travel taster service this evening. When I'm not on stage, I work as a sex educator and sales associate for a women-owned sex toy co-operative. I help men and women decide which dildos and vibrators work best for them.

As you can imagine, the most common question I get is – what size is right for me? Not for me, I mean for them. Now I can't tell what sort of dildo a person needs just from talking to them. So I tell customers to take a trip to the supermarket, and check out some vegetables. Long, thin vegetables. Then they've gotta take them home, and let them reach room temperature. Then put condoms on them and try them out. Once they've figured out which ones satisfy them the most, I tell them to measure them and then come back to me with this information, and then I can help them out.

Now talking to you about this have made me a little curious, so before I get to our questionnaire, let me ask you this. Let's say you're in the supermarket and you're in the cucumber section. There are the smooth, short waxy fat ones, and then there are the English kind, long with ridges. Which ones would you prefer? Can I see a show of hands for the regular cucumbers? How about the English ones?

What about zucchini? Or those yellow summer squash with the curved tip – great for G-spot stimulation . . .

End of Scene One

Coco stands by her small table. Spotlight on her. She puts on nerd glasses.

COCO [*reads a postcard*]: January 23, Portland, Oregon. Dear Audience, I think it's time to explain why we are so interested in Latin women and food. Actually, this piece about consumption – of our bodies and our myths – and food. Let's start with Anthropofagies. That's what the Brazilians use to call it in the 1920s. An-Thro- Po-Fa – Gi-A. That was supposed to be our great, creative, cannibalistic revenge. Absorb our sacred enemies and transform them into totems, they said. Take everything that is thrown our way and have our way with it. That's how we were supposed to live up to our ancestors. So when you come charging in our direction, running from whatever it is you're running from – you may not think that we who serve you could be eating as well. But we do. Gently but efficiently, we devour you. The more visceral your desires, the more physical our labor.

Lights out

Scene 2

Stage is dark

When Nao (customer 1) is on down-center mark.

Lights 10: spotlight on at down-center

Sound 7: tape #7 (voice over)

Customer #1 (Nao) (Hair pulled back, she wears a ripped 'Bahamas' T-shirt. She does yoga poses.)

VOICE-OVER: (*airy voice*) I hadn't really grasped why I felt so . . . empty. I just couldn't satisfy myself. Then, a true friend referred me to Triple E. I didn't know what to expect when I called. But everything was as promised, no surprises and no problems. I can tell I've made contact with the deepest parts of myself. My spiritual practice has grown and I feel desirable again. I'm eternally grateful to the Institute, and of course, to the goddess.

Sound 8: pause tape

Lights 11: light out

Customer #1 leaves the stage. Meanwhile, Coco is on her mark at table.

Lights 12: table light

Sound 9: continue to play tape 7

Coco (Wearing a black bathrobe, she is resetting the table.)

VOICE-OVER: The first lesson I learned about gringos when I was little was that their food tasted gross. I thought I was supposed to learn how to cook decent food as a matter of cultural survival. I ended up as the only one in my crowd who doesn't live on takeout. I'm the one who makes the big dinners for everybody. I got so into it that I never even complained when guys never did shit to help. I even told one guy I wanted to cook for all his friends, no matter how many stopped by unannounced. I said I wanted to cook for his family, even though I was terrified they wouldn't like my food. Once one of them showed up with a ham and cheese croissant that was oozing with mayonnaise, and I took it as a personal affront. When another one asked for a beer while I was cutting up the lasagna, and I knew there were no more in the fridge, I dropped the knife and ran out to the store and let my own food get cold. Every once in a while I would fall asleep at dinner while the guests were still around because I was so tired. And they say we use food to trap them.

Sound 10: pause tape

Lights 13: light out

Coco exits. Meanwhile, (Nao) customer #2 at stage left (book position).
Lights 14: book light up
Sound 11: continue to play tape #7
Customer #2 (Baseball cap, with dreads, and Human Race T-shirt.)

VOICE-OVER: [*Whiny voice*] Well, it's not exactly what I expected. Kind of a hodgepodge of stories, or, what do ya call 'em, ancient tales or something like that. I think it had to do with women and their sexual appetites, and well . . . I dunno. The corn was OK, nothing to write home about. The bit with the knife was cool. Did I say enough?

Sound 12: pause tape
Lights 15: light out
Customer #2 exits. Meanwhile Judy (Coco) is down stage-center.
Lights 16: light up down-center
Sound 13: continue to play tape #7
Slide 1: English translation slide is projected on screen
Judy (Coco) (wearing black bathrobe and wild wig, begins to style her hair and primp 'herself').

VOICE-OVER (*Spanish-speaking transvestite*): Me puedes llamar Judy. Me preguntas si me deprimo? Por supuesto que me deprimo. Pero esto es un trabajo, vieja. Qué puedo hacer? Nadie escogió vivir en medio de esta mierda. Trato de no pensar mucho en estas cosas. Cuando me siento mal, pienso en un peinado nuevo. A los italianos les fascina el pelo rizado, asi que me hize este permanente para estar más morena. Qué te parece? Es que chica, hay que comer, no?

   Mi familia? Ya estan acostumbrados. Cuando traigo un gallego a la casa, mi familia no lo ve a él – ven un pollo, arroz, frijoles, y platanos, ven un refri lleno. Les digo a los pepes que estoy haciendo esto para comprarme una libra de picadillo, y asi se sienten más culpables de mi situación y entonces me dan más plata. No digo que me gusta estar en un lugar con aire acondicionado. Yo pudiera estar en una oficina todo el día, como hacia cuando trabajaba en el banco. Pero que saqué de eso? Ay mi cielo, absolutamente nada.

(TRANSLATION SLIDE READS)

You can call me Judy. Depressed? Sure I get depressed. But it's a job, honey. What can I do? Nobody chooses to be born in the middle of a mess like this one. I try not to think about things too much. When I feel down, I start thinking about a new way to fix my hair. The Italians like wild hair, so I permed mine to look more *morena*, what do you think? We have to eat, right?

   My family? Oh, they're used to it. When I bring a *Gallego* home, my family doesn't see him, they just see a chicken, rice, beans and *platanos* – a full fridge. When I tell the guys that I'm doing it to buy a pound of ground beef, they feel better about giving me money, and they leave me more. I don't say I like to be in a nice room with air conditioning for a change. I could sit in an office all day – I did that when I was working in a bank. What did I get then? Oh darling, absolutely nothing.

Slide 2: slide out
Lights 17: light out
Judy exits.
Meanwhile Nao enters and sits at table.
Lights 18: light up over dining table
Sound 14: continue to play tape #7

[*She begins to pick her teeth with a toothpick.*]
VOICE-OVER: I once asked an astronaut what he missed most about Earth and he replied, 'Food and sex.' I can relate to that.
I am eating her and she tastes so tangy, a bit like a rusty papaya, unlike any other person I've tasted. Women taste strong, not like men. Men don't taste like anything if they are properly washed. Women always have a taste even if they are freshly bathed. When you consume a woman there is a taste and a smell left in your mouth and in your nose, which are connected by the way, as are your asshole and your mouth. But a woman's flavor changes depending on

what she has eaten, how aroused she is, where she is in her cycle and who is in her vicinity. They say it's the same for men, with semen, but whatever, to me the taste of semen is repulsive. I think those who enjoy eating women must enjoy the flavor and scent and juice of seriously potent fruit . . . . I've eaten both and it takes more raw talent . . . to eat a woman.

Sound 15: pause tape
Lights 19: light out
Nao exits. Meanwhile 'Marta' enters (Coco w/braids wig and rebozo).
Lights 20: light downstage center
Sound 16: continue to play tape #7
Slide 3: slide #2 on

[Marta (she lays out several dolls on top of a rebozo)]
VOICE-OVER (*in Spanish*): Yo he trabajado aquí en el zócalo desde los siete años. Así que conozco bien como son los turistas que vienen a este lugar. Primero les ofresco mis muñecos. Mi mama hace muy bonitos muñecos zapatistas, muy hermosos con pasamontañas de terciopelo. Nunca he visto a Marcos, pero tengo muñecos de Marcos, Ramona y Trini, Moises y David. Yo digo siempre que el dinero es para mi tortilla. Algunos compran al tiro. Si eso no funciona les muestro mis pulseras. La gente que ya conozco a veces no quieren comprar, entonces les pido una coca. A veces hay otros que me llevan a cenar. Siempre trato de ver si mis amigos y mi mamá pueden venir también. Así nos sentamos en los restaurantes donde a veces nos echan, y los meseros no pueden decir nada. Mi amigo Alex de Alemania me regaló este traje. Lo uso para trabajar. El también me retrató y me pagó 20 pesos por haberme tomado la foto. Ahora les cobro 30 pesos a los gringos por cada foto.

Sound 17: pause tape
Slide 4: slide out
Lights 21: light out

(TRANSLATION SLIDE)

I've been working here since I was seven, and I guess I've gotten to know what the tourists who come here are like. First, I offer them my dolls. My mother makes good Zapatista dolls, nice ones with velvet ski caps. I've never seen the real Marcos, but I have dolls of Marcos, Ramona, Trini, Moises and David. I tell people that the money is for my tortillas. Some people buy them right away. If that doesn't work I show them my bracelets. People I already know, though, sometimes they don't want to buy dolls or bracelets, so I ask them for a soda. Then sometimes there are people who will even buy me a meal, and then I always ask for chicken. I always try to see if my friends and my mother can come too. Then we can sit in the restaurants where we usually get thrown out and the waiters can't say anything. My friend Alex from Germany bought me my dress. This is what I work in. Alex also took my picture and paid me 20 pesos. Now I charge the gringos 30 pesos for one shot. [*She picks up her dolls and puts the bundle on her back. Marta exits. Meanwhile Customer #3 (Nao) enters.*]

Lights 22: light up stage left (book light)
Sound 18: continue to play tape #7

[Customer #3 (in sunglasses and a slick jacket)]
VOICE-OVER: If you really wanna know, I think Triple E is a crackpot. I can't believe what I paid for this. I didn't feel a thing. They said the camote was an aphrodisiac, so I ate five and all they gave me was the runs. I was hoping to get a a little more – you know what I mean. And those girls weren't exactly spring chickens. I thought it would be more like those kinds of places – it's like the way everybody moves, the way they let you know things with their hands.

You don't need to speak the language even – you can just get into the music. The girls there, the way they . . . . It's so . . . smooth, so . . . well, I'd to see a little more of that.

Sound 19: tape #7 ends here
Lights 23: light out
Customer #3 exits
Video 15: video on

248

Coco and Nao are at dressing tables changing into new costumes throughout sequence.
Lights 24: lights on over two dressing tables

EEE JONES (*video*): I gather from your comments that our next intensive program will be more to your liking. Our aim is to please all sorts of tastes, and we recognize that serving you a meal is only one of the ways of heightening your experience of the senses and your connection to the spiritual. Many of you out there are demanding more of an immersion in another way of living – in, of course, the safest setting possible. In fact, our current research suggests that intercultural growth areas are the ones that offer the highest degree of, shall we say, intimate personal contact.

Sound 20: start music tape #3 track 3 (Esquivel)

Therefore, in order to attend to our increasingly diversified client base, and, to satisfy your hunger for transformative physical encounters, we are upgrading our services to provide the most extensive and sophisticated multilingual intercourse you could imagine. Blanca, Rosa, would you like to give our studio audience tonight a preview?
BLANCA: Estoy lista, Triple E.
ROSA: Orale, jefito.
EEE JONES: Fine. Now, if a travel taster says, 'Je veux t'offrir un verre,' that means
BLANCA: I would like to buy you a drink.
EEE JONES: And you say –
BLANCA: Je voudrais de l'eau minérale.
ROSA: No, je veux un martini.
EEE JONES: If a travel taster says, 'come ti chiami?' you say –
ROSA: Mi chiamo Lola.
EEE JONES: Now if a travel taster says, 'Ist das dein Freund?' he means –
ROSA: Is that guy your boyfriend?
EEE JONES: And you say –
BLANCA: Das ist mein bruder.
EEE JONES: Which means?
BLANCA: He's my brother.
EEE JONES: When a travel taster says, 'De qué signo eres?' What does that mean?
BLANCA: What's your sign? So we say –
ROSA: Soy virgo, soy virgen.
EEE JONES: Good. So if he says, 'I'm married,' you say –
BLANCA: Oh, do you have an open relationship?

Sound 21: music out

EEE JONES: Yes, and if he says, 'Was magst du?' meaning –
BLANCA: What are you into?
EEE JONES: You'll answer . . .
ROSA: How do you want it – or – wie willst du es? Right?
EEE JONES: Very good ladies. I think you're ready. Can we have the lights up on our audience please?

Video 16: video off
Lights 25: audience lights up, general front, flashing colors from back
Sound 22: tape #4 track 1 (Herb Alpert and Tijuana Brass)
Blanca and Rosa go to get their 'mikes' and then go out into the audience.

BLANCA: Bienvenidos mis amigos, bienvenus mes amis, wilkommen mienen freunden, ahora queremos hacerles algunas preguntas, so let's see who's the most ready to participate in our new program. Dale Rosa!

Lights 26: lights stop flashing, colored lights stay on

ROSA [*standing in one of the aisles*]: Who knows how to say – 'Bring me another margarita' – in another language?

If an audience member answers, Rosa says: Let's have a round of applause for this gentleman.
If an audience doesn't answer, Rosa goes to one and says: Try saying: Tráeme otra margarita, por favor.
BLANCA: That was great! Does anyone know what this means? No puedo comer fritangas?
If an audiences answers, Blanca says: Let's have a round of applause for our friend!
If they don't she says: It means: I can't eat fried food.
ROSA [*standing next to a male audience member*]: OK, I have a feeling about you. Fuiste maestro de conga en tu vida anterior, no es verdad? Know what that means?
If the audience member answers Rosa says: Well, I can't wait to get up and dance with you baby!
If they don't she says: You may not know it but I can tell you were a bongo player in your past life.
BLANCA [*to a woman – she does a moño while saying*]: Quieres mover tu cintura como una mulata buena? Do you know what I said?
If the woman answers yes, Blanca says: (if not continue saying the phrase to other women until Blanca gets a yes): Well, I think all of you have done marvellously! Rosa, could I see you on stage for a moment?
Blanca and Rosa go back on stage. They whisper to each other briefly.
ROSA [*pointing to those in the audience who spoke*]: Would you please stand? Would you please stand? Would you, and you? Thank you! Congratulations, all of you have proven your multilingual potential. Please now join us on stage for an Afro-Frenetic Extravaganza.

Lights 27: lights flashing!
Four audience members go on stage.
Lights 28: lights stop flashing
Sound 23: music fades out

BLANCA [*pointing to guy marked as Congero*]: Ven aca Señor Congero.
Música por favor.
Sound 24: tape # 5 (afro frenetic)
Rosa grabs guy and sits him down, hangs him mini bongos, white cap, and a cigar.
She begins to show him the rhythm and he starts drumming.
Rosa signals for the audience to applaud.
Meanwhile Blanca puts other three audience members on their marks.
Blanca and Rosa take their positions in front of dancers. They begin to step and clap to the music.

BLANCA: Soy Blanca
ROSA: Soy Rosa
TOGETHER: . . . and we're going to teach you to rhumba!
BLANCA: Are you ready for an Afro-Frenetic dance extravaganza?
ROSA: Yeah, let's do it!
TOGETHER: Vámonos!
ROSA: This is the basic step you'll need. [*Blanca and Rosa start moving their feet only.*] We'll add the shoulders later.
[*Blanca goes around to back of dancers and starts correcting their positions.*]
ROSA: Fantastico, OK – let's add the shoulders!
BLANCA: Everybody!
ROSA: OK – Try to keep control of your upper body!
BLANCA: Yeah, no window washing!
ROSA: [*demonstrating*] And no funky chicken either!
BLANCA: Gimme a minute, I'm gonna check Maestro Bongo. [*Blanca goes over to Congero.*] OK, OK, That was great. Now you're ready to learn how to *moño*.
ROSA AND BLANCA: Moño!

Sound 25: quick change to tape #6 (Eddie Palmieri)
They start gyrating
Do it!
[*Dancers do moños. Rosa and Blanca motion for audience to applaud dancers.*]
ROSA: And now, it's time for the frenetic part. Let's go freestyle!

Sound 26: crank up the music
Lights 29: lights begin to flash, chaotic scene
Blanca, Rosa and dancers go bananas.
Sound 27: after 30 seconds (or so) of unbridled dance, music fades out
Lights 30: light go back to general and colors
Rosa and Blanca pull out fans and take dancers over to table.

BLANCA: You guys deserve a rest.
[*Rosa fans dancers*]
ROSA: And a drink!
[*Rosa serves drinks*]
BLANCA: Well, that was just great. Now travel tasters, Rosa and I are just beginning to develop this part of our repertoire and would like to ask for your help. Would one of you be willing to volunteer for a test dialogue to get us going?
[*Travel taster volunteers. Blanca, Rosa and T.T. Move to downstage center. She and Rosa set up to two chairs.*]

Lights 31: downstage center spot, coming from the front

BLANCA: OK, you're going to have a conversation with me and Rosa will show you what you need to say. Now, let's take our little game down here, so the two of us can get to know each other better.
Blanca and T.T. sit downstage center.
ROSA: We've been working on our conversational abilities with our fantastic HOT INTERNATIONAL guide, which comes with translations for love and sex in seven different languages. Tonight though, we're going to work on our Spanish. Ready? Or should I say listo? Now you've just come off the dance floor with Blanca and you're going to ask her if she liked the dance. Say, 'Te gustó el baile?'
T.T.: Te gustó el baile?
BLANCA: Sí! Eres buenísimo!
ROSA: She's saying that you're really great - so you ask her if she wants to go to your place. Say, 'Quieres ir a mi casa?'
T.T.: Quieres ir a mi casa?
BLANCA: Vamos a esperar a conocernos mejor, no?
ROSA: Oh, oh, she's say you have to get to know each other better. So make small talk. Ask her what her name is – 'como te llamas?'
T.T.: Como te llamas?
BLANCA: Me llamo Lola. Y tú de dónde eres?
ROSA: She wants to know where you're from. Tell her you're Nigel from England. 'Soy Nigel de Inglaterra.'
T.T.: Soy Nigel de Inglaterra.
BLANCA: Ya es tarde. Debo ir a mi casa.
ROSA: Oh oh, She wants to go home. You better offer to take her. Say, 'Te llevo?'
T.T.: Te llevo?
BLANCA: Bueno, vámonos.
ROSA: Lucky guy. She said yes! Ok, now you're home together, and you've gotten through the initial formalities. You've got to tell her to get on the bed. Say 'Echate en la cama!'
T.T.: Echate en la cama!
BLANCA: Ok.
ROSA: That was easy! Now, get her on her knees. 'Ponte en rodilla.'
T.T.: Ponte en rodilla!
BLANCA: Ya voy! Espérate, eres muy grande!
ROSA: She thinks you're a little big. You tell her to try another way. 'Vamos a probar otra cosa.'
T.T.: Vamos a probar otra cosa.
BLANCA: Que rico es asi!
ROSA: Great – she likes it.
BLANCA: Me estas volviendo loca!
ROSA: You're driving her wild. Now you can tell her to get some rope. 'Busca la cuerda.'

T.T.: Busca la cuerda.

BLANCA: No me ates, por favor!

ROSA: Oops, she doesn't want to be tied up. Tell her she's gotta be punished. 'Hay que castigarte!'

T.T.: Hay que castigarte!

BLANCA: Eres un animal!

ROSA: You better tell her to calm down. Say, 'cálmate!'

T.T.: Cálmate!

BLANCA: Vete al carrajo!

ROSA: She's very angry. Tell her you lost control and that you're sorry. 'Perdóname, perdí el control.'

T.T.: Perdóname, perdí el control.

BLANCA: Me estas usando!

ROSA: She thinks you're using her. Say it isn't true, that you're looking for love. 'No es cierto, busco amor!'

T.T.: No es cierto – busco amor!

BLANCA: Y yo estoy buscando apoyo financiero.

ROSA: And she's looking for financial support. Travel taster, why don't you suggest that you could live together in your country? 'Podemos ir a vivir en mi país.'

T.T.: Podemos ir a vivir en mi país.

BLANCA: Vamos a conocernos un poquito mejor.

ROSA: She still wants to get to know you better. But I think it's going very well. The next morning, you offer to take her out for breakfast. Say, 'Quieres ir a desayunar?'

T.T.: Quieres ir a desayunar?

BLANCA: Ay sí!

ROSA: She's game. Now, just to be sure, ask her for her name again. 'Como era que te llamabas?'

T.T.: Como era que te llamabas?

BLANCA: Me llamo Lola.

ROSA: Tell her you'll never forget her. 'Nunca me olvidaré de tí.'

T.T.: Nunca me olvidaré de tí.

BLANCA AND ROSA: Gracias guapo.

ROSA [*to the audience*]: Aren't they fantastic? Let's give them a hand.

Applause

Blanca and Rosa lead Travel Tasters back to audience.

Lights 31: house lights up till audience participants are seated,

MAN'S VOICE: Un momento, compañera. I saw you with that foreigner.

Lights change to cold spotlight on Blanca.

Como te llamas?

BLANCA [*walking back into the spotlight*]: Me llamo Lola.

MAN: Sure. Where do you live?

BLANCA: En Centro Habana.

MAN: Where do you work?

BLANCA: Wherever I can. [*She clasps her hands in prayer.*] Todos seguimos al Señor. You know, the man in charge here? [*She makes a gesture to show a beard on chin.*] He's bending every which way to keep things going. And we're following him.

MAN: What did you say your name was again?

BLANCA [*taking off her wig*]: Coco.

MAN: You know, that guy you talked to didn't seem like the kind of man who would take advantage of a Third World woman.

BLANCA: Not all the guys who come here are pigs you know.

MAN: Aren't you making light of a very serious situation?

BLANCA: What else can I do? Haven't you ever had sex with someone who had more than you?

MALE VOICE: More?

BLANCA: More. More power. More money. More food. More youth. More.

252

Coco wheels out the red velvet curtain and brings over the microphones.
BLANCA: Nao you've got to stop now.
ROSA: But I'm not finished yet. What about creamy foods, mushy ones?
BLANCA: Nao, stop. [*pause*]
And now ladies and gentlemen we've reached the grand finale of our program. We're going to have a very special live musical presentation straight from Isla Mujeres, from the divine, the one and only Rosa de la Rosa!

Sound 28: microphones on

ROSA: Thanks Blanca. You know, my friend Blanca, she's as beautiful on the inside as she is on the outside. So you can imagine what kind of liver she's got – gorgeous! Let's have some music!

Lights 33: cabaret style spot on platform

ROSA AND BLANCA'S SONG:
Señor John is a Malibu swinger
Who decided to take a trip south
His friends said he should first learn some Spanish
But that John insists that he's learned enough
I learned from my be - lov - ed maid
When I was a little muchacho
And then from the gardener, the butler,
The driver, the waiter and cook.

Yell: And John started singin':

Que me des unos Huevos rancheros
Yo quiero Bananas and nuts
Tu Quieres mi Concha-Biscocha
It's your pinche salchica I lust.

And with that he took off with his backpack.
Some days later he lands on our isle
and he stumbles right into our hangout
A hip bar called the Crocodile's smile

There we two girls work hard for our money
Putting up with a whole lot of schmucks.
We dance and sing, and grind our hips nightly
to be sure we take home lots of bucks.

Yell: And he says:

May I squeeze tu melón y papaya.
You can pinch my panocha if you want.
How I relish the zest of your chile.
That chamoya 'n' chorizo is enough.

Our poor John, he has never been sober.
But on holiday he gets much worse.
Married ladies must tolerate spouses
But drunk gringos are the island girls' curse.
[*This last line is repeated over and over while platform is wheeled off.*
Stage action: platform is wheeled off into wings, while Rosa and Blanca are still singing.]

Lights 34: spot fades into a general that can catch the exit of the platform

Applause
Music: tape #2 (Jorge Reyes) – 27
Video 17: video on

EEE JONES: Ladies and gentlemen, I am sure that you will agree with me that this has been an absolutely exceptional evening. I have no doubt that each and every one of you will go home transformed. Thank you for choosing our first-class travel tasters' service, brought to you by the Institute for Southern Hemispheric Wholeness. For complete tour information please pick up one of our brochures located in the lobby of the theatre. We also offer a frequent travellers' card that will allow you to accumulate a host of exotic and lustful benefits. Adios and bon appétit.

Video 18: Triple E smiles, video fades, then video off
Lights 36: all lights fade out with video to black
Music fades out – end
Lights 37: bow lights
Lights 38: after bow, lights back to preset

Props to be supplied by the space:
VCR and video projector with REMOTE CONTROL
slide projector
SOUND SYSTEM (two audio cassette decks or one DAT and one audio cassette deck)
3 MICROPHONES

dining table and four chairs
2 SMALL TABLES WITH CHAIRS (as dressing tables)
3 CLOTHING RACKS
FOOD CART on WHEELS

one stage hand
PULLEY SYSTEM TO FLY PROP(BOOK) FROM RIG

16

FOLLOWING ACCONCI/
TARGETING VISION

Christine Poggi

In 1969 Vito Acconci shifted the terrain of his artistic practice from poetry and art criticism to performances that took the streets of New York and his own body as their mutual ground. This shift entailed not so much a change of medium, as a newly conceptualized relation of self and other, self and social world. Crucial to this relation was an investigation of beholding, understood as necessarily corporeal, temporal, and implicated in the construction of subjectivity, power, and desire. Coming to visual art as an outsider, Acconci perceived it to be an open category, with no distinctive attributes or immanent laws. As he put it,

> Art for my generation was a kind of non-field. It didn't seem to have any inherent characteristics of its own. Art was a field into which you could import from other fields, so I felt free to come to it from the closed field of poetry, in which the parameters were set. Besides, I was interested in what all the arts had in common – the author mediating between the object and viewer.[1]

Focusing on the object/viewer relation, Acconci began to engage in a metacritique of the conventions of viewing works of art, especially those associated with 1960s formalism that privileged disinterested, purely optical, contemplation.

Acconci had become fascinated with the norms of formalist criticism while writing reviews for *Art News* from November 1968 to December 1970. Entering this new field of writing, Acconci characteristically set out to master its terms:

> I was feverish to know the rules of the field – you know, the rules of the game. And it's funny because a lot of the stuff that meant most to me at that time was real exaggerated formalist criticism – Michael Fried, whatever. Not so much that I agreed with it, but it made a certain position clear – what I wanted to resist.[2]

For Fried and Clement Greenberg, purity and quality in art derived from adherence to the laws of a given medium. In painting, by the late 1950s, this had come to mean an emphasis on opticality, on qualities that appealed to the eye alone without invoking tactile or sculptural sensations.[3] Optical art was ideally addressed to a disinterested beholder, and was intended to achieve 'presentness.' In the moment of viewing, desire and temporality, contingency and lack, would be forestalled. Fried's influential article of 1967, 'Art and Objecthood,' was above all famous for its concluding line: 'Presentness is grace.' Here the spiritual dimension of atemporal, disinterested beholding is clearly revealed. Through an instantaneous act of perception, the beholder sees the modernist work of art as fully unified and coherent. Its clarity of design and self-reflexivity manifest the autonomy and plenitude of the aesthetic sphere, which is then mirrored in the beholder's sense of subjective coherence and stability.[4] According to Fried, works such as Frank Stella's shaped paintings of the mid-1960s, or Morris Louis's *Veils*, exemplify this pictorial autonomy without demanding awareness of their status as objects in three-dimensional space. The eye that beholds these works is construed as the vehicle of a disembodied gaze. Rejecting this form of modernism, Acconci abandoned the criterion of medium specificity and the definition of the beholder as a disinterested, transcendent subject.

Vision, in Acconci's early work, is consistently situated within the matrix of the body and its physical constraints. The artist's critique of the disembodied gaze emerges clearly in his super-8 film, *Soap and Eyes* of June 1970 (Plate 16.1). In this three-minute performance, Acconci looks into the camera while pouring soapy water into his eyes. The film's duration was determined experientially, as the length of time it took Acconci to work the soap out of his eyes, so that he could look into the camera again. This 'looking at looking,' to use Acconci's words, calls attention to the physical processes of blinking, exhaustion, readjustment, and recovery.[5] It demonstrates the facticity and irreducible temporality of the body as the very grounds of vision.

Already during the summer and fall of 1969, Acconci had attempted to document the interaction of self and world through an analysis of the phenomenology of vision. In a series of photoworks he used a hand-held camera as a correlative of, and supplement to, vision. In *Blinks*, executed in lower Manhattan, Acconci walked a continuous line, attempting not to blink, while holding the camera ready at eye level. Each time he was forced to blink, he took a photograph, thereby equating the action of the shutter with the shutting of his eyes, and recording what he could not see while performing the piece. *Blinks* investigated the physical limitations of vision, as well as the ways in which the body's spatio-temporal position determines what is seen – how distance always inheres in objects as they are seen. Rather than posit a perceptually unified, transcendent gaze, *Blinks* gives us a sequence of views that index the changing locations of the body, even though the camera remains focused on a distant point and the body itself is not directly figured. As Kate Linker

Plate 16.1 Vito Acconci, still from *Soap and Eyes*, 1970. Courtesy of the Barbara Gladstone Gallery, New York

has observed, 'what is evident in these photoworks is that they present a view in which the self is made contingent, or relativized, inasmuch as it can only be known through another register, through its imprint in a surround.'[6]

In commenting upon his work in 1971, Acconci invoked Maurice Merleau-Ponty's analysis of the body's specific mode of 'inhabiting' or 'haunting' rather than merely existing in space. According to the artist:

> Actually you can't say a body is in space, or exists in space – it haunts space (that's a Merleau-Ponty phrase I just came across recently, but it clicked). A body is here, but while he's here he's also there. He's in a lot of places at once, making signs and leaving marks because of the way feelers go out from his body to things around him. It's like a presence, but a ghostly presence.[7]

These remarks refer to ideas articulated in *The Primacy of Perception*, which appeared in English translation in 1964. There one can read that 'the body is no longer merely *an object in the world*, under the purview of a separated spirit. It is on the side of the subject; it is our *point of view on the world*.' For Merleau-Ponty, moreover, this point of view involved the totality of the body's relation to space:

> We grasp external space through our bodily situation. A 'corporeal or postural schema' gives us at every moment a global, practical, and implicit notion of the relation between our body and things, of our hold on them. A system of possible movements, or 'motor projects,' radiates from us to our environment. Our body is not in space like things; it inhabits or haunts space.[8]

Acconci's photoworks can be interpreted as a series of such 'motor projects,' through which the artist investigates his postural relation to the environment. In *Stretch* (Plate 16.2), for example, Acconci took a series of four photographs, holding the camera as far as he could over his head, to his left, down to his feet, to his right. He then organized these photos and the explanatory text in a corresponding gridlike configuration, so that each photograph maps the limits of the body while connecting those limits to the larger visual field. In *Lay of the Land* Acconci lay on his side and took five photographs, with the camera held at this feet, knees, stomach, chest, and head. The resulting piece displayed these photos horizontally, the text indicating the position from which each was taken.

Merleau-Ponty had argued in *The Primacy of Perception*, that

> spatial forms or distances are not so much relations between different points in objective space as they are relations between these points and a central perspective – our body. In short, these relations are different ways for external stimuli to test, to solicit, and to vary our grasp on the world, our horizontal and vertical anchorage in a place and in a here-and-now.[9]

For Merleau-Ponty, the central perspective issued not from the eyes alone but from the body as a whole: 'After all, the world is all around me, not in front of me.'[10] Acconci's photoworks reveal a body that, at least initially, may seem 'anchored' in a spatial matrix, a 'here-and-now'; but they do so by subverting the normative hierarchy of the head as the privileged locus of vision, synonymous with consciousness itself. Refusing a single,

Plate 16.2 Vito Acconci, *Stretch*, 1969. Courtesy of the Barbara Gladstone Gallery, New York

totalizing point of view, the camera redistributes the function of seeing around the perimeter of the body, so that it describes its full span, or along its horizontally aligned axis, so that it more closely approximates the lay of the land itself. Paradoxically, the views presented in the final works remain discontinuous fragments; while pointing to a specific time and place, they do not replicate Acconci's own possibilities of seeing, and therefore fail to deliver a unified sign of his own visual grasp of his situation. As in *Blinks*, these photographs function as supplements to an act of perception construed as partial and contingent upon movement. They refer to the body as a 'central perspective' while simultaneously toppling and decentering that perspective. In an important sense, the self appears divided, caught in an effort to coincide with the physical traces of its presence in the world. As Acconci put it, 'I have to keep going to where I am.'[11]

While the works just analyzed address the phenomenology of vision in a world that seems inhabited by Acconci alone, other works performed simultaneously investigate the intersubjective structures of vision. In these works, the gaze is again situated in the body, but so as to reveal the corporeal enactment of a transgressive desire for knowledge of, and power over, the other. Significantly, in Acconci's early analysis of the act of beholding art, he compared it to targeting, which would become a recurring motif in his performances. He began by considering the viewing of art from a materialist standpoint, asking:

> 'What, how can I think of a generalized art condition?' It seems like in any kind of art situation, viewer enters exhibition space, viewer heads towards artwork, so viewer is aiming towards artwork. Viewer is treating artwork as a kind of target, so it seems to me this is a kind of general condition of all art viewing, art experience.[12]

According to this description, viewing is an act of aggression, comparable to the stalking of prey. Zeroing in on the work of art, hitting the mark, the viewer reveals a desire for tactile contact, for physical possession or control. The notion of targeting invoked here may be related to the early works of Jasper Johns, which were an important precedent for Acconci. From 1967 to 1969 he and Bernadette Mayer edited a journal called *0 to 9*, after the number paintings of Johns, which he has praised for their use of a common or shared vocabulary.[13] Yet Acconci must also have been struck by Johns's targets, in which viewing is figured as fetishistic, violent, and implicitly reciprocal. Many of Acconci's earliest performances issue from a similar understanding of beholding as a transgressive form of targeting, akin to touching, marking, or even biting.

Following Piece (Plate 16.3), one of Acconci's first street works, which he executed as part of a group show in 1969, exemplifies the transgressive power of the gaze.[14] For this performance, Acconci chose a series of individuals at random, one each day for a period of three weeks, and followed them until they entered a private place. Although the targeted individual presumably remained unaware of Acconci's presence, he or she was put in the position of controlling the artist's movements. In a sense Acconci relinquished his freedom to the other person, becoming dependent on him or her for reasons to move, to traverse the space of the city as he had once traversed the space of the page with writing. The artist has also compared his relation to the surveyed other in this piece, to the relation of reader to text, the one following the other faithfully as in a traditional model of reading. Yet this asymmetrical relation also implicated Acconci in a voyeuristic structure of desire for mastery and knowledge of the pursued individual. The FBI-style report on each of the followed individual's activities, which Acconci mailed to selected members of the art world the next month, assumed the objective language of dominance and control. According to the artist, by following a predetermined set of rules, he took on a positional role within an impersonal system. In his notes for *Following Piece* Acconci wrote: 'Fall into position in a system – I can be substituted for – my positional value counts here, not my individual characteristics.'[15] Yet the staged photos that Acconci had taken later, to 'document' this piece, reassert the intense particularity of focus required in this performance, so that the artist's eye/I remains historically specific, singular, and gendered male, even as it avoids overt displays of expressive subjectivity.

If *Following Piece* occured by definition in a public domain, governed by the grid of New York City's streets, in *Trademarks* of 1970 (Plates 16.4 and 16.5) Acconci installed himself in an initially private or self-enclosed space. Turning inward, he targeted his own body, employing it as a ground for an unusual kind of indexical writing. His activity consisted in biting as much of himself as he could reach; he then applied ink to the bites and stamped

Plate 16.3 Vito Acconci, *Following Piece*, from *Street Works IV*, 1969. Courtesy of the Barbara Gladstone Gallery, New York

'bite-prints' on a variety of other surfaces. The artist explained: 'The bites set me up as a target (I can shift the focus – apply printers' ink to the bites so that they can be made available – I can point out other targets by stamping bite-prints on paper, on a wall, on another body.')[16] As in Jasper Johns's *Target with Plaster Casts* (Plate 16.6) and his *Target with Four Faces* (Plate 16.7), both of 1955, this was an attempt to apprehend the self as a physical object, positioning it as the target of an 'other's' line of sight. In Johns's *Target with Four Faces*, the human surrogates are distanced, strangely replicated, fragmented; cut off just below the eyes, the plaster casts remain blind. The ability of these truncated 'visages' to return the viewer's gaze is displaced onto the eyelike target itself, as several drawings of the early 1960s make clear. In a lithographic version of this subject of 1960 (Plate 16.8), the viewer's eye finds itself addressed in turn, targeted by a work of art that functions as an uncanny mirroring device.

Similarly, Acconci's *Trademarks* establishes a dialectical movement in which subject/ object positions continuously shift. Acconci's self-inflicted biting was initially intended to enclose him within a self-reflexive circle, one part of the body marked by another, connected to the whole. By concentrating so exclusively on himself, Acconci hoped to

Plate 16.4 Vito Acconci, *Trademarks*, 1970. Courtesy of the Barbara Gladstone Gallery, New York

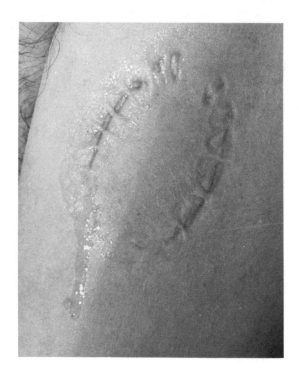

Plate 16.5 Vito Acconci, *Trademarks*, 1970. Courtesy of the Barbara Gladstone Gallery, New York

convince his viewers that he was unaware of the exterior world or the gaze of the other. Like the self-sufficient, modernist work of art, he appeared to exist within an autonomous, framed sphere. In the text that accompanies this performance, Acconci defined the self in physical terms, as a closed region, bounded by skin as if by a frame. The bites, which are

Plate 16.6 Jasper Johns, *Target with Plaster Casts*, 1955. Museum of Modern Art, New York

hard and break through the skin, open this closed region, transgressing the boundary between inside and outside.[17] As a form of writing, the bite-prints extend this principle, making a private activity available to the public, and setting up further targets. Through this process the body is made to signify, to participate in the circulation of signs, as the title *Trademarks* indicates.

262

Plate 16.7 Jasper Johns, *Target with Four Faces*, 1955. Museum of Modern Art, New York

But to what sort of trade – in the double sense of craft and economic exchange – do Acconci's marks point? Within the art world, the bitemarks function as surrogate gestural traces or signatures, guarantees of authenticity and value. The consumption of works of art, acording to a system of names, here receives a literal performance that undermines its ideality and the principle of aesthetic distance. One thinks of Marcel Duchamp's interest in

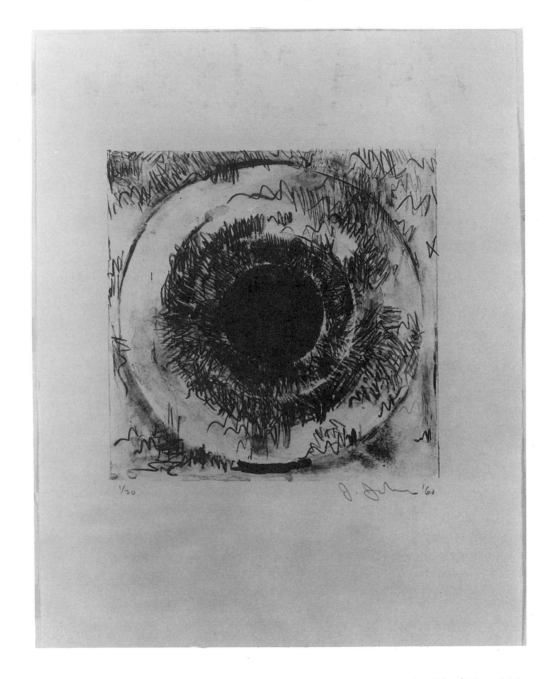

Plate 16.8 Jasper Johns, *Target*, 1960. Museum of Modern Art, New York. Gift of Mr and Mrs Armand P. Bartos

that which functions as a 'physical caustic' (*mordant physique*) – something that bites,[18] or of Johns's frequently quoted statement that '"Looking" is & is not "eating" and also "being eaten".'[19] As does Jasper Johns in his *The Critic Sees* of 1961, or in his other works which point to viewing as a form of sadistic oral consumption such as *Painting Bitten by a*

Man, also of 1961 (Plate 16.9), Acconci draws a parallel between biting and seeing. Johns's enigmatic title, *A Painting Bitten by a Man*, leaves open the question of who has done the biting, the artist or the viewer/critic. We know only that he is male, and that his relation to this work has overstepped the boundaries of decorum. In its suppression of identity, and in its marking of a painful attempt at oral incorporation, we might also see a reference to the difficulty of finding a language for the expression of repressed or forbidden desire – including, but (I would argue) not limited to, gay desire. Nor is it clear if this work speaks of rage against an other, or renders manifest the artist's experience of having been the object of such rage (or both). At the very least, viewing has been enacted as a form of wounding that ruptures corporeal integrity: it is this gesture that the painting preserves as the single iconic image/sign on the pictorial field.

As in Acconci's *Trademarks*, in Johns's work the bite is literal, leaving its trace on a canvas whose encaustic surface simulates human skin – now congealed and reified. As many critics have noted, Johns's use of encaustic evokes analogies to the human body, especially to the layer of skin that is both its protective armor and its vulnerable, sensate opening to the world. The encaustic/skin analogy allows the artist to treat the pictorial surface as a site that can visibly register physical and psychic events, while paradoxically distancing and objectifying those events. Johns would also at times treat his own body as a printing template, whose 'inked' forms could be transferred to other surfaces. In each of a series of four works titled *Study for Skin* of 1962, Johns pressed his oil-covered face and hands onto a sheet of drafting paper, then dusted it with charcoal to create a fragile monotype (Plate 16.10). The choice of ground is significant, for the drafting paper, intended to receive a far less personal imprint, establishes an incongruous context for the display of expressive gestures. The traces of the artist's skin convey a sense of the body striving to constitute an image, yet remaining constrained and deformed by the flatness of the ground and its objectifying format. By the fourth work in the series, the ghostly residues of Johns's corporeal presence have become nearly illegible, pointing to the self's effacement, its non-presence and non-coherence in an external image. *Painting Bitten by a Man* engages a similar dialectic of image and ground, presence and absence. That Johns thought of biting as a form of somatic writing may be surmised from the fact that this painting is roughly the size of a sheet of paper and that beneath the encaustic, and the canvas it nearly covers, its ground is a $9^{1}/_{2}$ by $6^{7}/_{8}$ inch typeplate. The scale of *Painting Bitten by a Man* is crucial to its mode of signifying: the work establishes a charged relation to the viewer's body by preserving the dimensions of the object/ground (typeplate) and the act (biting) that constitute it. This literalness, and the fact that the bitemark relates to no other sign or mark on the encaustic surface, casts it in direct relation to the spectator before it. Centered in the upper third of its field of presentation, the bitemark takes on a stark force, equivalent in its way to the unwavering address of a Dutch seventeenth-century portrait.

Yet the status of the bitemark remains ambiguous – it is simultaneously a unique indexical mark, which preserves the gesture that produced it, and a seemingly timeless, universal sign – like the handprints in Jackson Pollock's *No. I* of 1948, or indeed the handprints and face in Johns's *Study for Skin I*. The act of biting itself has a multivalent character, suggesting the primal oral phase in the sexual development of a child, as well as adult sexual regression – or it may be the sign of a more general frustration in the ability to communicate verbally. Johns's painting – and he is careful to call it a painting – raises the question of the relation of pictorial and verbal fields, of visual image and verbal sign. The bitemark, for this viewer, evokes a desire to bring the body to signification, to make its

Plate 16.9 Jasper Johns, *Painting Bitten by a Man*, 1961. Collection of the artist. Photograph by Rudolph Burckhardt

Plate 16.10 Jasper Johns, *Study for Skin 1*, 1961. Collection of the artist. Photograph © Dorothy Zeidman

gestural language into a form of writing, while retaining its corporeal immediacy – its life. But the gesture remains enigmatic, refusing to deliver its meaning fully, and Johns seems just as interested in this possibility of illegibility. According to the artist,

> Painting has a nature that is not entirely translatable into verbal language. I think painting is a language, actually. It's linguistic in a sense, but not in a verbal sense. 'I think that one wants from painting a sense of life.' And I think that is true.[20]

The title – *Painting Bitten by a Man* – points to the work with a banal literalness that stands in contradiction to its unprecedented method of construction, and its multiple and even contradictory associations. If looking is (and is not) like biting, and biting is (and is not) like writing, is any act of interpretation a potential form of consumption? This work makes me conscious of my own attempt to incorporate Johns's painting into a system of meanings and uses, surely in part (and inevitably) foreign to his own.

Where Johns's works at times put the viewer in the position of aggressor, as the purported maker of the mark, Acconci exposes his punctured body, saliva dripping from his wounds, to the gaze of the viewer in an act of apparent masochism. Yet even while concentrating most exclusively, most narcissistically on his own body, the artist breaks through its contours and exposes this process to the documentary eye of the camera. As Amelia Jones has observed, in many of Acconci's pieces, he becomes an objectified, 'feminized' spectacle, whose insistent (and sometimes abject) corporeality unhinges the performance of a transcendent subjectivity.[21] The oscillation of subject and object, active and passive positions, enacted in Acconci's relation to his body, produces a secondary dialectic with the viewers of this work. As in Johns's works, we are induced to participate in the activity of targeting, making his photographed image and biteprints the objects of our gaze, while simultaneously witnessing Acconci's control over his body and its display, as well as its production of a self-referential code.

In *Pull* of April 1971, Acconci established a potentially more dialogical situation, which significantly was structured around a mutual, highly charged, and gendered exchange of gazes. Performed with Kathy Dillon, the woman he was living with at the time and a frequent collaborator in his activities and videos, this work also tested a private relationship. During the thirty-minute piece, executed before an audience at New York University, Acconci walked in a circle around Dillon, who rotated in the center. Each participant sought to hold the other's gaze while following the other's direction, or attempting to initiate a new direction (or change in speed). The encounter took place within a ten-foot square, marked by masking tape on the floor, and harshly lit by a 500-watt bulb, the audience remaining nearly invisible in the darkness. The activity and its mode of presentation were intended to install Dillon and Acconci in a seemingly private, even 'personal'[22] space; within this space they exerted 'pull' on each other, playing out the chiasmic roles of subject and object, each playing the role of mirror to the other. According to Acconci:

> She might be trying to gain strength, remaining a fixed point – I might be trying to crowd her, drive her to a standstill – she might be trying to draw me into her, stop me from circling – I might be trying to remain an observer, detached, on the outside.[23]

The circular structure of the work offers alternate interpretations of the power implied in mobilizing the act of looking within a confined space. Dillon, whose field of action was restricted to a point, might be viewed as a target, prey to Acconci's more aggressive circling. Yet Dillon also appears as a subject by virtue of being centered, while Acconci becomes an object on her horizon. Acconci's text, with its own oscillatory movement and exploration of these possibilities, suggests an equal playing field. But this is to ignore the fact that men have traditionally enacted their transcendence by moving through and claiming space, charging it with intentional meaning, while women have been comparatively immobilized and thereby objectified.[24] While revealing the instability of the subject/object relation, and the way in which each of these terms implies and requires its complement, *Pull* never shatters the Western subject/object paradigm. Vision remains an instrument of power and control, whose grip is broken only by the just-audible words of Acconci to Dillon towards the end of the performance, that it was almost over.

The aggression evident in *Trademarks* and *Pull* became even more pronounced in *Claim* of September 1971. For this performance, Acconci sat on a chair at the foot of the stairway in the basement of Willoughby Sharp's loft. The artist was blindfolded, but equipped with two metal pipes and a crowbar; he thus alternated ambiguously between a position of vulnerability to the gaze and the approach of the other, and a position of dominance from which he laid 'claim' to the space of the basement. Viewers were alerted to Acconci's threatening posture and territorial demands by a video monitor situated next to the stairway door at street level. On the monitor they could observe the artist talking to himself, working himself into a state of 'possession obsession':

> I'm alone down here in the basement . . . I want to stay alone here . . . I don't
> want anyone with me . . . I'll stop anyone from coming down the stairs . . . I have
> to keep talking . . . I've got to believe this . . . I've got to make myself believe this
> . . .

Despite this warning, occasionally an intrepid visitor would open the door and approach
the stairway. Acconci responded violently, brandishing his weapons and escalating the tone
of his rhetoric:

> I hear him – someone's coming down the stairs – I swing the weapon in front of
> me – it pounds against the stairs, against the wall – he backs off . . . I'll keep you
> away . . . I'll do anything to stop you . . . I'll kill you . . .[25]

Delivered from the basement of the two-level loft, Acconci's obsessive monologue seems
to erupt with the blind power of the unconscious – recalling the insane ravings of the
'mother' in Hitchcock's *Psycho*, a film Acconci acknowledges as a reference. His
monologue also rehearses the oppressive authoritarianism he experienced during the time
he spent training (unsuccessfully) for the marines in Quantico, Virginia, where fighting
exercises were accompanied by a broadcast voice seeking to drive the men into a predatory
state of mind: 'You're a tiger. Kill'em. Kill'em.'[26] These models of violent rhetoric inscribe,
however mockingly, Acconci's fascination with violence within a disturbingly masculinist
sphere. As Amelia Jones has argued in relation to Acconci's flirtation with a hyperbolic
masculinity, as well as with a theatricalized masochism, 'any performative act is always
recuperable to its non-parodic base-line effects.'[27] This is the danger that Acconci's most
notorious activities court and that he perhaps even desires at times – though here I would
like to resist the temptation to collapse his work into a single reductive interpretation. I
choose, as Jones and Linker have done, to focus on the ambivalent character of Acconci's
critique of masculine subjectivity, and in this essay, his critique of the formalist ideal of a
disinterested, gender-neutral (though always implicitly white and male), beholder.

Claim can be seen as a minimalist sculpture par excellence. It literally enacts what
Michael Fried had found so deplorable in the work of artists such as Donald Judd, Robert
Morris, and Tony Smith. For Fried, their sculptures laid claim to the surrounding space,
confronting viewers with all the disturbing presence of anthropomorphic objects.
Encountering one of these objects meant becoming immersed in a situation. One felt,
moreover, that this situation was open, waiting for the viewer, perhaps even lying in wait.
In 'Art and Objecthood' Fried declared that 'literalist [minimalist] works of art must
somehow *confront* the beholder – they must, one might say, be placed not just in his space
but in his *way*,' and he further argued that this was a function, 'not just of the obtrusiveness
and, often, even aggressiveness of literalist work, but of the special complicity that that
work extorts from the beholder.'[28] Acconci seems to have deduced that if a situation could
be constructed around a sculptural object as if it constituted a form of violent
interpellation, he could intensify this encounter by involving a real threat.

The territorial instinct that drove this performance is one that also carries political
meanings. As Kurt Lewin argued, 'Political struggles as well as struggles between
individuals are nearly always struggles over the boundary of the space of free movement.'[29]
Central to this concept was the permeability of perceived boundaries between spaces or
regions, and the amount of resistance these boundaries offered to being crossed.[30] In

Claim, Acconci established a power field around his presence that could only be penetrated at great danger. Acconci has asserted that he only wanted to meet his audience, to say hello, but it turned out that he kept saying goodbye.[31] The viewer who attempted to encounter the artist, positioned as a blind target within an enclosed region, would only experience Acconci reverse the terms and target the viewer. At stake was a set of relations defined by the marking of limits, control over access to a given space, and the power associated with the gaze. By exerting this control so violently, *Claim* parodied the museum's injunction against approaching works of art or touching them. It inscribed this interdiction within both the individual's unconscious and the larger arena of political struggle over territory and freedom of movement.

In their exploration of the corporeality and temporality of vision, Acconci's early works violated the tenets of high modernism, as defined by the formalist critics of the 1960s. Rather than affirm the transcendence of the subject in an idealized moment of disinterested viewing, Acconci set out to explore the act of looking in its phenomenological and social implications. By targeting vision itself, he challenged the assumption that one can bracket the material conditions of viewing or suspend the desire that motivates the constitution of subjectivity. His works participate in a broader shift that marks a rupture with the idealist claims of a certain modernism, now itself a contested category. But in the late 1960s, even in the absence of the term postmodernism, Acconci's work exemplified a new paradigm for questioning the act of beholding and the ways in which it structures the contingent relation of self and other, self and world.

In this essay I have attempted to 'follow' Acconci, as he followed those individuals he selected in October 1969 for *Following Piece*, notebook and pen in hand, turning an ostensibly simple act of 'reading' a text into the writing of another, and the act of writing into a performance of invested beholding. Reading, writing, beholding and performance are inextricably linked in Acconci's works of the late 1960s and early 1970s; moreover these activities are mapped within a conflicted social arena that opens their significance to multiple interpretations. My attraction to the visual practices of this period of recent history, and to Acconci's work in particular, stems from my own postmodern conviction that art is a 'family of uses' – to use Acconci's term – rather than an occasion for the experience of transcendent viewing. Yet I am aware that this version of postmodernism gains its own coherence most powerfully when articulated in opposition to the canonical texts of formalist criticism – whose terms I remain fascinated with. Beginning to define my stake in this debate (an ongoing project) was one of my motives in writing about/ performing my relation to Acconci's work and the problematic of the beholder it puts into motion.

NOTES

1   Cited in E. Schwartz, 'Vito Acconci: "I Want to Put the Viewer on Shaky Ground,"' *Art News*, Summer 1981, vol. 80, no. 6, p. 95. Acconci's interest in what the various arts share, rather than in what distinguishes them, is revealing. He refuses to grant art an essence, either by affirming the specificity and separateness of a given medium, or by citing a stable lineage of great masters from the past. In 1971 Acconci told Cindy Nemser, 'There is no essence of art. Art is just a family of uses.' See: 'An Interview with Vito Acconci,' *Arts Magazine*, March 1971, vol. 45, no. 5, p. 23.
2   Cited in K. Horsfield, 'On Art and Artists: Vito Acconci,' *Profile*, Summer 1984, p. 7.

3   For an insightful analysis of important shifts in Greenberg's thinking on these issues, see Y.-A. Bois, 'The Limit of Almost,' in *Ad Reinhardt*, Museum of Contemporary Art, Los Angeles and Museum of Modern Art, New York, 1991, pp. 11–33.

4   M. Fried, 'Art and Objecthood,' *Artforum*, Summer 1967, vol. 5, no. 10, pp. 12–23; reprinted in G. Battcock (ed.), *Minimal Art: A Critical Anthology*, Berkeley, University of California Press, 1968, pp. 116–47. Among Fried's other important essays to address the related issues of pictorial autonomy, unity, and the ideal of opticality, see especially: 'Shape as Form: Frank Stella's New Paintings,' *Artforum*, November 1966, vol. 5, no. 3, pp. 18–27, and *Three American Painters*, Fogg Art Museum, Harvard University, 1965. Also relevant in this context are Clement Greenberg's essays of the late 1950s and early 1960s in which opticality begins to displace flatness as the irreducible essence of painting. See for example: 'The Pasted-Paper Revolution,' *Art News,* September 1958, vol. 57, no. 5, pp. 46–9ff, reprinted as 'Collage,' in *Art and Culture*, Boston, Beacon Press, 1961, pp. 70–83, and 'The New Sculpture' [1958], in *Art and Culture*, pp. 139–45.

5   V. Acconci, 'Body as Place – Moving in on Myself, Performing Myself,' *Avalanche*, New York, special Acconci issue, Fall 1972, no. 6, p. 20.

6   K. Linker, *Vito Acconci: Photographic Works 1969–1970*, Chicago, Rhona Hoffman Gallery and New York, Brooke Alexander Gallery, 1988, n. p.

7   Cited in C. Nemser, 'An Interview with Vito Acconci,' *Arts Magazine*, March 1971, vol. 45, no. 5, p. 20.

8   'An Unpublished Text by Maurice Merleau-Ponty,' 1962, in *The Primacy of Perception*, James M. Edie (ed. and intro.), Evanston, Northwestern University Press, 1964, p. 5.

9   Ibid. See also Merleau-Ponty's discussion of this issue in 'The Child's Relation with Others,' ibid., pp. 116–18.

10   'Eye and Mind,' ibid., p. 178.

11   Acconci, 'Early Work: Moving My Body into Place,' *Avalanche*, Fall 1973, p. 6.

12   Acconci, 'Interview by Robin White at Crown Point Press,' *View*, October–November 1979, p. 15.

13   Acconci recalls that, at the time, he had the title wrong. It should have been *0 Through 9.* Interview with the author, 5 October 1991. In this interview, Acconci further remarked that Johns's paintings provided a model for his own use of *Roget's Thesaurus* and *Webster's Third International Dictionary* as common or conventional systems with which to work in the late 1960s. In an interview with Ellen Schwartz, the artist stated: 'When I first saw the work of Jasper Johns in 1965, it jolted me. Johns' numbers and flags were flat paintings of flat objects, and that seemed just perfect. I began to experiment with idioms like "from the horse's mouth" because they didn't exist except as language.' Cited in: E. Schwartz, 'Vito Acconci: "I Want to Put the Viewer on Shaky Ground,"' p. 95.

14   *Following Piece* was Acconci's contribution to 'Street Works IV,' sponsored by the Architectural League of New York and coordinated by Marjorie Strider, Hannah Weiner, and John Perrault. 'Street Works IV' was a citywide project that took place during three weeks in October 1969. Other artists who participated include Stephen Kaltenbach, Arakawa, Abraham Lubelski, Bernadette Mayer, Les Levine, Scott Burton, Eduardo Costa, Hannah Weiner, Marjorie Strider, and John Perrault.

15   Acconci, 'Peopled Space – Performing Myself through Another Agent,' *Avalanche*, Fall 1972, p. 31.

16   V. Acconci, 'Body as Place – Moving in on Myself, Performing Myself,' *Avalanche*, p. 11.

17   'Finding myself – getting to a region, getting through a region . . . Opening a closed region: building a biography, a public record . . . Make my own outside – send my inside outside (I can slip outside, then, because I am still moving inside), (ibid.).

18   In a note of 1913, under the heading 'Possible,' Marcel Duchamp wrote: 'Le *possible* est seulement un *"mordant" physique* (genre vitriol) brûlant toute esthétique ou callistique.' ('The possible is only a physical 'caustic' (the vitriolic kind) burning all esthetics or sense of beauty.') See Marcel Duchamp, *Duchamp du Signe: Écrits*, Michel Sanouillet (ed.), Paris, Flammarion, 1994, p. 104. In the context of his notes of 1913, Duchamp's use of the term 'possible' seems to refer to the desired (and deferred) object, and the term 'mordant' ('caustic') to the corrosive effects of desire. For remarks on the interrogation of the shop window, and of the 'pain' which consists in 'cutting the glass and experiencing regret (biting one's thumbs) until the possession

is consummated,' see: 'Spéculations,' 1913, ibid., 105–6. What Johns and Duchamp share, in my view, is a strong sense of the reciprocal, corporeal effect of desire, a sense that in the act of desiring or possessing, one is also consumed (bitten).

19 Jasper Johns, 'Book A, p. 55, 1964,' *Writings, Sketchbook Notes, Interviews*, Kirk Varnedoe (ed.), Museum of Modern Art, New York, 1996, p. 59; first published as 'Sketchbook Notes,' *Art and Literature*, Lausanne, Spring 1965, no. 4, p. 185.

20 Jasper Johns, statement made in an interview with Yoshiaki Tono in 1975, *Writings, Sketchbook Notes, Interviews*, p. 149.

21 A. Jones, *Body Art/Performing the Subject*, Minneapolis, University of Minnesota Press, 1998, chapter 3, 'The Body in Action: Vito Acconci and the "Coherent" Male Artistic Subject.' I would like to thank Amelia Jones for generously allowing me to read this chapter of her book prior to its publication. As is evident throughout this essay, my own reading of Acconci's work is informed by hers.

22 Acconci was interested in Edward Hall's distinctions between intimate, personal, social, and public distances. Hall defined personal distance (close phase) as lying between one-and-a-half and two-and-a-half feet. This distance allowed for a small protective sphere around each individual but also implied a 'kinesthetic sense of closeness' and an ability to regard the other person without the distortion of intimate distance. The 'far phase' of personal distance, between two-and-a-half and four feet, set the limit of physical domination. See: *The Hidden Dimension*, Garden City, New York, Doubleday, 1966, pp. 107–22. In *Pull*, Acconci remained within the sphere of personal distance, hovering around the boundary between the close and far phase. Towards the end of the performance, however, he moved closer to Dillon as his circling grew more aggressive.

23 Acconci, 'Occupied Zone, Moving In, Performing on Another Agent,' *Avalanche*, Fall 1972, p. 52.

24 Acconci analyzes the spatial myths that structure gender differences in Western culture in 'Projections of Home,' *Artforum*, March 1988, vol. 26, no. 7, pp. 126–8. I discuss this essay in the context of Acconci's fear of domesticity in: 'Vito Acconci's Bad Dream of Domesticity,' in Christopher Reed (ed.), *Not at Home: The Suppression of Domesticity in Modern Art and Architecture*, London, Thames & Hudson, 1996, pp. 237–52. Amelia Jones also analyzes this issue in *Body Art/Performing the Subject*, pp. 122–4.

25 Acconci, 'Concentration – Container – Assimilation,' *Avalanche*, Fall 1972, p. 55.

26 For a discussion of Acconci's brief stint as a trainee in the Marine Platoon Leaders Corps, see K. Linker, *Vito Acconci*, New York, Rizzoli, 1994, p. 11.

27 Jones, *Body Art/Performing the Subject*, p. 104.

28 Fried, 'Art and Objecthood,' in Battcock (ed.), *Minimal Art: A Critical Anthology*, p. 127.

29 K. Lewin, *Principles of Topological Psychology*, New York and London, McGraw-Hill (1936) 1966, p. 47. Acconci's early performance activities were influenced by his reading of Lewin and his theory of social relations as a structurally dynamic field governed by regions, boundaries, and power fields. This vocabulary turns up frequently in Acconci's writings. For a discussion of Lewin's theories and their influence on Acconci, see Linker, *Vito Acconci*, pp. 30–5, 47–8.

30 Lewin, *Principles*, p. 123.

31 Acconci made a remark to this effect on the first occasion when I heard him speak to a group of art students, some time in the early 1980s, in a crowded basement room at Yale University. As I recall, though I took no notes at the time, he was referring to *Claim*.

17

PERFORMING VISION IN THE THEATRE OF THE GAZE

The work of Douglas Gordon

Joanna Lowry

> What determines me, at the most profound level, in the visible, is the gaze
> that is outside. It is through the gaze that I enter light and it is from the gaze
> that I receive its effects. Hence it comes about that the gaze is the instrument
> through which light is embodied and through which – if you will allow me to
> use a word, as I often do, in a fragmented form – I am photo-graphed.[1]

Lacan's description of the subject trapped in the field of the gaze constructs the 'visible' as a kind of theatrical space, a space in which the subject, rather like an actor on the stage, enters the light of the gaze and performs his or her desire within that light. It is a theoretical description of the subject's relationship to visuality which is dependent upon a metaphorical inscription of spatial and temporal dimensionality: a theatre of the gaze. It is also a description which invokes the image of technology: the subject is 'photo-graphed'. The space of the visible is described here, metaphorically, as a kind of camera. Lacan uses the language of technology to emphasize the fundamental 'otherness' of the space of the visible in its relationship to the subject.

This essay attempts to explore the relationship between these two ideas – first, the idea that Lacan's description of the subject's position within the field of the gaze implies an understanding of the act of looking as fundamentally 'performative', and, second, the idea that this very 'performance' of looking takes place within a field of the visible that is haunted by the spectre of technology: visuality is staged within a kind of apparatus. These two questions seem particularly relevant to our understanding of the way in which certain forms of contemporary video installation themselves stage the act of spectatorship. Lacan's description of the field of the visible provides us with a way of understanding how such installations operate as metaphorical spaces articulating the relationship between the eye and the gaze, thereby impelling the spectator to recognize the performativity of the act of looking itself. His description also draws our attention to the way in which such installations necessarily take place within a field of the visible that is constituted through technology. What role does this technological presence – this apparatus – play in the way we understand the act of looking and the relationship of the subject to the field of vision?

The video installations of Douglas Gordon provide an example of a practice which in many ways seems to exemplify the Lacanian model of the gaze: they provide a space in which the spectator literally acts out his or her relationship to vision. In his installation *24*

273

Hour Psycho (1993) a huge screen, upon which a slowed-down, halting version of Hitchcock's film *Psycho* is being endlessly replayed, hangs, as if invisibly suspended in the air in the middle of the gallery (Plate 17.1). It is slightly too high and at an oblique angle to us as we enter the gallery so that our first impression is of the distortion effect of the screen. We are struck by the seemingly paradoxical conjunction of a three-dimensional hallucinatory object that invites us to walk around and under and behind it with the almost evanescent thinness of the two-dimensional image whose body is belied by this distortion. There is thus an immediate putting into question both of the body of the spectator, who must move around and negotiate a place from which to view the screen, and of the body of the film itself, which is presented to us to us both as object and as an illusion. Significantly, though, the spectacular hallucinatory presence of Gordon's installation distracts us from the fundamental role played by the technological apparatus itself in sustaining a model of vision. The space within which the spectator performs the act of looking is implicitly defined by the presence, not only of the screen, but also of the technology of projection.

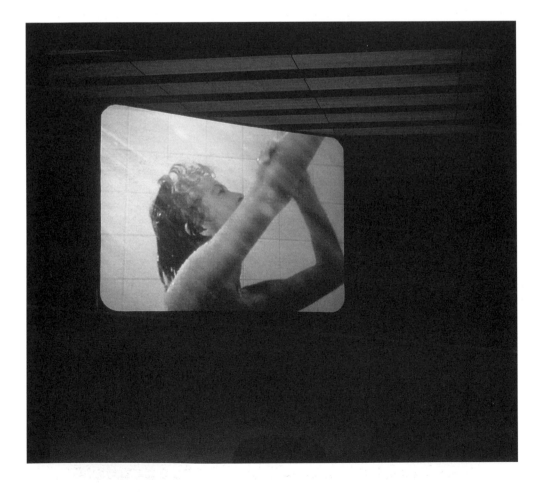

Plate 17.1 Douglas Gordon, *24 Hour Psycho*, 1993. Photograph by John Riddy. Courtesy of the Lisson Gallery, London

In *Babylon* (1996) Gordon stands two screens, slightly at an angle to each other, each showing footage from a 1960s stag film depicting a woman stripping. Each image has been slowed down so that the seamlessness of the viewing process is broken, and one screen, larger than the other, shows the image inverted. Gordon often employs this device of paired screens, each in some sense deflecting the image onto the other, situated in the middle of the floor space, up to and between which the spectator can walk. It is a device that he also employs in *Hysterical* (1995) (Plate 17.2). Here, excerpts from early twentieth-century scientific film footage depict two doctors restraining a hysterical masked woman and laying her down upon a bed. This violent and enigmatic scene is once again simultaneously projected onto two screens, one slowed down and slightly enlarged so that the two sequences occasionally but rarely achieve synchrony. Both these installations, which take as their subject found footage in which women are the victims of a sadistic or voyeuristic male power, are parallelled by similarly staged installations featuring a troubled male body. *10ms⁻¹* (1994) uses medical footage of a First World War victim of shell-shock and we witness him as he tries repeatedly and unsuccessfully to pull himself up off the floor. In *Confessions of an Unjustified Sinner* (1996) an excerpt from an early Jekyll and Hyde film is used to dramatize the instability of masculine identity: Jekyll is continuously replayed, on double screens, in the process of transforming into Hyde.

In essence, therefore, Gordon's theatre of vision is constructed around scenes of sexual violence: his recent video pieces seem to revolve either around the exercise of male power over the woman's body, or around the failure of the male body itself. In this sense it is an essentially perverse theatre. I shall argue that the technological apparatus that sustains this

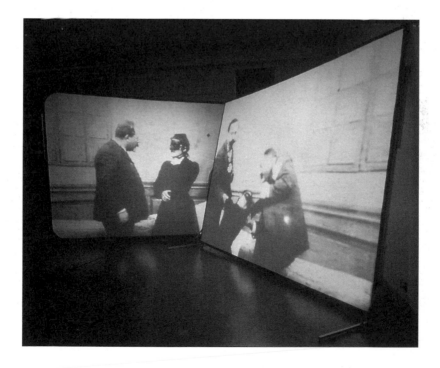

Plate 17.2 Douglas Gordon, *Hysterical*, 1995. Courtesy of the Lisson Gallery, London

theatre of vision plays a key role in sustaining that perversity.[2] The performance of vision within these installations takes place within a visual field that is structured by the triangular relationship between the viewing subject, the screen, and the technological apparatus. The work itself is defined by this very space of encounter between the embodied spectator and the space of projection. Gordon's screens can be seen as peculiarly hybrid objects which exist simultaneously within the spaces of sculpture, cinema, and video – each of these representational forms implying a distinctive relationship to the spectator and a specific delineation of the visual field. It is therefore worth considering briefly the theoretical frameworks that have emerged for dealing with the problem of spectatorship in relation to these different forms.

If we consider the video installation that Gordon presents us with to be sculptural then our approach must be informed by Michael Fried's critique of Minimalism in his 1967 essay, 'Art and Objecthood', which drew attention to the theatrical way in which Minimalist sculpture addressed the body of the spectator in real time. This required a negotiation of the encounter with the object which, for Fried, represented a betrayal of the pure optical space of modernism.[3] Fried's critique, in a curious way, offered a paradigm for the theorization of space of post-Minimalist sculpture, performance art, and video. It drew attention (albeit disparagingly) to precisely the question of the embodiment of the spectator, to the sharing of real time between the object and the spectator, and to the performative nature of the relationship between them.

If, however, we view Gordon's installations primarily in the context of video art, then it is important for us to consider the extent to which the performative space of encounter in video theory has been structured as a space of psychology. A key text here is Rosalind Krauss's essay 'Video: The Aesthetics of Narcissism'[4] in which she argued that video was indeed primarily a psychological rather than a technological medium. She argued that, in its emergence as an art form during the 1970s and 1980s, video art inscribed itself within a space of narcissism. This was a space in which the attention of the spectator was diverted from an encounter with the external object as Other and redirected towards the parameters of the psychological situation within which the self was constructed. The video practices she was concerned with invariably addressed in a self-referential way the relationship between the artist and the image or, in the case of installation work, the relationship between the spectator and the image. She drew attention, for instance, to Peter Campus's companion installations *mem* and *dor* (1974) in which a live-feedback recording of the spectator was projected onto the screen in such a way that the image itself could only be glimpsed either, in the former, as the person was leaving the room, or, in the latter, if they were to move right up to the surface of the screen. Krauss argued that this installation acknowledged the narcissistic drive that propelled the viewer to see him or herself while simultaneously emphasizing the difference between the body and the screen – between the body and the world of objects external to the self. Her discussion drew attention to the instability of the image on the screen as an object poised between different forms of spectatorial encounter.

Both Fried and Krauss, in their attempts to describe the parameters of our encounters with the Minimalist object and the video installation respectively, deal with the spectator as a kind of performer in the space of the object. More importantly, both of these models are premised upon the idea of a failure in the optical system at the moment of the bodily encounter. But neither of these models offer us a theorization of the relationship of technology itself to the performance of looking. In order to engage with a discussion of the significance of the apparatus of production for a theorization of the gaze we need to turn to some of the discussions concerning the concept of the 'apparatus' in film theory.

An important component of film theory during the 1970s was the discussion about the theory of the cinematic apparatus advanced by writers such as Christian Metz and J. L. Baudry.[5] This theorization of the institution of cinema conceived of it as a vast apparatus constructed so as to produce a simulacrum of the structure of the unconscious. The term 'apparatus' was used to describe comprehensively the technologies of production and projection and the whole social system of production and distribution that constituted 'cinema'. The term was employed, therefore, as a technological metaphor which clearly implied a fantasy investment in technology.[6] The film spectator who is locked into this apparatus regresses to an infantile stage that has been described as akin to the Lacanian mirror stage, hallucinating an imaginary unifying relationship to the screen and experiencing a sense of identificatory mastery over the field of vision.

This model of the cinematic apparatus has been forcefully criticized by theorists including Joan Copjec and Constance Penley. Penley relates the metaphor of the machine to the concept of the 'bachelor machine', a fantasy of the anthropomorphic machines constructed within fiction and art to represent the relationship between the body and the social. As Penley points out, such machines are typically self-contained systems, locked into perpetual motion and reversible time, subject to a fantasy of an omniscient and omnipotent producer. She argues that this apparatus metaphor is linked to a construction of male spectatorship that represses issues of sexual difference.[7] Joan Copjec points out that there are similarities between the apparatus model and those paranoid machines that are described by schizophrenics as being the originators of their delusions, machines that operate as anthropomorphized phallic constructions to deny the reality of sexual difference.[8] For both of these writers the concept of the 'apparatus' within film theory is dependent upon the construction of the act of spectatorship as a narcissistic identificatory moment of plenitude, a denial of the difference between the image and reality, involving a suppression of the issues of sexual difference which lie at the heart of representation.

There is a sense in which this feminist-based critique of the cinematic 'apparatus' makes us aware of the way in which it invokes a fundamentally 'perverse' fantasy of spectatorship, one which is dependent upon a structure of disavowal and a suppression of a sexual politics. Video installation, however, as I have suggested above, often involves a disruption of the identificatory models of spectatorship that are associated with film theory: the embodied spectator is forced into literally acting out their engagement with the image. In this context the role of Penley's 'bachelor machine', the apparatus that subtends that perverse form of looking, is pushed into a new kind of visibility and we are able to re-evaluate its relationship to the performance of looking.

Ironically one of the clearest illustrations of this relationship between the apparatus of cinema and the performance of looking comes from within cinema itself. Michael Powell's film *Peeping Tom* (1960) explored precisely the innate perversity of the visual field of cinema. In the film a young cameraman, Mark Lewis, having been deeply disturbed by a traumatic childhood at the hands of a sadistic father, stalks and murders a series of young women with a blade attached to his camera. This camera is like a kind of prosthetic device that he is never detached from. He films his victims at the moment of their death, their terrified eyes at the moment of extinction seeing their own reflection in a mirror attached to the camera lens. Night after night he sits alone in his room at the top of his old family home replaying these scenes. It is as though through repetition he might get closer to the real event, might experience that elusive catharsis for himself. In this context the camera and the projector are represented as a complex apparatus for the simultaneous representation and displacement of the women's deaths, the reality of which can never quite be grasped. At the moment of filming – also the moment of death – the cameraman/spectator is displaced: he sees her death but she doesn't see him – he is 'out of the picture'. The traumatic scene is revisited in cycles of repetition which, ironically, can only revisit that moment of loss, a loss which has parallels with the failure of opticality implied by Krauss and Fried.

A key moment in the film occurs when the blind mother of Lewis's girlfriend visits the room in which he projects his films. Her presence ruptures the cycle of repeated screenings. It is precisely because she is blind and cannot see that she is able to intervene in the relationship between Lewis, the screen, and his projector. Her blindness is given symbolic power when she stands in front of the screen on which the young woman's death is being replayed, standing in front of Lewis's own shadow which itself falls like a stain across the image of the dying woman's face. 'What am I seeing?' she asks; 'What am I looking at?' And in the impossibility of an answer we experience the collapse of the structuring of the relationship between the technology which produces the image, the spectator, and the image on the screen which sustains this perverse viewing – and therefore the beginning of the denouement which will culminate in Mark Lewis killing himself.[9]

What Powell effects in this film is a scenario in which the perversity of the cinematic apparatus is stripped bare, centring upon the fundamental impossibility of a meeting between the desiring eye of the viewing subject and that subject's embodied presence as a kind of shadow across the screen, blocking out what is most desired to be seen. What he also exposes of course, to the disquiet of contemporary audiences, is the complicity of cinematic pleasure with the structuring of sexual difference and with the exercise of violence upon the woman's body. But what is even more significant for our argument here is the way in which Powell presents us with a narrative in which the act of looking at the screen is a compulsive kind of performance that has to be enacted again and again within the machine-filled space of the projection room.

The space that Douglas Gordon's installations occupy seems to me to bear some resemblance to the projection room presented to us in *Peeping Tom*. We, too, are compelled to watch the often violent and voyeuristic footage that is repeatedly projected onto the screen; and when we enter the space of his installations it is often our own shadow that falls across the screen as we try to get a closer look. We are the ones who, unable to synthesize the series of displaced projections with which Gordon presents us, have our moment of narcissistic identification interrupted or blocked. What he constructs for us is a space which is implicitly, if invisibly, defined by the cinematic apparatus, in which the technologies of recording and projection are integrally related to the act of looking itself.

But the relationship of the spectator and technology that Gordon invokes in his work is not only situated within a space of sexual violence and voyeurism. This is also sometimes a space of scientific observation. Alongside the video installations that use material derived from Hollywood cinema are those, like *Hysterical* and *10ms⁻¹*, which feature excerpts from medical and scientific archives. These are pieces of film footage produced within the discursive framework of scientific method where the capacity of optical technologies for offering up the world to objective, dispassionate scrutiny is taken for granted. Gordon's brutal severing of these films from their original contexts makes the viewer even more aware of the alienated spectatorial position being constructed through them. What is discomfortingly foregrounded for us in these works is the discursive presence of film as an apparatus designed to bring us to a closer knowledge of the body – an apparatus that allows us time for scrutiny, an apparatus that allows us to look because it allows us to look through the eyes of a machine.[10]

One of the earliest examples of this model of vision is found in Eadweard Muybridge's photographic sequences examining the human body in motion, produced between 1872 and 1887. The complexity of Muybridge's apparatus for arresting vision is well known: the extended screen with its gridded surface against which the movement of the bodies could be monitored and compared, the banks of cameras , both fixed and mobile, which were coupled to an elaborate timing device. Muybridge's project exemplifies the way in which the spectator is displaced by the camera, the very frame of each image is an index of a mechanical intervention, splicing through time and space. There is a sense in which Muybridge's experiment dramatizes the displacement of vision as located in the body – 'the denial of the body, its pulsings and phantasms, as the ground of vision'.[11] Vision in these early experiments is literally displaced by the apparatuses of photography and projection which substitute for, and extend, the functions of the eye. In this construction of a perverse relationship to vision there is an incitement both to the voyeuristic – in that extended gaze that the mechanism allows us – and to the fantastic – in our awareness of that which is excluded, our searching of the image for its excess.[12]

However, while Muybridge situated his bodies in front of a gridded screen, emphasizing the scientific ordering of vision, he also took a parallel, simultaneous set of pictures from the side. From this perspective the screen cannot be seen clearly, its control over the body is broken, and the spectator catches a glimpse of the studio beyond the frame. This angle then exposes the 'blind field'[13] beyond the frame of the image. We are made aware of the contingency of the 'real' which is fleetingly caught by the camera but which has no meaning within the picture. Muybridge's tangential images reveal the disjunction between these two potential viewing positions. The frame of the image is revealed as being an index of the machine, as being a function of the place that the viewing subject cannot fully occupy.

Douglas Gordon repeatedly employs the device of the screen placed at an oblique angle to the spectator. This angle of distortion is similar to the skewed angle of vision offered to us by Muybridge. It represents an abdication of a position of visual mastery over the image. The viewing subject is displaced from an identification with the site of projection and becomes, as it were, re-embodied in relationship to the screen and particularly to the contingency of the blind field beyond its frame. The performance of looking at the screen in the context of these installations always, therefore, involves an awareness of two kinds of vision – one centred on the technological apparatus, in this case the video projector, which produces and controls the image within the frame, the other centred on the embodied spectator, who is always displaced from this site of production, always drawn by the anamorphic structure of the installation into a desire to see beyond the edge of the screen.

This model of two kinds of relationship to the visual world bears a striking relationship to that proposed by Lacan in his essay 'The Split between the Eye and the Gaze'.[14] Lacan suggests that while as subjects we imagine ourselves to be the originary centre of the visual, projecting an image of the visual world out onto a virtual screen, we are in fact simultaneously caught within the visual world of the 'Gaze', a regime of the visual which preexists and envelopes the spectator. The subject is positioned in vision: 'In the scopic field the gaze is outside. I am looked at, that is to say, I am a picture.'[15]

Lacan suggests a correspondence between the Gaze and the Real, or what he calls the 'tuché', that momentary, searing, access to an encounter beyond the system of symbolic signifiers that normally position us as subjects. The 'tuché' is associated for him with the loss of the parental gaze and with the site of all those infantile losses that are the precursors of our entry into subjecthood. The 'tuché' is above all associated with the idea of trauma, of a painful encounter with the Real that is outside signification, an encounter which we cannot assimilate and to which, therefore, we compulsively return again and again. He discusses at length the way in which vision is fissured by Holbein's painting of *The Ambassadors*.[16] He describes how the anamorphically distorted skull that hovers in the foreground of the picture can be seen clearly only when we abdicate a position of visual mastery over the picture: it is only from an oblique perspective that the image forms itself into a skull, a reminder of mortality and death. This phenomenon symbolizes for Lacan the relationship between the subject and vision: in our imaginary positioning of ourselves as controllers of the visual world we are never quite secure. We are always aware of another position, of something beyond the screen, something which cannot be controlled, the unsymbolizable Real.

Gordon's installations present us with fragments of film footage that are enigmatically decontextualized. They are troublingly unassimilable and are usually presented on video loops which endlessly repeat. In their fragmented form and in their repetition they recall Lacan's definition of the trauma as that which cannot be made sense of or be symbolized within representation: 'a kernel of nonsense at the heart of the subject'.[17]

The found images that Gordon selects for these installations all focus upon some issue of sexual difference and identity: where women are depicted the scenes focus upon a violence against the woman's body, a desire to see more of it, or a desire to know and control it; where men are represented their bodies seem to be subject to some narrative of failure and instability. These scenes have a curious mad arbitrariness that can only be tamed by repetition. Gordon's screens, in Lacanian terms, seem to operate not so much as sites of representation as they do as sites that 'screen' us from something: from the missed en-counter with the Real.

Moreover, our experience of these installations is dominated by the presence of the technological apparatus as a device for splitting the Eye and the Gaze. We look at the image through a series of mechanisms of displacement: repetition, the close-up, slow motion, the oblique screen. These manipulations of the image, these forms of *trucage*, represent an obsessive interrogation of the limits of the image, of its materiality; a reminder of the way in which the image tethers our desire. In his crude deployment of these visual tricks Gordon draws attention to the strategies of deferrment and disavowal at work within the act of spectatorship and of the essentially perverse relationship between vision and desire. Moreover these manipulations, which are in one sense outside film and supplementary to it, are revealed here as central to an understanding of our engagement with it. These devices, as indices of the presence of the technology itself, compel us to revisit the place from which we cannot see, beyond the edge of the screen. The edge of the screen marks a deictic gesture towards both the embodied spectator whose visual field has been displaced and also towards that moment of rupture with the space beyond – what Lacan refers to as the 'tychic', the 'Real', the unsymbolizable.

As spectators in the space of these installations, therefore, it seems that we are not so much engaged with the screens that hover before us in all their phantasmic presence, but by the dark space outside them within which we stand, the space outside the frame, the space of the Gaze in which we are caught, like Powell's Peeping Tom, in the act of looking. Our position as viewers within this space is controlled by the constant presence of an almost invisible technology to which we are in thrall and which constructs the very conditions of our fascination. We walk up to the screen, pass under or around it, our shadow falls across it. Yet, while we thus engage in a performance of looking that emphasizes the perversity of its own desire, we are aware that we do this within a space that is constituted by the apparatus of projection – the invisible bachelor machine that endlessly repeats, with an obsessional voyeurism, the miraculous re-animation of the image. It is this machinery that produces the conditions within which we have to perform our missed encounter with the Real.

NOTES

1 Jacques Lacan, *The Four Fundamental Concepts of Psychoanalysis*, ed. Jacques-Alain Miller, trans. Alan Sheridan, Harmondsworth, Penguin, 1987, p. 106.
2 'Perversion' is here used in the psychoanalytic sense, implying a structuring of pleasure based upon a deviation from typical genital sexuality, one which may be based, for example, upon voyeurism, fetishism or scopophilia. It implies a systematic structuring of avoidance and is necessarily predicated upon a structure of disavowal which puts the relationship between the subject and the Real at risk. Linda Williams has argued that from its very inception the cinematic apparatus involved an 'implantation of perversions', employing the image of the female body to stand in fetishistically for a traumatic awareness of sexual difference posed by the apparatus itself, L. Williams, 'Film Body: An Implantation of Perversions', in *Narrative, Apparatus, Ideology: A Film Theory Reader*, ed. Philip Rosen, New York, Columbia University Press, 1986, pp. 507–34. Parveen Adams has commented upon the extent to which cinema is fascinated by the representation of perversion and, in an essay on Michael Powell's film *Peeping Tom* which has some relevance for the argument I am presenting here, discusses the relationship of the film's spectator to the structure of perversion represented within it; P. Adams, 'Father, Can't You See I'm Filming?', in *The Emptiness of the Image*, London, Routledge, 1996, pp. 91–108.
3 Michael Fried, 'Art and Objecthood', *Artforum*, vol. 5, no. 10, 1967, pp. 12–23.
4 Rosalind Krauss, 'Video: The Aesthetics of Narcissism', *October*, no. 1, Spring 1976, pp. 51–64.
5 Christian Metz, *The Imaginary Signifier*, trans. Ben Brewster, Bloomington, Indiana University Press, 1982. Jean-Louis Baudry, 'The Apparatus: Metapsychological Approaches to the Impression of Reality in Cinema', trans. Jean Andrews and Bertrand Augst, *Camera Obscura*, no. 1, Fall 1976, pp. 104–26.
6 For a discussion of the different ways in which the term 'apparatus' was used see Joan Copjec, 'The Anxiety of the Influencing Machine', *October*, no. 23, Winter 1982, pp. 43–59.
7 Constance Penley, 'Feminism, Film Theory, Bachelor Machines', in *The Future of an Illusion: Film, Feminism and Psychoanalysis*, London, Routledge, 1989, pp. 57–82.
8 Joan Copjec, 'The Anxiety of the Influencing Machine', pp. 55–6.
9 For a detailed analysis of the way in which a process of perverse looking is structured within this scene see Parveen Adams, 'Father, Can't You See I'm Filming?', pp. 101–2.
10 For an analysis of the significance of such 'scientific' discourses for the history of cinema see Lisa Cartwright, *Screening the Body: Tracing Medicine's Visual Culture*, Minneapolis, University of Minnesota Press, 1995.
11 Jonathan Crary, *Techniques of the Observer: On Vision and Modernity in the Nineteenth Century*, Cambridge, Massachusetts, MIT Press, 1992.
12 Linda Williams has demonstrated the extent to which Muybridge's experiments instituted a 'perverse' fetishization of the woman's body within the discursive formation of cinematic spectatorship. L. Williams, 'Film body', p. 522.
13 For a discussion of the 'blind field' in relationship to photography see Roland Barthes, *Camera Lucida*, trans. Richard Howard, New York, Hill & Wang, 1981, pp. 55–6, and Christian Metz,

'Photography and Fetish', in *The Critical Image*, ed. Carol Squiers, Seattle, Bay Press, 1990, pp. 155–65.

14 Jacques Lacan, *The Four Fundamental Concepts of Psychoanalysis*, pp. 67–119.
15 Ibid., p. 106.
16 Ibid., p. 92.
17 Margaret Iverson, 'What Is a Photograph?', *Art History*, vol. 17, no. 3, September 1994, p. 455.

18

WHAT SENSE DO THE SENSES MAKE?

Aspects of corporeality in the works of Miriam Cahn and Maureen Connor

Barbara U. Schmidt

Over the last few years there has been a proliferation of articles, conferences and exhibitions centering on the body. This trend, which was apparent at Documenta IX in 1992 and the Whitney Biennial in 1993, has literally exploded since then. Current developments in media and genetic technologies as well as in theories of representation have given rise to intensive debates concerning the body and its conceptual understanding. Since the body supposedly disappeared along with performance art around 1980,[1] this trend is being celebrated as its rediscovery. Apparently, the art establishment needs such clear distinctions between presence and absence, in order to perpetuate the avant-garde myth of radical innovation and progress.[2]

But did various elements of performance art and the intrinsically linked presence of the 'real' body ever disappear at all? I think not. Moreover, I would challenge the assumption that contemporary forms of artistic casting, photographing, X-raying, mutilating, and fragmenting the body imply a rediscovery of the body. On the contrary, I would characterize these actions as related to now conventional ideas about subject formation and corporeality. Such approaches, namely, uphold the Lacanian concept that the identification of the subject is exclusively constituted through a distanced specular process and mediated through language.[3]

Two aspects of this engagement with the Lacanian model of identity seem problematic to me. First, the assumption that the presentation of the body as remnant or loss is a subversive act. Although the body's coherence is, of course, questioned and destabilized in Lacanian theory, the ideal of wholeness remains intact and gives the act of destruction its meaning. Thus, the concept of corporeal identity itself is not basically changed through this notion of subjectivity. It is merely viewed from the opposite side. Second, I am skeptical about the insistence on the language-based construction of identity and its domination by processes of differentiation and hierarchical distinctions. The claim that there is no 'outside' of the basic law of symbolic order devalues as essentialist every approach which tries to integrate the reality of embodied experience into the concept of 'subject' and 'gender.' For this reason these concepts are kept 'outside' the dominant discourse, which concentrates on presenting normative structures of identity as contingent cultural constructions.[4]

An advantage that feminists can derive from Lacanian models of identification is that sexual identity as related to the body is no longer understood ontologically but rather is viewed as an interpretation within the realm of signs and discourses. However, to describe embodied subjectivity only as the result of symbolic operations would be to exclude the subversive aspects of concrete, existential experience and corporeal perception. One means of access to this concept of 'embodied experience' can be found in the philosophy of phenomenology as practiced by Maurice Merleau-Ponty, 'whose contribution to phenomenology', as Vivian Sobchack has noted, 'has been an insistence upon an elaborate description of human embodiment as the ground of all meaning and semiosis.'[5] Merleau-Ponty strives toward an understanding of the body itself as perceiving, and for that reason connected with and not differentiated from consciousness. Subsequently, this leads to a localizing of subjectivity and meaning in actual and embodied existential practice. Thus, subjectivity and meaning are not based on a distanced self-image and or a fixed law. On the contrary, they are understood as the result of a specific relation between embodied consciousness and the exterior world, and therefore always remain contingent and temporal, unfinished, and in motion.[6] As Sobchack has argued in her critical assessment of Merleau-Ponty's theoretical approach, this does not imply the existence of a natural or authentic perception. Rather, in her opinion, experience is always determined by social constructions. Moreover, she describes the body not as a universal instrument of perception but as always marked, for example, by age, sex, and skin color with the understanding that the significance of these also varies according to the context.[7]

In the following I will argue that the works by Miriam Cahn and Maureen Connor – in the sense just described – simultaneously explore the body and gender as discursive products and focus on the excluded ambiguities of gendered identity and the influence of the 'real' – of corporeality – on representation. Although I use phenomenological concepts such as 'embodied existence' as a basis of my examination, it is not my intention to develop a phenomenological art or body theory, but rather to draw attention to latent approaches. I will use this model in an attempt to trace the way artistic practices disrupt and subvert the aesthetics of perfection and homogeneity in order to make visible excluded aspects of corporeal experience and perception.

The discussion about the politics of aesthetics is anything but homogeneous. In the early 1980s, for example, artists and adherents of New Image painting and Neo-Expressionism tried to preserve regressive concepts of art such as subjective expression, authenticity, and originality. Additionally, the categories of work and material were celebrated as autonomous source for authentic experience and 'aura.'[8] Those artists who, on the contrary, understood themselves as producing recipients of pre-given regulative structures turned to other modes of production like film or photography. One of the early supporters of this kind of approach – very generally labeled appropriation art – was Douglas Crimp. In his essay 'Pictures' from 1979 he emphasizes that performance, a dominant mode of expression earlier in the 1970s, has given way to more distanced media and strategies, which in turn aim to 'give the presentation of an event in such a manner and such a distance that it is apprehended as representation – representation not, however, conceived as the re-presentation of that which is prior, but as unavoidable condition of intelligibility of even that which is present.'[9]

As the editors point out in their introduction to this volume, practices of citation and performativity avoid the traps of false authenticity. But the price is the 'unavoidable condition of intelligibility' itself – that which is excluded from the realm of representation is suppressed, made unintelligible. This process entails a separation of representation and subjective experience which is problematic from a feminist view, as this mode of deconstruction can be easily co-opted by 'non-specific critiques of the institution of authorship.'[10] I would like to show how Cahn and Connor explore in their work possibilities of overstepping the gendered distinction between sensual and conceptual, subjective and critical, by integrating the multiple and contradictory sensual qualities of the media and materials into dominant patterns of representation.[11] Through this strategy the term 'aesthetic,' which is often rejected as idealizing and even regressive, regains the complexity of the originally Greek word aisthesis, which signifies equally perception, feeling, and knowledge.

Miriam Cahn (born in 1949 in Basle, Switzerland) has unfortunately had only one large exhibition in the United States, at the Renaissance Society in Chicago in 1991. I have chosen to concentrate on a drawing installation from 1982. The title of the exhibition is *Wach Raum II* (Guard Room) – whereby *wach* (guard) is meant both in the sense of control and alertness. The installation consisted of sheets of paper covering the walls. It was installed at the Documenta VII in Kassel, Germany but withdrawn by the artist shortly before the opening.[12] On one wall could be seen what Cahn calls 'masculine' signs (for example, missile heads, warships, the twin towers of the World Trade Center). On the opposite wall smaller-sized 'feminine' signs (for example, tables, houses, boats) and a series of seemingly sketchy, gesticulating, distorted female figures were rendered (Plates 18.1– 18.3).

At first glance the 'signs' appear as simple and schematic reproductions of the given

Plate 18.1 Miriam Cahn, from *Wach Raum II*, 1982, Kassel, Germany. Photograph by Miriam Cahn

Plate 18.2 Miriam Cahn, from *Wach Raum II*, 1982, Kassel, Germany. Photograph by Miriam Cahn

objects. Cahn seems to forfeit any direct narrative links between them. Additionally, it should be mentioned that Cahn repeats signs that she has sketched almost identically in various other works. This suggests a repetitive, symbolic language as developed by Charles S. Peirce, who started from the assumption that the power of symbolic signs to signify is an effect of conventions.[13] The simplification of the images would serve then to make visible such socio-cultural conventions and the way they function as meaning systems.

The principle of masculinity is represented by an apparently homogeneous choice of signs. The skyscrapers, for example, with their phallic shape and eruptive thrust, can be compared to silos containing rockets or warheads. The weapons and antennas that rise from the decks of the merchant ships in aggressive stiffness can also be read in this manner. In contrast to the huge papers and dynamic, upright 'masculine' signs the 'feminine' drawings have a very small size and more centralized forms. This difference refers to the gendered concepts of the socialized body and subjective identity which are supported by naturalized oppositions that strengthen each other – such as active/passive, upright/centered, armed/vulnerable. Cahn thus exposes the fact that the unequivocal division of signs – into 'masculine' on the one hand, with connotations of monumental scale and high technology, and 'feminine' categories characterized by private and simple structures on the other – is crucial for the coherence and common understanding of gender-specific discourses.

At the same time Cahn subverts the system of bipolar distinction by strategies that 'cross out' its logic: the realms of war, economics, technology, and medicine – represented by the 'masculine' signs – are lined up one after the other forming a monumental block and linked

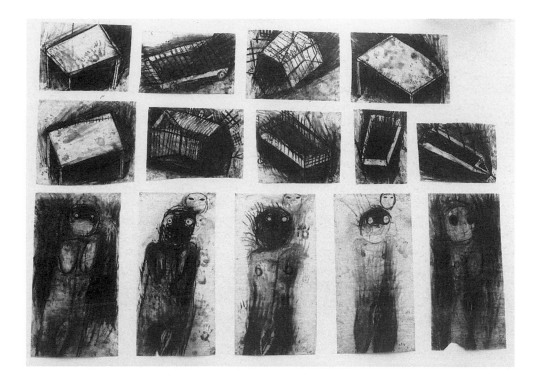

Plate 18.3 Miriam Cahn, from *Wach Raum II*, 1982, Kassel, Germany. Photograph by Miriam Cahn

through formal and thematic counterparts. This representation of strength can at the same time be read as unstable and ambiguous. The skyscrapers, for example, seem fragile, almost collapsing. The impression of a monumental block of drawings is subverted as the strong dynamic movements of the single signs is not completely unified. While the shapes of the sickbed and the skyscrapers are integrated into a parallel composition, their spatial dynamic seems to collide with that of the warship.

This incoherent structure of relations and these formal contradictions may remind the viewer of Foucault's description of power

> as the multiplicity of force relations immanent in the sphere in which they operate and which constitute their own organization; . . . as the support which these force relations find in one another, thus forming a chain or a system, or on the contrary, the disjunctions and contradictions which isolate them from one another. . . .[14]

Cahn leaves it to the viewer to consider possible relations between the different signs and the 'systems' of power they represent. Concerning the contemporary context of Cahn's installation, it is important to mention that in Germany in 1982 debates about power strategies were especially heated due to public discussions about and protests against the state's decision to arm the military with Pershing II rockets.

Terror and fear, the emotions that the female figures in Cahn's drawings express at first glance, seem to be a result of the presence of a threatening, superior power. The dynamic diagonal lines, sharp-angled shapes, and enormous size of the 'masculine' signs – such as the merchant ship – connote their aggression and danger. Moreover, the ship seems to be invincible because it is not anchored, either by a background or by a frame, in relation to pictorial space or surface. At the same time, distortions in the presentation subvert this rhetoric of power. An interaction takes place between the two-dimensional surface elements and those which are clearly rendered to look voluminous. This tension between surface and space is especially blatant in the perspective drawing of the rocket warhead. The highest edge of the towering pipe is indicated by terse strokes, which disrupt the illusion of the representation and expose it as a construction. Broken lines can be detected everywhere; these convey the impression of insecurity and instability. The thin paper hanging loosely on the wall reinforces this impression.

The heterogeneity of the drawings is a result of the process of their production itself. Cahn abandons the position of a distant overview from which a unified representation is possible. She rolls out the extremely large paper up to 8 square meters onto the floor of her studio and, kneeling on it, draws her signs and figures in quick, spontaneous strokes. The black chalk and chalk dust with which Cahn creates her drawings are not set afterward; therefore, while in the process of drawing, she must rub the chalk into the paper with appropriate bodily force. The corporeal power and affect that constitute her gestures are clearly a part of her drawings, which cannot thus be subordinated to the emotionless, rigid technological order. Thus the perceiving and experiencing body is exposed as a site of meaning as Cahn's process of production integrates the illusion of technical perfection and power into the instability of a corporeal gesture. Cahn's marking of the presence of her body thus does not produce the establishment of a counter-norm, but rather introduces an irreducible ambiguity that subverts the homogenous functioning of conventional symbolic systems.

As in the practice of appropriation art, Cahn does not create subjective, autonomous images but uses stereotyped signs and meaning systems. In her re-presentations she explores the functioning of those systems, but – in contrast to strategies of appropriation art – abandons the separation of meaning and being. Rather, she articulates meaning as existential experience, as the outcome of a situated relation of the subject to a codified world. Sobchack describes such a process of phenomenological semiotics as follows:

> Meaning is reducible neither to a location in consciousness . . . , nor a location in the objects of consciousness. . . . Rather it emerges in situ, as the intersection and correlation of consciousness and object whose location is in the inhabited and intentional space lived temporally as the body-being-in-the-world.[15]

The concepts that various, intersubjective and dynamic positionalities are held by the embodied subject and that the production of meaning is situated subvert the (illusive) coherence of specular identity and the static system of differentiation found in models of identification derived from Lacan. The intersection of symbolic meaning and existential experience also deviates from the concept of an artwork as an autonomous 'object' and proffers in its stead the idea of the work of art as determined through a reflective process of perception.

Cahn's use of materials and her concept of form correlate with this observation: for example, since the paper is not forced into a frame and the chalk is not set, the materials retain a high degree of openness. This is especially clear with respect to two of Cahn's sketchbooks with drawings similar to those on the walls and which Cahn laid on the floor for visitors to page through. Here too, the chalk-strokes are never fully incorporated into the illustration; they continually remain present as material. The lines and surfaces suggest a velvety quality, which fluctuates according to the thickness of the application. With respect to the larger interconnected black sections it is often impossible to differentiate between a surface structure or unfathomable depth. Also, the drawings disintegrate in a process of appropriation – through touch and the turning of pages; the drawings get smudged and each finger that has contact with them takes a little chalk away with it. The sensual or even synesthetic experiences are part of the process of perception in which the spectator gets involved. As becomes clear, the process of perception is, like the process of artistic production, an intersubjective one: the spectators leave their fingerprints on the drawings when turning the pages of the sketchbook and they, in return, get 'dirty' fingers.

This 'dirt' (actually chalk) cannot be understood as abjected or excluded from a bound system as Mary Douglas presents it in her ethnological study *Purity and Danger*: 'if uncleanness is matter out of place, we must approach it through order. Uncleanness or dirt is that which must not be included if a pattern is to be maintained. To recognize this is the first step towards insight into pollution.'[16] For Cahn intersubjective 'formation' neither implies the subordination and control of the materiality nor leads to a final, fixed, and coherent construction. Thus there is no stable demarcation-line along which the differentiation between inside and outside, form and its 'other' could be made.

The concept of difference and the exclusion of the other also concerns the artist Maureen Connor (born in 1947 in Baltimore, Maryland, United States) in her series of bottle-rack pieces from 1988–9, which allude to Duchamp's 'found' object, his ready-made bottle-rack, of 1914. Connor by no means cites the conceptual art tradition in an affirmative manner. On the contrary, she questions this tradition by reproducing it (Plate 18.4). The machine-made, functional shape of the bottle-racks is enlarged approximately to shoulder height. As Amelia Jones has suggested, this anthropomorphizing of the bottle-racks results in a phenomenological effect: 'they both solicit and repel the visitor's engagement with their skeletal and corset-like hoops of steel and menacing hooks.'[17]

The confrontation between corporeality and technological construction is also the theme of the piece *Penis* from 1989 (Plate 18.5). The dominant, phallic shape, illuminated from within, alludes to the fluorescent tubes of Minimalist art. In her feminist critique of Minimalism, Anna Chave points to Dan Flavin's Minimalist tubes as 'fetishes,' the fetish being 'a talisman against castration and impotence, a symbolic surrogate for the female body's absent penis'; Flavin's dependence on 'technological artifacts' thus 'may evince the sense of impotence visited on the once sovereign, universal (read: male) subject by the ascendancy of technology.'[18] Also Connor's fluorescent tube is not a pure construction of 'neutral', industrial materials like plexiglass or metal. Rather, the phallic symbol of power is given corporeality and fragility by a delicate covering of cloth and wax. The bodily effect is heightened by the pale pink color of the inserted material. Alluding to the specific body organ, the piece *Penis* creates a tension-packed opposite to the abstract phallus and the assumption of its being a unified and unambiguous representation.

Like Cahn, Connor confronts the abstract symbolic order of meaning with the corporeal-sensory disorder. By citing the phallus as the primary signifier of the symbolic order, Connor refers to the Lacanian model, according to which the subject is defined through language, which itself takes its structure in relation to the presence or absence of the phallus. Because it reduces the body to a mere object of symbolic inscription, this

Plate 18.4 Maureen Connor, *Discrete Objects*, installation view, 1995. Includes, from left: *Untitled*, 1990 (with bras), *Lung Rack*, 1989, *Untitled*, 1989 (with body suit), *Untitled*, 1989 (with rubber straps), *No Way Out*, 1990, and *Untitled*, 1989 (with G-strings). Photograph by Larry Lamay

model ignores the possibility of the subversive power of sensory, corporeal experience. As I indicated earlier, because the defining function of language does not reference a reality outside of its own system, this model appears to ensure a liberation from biological determinism. But the psychoanalytical model, in its reliance on the phallus as the determining signifier, is not able to remove phallic authority from its position.[19] As Joan Scott has argued, this approach 'rests on the assumption that meaning is conveyed through implicit or explicit contrast, through internal differentiation. Positive definitions rest always . . . on the negation or repression of something represented as antithetical to it.'[20]

Connor avoids establishing a definition of femininity as an opposite pole to the penis/phallus or mourning its absence. On the contrary, from the perspective of corporeal existence she describes the phallus itself as a deficient construction. Through the corporeal staging of 'penis' the construction of masculine strength, perfection, or transcendence is not only exposed in its function of excluding contradictory elements. The binary oppositions 'inside/outside' are also revoked, since the material doesn't only mark a covering, but also functions as a transparent cloth from within. Through its potential malleability the wax alludes to aspects of instability and process; in this way the wax in Connor's piece is similar in effect to that of the chalk that Cahn uses in her works. In Sobchack's terms the 'exclusion of the invisible from the existential activity of vision and exclusion of the lived-body's introceptive and subjective experience from its extroverted and objective appearance' which are traditionally generated by patriarchal discourse are thus dismantled as an oppressive fiction.[21]

Plate 18.5 Maureen Connor, *Penis*, 1989. Collection of the artist. Photograph by Susan Salinger

In closing I want to consider whether there is a difference between Duchamp's bearded 'Mona Lisa' (his altered ready-made *L.H.O.O.Q.* from 1919) and Connor's *Penis*, which is garbed, so to speak, in a transparent, pink negligée. More precisely formulated, I would like to ask the following question: Isn't it more radical to mark the sexually coded body with an irreducible instability, than to bring gender as a variable factor into play? As already mentioned in my introduction, I see a central problem in denaturalizing models of fragmenting the body or strategies of sexual parody, as they only focus on the analysis of coding practices. By delineating the crucial role that embodied experience plays in the works of Cahn and Connor, I have attempted to argue that a fundamental transformation in our symbolizing systems requires a change of the categories of meaning and perception, which can be realized on the basis of existentialist phenomenology. As my, certainly incomplete, examinations of the works of Cahn and Connor show, the inclusion of the perceiving body doesn't necessarily have to imply an essentialist conception of femininity.

It is important for me to emphasize once again that such concepts of tangibility and body perception do not demand the death of the author but rather the demise of a distant and controlling authorial subject. Subsequently the idea of the art work as object becomes obsolete, and the unfinished, processual structure of Cahn's and Connor's installations mark the work's relation to the producer and recipient as an intersubjective experience of perception and signification. An art historical examination of such modes of representation can be realized not through an objectified formal description, but through a simultaneous tracing and analyzing of the work as process. This recognition demands a 'viewer' who gives up the illusion of a distant and supposedly independent gaze in favor of an existential act of perception as basis for interpretation and signification. Such a mode of interpretation is a challenge that mainstream art discourse, or better, its representatives have up until now generally evaded.

NOTES

1 See for example Douglas Crimp, 'Pictures,' *October*, Spring 1979, vol. 8, pp. 75–88.
2 On the functioning of this male-centered ideology and its misogynist effects see Carol Duncan, 'The MoMA's Hot Mamas,' in Carol Duncan, *The Aesthetics of Power: Essays in Critical Art History*, Cambridge, Cambridge University Press, 1993; and Griselda Pollock, *Avant-Garde Gambits: Gender and the Colour of Art History*, London, Thames & Hudson, 1992.
3 In his essay, 'The Mirror Stage as Formative Function of the I' (in Jacques Lacan, *Écrits. A Selection*, tr. Alain Sheridan, New York and London, W.W. Norton & Company, 1977), Lacan writes of the specular process as follows: '[T]he fact is that the total form of the body by which the subject anticipates in a mirage the maturation of his power is given to him only as Gestalt, that is to say, in an exteriority in which this form is certainly more constituent than constituted, but in which it appears to him above all in a contrasting size (*un relief de statue*) that fixes it and in a symmetry that inverts it, in contrast with the turbulent movements that the subject feels are animating him' (p. 2). Regarding the mediation of identity through language, see especially Lacan's essay, 'The Signification of the Phallus' (also in *Écrits*), where he argues the following: 'Conversely, it is Freud's discovery that gives to the signifier/signified opposition the full extent of its implications: namely, that the signifier has an active function in determining certain effects in which the signifiable appears as submitting to its mark, by becoming through that passion the signified. This passion of the signifier now becomes a new dimension of the human condition in that it is not only man who speaks, but that in man and through man it speaks (*ça parle*), that his nature is woven by effects in which is to be found the structure of language, of which he becomes the material' (p. 284).

4   See Judith Butler, *Gender Trouble: Feminism and the Subversion of Identity*, London and New York, Routledge, 1990, especially chapter 3, section IV, 'Bodily Inscriptions, Performative Subversions,' pp. 128–41.

5   Vivan Sobchack, *The Address of the Eye*, Princeton, NJ, Princeton University Press, 1992, p. 148.

6   Sobchack writes, 'Merleau Ponty's system accounts for subjectivity as intersubjectivity, whereas Lacan's schema accounts for subjectivity as objectified' (ibid., p. 123).

7   See Sobchack in ibid., p. 144.

8   The affirmation of this masculine myth of creative genius and the corresponding modernist aesthetic categories are, for example, still prevalent in the stylization and idealization of the protagonist in Julian Schnabel's film *Basquiat* from 1996.

9   Crimp, 'Pictures,' p. 77.

10 Amelia Jones, '"Post-Feminism" – A Remasculinization of Culture?,' in *M/E/A/N/I/N/G*, May 1990, vol. 7, p. 36.

11 In her essay about the critique of representation and its relation to painting, Mira Schor delineates how the analysis of discursive socio-cultural processes goes along with a subordination of materiality and sensuality. Further, Schor compares the subordination of sensual qualities of material to the subordination of woman as it is a concept structurally impossible within the symbolic and therefore identified with equally negative concept of the body; see Schor, 'Figure/Ground,' in her book *Wet: On Painting, Feminism, and Art Culture*, Durham and London, Duke University Press, 1997, especially p. 152.

12 The installation consisted of three walls covered with 'masculine' signs and one wall with 'feminine' signs. Rudi Fuchs, the chief curator of Documenta VII, described his concept as effecting dialogue among artists, but he did not respect the elucidating dialogue that Cahn initiated between the gender stereotypes. Instead he removed the drawings showing 'female' signs in order to combine Cahn's images with the work by another artist. Douglas Crimp pointedly characterizes his attitude as an 'inflated self-image as master artist of the exhibition' and emphasizes that '[w]hether the participating artists intended it or not, Fuchs would endeavour to ensure that their works would in no way reflect on their environment: the world around them, customs and architecture, politics and cooking.' Douglas Crimp, 'The Art of Exhibition,' in his book *On the Museum's Ruins*, Cambridge, Mass., MIT Press, 1993, p. 240. After Cahn's protest remained without success, she consequently removed the 'masculine' signs as well and left the Documenta.

13 *Collected Papers of Charles S. Peirce*, vol. II, *Elements of Logic*, ed. Charles Hartshorne, Paul Weiss, Cambridge and New York, Cambridge University Press, 1932, pp. 165–9.

14 Michel Foucault, *The History of Sexuality*, vol. 1, New York, Vintage, 1990, p. 92.

15 Sobchack, *The Address of the Eye*, p. 66.

16 Mary Douglas, *Purity and Danger*, London, Boston, and Henley, Routledge & Kegan Paul, 1980, p. 40.

17 Amelia Jones, 'The Flesh of the World: Maureen Connor's Phenomenological Feminism,' in *Maureen Connor – Discreet Objects*, exhibition catalogue, New York, Alternative Museum, 1995, p. 7. This intersection of the inner and outer perception is also elicited in Connor's installation *Untitled*, of 1989 (consisting of body suits, wax casts of the muscular structure of the arm, glass and wax casts of sheep lungs, and mirrors). The installation exposes the violence inherent in the compulsion of giving 'body' to fictitious norms.

18 Anna C. Chave, 'Minimalism and the Rhetoric of Power,' in *Arts Magazine*, January 1990, vol. 64, no. 5, p. 45.

19 As Jane Gallop argues, the phallus clearly has 'a relation to the penis: the phallus symbolizes the penis. But even this link does not constitute a special relation between phallus and penis, for the phallus also symbolizes the clitoris;' in *Reading Lacan*, Ithaca and London, Cornell University Press, 1985, p. 136.

20 Joan Scott, *Gender and the Politics of History*, New York, Columbia University Press, 1988, p. 7.

21 Sobchack, *The Address of the Eye*, p. 158.

AUTHOR/ARTIST INDEX

Note: page numbers in italics refer to illustrations where these are separated from the text

SUBJECT INDEX

Note: page numbers in italics refer to illustrations where these are separated from the text